HEALTH ECONOMICS WORLDWIDE

Developments in Health Economics and Public Policy

VOLUME 1

Series Editors
Peter Zweifel, *University of Zurich, Switzerland*
H.E. Frech III, *University of California, Santa Barbara, U.S.A.*

HEALTH ECONOMICS WORLDWIDE

Edited by

Peter Zweifel

University of Zürich, Dept. of Economics, Switzerland

and

H. E. Frech III

University of California, Dept. of Economics, U.S.A.

Kluwer Academic Publishers

Dordrecht / Boston / London

338.433621
H4342

Library of Congress Cataloging-in-Publication Data

Health economics worldwide/edited by Peter Zweifel, H.E. Frech III.
    p. cm. – (Developments in Health Economics and Public Policy; v. 1)
    Papers from the Second World Congress on Health Economics, held at
the University of Zurich, Sept. 10–14, 1990.
    ISBN 0-7923-1219-8 (hb : acid free paper)
    1. Medical economics – Congresses. I. Zweifel, Peter. II. Frech, H. E. III. World
Congress on Health Economics (2nd : 1990 : University of Zurich) IV. Series.
RA410.A2H46 1991
338.4'33621–dc20   91-11942

ISBN 0-7923-1219-8

Published by Kluwer Academic Publishers,
P.O. Box 17, 3300 AA Dordrecht, The Netherlands.

Kluwer Academic Publishers incorporates
the publishing programmes of
D. Reidel, Martinus Nijhoff, Dr W. Junk and MTP Press.

Sold and distributed in the U.S.A. and Canada
by Kluwer Academic Publishers,
101 Philip Drive, Norwell, MA 02061, U.S.A.

In all other countries, sold and distributed
by Kluwer Academic Publishers Group,
P.O. Box 322, 3300 AH Dordrecht, The Netherlands.

JK

Printed on acid-free paper

Printed in the Netherlands

Table of contents

Preface

This volume reflects both the main issues confronting health economics and the state of the art in health economics a decade before the end of the twentieth century. It contains a selection from almost 150 papers presented at the Second World Congress on Health Economics, held at the University of Zürich, Switzerland, 10–14 September 1990. This is ten years after the last Congress (held in Leiden, The Netherlands) and more than 17 years after the Tokyo meeting organized by the International Economic Association (which might be called the First World Congress were it not for its small size and symposium-like character).

Out of the 16 papers appearing in this book, only four were invited, and they were refereed like all the others. The remaining contributions are survivors of stiff competition. However, in spite of the large sample of papers we were able to draw from, certain gaps of coverage persist. In particular, environmental impacts on health were designated as a field of priority interest in the call for papers to this Congress. Yet, not even half a dozen contributions were submitted, which is remarkable in view of the intense interest of the public in the health effects of environmental degradation, ranging from noise level to ozone concentration. Another specially designed field was the political economy of health, dealing with the behavior of policy makers when deciding about changes in the health care systems. It did not attract as many contributions as we had hoped for or expected.

The papers contained in this volume can be grouped in the following topics:

I.   Issues in health insurance
II. Criteria for allocating health care resources
III. Administrative and market allocation in health care
IV. Health care in the political arena

The reader will notice a preponderance of contributions from the U.S. in topics I and III whereas contributions from other countries (where systems of national health insurance and of public provision of health care are more common) tend to be found in Sections II and IV. Thus, prevailing institutional arrangements seem to influence research in health economics. We join authors in the quiet hope that the converse may become true as well: that the results of research presented in this book will contribute to the future shaping of institutions in the health care sector.

P.Z.
H.E.F.

Sponsors of the second world congress on health economics

Interpharma (Ciba Geigy, Roche, Sandoz)
Konkordat der Schweizerischen Krankenkassen
Medizinisch Pharmazeutische Studiengesellschaft (Bayer, Boehringer
   (Ingelheim), Boehringer (Mannheim), Hoechst, Knoll, Merck, Schering)
SAF (Swiss Auditing and Fiduciary Company)
Basler Insurance Company
Swiss Reinsurance Company
FMH, Federation of Swiss Medical Doctors
VESKA, Swiss Hospital Association
Upjohn (Germany)

PART ONE

Issues in health insurance

Pricing and imperfections in the medical care marketplace*

G22   I 11 I 18
uc s

JOSEPH P. NEWHOUSE

Division of Health Policy Research and Education, Harvard University, Boston, MA 02115, U.S.A.

Many well-known papers in the literature of health economics assume that prices paid to providers (gross prices) approximate those that would be set in a competitive market (*e.g.*, Pauly 1968; Feldstein 1973) or that any deviation from competitive prices is well understood (Crew 1969). In the policy arena, however, this view has not predominated; for example, in the United States Medicare payments to physicians have recently been changed on the premise that prices do not resemble those set in a competitive market (Hsiao *et al.*, 1988; PPRC, 1987).

In this paper I argue that one cannot assume hospital and physician prices mimic those of a competitive equilibrium. Indeed, in most countries hospital and physician prices are set through some sort of administered price system or are implicit in a total budget. Even if the intent were to approximate an optimal price, systems such as the Prospective Payment System or the Resource Based Relative Value Scale will make errors. In light of such errors I argue that it will be welfare improving to adopt a mixed mode of reimbursing health care providers.

In particular, I make the following arguments:
1. In countries that rely on insurance, as opposed to a national health service, insurers' behavior is important for price setting. In countries with a national health service, the behavior of the government agency operating the service will *ipso facto* be important in setting prices for factors that are specialized to the health sector.
2. The usual market mechanism for establishing an optimal price – competition among suppliers for an informed consumer's dollar – often does not operate in medical care, either because: a) prices are negotiated between an insurer or public agency and providers; or b) prices are set by fiat; or c) the consumer spends the insurer's dollar. As a result, prices paid providers

*I would like to thank Randy Ellis, Ted Frech, Emmett Keeler, and Edward Norton for comments on an earlier draft. Having not seen this draft, they cannot be responsible for any of its shortcomings.

P. Zweifel and H. E. Frech III (eds.), Health Economics Worldwide. 3–22.

may well not be identical to those that would emerge from a competitive marketplace; indeed, they may not even closely approximate them.

3. The problems caused by errors in administered prices are compounded by the heterogeneity of consumers if pricing does not recognize this heterogeneity, as is often the case, probably because it is too costly to do so.

4. Several empirical phenomena can arguably be explained by these observations:

    a. The alleged overprovision of certain services by fee-for-service physicians and, less commonly, the underprovision of others;

    b. Excess capacity in surgery in the United States;

    c. Selection behavior in capitated plans;

    d. Allegations of skimming and dumping in the American Prospective Payment System.

5. Welfare losses from errors in price setting may be mitigated by adopting a mixed mode of reimbursement, for example, partly fee-for-service and partly capitation.

THE IMPORTANCE OF INSURERS

In this section I argue that prices in the medical marketplace should be thought of as administered prices rather than the outcome of a competitive marketplace. Many readers may find this observation obvious; they should simply skip on to the next section.

Several institutional facts about health insurance make the insurer's pricing behavior relevant:

    1) Insurance is nearly universal; it is not a small part of the market;

    2) The price to the patient may be unaffected by provider choice. Insurers generally do not make lump sum payments to individual patients who then shop for providers, though some patients may face coinsurance. Moreover, providers may not be allowed to extra bill; that is, the price the insurer names may be the effective price;

    3) Insurers traditionally have not attempted to influence patient choice of provider on the basis of price charged to the insurer, although the advent of Preferred Provider Organizations in the United States is changing this somewhat; and

    4) Both product and factor markets are not predominantly international.

Universality. If insurance were not universal and insurance payments were a small part of the market, as they were many years ago, the insurer could observe and pay the market price. Suppliers would have no reason to accept less, and competition in the insurance market (or the political market) would mean the insurer would not pay more.

However, in most OECD countries there is universal or nearly universal public coverage of inpatient and ambulatory services (Poullier 1989). Even in the United States, the country that relies on out-of-pocket payments more than any other OECD country, only 5 percent of hospital costs and 19 percent of physician costs are paid out-of-pocket (1988 figures, from the Office of National Cost Estimates, in press).

Form of Insurance Payment.   Even with universal insurance, if insurers paid a lump sum conditional upon the injury or illness of the patient, the market would play a role in price setting because the consumer would benefit from seeing a lower cost provider. Indeed, this is approximately how the auto-mobile insurance market operates in the United States. Drivers whose cars are damaged may be given a lump sum depending upon the insurer's estimate of the market cost to repair the automobile and thus are fully responsible for the marginal dollar of the cost of repair. Alternatively, they may be required to seek several estimates of the cost of repair.

Although there are some attempts to implement such a principle in medical care, especially United States employees who are given a lump sum by an employer toward the choice of a health care plan such as an HMO, they are generally exceptional.[1] Even in the case of the consumer's facing the full price of a premium difference for an HMO, the price to the consumer will not necessarily reflect his or her expected cost because of the heterogeneity of risk across consumers (more on that below).

Indeed, in most instances hospital insurance is the exact opposite of a lump sum payment to the consumer; the consumer often bears none of the cost of provider price differences. For example, in the United States the patient's insurance arrangement is such that the patient's out-of-pocket pay-ment, if any, is independent of the hospital chosen in the majority of hospital admissions.[2] In the case of physician services in the United States it is more common for the patient to face a coinsurance rate, usually in the range of 20 percent, which means some of the provider price difference will be borne by the patient. In other countries such arrangements are less common, either because there is no out-of-pocket payment or because any payment is the same irrespective of provider choice (a copayment).

In many countries the insurance payment is the sole reimbursement to the provider; that is, so-called extra billing is not allowed. Thus, the amount the insurer pays the hospital or physician is often the relevant price from the supplier's point of view. If extra billing is allowed, departures from a competi-tively determined price will be asymmetric, assuming rebates are not given, if the insurer's price is above the competitively determined price. To simplify, I will assume extra billing is not allowed in what follows.

No Restrictions on Choice of Provider. Price competition in the provider market could still in principle come about through the insurance market if insurers passed through to consumers the provider prices they faced, but they generally do not. As noted above, one exception in the United States is a Health Maintenance Organization. Another example from the United

States is the Preferred Provider Organization; consumers pay more out-of-pocket to see physicians whose price to the organization is higher. The implementation of this principle through Preferred Provider Organizations, however, has been flawed.[3]

Little International Trade. If markets were international and competitive, even dominant insurers at the national level, such as the National Health Service in the United Kingdom, would be price takers. In fact, however, patients rarely cross national borders. Although labor does migrate, it is hardly the case that there is one price throughout the world for, say, physicians. Even when goods are internationally traded, as in the case of drugs, the situation may be one of bilateral monopoly rather than one world price competitively determined.

INSURER'S REIMBURSEMENT LEVELS AND MARKET OUTCOMES

In a standard market with several suppliers the consumer will search for the lowest cost provider up to the point where (ignoring risk aversion) the expected gain from further searching equals its marginal cost (Stigler 1961). A component of the gain from search in such a market is an expected reduction in the price of the service (there may also be improved quality). If search costs and travel costs were zero, suppliers would price at marginal cost except in cases of increasing returns to scale. Non-zero search and travel costs allow for departures from marginal cost, but these are a function of the magnitude of such costs, which are typically small (Pratt, Wise, and Zeckhauser 1979).

If the patient's out-of-pocket payment is independent of the supplier chosen, however, and the patient chooses the supplier, there is no incentive for the provider to price at cost, that is, no reason to bill the insurer at an amount that equals cost. Indeed, if the patient's payment is not a function of the provider's price, the provider has an incentive to charge the insurer an infinite price.[4] Hence, insurers have developed administrative rules for setting reimbursement rates. In what follows I wish to focus on such administered price systems.

In the United States administered prices tend to be formula based. Examples include the Prospective Payment System for hospital prices, the Resource Based Relative Value Scale for physician prices (Hsiao, *et al.* 1988), and the Adjusted Average Per Capita Cost for HMO reimbursement. Other countries tend not to use such explicit formulas. In many countries prices may be negotiated (*e.g.*, physician fees in Canada), and in other countries they may be implicit in expenditure limits (*e.g.*, physician prices in the Federal Republic of Germany). In countries such as Canada where hospital budgets are negotiated with or determined by public authorities, the price for admitting a given patient will be implicit in how next year's budget

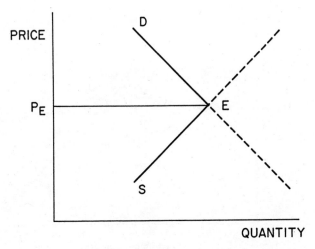

Figure 1. Demand and supply constrained equilibria. Demand constrained equilibria lie along DE, supply equilibria along SE.

is expected to change, if at all, as a function of this year's volume and case mix. In other words, there is a shadow price for admitting various types of patients; the shadow price, however, may be uncertain.

To make headway I suppose that the insurer sets a constant price and extra billing is not allowed (abstract for now from the basis of payment). Quantities may be supply constrained or demand constrained. Four cases can be distinguished.

Case 1. The price set is less than marginal cost at zero quantity and marginal cost does not fall as quantity rises. (To simplify matters I will continue to make the assumption that marginal cost does not fall as quantity rises.) In this case the service will not be provided, unless the provider is willing to cross subsidize the service from other services priced above marginal cost. Willingness to cross subsidize will depend upon the organization's objectives and the competitiveness of the market it faces, but it is more plausible in markets dominated by non-profit firms (Newhouse 1970; Weisbrod 1977).

Case 2. The price is above marginal cost at zero quantity; there is no inducement and no competition, and the product cannot be altered.[5] One standard analysis distinguishes demand- and supply-constrained equilibria, as shown in Figure 1. In that Figure prices above price p(E) result in an outcome on the line segment DE; the outcome is demand constrained. Similarly, prices below p(E) lead to supply-constrained equilibria. In the supply-constrained equilibria the maximizing provider reveals marginal cost by producing to the point where marginal cost equals price. The observed outcome may differ from the equilibrium shown in Figure 1 to the degree that not-for-profit firms use "profits" to subsidize additional quantity or to the degree that search is incomplete.

In the medical marketplace, however, the price to the consumer rarely

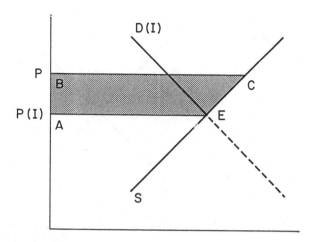

Figure 2. Rents from an administered price = ABCE.

equals the reimbursement to the provider. Indeed, in many countries the price to the consumer is zero. To simplify matters I will assume that the price to the consumer is zero and also will assume (for Cases 2 and 3) that demand is not a binding constraint; *i.e.*, demand at zero price exceeds what the provider wishes to supply at the price named by the insurer. The demand curves shown in the Figures are thus hypothetical in the sense that they show the quantity that would be demanded were the consumer paying the entire price; *i.e.*, were there no insurance.

For purposes of welfare analysis, I slightly extend Mark Pauly's (1980) notion of demand curves of informed consumers to the demand curves of informed consumers whose incomes reflect optimal lump sum transfers to the state of the world that actually occurs. This demand curve D(I) cuts the supply curve (the marginal cost curve) at an optimal quantity. Call the resulting price p(I). If the insurer picks a price above p(I), the firm simply pockets rents relative to a market with an unsubsidized demand curve (ABCE in Figure 2).

If the product can be altered but there is no competition, the firm chooses product characteristics so as to maximize profits; the above analysis does not fundamentally change.

Case 3. The price is above marginal cost at zero quantity, there is competition over product characteristics, but there is no inducement. As compared with Case 2, any rents are dissipated in competition over product characteristics; for an analysis see Held and Pauly (1983) and Joskow (1983).[6] I suspect that the product can usually be altered, so that Case 3 rather than Case 2 is the usual situation. For example, the physician can spend more time with the patient; clinics can be more numerous and therefore closer to an individual's place of residence or work.

Case 4. The price is above marginal cost at zero quantity, there may or may not be competition, but there is inducement. Pauly (1980) provides an analysis of this case. There is an incentive to induce demand if the quantity demanded with no inducement is less than the amount the producer wishes to produce given the price the insurer chooses (*i.e.*, inducement arises in a demand-constrained world). Inducement may or may not suffice to shift demand to the intersection of the price with the marginal cost curve.

DEPARTURES FROM THE OPTIMAL PRICE AND REAL WORLD PHENOMENA

There is little or no reason to think that the price the insurer sets will equal the optimal price P(I), and departures from the optimal price may explain a number of observations.

As Pauly (1980) has pointed out, if the insurer names a price above the optimal price, there may be an incentive for inducement (Case 4). Fees above marginal cost are thus consistent with a seemingly high proportion of inappropriate procedures (Chassin *et al.*, 1987), especially in the case of non-invasive tests or other services that do not involve the physician's time.[7] Contrary to what is often claimed in casual conversation, it is not the basis of payment (fee-for-service) that is potentially responsible for the inducement; it is the payment above marginal cost. However, inappropriate actions may reflect physician uncertainty or errors, as well as fees above p(I). For example, in the RAND Health Insurance Experiment the hospital setting was considered inappropriate the same percentage of the time (12.3 percent) in both the fee-for-service and HMO systems of care, even though the marginal price in the HMO setting was zero (Siu *et al.*, 1988).

Fees below marginal cost at zero quantity, as noted above, mean the service will not be provided without a cross subsidy; a real world example is cochlear (inner ear) implants in the United States Medicare program (Kane and Manoukian, 1989).

Payment above P(I) and demand-constrained equilibria are consistent with the excess capacity that Hughes *et al.* (1972) found for surgeons in the United States in the late 1960's. Because inpatient physician services were at that time typically much better covered by insurance than were outpatient services, it is plausible that surgeon's fees departed from P(I) to a greater extent than did fees for physicians whose services were outpatient-intensive, such as pediatricians. This would have induced entry into surgery, thereby reducing or eliminating the rents.

PATIENT HETEROGENEITY AND THE BASIS OF PAYMENT

Up to now nothing has been made of patient heterogeneity, but patients are, of course, heterogeneous with respect to the cost of treating them. For example, coefficients of variation for charges within the various DRG's of the Prospective Payment System in the United States are frequently 1.0 or more.

The inability to match reimbursement to marginal cost at the patient level explains additional real world phenomena. Most fundamentally, it is consistent with the persistence of many bases of reimbursement of medical providers throughout the world, including fee-for-service, capitation, and salary.[8] Each can be seen as a second-best method for coping with the problems of patient heterogeneity and errors in setting price.[9]

Fee-for-service has the advantage of accounting for patient heterogeneity more naturally than the other bases of reimbursement; the provider will be paid more for the patient whose medical condition indicates that more services should be delivered. As just argued, however, it is vulnerable to distortions in the provision of particular services from errors in price setting, simply because many fees must be set with poor information on cost.

Capitated systems may combine inputs more efficiently. Pauly (1980) has argued that physicians will combine inputs efficiently if they can capture the gains from that efficiency, irrespective of the payment system. This is, in general, the case in capitated organizations. It is not necessarily the case in fee-for-service environments, however, if the markup over $P(I)$ varies by service, which may well be the case in practice. In effect, the capitated program internalizes the pricing of individual services to the organization.

On the other hand, capitation as a basis of payment usually does not account for patient heterogeneity or does so only minimally, as in the case of the United States Medicare program that adjusts payments to capitated organizations for age, sex, location, and institutional status.[10] These variables, however, only account for a tiny fraction, roughly 10 percent, of the explainable variance in cost across people (Newhouse *et al.* 1989).

Moreover, in both capitated and salaried systems there is no marginal revenue for providing another service, with the consequent incentive to underprovide or welch on the contract to provide "necessary services." This requires capitated systems to incur monitoring costs in order to minimize shirking or that informed consumers monitor underprovision; *see* Pauly (1980). By contrast, fee-for-service may incur monitoring costs to minimize overprovision.

Salaried employees are found in the context of a national health service or a privately organized delivery system, such as a health maintenance organization.[11] How the salaried basis of payment for the employees affects outcomes depends upon what the health service or delivery system rewards in its personnel promotion and salary setting methods. For purposes of my argument here, I will only assume that the organization makes errors in implementing its objectives at the level of the individual provider, perhaps because it cannot monitor perfectly.

PATIENT HETEROGENEITY AND ADVERSE SELECTION

There is a considerable theoretical and empirical literature on adverse selection (Rothschild and Stiglitz 1976, Luft 1981, Pauly 1986, Langwell and

Hadley 1989, Freund *et al.* 1989). It is well accepted that equal premiums per person can induce selection behavior in the choice of insurance plan, including choice of a health maintenance organization. As an example, health maintenance organizations have a clear incentive not to enroll patients whose expected costs are above average. This possibility has led advocates of capitation, such as Enthoven, to suggest that sponsors monitor the extent of selection behavior, and, if such behavior is found, disqualify the organization as an option (Enthoven 1986, 1988).

Most empirical literature on selection behavior is based on American Health Maintenance Organizations. The National Health Service in the United Kingdom, however, capitates general practitioners. In light of the literature, it would seem reasonable to expect selection behavior in the National Health Service. Unlike the United States case, however, where selection takes the form of not enrolling the patient in the capitated organization, selection in the National Health Service case could take the form of excessive referrals by general practitioners of patients who require extensive resources to treat ("dumping" patients to the specialist).[12] Whether referral rates are higher than they would be if general practitioners were not capitated but were reimbursed entirely on a fee-for-service basis must remain a thought experiment. In principle, however, one could investigate whether referrals in the National Health Service are inappropriately high.

Selection behavior, however, can arise in contexts other than capitation, for example, the so-called dumping that the United States Prospective Payment System may have brought about. Because the System pays a fixed amount conditional on diagnosis but patients are heterogeneous, there is a financial incentive for the hospital to shun those whose treatment is expected to prove more expensive than the fixed amount. A necessary condition is that the hospital be able to predict those who are more likely to be high cost cases at admission, a condition that Keeler, Carter, and Trude (1988) have shown is satisfied.

Both statute law and regulations recognize the Prospective Payment System's incentive to dump certain patients and attempt to blunt its impact; for example, all transferred cases are reviewed by an external agency. Nonetheless, anecdotal and some more systematic evidence suggests that these attempts have not been wholly successful (Newhouse 1989).

Another example of selection could arise if the proposal in the United States to reduce the number of physician visit codes in order to minimize upcoding were adopted.[13] Heterogeneous patients within a given code could well induce selection behavior.[14]

TOWARD MINIMIZING THE CONSEQUENCES OF ERROR

Clearly inefficiencies and distortions can arise from setting the wrong price, a problem that potentially applies to hospital and physician prices in many countries. I have mentioned a number of phenomena that are consistent with such distortions. Even if one were unconvinced by such phenomena that prices departed from those that would be observed in a standard market, one might agree that public and private insurers are operating administered price systems and that administered price systems over time usually lead to distorted prices. The rapid rate of technological change in medicine only serves to increase the likelihood of errors in pricing.

I now want to turn the prescriptive side; if one agreed with the conclusion that price setting induces distortion, what if anything would one do about it? I argue in this section that a mixed mode of reimbursement can reduce welfare loss; for concreteness, I take a blend between a capitated rate and a fee-for-service rate as an example of a mixed mode of reimbursement. Although my example is a case in which prices are set explicitly, the basic idea could be adapted to methods for setting budgets (*e.g.*, for a hospital).[15]

Before coming to the argument for a blend, consider three alternatives. One quite different alternative is to have price setting done through a competitive process, that is, to rehabilitate the market. A possible scenario is that competitive insurers would negotiate with providers over price. They would then offer the panel of providers with whom they had negotiated contracts to consumers, who would face the full price differences in choosing insurers.[16] Another scenario is that the insurer would ask for bids, for example, for laboratory services.

If competitive prices are feasible, the distortions I wish to focus on in the remainder of the paper can potentially be eliminated. Indeed, it may well be that in some areas of medical care competitive pricing is feasible. But it remains to be seen if problems of selection preclude competitive pricing throughout medical care.[17]

There is a potential further problem if some consumers wish to pay something for freedom of provider choice (*i.e.*, no price differences at the point of service).[18] Although there is clearly a limit to what consumers would be willing to pay for such choice, insurance contracts that do not limit choice on the basis of price and do not permit balance billing would appear to require administered prices of the type I have been discussing.

A second alternative, implicit in some literature, is that the insurer should simply set the optimal price. It should be obvious that this is utopian; we cannot estimate cost functions without error, probably substantial error, for many reasons. Most importantly, the commonly available data for estimating such functions are accounting costs and not economic costs. Furthermore, even if one had data on economic cost, one must allow for economies of scale and scope, which may well place greater demands on the data than they can bear. Finally, if cost varies with scale, one must know the informed consumer's demand curve in order to set the optimal price.

A third alternative is for the insurer to set a price, see what happens, and adjust the price accordingly. One suspects that this is in fact what usually happens (ignoring issues of political economy and rent seeking). There remains, however, a question of the basis for the price the insurer sets, for example, capitation or fee-for-service.

The recent literature has emphasized various blended rates or prices. Ellis and McGuire (1986) is perhaps the best known example. They advocated a two-part pricing strategy for hospital payment, or what they termed supply-side cost sharing. The hospital's payment was to be a linear function of its costs, the traditional reimbursement method in the United States, and a fixed payment according to characteristics of the patient, for example, the DRG. In their framework a pure cost-based method was equivalent to no supply-side cost sharing, whereas the Prospective Payment System was equal to full supply-side cost sharing (a coinsurance rate of 1 at the margin). The former tended to overprovide services; the latter to underprovide if the physician was an imperfect agent. They developed a model of provider decision making in which the hospital (physician) would be induced to provide an efficient supply of services with a linear combination of a prospective rate and cost-based reimbursement.

Several other papers have recently taken up the notion of a blended rate. Ellis and McGuire (in press), Goodall (in press), Keeler (in press), and Pope (in press) have all extended the ideas of the original Ellis and McGuire paper in the context of the Prospective Payment System. Selden (in press), partly following an earlier conjecture of mine (Newhouse 1986), has developed a model showing that a blend between capitation and fee-for-service would be an optimal method for reimbursing HMO's.

I would like to end by suggesting a reason for a mixed or blended reimbursement system that is different from Ellis and McGuire's, though it has some analogies with Pope's. This argument is essentially an application of the law of large numbers, together with the argument that departures from the optimal price cause squared error losses in welfare. It focuses on reducing error in administered price systems and hence is compatible with a wide variety of models of behavior of medical care providers. Because the argument relies only on the existence of random errors in price setting, it would appear to strengthen the conclusion that a mixed or blended basis of reimbursement is an improvement.

Consider a pure fee-for-service system. Let Pauly's optimal price be denoted as P(I). Let the actual price be P; it is set by whatever administrative mechanism is in place, for example, the Resource Based Relative Value Scale. The argument is that in Cases 2, 3, and 4 described above, welfare losses are proportional to the square of the deviation from the optimal price. This is shown graphically in Figures 3 and 4.

This argument requires the assumption that those with the greatest "willingness to pay" as indicated by the demand curve are those who receive the service. Willingness to pay is in quotation marks because the demand curve could in principle include the willingness to pay of others (externalities). To the degree that those with the greatest willingness to pay do not receive the service – that is, to the degree that some other rationing principle is followed – welfare loss will be larger. And it may well be the case that some other rationing principle is followed.

For the purposes of this paper, the key issue in this context is whether

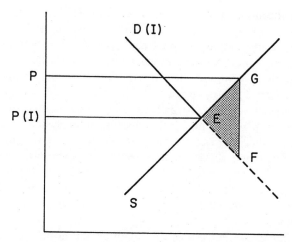

Figure 3. Welfare loss from too high a price.

any differences among the various bases of payment in the rationing principle employed lead to the superiority of one payment method. Following on the earlier discussion of the various bases as second (or third) best and the empirical fact that there are many bases of payment in use in the world, it seems reasonable to assume that this is not the case, but I do not try to prove this. To keep the subsequent exposition simple, I will assume the usual type of rationing; *i.e.*, those with the greatest social valuation are those who receive care.

In Figure 3 a price set at P above P(I) leads to an outcome at G, with a corresponding welfare loss of GEF relative to a situation where the optimal price P(I) clears the market at E.[19] In Figure 4 a price set below P(I) leads to a welfare loss GHE. As price moves away from P(I) in these diagrams,

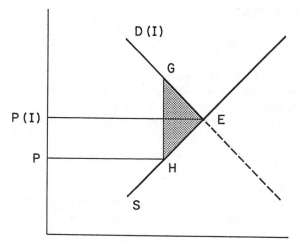

Figure 4. Welfare loss from too low a price.

the welfare loss increases to a first approximation as the square of the deviation from P(I). The exact result requires linear supply and demand curves, which I assume in what follows.

Assume for the moment that the method for choosing a price, for example, the method used to set the Resource Based Relative Value Scale, is an unbiased estimator of P(I). Thus, P(I) + error = P, and E(P) = P(I). Under these circumstances the welfare loss is proportional to the variance of the error in setting prices.[20]

Suppose, however, the method for choosing price is a biased estimator of P(I); for example, the government consistently picks too low a price. Relative to the welfare loss from an unbiased estimator of P(I), the welfare loss becomes proportional to the variance plus the square of the bias.[21] This calculation, however, ignores any welfare loss that might be incurred in raising the marginal dollar of revenue to pay providers, as would be the case if those revenues come from taxes or mandated premiums. If that welfare loss were accounted for, a downward biased estimator of P(I) may well be globally optimal. Monopsony might therefore be welfare improving! In order to simplify matters, however, in what follows I will ignore the welfare loss, if any, from raising revenue.

The calculations I have just made ignored the censoring of negative errors; if price is set below marginal cost at zero quantity, the service will not be supplied (Case 1). I presume this would happen only in cases in which it was efficient not to supply the service; otherwise the insurer would observe that the service is not supplied and adjust the price upward accordingly. If Case 1 only occurs when it is efficient not to supply the service, there is no need to correct the formula for welfare loss from censoring.

The calculations also ignored the possibility that product characteristics (quality) may adjust to clear the market at whatever price is set (Case 3); in this case instead of deviations from the optimal price, one should rephrase the argument in terms of deviations from the optimal quality, taking account of various willingness to pay for different qualities. (As before, willingness to pay and supply price must be linear in quality for squared error loss to hold exactly.).

The argument thus far has been couched in terms of fees. The argument for a pure capitation system is analogous. There are potentially the other issues in capitation noted above such as selection behavior (because price differs from the expected cost for an individual) or underprovision of services (because of no payment on the margin and imperfect ability to monitor the contract to provide necessary services). I am, however, abstracting from both these problems to focus on errors in the setting the rate, for example, errors made in calculating the Adjusted Average Per Capita Cost in the United States Medicare program, where an error is any departure from the optimal rate. Analogously to the fee-for-service case, if errors in setting this rate are unbiased, there is squared error loss; if not, a term for the square of the bias must be taken into account.

There is also an analogous argument for censoring with the capitated rate;

unless the capitated organization breaks even or makes a profit, it will not stay in business. As in the fee-for-service case, however, the organization may well be able to make adjustments in the quality dimension. And if this is impossible (for example, because of legal liability), that would mean that only positive errors would be observed (*i.e.*, p would always be at or above p(I)), in which case it would still be true that with unbiased prices welfare losses would be proportional to the square of the deviation of the error from the optimal price.

I now consider a blend of fee-for-service and capitation payments. Suppose the fee-for-service and capitation payments are scaled such that the variance of each error (*i.e.*, errors in setting fees and errors in capitation rates)is σ^2, and suppose for now that errors are either unbiased or the bias is the same in the two methods.[22] If the errors are independent, a 50–50 blend of a fee-for-service and capitated rate will have a loss proportional to $0.5\sigma^2$ plus any bias term, whereas either pure system will have a loss proportional to σ^2 (with the same proportionality factor) plus any bias term.[23] Weights other than 0.5 would change the amount of gain from a mixed basis of reimbursement, but not the fact of a gain.[24] Positive covariance between the errors would reduce the amount of the gain, but the gain is eliminated only if there is complete dependence.

The assumption that price setting is unbiased or that there is the same bias in each method can be relaxed. Suppose the bias in each method is random but has the same variance. Then by the same argument just employed there is an additional gain from a mixed method of reimbursement.[25]

Additional bases of payment beyond a capitation and a fee would further increase the gain. There are clearly diminishing returns to additional bases, and there may well be transaction costs to computing prices in other bases that would outweigh the gain from adding additional bases.[26] The only commonly used other base of payment is a salary or other fixed payment. Although it is reasonably apparent how one might use a salary in the case of an employed physician, it is less clear how one would use it to reimburse a delivery system such as a Health Maintenance Organization.[27]

Multiple bases of payment do exist. For example, general practitioners in the British National Health Service receive both a capitation payment and fees for selected services. Such payments have also been used in Denmark for many years.

The argument for using multiple bases of payment potentially applies in any context in which prices are set administratively. For example, in imperfect labor markets it may be welfare improving to have multiple bases of payments, such as a wage rate and a piece rate. Such a conclusion, however, would be dependent upon the incentive effects of each pure basis of payment.

The latter caveat, of course, applies in the medical care context as well. In other words, I have focused on the error term in this discussion, but a complete treatment of the welfare properties of a blended formula must also encompass the consequences from using a weighted average of $p(I_1)$ and p(I$_2$) relative to full reliance on either. Ellis and McGuire (1986) and the related articles cited in the text discuss those consequences. For my purposes it is only important to note that in the models considered in these papers it is welfare improving to use a mixture of p(I$_1$) and p(I$_2$) relative to sole reliance on either.[28]

In addition to the literature in health economics, there is a related industrial organization literature; it concludes that a linear payment scheme, *i.e.*, a fixed payment plus a payment that is a (linear) function of output, is optimal for a regulated firm that has better information about cost than the regulator who determines the contract. For an example see Laffont and Tirole (1986) and the literature cited there.

To this point I have not taken up distortions in price setting from the political process. For example, self-interested behavior by rent-seeking parties may lead to such distortions. The major response to this problem is that, to the degree it is an issue, it may well apply equally to either mode of payment; if so, it would not undercut the argument for a mixed method of payment.[29] Thus, I do not think that considerations of the political process much undermine the argument for a mixed mode of reimbursement.

To summarize: Some economic literature treats price determination in the medical marketplace as if it were similar to that of a standard marketplace. It seems more realistic to treat it as an outcome of one or more administered price systems. Such systems, may be formula-based, as is common in the United States (for example, the Prospective Payment System), or not (for example, a negotiated budget). In either case, however, the actual price is likely to deviate from the ideal price in part for lack of information. Plausible deviations can explain some observed phenomena. The inability to attain the ideal price, together with heterogeneity of patients, may also explain why in practice we observe several different bases of provider payment; for example, fee-for-service, capitation, and salary. All of these may be attempts to arrive at second best prices.

Ignoring any welfare loss from raising revenue and assuming those with the largest marginal social valuation for the service are served first, errors in price setting lead to a welfare loss that is approximately proportional to the square of the deviation from the ideal price. If price setting is unbiased (*i.e.*, errors have a mean of zero), the welfare loss is approximately proportional to the variance of the error in setting price. If price setting is biased, welfare loss is approximately proportional to the variance plus the square of the bias. Taking account of welfare loss from raising revenue may make monopsonistic pricing optimal.

If one uses multiple bases of payment, for example both fee-for-service and capitation, one can average the errors that arise in each basis. This creates a gain from using a mixed system, in addition to those gains cited by other analysts, who focus on the method of reimbursement assuming what, in the present context, could be termed error-free price effects. The gains from averaging errors would appear available in any administered price system and are compatible with a wide variety of models of provider behavior.

NOTES

1. Some other programs attempt to emulate this principle, but have the wrong basis for price to implement it. For example, the participating physician program in the United States Medicare program offers to publicize that a participating physician will not extra bill above the Medicare fee schedule. The intent is to create price competition in the physician marketplace. However, as many have pointed out, if the basis of a price comparison is the quality-adjusted treatment of a given problem, this type of program falls short because it does not price the treatment of the entire medical problem, and in particular the quantity of inputs (services) used to treat the problem. Thus, the total amount spent during a year to treat, say, hypertension, could be lower for physician A than physician B, even if A's fees are uniformly higher than B's. Moreover, as part of its shift to a relative value scale, the Medicare program has recently placed limits on physicians' ability to extra bill. As a result, physician prices under the program will even more closely resemble an administered price.

2. This is true of all admissions to the Medicare program, which in 1988 paid for over a third of admissions to community hospitals. Additionally, the patient's cost sharing (generally none) is unaffected by the choice of provider in the Medicaid program, which accounts for another 11 percent of admissions, although in some states, most notably California, the price of the hospital may matter to whether the hospital receives reimbursement from Medicaid. The patient's cost sharing is also immaterial for patients covered by private insurance plans that either cover hospitalization completely or contain a stop loss provision that is exceeded during the stay. Many private insurance plans contain such a stop loss provision (98 percent of plans in a non-random survey done by Hewitt Associates (American Hospital Association, 1988).

   In terms of documenting the above figures, the share of Medicare admissions is calculated from the American Hospital Association (1989), which shows that the over 65 accounted for over 11 million of the 33.5 million admissions to community hospitals, and statistics from the Health Care Financing Administration, showing that Medicare covers 99 percent of those over 65 for hospital services (Mariano 1989) and that under 65 Medicare eligibles accounted for around 1.1 to 1.2 million discharges in each year from 1978 to 1986, the latest year for which statistics are available ((Helbing and Keene 1989). The number of Medicaid admissions is from Ruther and Reilly (1989) and is for 1985. In light of recent expanded eligibility for Medicaid, the estimated Medicaid share is probably low.

3. Apart from the issue of the availability of such organizations, there is no generally accepted methodology for assessing the cost that various physicians incur to treat a given medical problem or episode of illness, which is ultimately the good being purchased. The principal difficulties are that: a) Pricing is per service rather than per episode. Although additional services per episode may result in a quality difference (perhaps sometimes negative), such a difference is properly treated by a hedonic adjustment to an episode price. In a world of administered prices, such an adjustment need not equal the fees charged for the additional service(s); b) Per episode pricing requires that the physician's costs be adjusted for case mix; otherwise the physician with a sicker case mix will be penalized (see the discussion on heterogeneous risks below). The technology for such adjustment, however, is primitive; and c) Many physicians may treat a small number of patients with a given problem. Thus, even if there were no systematic sorting of patients across physicians according to the degree of sickness, small numbers will tend to make observed costs of each physician noisy. As a result of these problems, Preferred Provider Organizations have in practice tended to simply

negotiate for a discount off the list price of a variety of services rather than choose physicians with a "conservative" practice style.

4. Some of the economics literature (*e.g.*, Frech and Ginsburg 1975) uses the average out-of-pocket share to bound the price the provider charges the insurer. This, however, ignores the fact that in many countries there is no out-of-pocket payment and even in the United States there are insurers, most notably Medicare in the case of hospital services, for whom out-of-pocket payment is independent of the provider's price, as pointed out in a previous footnote. A corollary is that the out-of-pocket payments for Medicare hospital services (now over $500 for each hospitalization in a spell of illness, though this is frequently covered by supplementary or so-called Medigap insurance) are irrelevant to price determination. (It is not even the case that there is necessarily a second order effect of these payments through the effect on aggregate demand, because there is no guarantee that the insurer sets a market clearing price and the equilibrium may be supply constrained.)

5. By inducement I mean that the provider attempts to influence the consumer to demand a greater quantity than a consumer who is as well informed as the provider would demand at the prices facing the consumer and with the consumer's income.

6. Complete dissipation of rents assumes free entry of perfect substitutes.

7. The importance of the physician's time is that at some point there is almost certainly a rising supply price for time, whereas for a number of tests there may well not be a rising supply price over the relevant range (*i.e.*, up to the number of patients being seen) and in the case of non-invasive tests there is no risk of an adverse outcome to act as a deterrent. There may be a time price to be paid by patients, but even the opportunity cost of the patient's time may be near zero for a hospitalized patient or one too sick to engage in any productive activity.

8. Listing only three modes of reimbursement is an oversimplification because the fee-for-service category leaves open the question of the degree of aggregation of the service. For example, a hospital could bill for services defined quite narrowly, that is, so much per day for room and board, so much for use of the operating room, so much for drugs, laboratory tests, and so forth. Alternatively, it could bill so much per stay irrespective of the length of stay or laboratory test usage, as is the case with the Prospective Payment System. In this case, the service is the stay.

9. I have not attempted to explain why one country relies to a greater degree on a given mode of reimbursement than another.

10. There is also an adjustment for eligibility for the Supplemental Security Income program, a program that supplements the income of low income elderly.

11. The private or public delivery system may receive its revenues through fee-for-service or capitation, or it may receive tax revenue.

12. Referrals, of course, will often be medically appropriate; those are not at issue here. General practitioners could also engage in the usual form of selection discussed in the American literature; *i.e.*, discouraging the enrollment on their list of those (generally sick) individuals for whom above average effort would be required.

13. *See* the Omnibus Reconciliation Act of 1986, P.L. 99–509, Section 9331 (d)(2).

14. The Physician Payment Review Commission has faulted this proposal on other grounds, namely its potential inequity across physicians and its potential greater encouragement to fraud. To date the proposal has not been adopted. *See* Physician Payment Review Commission (1989).

15. The budget could be set as if there were explicit prices.

16. For a description of an intended reform of this nature in the Netherlands, *see* Van de Ven (1990).

17. The bidding scenario would appear to work best in cases in which the product is reasonably standardized and the consumer does not have preferences among providers. Laboratory services are an example. In my view the majority of medical services probably do not fall into this category.

18. After all, Health Maintenance Organizations have not taken over the United States market,

and, although Preferred Provider arrangements are growing, I suspect it still may be more common than not to have consumers' premium payments independent of provider choice. *See* the discussion in the first section of the paper.

19. Inducement may not be necessary to reach G; demand at the price facing the consumer (*e.g.*, zero) may mean that G is still a supply-constrained outcome. If not, and if inducement is not sufficient to reach G, the welfare loss will be less (ignoring the costs, if any, to induce demand).

20. For proof *see* the next footnote.

21. Let e = error = P - P(I). It is clear from Figures 3 and 4 that (with linear supply and demand curves) the welfare loss is proportional to e^2. Let e be scaled so the constant of proportionality is one; then the expected loss = $E(e^2)$. Let e have a mean of k, the bias in e. Then var(e) = $E(e^2) - k^2$, or $E(e^2)$ = var(e) + k^2. In the special case of no bias in e, the welfare loss is proportional to var(e).

22. The schedule of fees and capitation rate that I have in mind are for a desired bundle of services (desired by the insurer or government). For this to be possible it is necessary that the desired bundle be in the feasible set of fees and capitation rates.

23. Let the mixed or blended payment be $0.5p_1 + 0.5p_2$, where 1 and 2 index a fee-for-service basis of payment and a capitation basis of payment respectively. Let $p(I_1)$ and $p(I_2)$ correspond to the P(I) of Figures 2–4 for the two different bases of payment. Then $p_1 = p(I_1) + e_1$, where e_1 is error, and similarly for p_2. If the e_i have a mean of zero and have the same variance, then the welfare loss from using p_1 or p_2 exclusively is proportional to var(e) = σ^2. Substituting in for p_1 and p_2, the mixed basis of payment is $0.5p(I_1) + 0.5p(I_2) + 0.5(e_1 + e_2)$. Assuming e_1 and e_2 are independent, the last term has variance $0.5\sigma^2$. As long as the bias is the same in the two bases of payments, any bias would add the same amount to each formula.

24. *See* Pope (in press) and Goodall (in press) for a method of determining weights. In the case of systems that are not paid on the basis of fee-for-service (*e.g.*, Health Maintenance Organizations in the United States, hospitals in Canada), making a portion of revenues dependent on fees also has the benefit of making utilization easier to monitor. This is useful both for monitoring quality and cost.

25. *See* footnote 21, which shows that welfare loss is proportional to the square of the bias (hence squared error loss). Then the result in the text follows because the blend is averaging the random component of the bias terms, just as it is averaging the random errors in pricing.

26. Note, however, that in the case of the United States Medicare program, the Health Care Financing Administration already computes prices on fee-for-service and capitation bases.

27. One is tempted to make the analogy to a fixed periodic payment; if such a payment were adjusted for volume, however, it would resemble a capitation rate.

28. The results in these papers, however, do not necessarily extend to a case in which quality adjusts to clear the market (Case 3).

29. I am arguing that any bias arising from the political process may be equal in both modes of payment. If so, as shown in a previous footnote, the bias term in the expression for welfare loss is the same in the mixed or blended mode as in the pure mode.

REFERENCES

American Hospital Association, "Digest of National Health Care Use and Expense Indicators", Chicago: American Hospital Association, 1988.

American Hospital Association, "Digest of National Health Care Use and Expense Indicators", Chicago: American Hospital Association, 1989.

Chassin, Mark, Jacqueline Kosecoff, R.E. Park, *et al.*, "Does Inappropriate Care Explain Geographic Variations in the Use of Health Care Services? A Study of Three Procedures", *JAMA* 258:2533–2537, 1987.

Crew, Michael, "Coinsurance and the Welfare Economics of Medical Care", *American Economic Review* 59:906–908, 1969.

Ellis, Randall P. and Thomas G. McGuire, "Provider Behavior Under Prospective Reimbursement", *Journal of Health Economics*, 5:129–152, 1986.

Ellis, Randall P. and Thomas G. McGuire, "Optimal Payment Systems for Health Services", *Journal of Health Economics*, (in press).

Enthoven, Alain, "Managed Competition in Health Care and the Unfinished Agenda", *Health Care Financing Review*, Annual Supplement, 1986.

Enthoven, Alain, "Managed Competition of Alternative Delivery Systems", *Journal of Health Politics, Policy, and Law*, 13:305–321, 1988.

Feldstein, Martin, "The Welfare Loss of Excess Health Insurance", *Journal of Political Economy* 81:251–280, 1973.

Frech, H. E. and Paul B. Ginsburg, "Imposed Health Insurance in Monopolistic Markets", *Economic Inquiry*, 13:55–70, 1975.

Freund, Deborah, Louis F. Rossiter, Peter D. Fox, *et al.*, "Evaluation of the Medicaid Competition Demonstrations", *Health Care Financing Review*, 11(2): 81–97, 1989.

Goodall, Colin, "A Simple Objective Method for Determining % Standard in Mixed Reimbursement Systems", *Journal of Health Economics*, (in press).

Helbing, Charles and Roger Keene, "Use and Cost of Short-stay Hospital Services Under Medicare, 1986", *Health Care Financing Review*, 10(4):93–109, 1989.

Held, Philip and Mark Pauly, "Competition and Efficiency in the End Stage Renal Disease Program", *Journal of Health Economics*, 2:95–118, 1983.

Hsiao, William, Peter Braun, Douwe Yntema, and Edmund R. Becker, "Estimating Physicians' Work for a Resource-Based Relative Value Scale", *New England Journal of Medicine*, 319:835–841, September 29, 1988.

Hughes, Edward F. X., Victor R. Fuchs, John E. Jacoby, and Eugene M. Lewit, "Surgical Work Loads in a Community Practice", *Surgery*, 71:315–327, 1972.

Joskow, Paul, "Reimbursement Policy, Cost Containment, and Non-Price Competition", *Journal of Health Economics*, 2:167–174, 1983.

Kane, Nancy and Paul Manoukian, "The Effect of the Medicare Prospective Payment System on the Adoption of New Technology – The Case of Cochlear Implants", *New England Journal of Medicine*, 321:1378–1383, 1989.

Keeler, Emmett B., "What Proportion of Hospital Cost Differences is Justifiable?", *Journal of Health Economics*, (in press).

Keeler, Emmett B., Grace M. Carter, and Sally Trude, "Insurance Aspects of DRG Outlier Payments", *Journal of Health Economics*, 7:193–214, 1988.

Laffont, Jean-Jacques and Jean Tirole, "Using Cost Observation to Regulate Firms", *Journal of Political Economy*, 94:614–641, 1986.

Langwell, Kathryn M. and James P. Hadley, "Evaluation of the Medicare Competition Demonstrations", *Health Care Financing Review* 11(2):65–80, 1989.

Luft, Harold, *Health Maintenance Organizations*, New York: John Wiley & Sons, 1981.

Mariano, L. Antonio, "Growth of the Medicare Population", *Health Care Financing Review*, 10(3):123–124, 1989.

Newhouse, Joseph P., "Toward a Theory of Nonprofit Institutions: An Economic Model of a Hospital", *American Economic Review*, 60:64–74, 1970.

Newhouse, Joseph P., "Rate Adjusters for Medicare Under Capitation", *Health Care Financing Review*, Annual Supplement, 1986.

Newhouse, Joseph P., "Do Unprofitable Patients Face Access Problems?", *Health Care Financing Review* 11(2): 33–42, 1989.

Newhouse, Joseph P., Willard G. Manning, Emmett B. Keeler, and Elizabeth Sloss, "Adjusting Capitation Rates Using Objective Health Measures and Prior Utilization", *Health Care Financing Review* 10(3):41–54, 1989.

Office of National Cost Estimates, "National Health Expenditures, 1988", *Health Care Financing Review*, Summer 1990, in press.

Pauly, Mark V., "The Economics of Moral Hazard: Comment", *American Economic Review*, 58:531–537, 1968.

Pauly, Mark V., *Doctors and Their Workshops*, Chicago: University of Chicago Press, 1980.

Pauly, Mark V., "Taxation, Health Insurance, and Market Failure in the Medical Economy", *Journal of Economic Literature*, 24:629–675, 1986.

Physician Payment Review Commission, *Annual Report*, p. 40, Washington: The Commission, 1987.

Physician Payment Review Commission, Annual Report, pp. 67–70, Washington: The Commission, 1989.

Pope, Gregory, "Using Hospital Specific Costs to Improve the Fairness of Prospective Reimbursement", *Journal of Health Economics*, (in press).

Poullier, Jean-Pierre, "Health Care Expenditure and Other Data: An International Compendium from the Organization for Economic Cooperation and Development", *Health Care Financing Review*, Annual Supplement, 1989.

Pratt, John W., David A. Wise, and Richard J. Zeckhauser, "Price Differences in Almost Competitive Markets", *Quarterly Journal of Economics*, 93:189–211, 1979.

Rothschild, Michael and Joseph Stiglitz, "Equilibrium in Competitive Insurance Markets: An Essay on the Economics of Imperfect Information", *Quarterly Journal of Economics*, 90:629–649, 1976.

Ruther, Martin and Thomas Reilly, *Medicare and Medicaid Data Book*, 1988, Washington: Government Printing Office (HCFA Publ. No. 03270), 1989.

Selden, Thomas, "A Model of Capitation", *Journal of Health Economics*, (in press).

Siu, Albert, Arleen Leibowitz, Robert H. Brook, *et al.*, "Use of the Hospital in a Randomized Trial of Prepaid Care", *JAMA*, 259:1343–1346, 1988.

Stigler, George, "The Economics of Information", *Journal of Political Economy*, 69:213–225, 1961.

Van de Ven, Wynand P.M.M., "From Regulated Cartel to Regulated Competition in the Dutch Health Care System", *European Economic Review*, 34:632–645, 1990.

Weisbrod, Burton, *The Voluntary Non-Profit Sector*, Lexington: D.C. Heath, 1977.

How can we prevent cream skimming in a competitive health insurance market?
*The great challenge for the 90's**

WYNAND P.M.M. VAN DE VEN and RENÉ C.J.A. VAN VLIET

Department of Health Policy and Management, College of Medicine and Health Sciences, Erasmus University, P.O. Box 1738, 3000 DR Rotterdam, The Netherlands.

1. INTRODUCTION

Recently in many countries market oriented strategies have been implemented or proposed in order to improve efficiency in health care. In several countries (*e.g.* the Netherlands, Australia, Germany, Israel, Switzerland and the United States of America (USA)) an essential aspect of these strategies is that competing insurers receive a risk-adjusted premium-replacing payment per insured. In return the insurers are responsible for paying for or delivering the services as described in the benefits package. The payment per insured is dependent on the risk category to which the insured belongs and provides the insurer with an incentive for efficiency. However, if the risk groups are heterogeneous, *cream skimming* may arise, resulting in adverse effects to society in terms of reduced (incentives for) quality and efficiency of care.

By cream skimming (or preferred risk selection) we understand selection by the insurer of so-called preferred risks, *i.e.* those insureds for whom the insurer considers the risk-adjusted per capita payment to be (far) above the expected cost level. Cream skimming may occur if the insurers can distinguish several subgroups of individuals with different expected costs within a risk group for which the risk-adjusted per capita payment is the same. The potential to cream skim the insureds is greater the less homogeneous the risk groups are.[1]

Pauly (1984) correctly notes that cream skimming is the result of *regulation* and not of *competition*. If the insurers are free to set their premiums in a competitive market, the result is premium differentiation rather than cream skimming. However, premium differentiation in a free market would imply that an 80-year old person would pay on average ten times the premium of

*This paper has been presented at the Second World Congress on Health Economics, September 1990, in Zürich. The authors wish to thank Brad Kirkman-Liff, Andrew Street and Peter Zweifel for their valuable comments on a previous draft.

a 20–year old person and that a chronically sick person would pay, say, one hundred times the premium of a chronically well person of the same age. In most societies this is considered undesirable. Risk-adjusted per capita payments (or vouchers) can be seen as a form of regulation that attempts to simulate the premium structure in a competitive health insurance market without having the adverse effects of (extreme) premium differentiation. However, if the system of risk-adjusted premium-replacing payments is not sufficiently sophisticated, cream skimming may occur.

The adverse effects of cream skimming are threefold. Firstly, for the (chronically) sick the access to good health care will be hindered. Insurers will try to attract the preferred risks and deter the non-preferred risks. If the capitation payment system does not adequately compensate for health status, insurers will prefer not to contract with providers of care who have a good reputation of treating patients with cancer, diabetes or high blood pressure, for instance, because the insurers do not want the patients who are attracted by these providers to be their insureds. In case of any risk sharing between the insurers and the contracted providers of care, the latter also have a financial incentive to attract the preferred risks and deter the non-preferred risks. This could be done, for instance, by providing poor care to the (chronically) ill. So, one possible outcome of an insufficiently sophisticated payment system is poor (access to) care for high risk persons. If the insurers are allowed to increase their revenues by asking an additional premium from their insureds, another possible outcome is higher premiums for the poorer risks.

Secondly, in the case of an insufficiently sophisticated payment system efficient insurers might be driven out of the market by inefficient insurers who are successful in cream skimming. Investments in cream skimming might have higher returns than investments in improving efficiency in the insurer's organization and in health care provision such as selectively contracting and stimulating managed care activities.

Thirdly, whilst individual insurers can gain by cream skimming, they only shift the costs to others,[2] so there is no social gain. In fact, because of the costs of cream skimming, there are only social welfare losses.

In sum, if cream skimming takes place, it is counterproductive with respect to three supposedly positive effects of competition, *i.e.* improving the quality and efficiency of care and becoming more responsive to the consumers' preferences. Therefore, an effective prevention of cream skimming is a *necessary* condition in order to reap the fruits of a competitive health insurance market with a regulated premium structure.[3]

In this paper we address the question of how to prevent cream skimming.[4] As a framework for our analysis we use the proposals of the Dutch government for a radical reform of the health care sector. These proposals are described in section 2. In section 3 it is shown that in case of an insufficiently sophisticated capitation payment system the potential profits of cream skimming based on information that is available to every insurer, are large.

Several examples are given of ways in which insurers can easily select the healthy people within (heterogeneous) risk groups based on age, gender and region, despite the requirement to accept anyone who wants to enroll (section 4). A first way to prevent cream skimming is to make the risk groups more homogeneous by including health indicators or other predictors of future expenditures as parameters in the capitation payment formula. An overview will be given of the huge progress made in this field during the last decade (section 5). As a second strategy several forms of additional procompetitive regulation are suggested (section 6).

In our opinion there are, in principle, enough solutions to the problem of cream skimming. However, in order to achieve these solutions the problem deserves high priority from both policy makers and researchers.

2. BUDGETS FOR COMPETING INSURERS

In the late 70's Enthoven (1978) launched his Consumer-Choice Health Plan (CCHP): a "national-health-insurance proposal for the USA based on regulated competition in the private sector". In CCHP all individuals would receive a subsidy from the government in the form of a refundable tax credit or a voucher to help them buy health insurance. The subsidy would be about 60% of the "actuarial cost", *i.e.* the average per capita costs for covered services for persons in each actuarial category. The subsidies would only be valid for premiums in qualified health insurance or delivery plans operating under procompetitive rules. These rules included periodic open enrollment, community rating by actuarial category (where the categories would match the categories used for setting subsidies) and a limit on each person's out-of-pocket payments.

In the late 80's the Dutch government and parliament decided to start with the implementation of a national health insurance based on regulated competition in the private sector, which showed a resemblance to Enthoven's CCHP. An essential element of the health care reforms is that direct government control over prices and productive capacities will make way for regulated competition among insurers and among health care providers. The benefits package will be broad, covering about 96% of all acute care (hospital, physician, drugs, physiotherapy and some dental care), long term care (nursing home care, care for mentally and physically handicapped persons) and health care related social welfare (old people's homes). According to the government's proposals,[5] all individuals will receive a subsidy to help them buy their insurance from one of the competing insurers. The subsidy will come from a Central Fund, which will be filled with mandatory income-dependent premiums, to be paid to the tax-collector. From the Central Fund the subsidy will go directly to the qualified insurer chosen by the insured. Qualified insurers are obliged to have an open enrollment period once every two years and to obey other procompetitive regulation. The subsidy per individual is independent of the chosen insurer and will be equal to the risk-adjusted per capita costs of the covered benefits for the risk group to which the insured belongs, *minus* a fixed amount. This fixed amount is equal for all individuals and will be about 15% of the average per capita costs of the covered benefits. The deficit created by this deducted fixed amount is met by a flat rate premium to be paid by the insureds directly to the insurer of their choice. In other words, the insurers will receive a risk-adjusted per capita payment from the Central Fund, supplemented by a flat rate premium to be paid by the insureds. The difference between the actual costs and the risk-adjusted capitation payment will not be the same for all insurers and will be reflected in the flat rate premium that the competing insurers will quote. This creates the incentive for insurers to be efficient. So the insurer's *budget* to cover the insureds' health expenditures consists of the payment from the Central Fund plus the flat rate premium from the insureds. Because an insurer determines the level of the flat rate premium to be paid by his insureds, it is the insurer himself who ultimately determines his budget. For the sake of solidarity between the healthy and the unhealthy people an insurer is obliged to quote the same flat rate premium to all his insureds who choose the same insurance option. Cost sharing arrangements may reduce this premium. Figure 1 shows schematically the financial flows of the proposed national health insurance.

The benefits package will not be described in terms of institutions like hospitals or nursing homes, but rather in terms of functions of care. Any supplier meeting certain quality standards is allowed to provide these services. This will greatly increase the possibilities for substitution of care. Insurers will be allowed to contract selectively with providers and to offer

Figure 1. Financial flows of the proposed Dutch national health insurance[a]

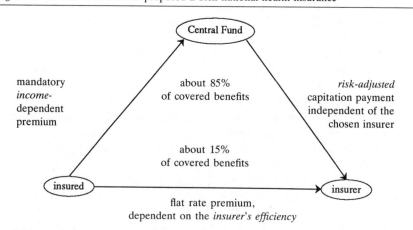

[a]The benefits package covers about 96% of total health care costs and health care related social welfare.

different insurance options as do, for instance, HMOs, preferred provider organizations or traditional health insurers, provided the insurance conditions conform to the functionally described legal insurance rights.

An important question, of course, is: For which risk factors will the capitation payment be adjusted? In answering this question it is important to realize that health care costs are determined by utilization and the prices of medical services; and that utilization is determined by factors such as health status,[6] supply, money- and time-prices, income, insurance coverage and propensity to use medical services. In the long term health status will be the only risk factor for which the capitation payment will be adjusted. So the subsidy from the Central Fund will be based on the Health Adjusted Per Capita Costs (HAPCC). Differences in costs caused by all other risk factors can be considered to be influenceable by the insurer or by the insured and will be reflected in the flat rate premium.[7] In the short term, however, it is to be expected that the payments from the Central Fund will be adjusted also for existing differences in costs caused by other risk factors, for instance supply and prices, because the insurers are not considered to be (fully) responsible for these differences, which cannot be expected to disappear instantly.

The HAPCC-capitation payment bears a striking resemblance to the AAPCC-capitation payment that HMOs in the USA receive for Medicare patients. This payment is based on the Adjusted Average Per Capita Cost (AAPCC). An essential difference is that the AAPCC payment rate is supposed to represent the local per capita fee-for-service costs that would have been expended, if the individual Medicare recipient had remained in the fee-for-service medical care system instead of enrolling in the HMO, while the HAPCC-payment reflects the health status of the individual insured. Although the starting points for calculating the payments are different, a common aspect in both capitation systems is the need for a sufficient refinement of the capitation formula for differences in health status. Without such refinement cream skimming might cause the problems described in section 1.

Before considering strategies to prevent cream skimming, we will first look at the potential profits of cream skimming for the insurers and the ways in which they may cream skim the insureds.

3. POTENTIAL PROFITS OF CREAM SKIMMING

It is self-evident that the potential profits of cream skimming depend crucially on the risk-adjusters included in the capitation payment formula as well as on the degree to which insurers can *predict* which insureds will have relatively high or low costs within each risk group. The adjusters included in the AAPCC-formula are age, gender, county, welfare status and institutional status. The Dutch government has suggested the following adjusters: age, gender and region. From the studies discussed below, it will become clear that the potential profits of cream skimming are very high if the payment formula is based solely on these risk-adjusters.

Newhouse et al. (1989) showed that the short term profits an HMO might achieve under the current AAPCC-formula can be substantial. In doing this they assumed that the HMO could predict all predictable differences in expenditures among its (potential) enrollees and that the HMO is interested only in short-run pecuniary gain and is risk neutral. Ignoring any costs associated with active selection (including the long term cost of a worsening reputation), Newhouse et al. found that the HMO would maximize short term profits if the HMO could reject that third of applicants whose predicted costs are above the AAPCC-capitation payment. The costs of the remaining two-thirds are only about 50% of the AAPCC-payment. Even with more sophisticated payment formulas the potential short term profits remained not inconsiderable. Although Newhouse et al. state that their assumptions are unlikely to hold, the presented results point to a serious potential problem.

Van Vliet and Van de Ven (1990) analyzed hospital and specialist expenditures of 35,000 privately insured persons in the Netherlands. They found that the mean expenditures in 1980 of those insureds who had above average expenditures in 1976, was 119% above the overall 1980 average expenditures.[8] Capitation payments based on age, gender, insurance coverage and region, would reduce this "loss" from 119% to 70% of the average per capita payment within the group (see table below). The inclusion of these risk-adjusters would have reduced the profit in 1980 within the group of persons who had no costs in 1976, from 32% to 24%. These results indicate that in the case of a payment formula based only on age, gender, insurance coverage and region, the potential profits that an insurer can make as the result of selecting "preferred risks" by using prior costs as a predictor of future costs, can be significant over a long period. From the same study it appeared that it would be very profitable for the insurers to select their preferred risks on the basis of risk factors (known to the insurers) such as prior costs of physiotherapy, of psychiatric outpatient care and of prescription drugs, and prior number of physician consultations.

4. POSSIBLE FORMS OF CREAM SKIMMING

Now that it is clear that cream skimming can be a very profitable strategy for insurers to lower their expenditures whilst maintaining their revenues, the question arises of how insurers can do this. In dealing with this question we will make some assumptions. These assumptions are derived from the current proposals for health care reforms in the Netherlands (see section 2). This implies that we assume a compulsory health insurance with a broad benefits package. Following the government proposals [9] we further assume that the insurers will receive a capitation payment for the cost of acute care

Table 1. Potential profits and losses per subgroup based on prior expenses, in the case of a capitation payment based on age, gender, region and insurance coverage.

| | 1976 | | Profits (+) and losses (−) as a percentage of average per capita payment in the subgroup, with the payment based on the following risk-adjusters: | | | |
| | | | NONE | | age, gender, insurance coverage and region | |
Cost interval in Dfl.	N	Mean cost in Dfl.[a]	1977	1980	1977	1980
0	21,007	0	+49%	+32%	+43%	+24%
1–500	9,135	158	−8%	−10%	+1%	−2%
>500	4,805	3318	−199%	−119%	−128%	−70%

[a] Overall mean costs in 1976 are Dfl.497. Source: Van Vliet and Van de Ven, 1990, Table 1 and 3.

based on age, gender and region. It is assumed that the costs of long term care and health care related social welfare will be financed in another way. Finally we assume that there is an open enrollment period every two years.

Looking at the possible forms of cream skimming we will make a distinction between selection of preferred risks at enrollment and at disenrollment.

At the *enrollment* of new insureds cream skimming could take place as follows:

1. Insurers could contract with a specialty mix of different quality and reputation, for instance good paediatricians and obstetricians and less well trained cardiologists, oncologists or diabetes-specialists. Insurers also could contract with providers who have no interpreters, who practice in "healthy" districts, and whose facilities have no disabled access. Such a strategy would attract the healthy and repel the sick (Enthoven, 1978, p. 711 and Luft, 1982, p. 292).
2. Insurers can attempt to select preferred risks by design of the benefit packages, as long as the insurance conditions are in accordance with the functionally described legal insurance rights. Another possibility is the design of the supplementary insurance: extensive maternity benefits to attract young, relatively healthy families; dental benefits if it is found that those who still have their teeth use less hospital care than those with dentures; and no extensive mental health (Enthoven, 1978; Luft, 1982 and 1986).
3. The insurance agent who helps people with their claims' processing and knows the health status of the family quite well, could advise the relatively unhealthy people to buy health insurance from another company, if that insurer has better insurance conditions for them or has contracted with physicians who specialize in the illness they have.
4. Insurers could attract the preferred risks by a package deal of health insurance and other forms of insurance bought mostly by relatively healthy people or people with a high income, such as insurances for sailing-yachts and winter-sports.

5. Insurers also could attract the preferred risks by selective advertising and direct mailing.
6. In the proposals for reforming the Dutch health insurance system people are offered a choice between paying the flat rate premium and having a deductible. By raising the level of the flat rate premium an insurer can make himself unattractive for high risk insureds. This could ultimately lead to a situation where no insurer is willing to offer the high option for a reasonable flat-rate premium.[10]

At *disenrollment* cream skimming could take place as follows:
1. Besides the insurers also the providers can make insureds leave a plan. Health care providers, who have a contract with insurers that contains elements of risk sharing, have the same financial incentives for cream skimming as the insurer has. However, providers have more subtle tools to cream skim the patients, such as keeping the patient in uncertainty about the correct diagnosis, making the patient wait for an appointment, making the patient wait in the office and being discourteous to the patient. The most famous (theoretical) example is the "mother with her asthmatic child" described by Newhouse (1982, p. 113). (To our knowledge, however, there is no well documented evidence that such behavior has occurred).
2. Insurers can encourage the "bad risks" to leave by not including in the benefits package some follow-up care that affects people after they had an illness, like for instance reconstructive breast surgery.
3. Insurers also can encourage the bad risks to leave by providing them with poor services such as delayed payments of reimbursement.
4. Finally, insurers could give their bad risks a "golden hand shake". Both an insurer and an insured who forms a bad risk might come up with the proposal that the insured receives a part of the expected future losses from the insurer if the insured will choose another insurer during the next open enrollment period.

Undoubtedly the most adverse effect of the theoretical possibilities of cream skimming mentioned above, is that access to good health care might be denied to some unhealthy people. However, the insurers will make a trade-off between the profits of cream skimming and the costs associated with it, including the worsening of their reputation. Consumer organizations will closely monitor the developments and give ample publicity to undesired situations. A bad reputation might result in a loss of insureds/patients [11]. Therefore the most extreme and most obvious forms of cream skimming probably will not occur. However, because of the high potential profits of cream skimming associated with a capitation payment adjusted for only age, gender and region (as illustrated in the previous section), one should seriously consider the several subtle forms cream skimming might take. Because of the large financial interests involved, one should not set the fox to watch the geese.

In principle there are two ways to prevent cream skimming: refining the capitation payment formula (*i.e.* extending the capitation formula with a set of relevant risk-adjusters) and additional procompetitive regulation. These strategies will be discussed in the next two sections.

5. REFINING THE CAPITATION FORMULA

5.1 *How far should the capitation formula be refined?*

An important question is: "How far should the capitation formula be refined to prevent cream skimming?" In theory the capitation formula should be refined to such an extent that the risk-adjusters create homogeneous risk groups such that the insurers expect the cost of cream skimming (including the cost of losing one's reputation) to exceed its profits. By refining the capitation formula, *i.e.* making the risk groups more homogeneous, the insurer's cost of cream skimming will increase – it is more difficult and therefore more costly to determine who are the preferred risks and the process of cream skimming would have to be more sophisticated, which makes it more expensive – whilst on average the profits of cream skimming will decrease (*see* for instance Table 1).[12] Therefore, refining the capitation formula on balance lowers the financial attractiveness of cream skimming to the insurers.

However, one might also question: "But can't we be *too* successful in refining the capitation formula? For, if we succeed in *exactly* predicting each individual's future health care expenditures, the ex-ante determined capitation payment is exactly equal to the future actual costs, thus making this payment system equivalent to a system of full reimbursement of all costs". The consoling answer to this question is that it is absolutely impossible to exactly predict each individual's future expenditures. It appears that the maximum explainable variance in annual acute health care expenditures per individual is around 15% and is unlikely to be more than 20% (Newhouse *et al.*, 1989; Van Vliet and Van de Ven, 1990). By far the largest part of variance in the annual expenditures of *individuals* is unpredictable. At the *aggregate* level, however, the differences between group averages are quite predictable. Based on the law of large numbers the group average is more predictable the more individuals are included in the group. However, to develop a risk-adjusted *per capita* payment that significantly eliminates cream skimming, it is important to have a good predictor of the *individual* health care expenditures.

Although the maximum explainable variance in annual acute health care expenditures per individual is relatively low (at most 20%), the potential profits in case of an insufficiently sophisticated capitation formula are very large. The more close we come to that maximum explainable variance, the lower is the financial attractiveness of cream skimming to the insurer. Only experience, however, will tell which refinement suffices in practice.

5.2 *Requirements for ideal risk-adjusters*

Ideally the risk-adjusters used to refine the capitation formula should meet the following requirements (Thomas *et al.*, 1983; Anderson *et al.*, 1986; Ash *et al.*, 1989):
* *validity*: they should predict the need for health services utilization and define a system of adjustment in which the cells are relatively homogeneous;
* *reliability*: they should be measured without measurement errors;
* *invulnerability to manipulation*: they should not be subject to manipulation by insurers, providers, or insureds;
* *obtainability*: they should be obtainable for all potential enrollees without undue expenditure of time or money and without making the administrative system unfeasible;
* *no perverse incentives*: they should not provide incentives for inefficiency or for low quality care;
* finally, they should not conflict with the right to *privacy* of insureds and health care providers.

It probably will be necessary to weigh these desirable properties one against another. There is considerable controversy over which of these properties is more critical (*see* for instance Gruenberg *et al.*, 1986).

5.3 *Potential risk-adjusters*

In the last decade huge progress has been made in the search for potential risk-adjusters. The most promising risk-adjusters seem *prior utilization*[13] combined with *diagnostic information*, *disability*, *functional health status* and indicators of *chronic medical conditions*. We will discuss each of these adjusters.[14]

Although *prior utilization* appears to be the best single predictor of an individual's future health expenditures, there are two major criticisms to using this predictor as a risk-adjuster. Firstly, some differences in prior use among individuals could reflect differences in physician discretionary practice patterns. A capitation payment based on prior utilization would pay insurers in direct proportion to the prior utilization of their insureds without regard to the appropriateness of the care (McClure, 1984). Secondly, the payment would be based on an average relationship between prior use and subsequent medical expenditures. The expected future costs, however, may differ widely for persons with high prior use associated with chronic medical conditions in contrast to those with one-off acute conditions. This might lead to perverse provider incentives or to new selection problems (Beebe *et al.*, 1985).

In order to solve both problems Ash *et al.* (1989) constructed so-called Diagnostic Cost Groups (DCG's). People were allocated to DCG's according to the principal diagnosis of their prior year's hospitalizations. DCG's were formed using empirically determined similarities in the future costs of individuals hospitalized for different reasons. One DCG was for those who had no prior year hospitalization as well as for those hospitalized with diagnoses thought to involve too much discretion in the hospitalization decision (*e.g.* pneumonia and influenza). A classification scheme with 5 DCG's appeared to suffice and was a relatively good predictor of future costs. The addition of this predictor to the model with only demographic predictors raised the percentage of explained variance of individual expenditures *in the next year* from 0.5 to 4.7%. The cost in the subsequent year of those individuals who had a non-discretionary prior hospitalization appeared to be three times as high as the cost of those without prior hospitalization (or with a discretionary hospitalization). This difference in cost appeared to persist over an extended period (*see* also Gruenberg *et al.* 1989), suggesting that the DCG designation captures some element of long-term chronicity.

Another prior hospitalization model has been developed by Anderson *et al.* (1990). Their Payment Amount for Capitated Systems (PACS) is based on the individual's health status and the input costs faced by the insurer. Health status is measured using a combination of demographic characteristics (age and sex), disability status, and three variables that together define prior utilization: 1) the major diagnostic category associated with each hospitalization in the previous years, 2) the chronicity of each clinical disorder that resulted in a hospitalization, and 3) a patient's level of ambulatory resource use in the base year. In terms of predictive accuracy the PACS-model surpassed the DCG-model. The PACS-risk adjusters explained twice as much variance of next year's individual expenditures as the DCG-risk adjusters.

Disability and *functional health status* have been shown to be relatively good predictors of future expenditures (Thomas and Lichtenstein, 1986). Indicators of functional health status reflect someone's ability to perform various activities of daily living and the degree of infirmity. Disabled and functionally impaired persons appeared to have roughly twice the health care expenditures of those who are unimpaired (Lubitz *et al.*, 1985; Gruenberg *et al.*, 1989). Impairment level continued to be a significant contributor to high Medicare expenditures after controlling for demographic factors and prior utilization (Gruenberg *et al.*, 1989). Newhouse (1986) suggested the use of functional health status and other measures of health status to try out in a demonstration. He considered disability to be an almost ideal adjuster, whose introduction as an adjuster may be so straightforward as not to warrant a demonstration.

The number of *chronic medical conditions* experienced by the individual, weighted with expected costs, appeared to be a powerful predictor of health expenditures (Van Vliet and Van de Ven, 1990). Besides direct measurement of chronic conditions it is also possible to have several indirect measures of it. For instance, Ash *et al.* (1989, p. 23) concluded that their DCG designation probably captured some element of long-term chronicity. An alternative would be to count the times that an individual has, in the last three years (say), exceeded an X-amount of expenditure, a given total, or a specified cost category. Suggestions for some of these categories are given by Freeborn *et al.* (1990), who found several conditions that were significantly more frequently reported by consistently high users than low users of medical care among the elderly.

Perceived health status, which is commonly derived from the answer to a single question, such as: "Compared to other people of your age, would you say that your health is excellent, good, fair, or poor?", predicts a few percent of the differences in medical costs between individuals. Although it appears to be a reasonable predictor of future health expenditures, perceived health status is not an ideal adjuster because it might be vulnerable to manipulation.

A restricted set of *physiological measures* such as whether the insured has diabetes, hay fever, hernia, angina or hypertension, appears to raise the explained variance with a few percentage points (Howland *et al.*, 1987; Newhouse *et al.*, 1989). However, because of problems associated with these measures, Newhouse *et al.* are skeptical about salvation lying in a much more complete battery of physiological measures, although there would undoubtedly be some gains from a more complete battery.

Sociodemographic characteristics such as age, gender, region, income, education, family size and unemployment status, appear to be relatively poor predictors of future individual health expenditures. They explain up to only 3% of the variance of health care expenditures.

In order to assess the relative strength of various predictors of medical utilization Epstein and Cumella (1988) reviewed more than 40 empirical studies published in the period 1975–1985. The studies were restricted to the elderly population. With respect to the percentage of variance in total individual medical costs explained by the various predictors, Epstein and Cumella came to the following conclusions:

* prior utilization: between 4 and 10%;
* functional health status: at most 3 to 4%;
* routine clinical and diagnostic information: between 2 and 4%;
* perceived health status: 2 to 3%;
* sociodemographic characteristics: up to 2%.

Finally, risk adjustments are not necessarily *prospective*, they may also be done *retrospectively* (Luft, 1986, p. 580; Enthoven, 1988, p. 86). Enthoven suggested that after the patient has been diagnosed and treatment has begun, one might use diagnostic information to put some people into more refined categories with associated fixed payments, for example, for "60–65–year-old breast cancer patients". These payments would be based on diagnoses that are relatively invulnerable to manipulation and for which high cost treatment is relatively non-discretionary. For predictable episodes of illness this suggestion may be a valuable addition to the DCG's developed by Ash *et al.* (1989).

5.4 *Simultaneous predictive power of various risk-adjusters*

Because the above mentioned risk-adjusters are not independent of each other, the percentages explained variance may not be added up. To assess the total variance that can be explained by a combined set of adjusters, we have to look at studies that include several adjusters simultaneously. Four of these studies will be discussed below.

Newhouse *et al.* (1989) analyzed data of about 4,000 persons between 14 and 65 years of age enrolled in the RAND Health Insurance Experiment. They estimated that at most 14.5% of the variance in individual health expenditure can be predicted. In order to illustrate the relative strength of various predictors, they started with a basic model and added several sets of predictors to it. The basic model contained as predictors only age, gender, site and AFDC-status (Aid to Families with Dependent Children). These predictors together explained 1.6% of the variance in annual individual health expenditures. The addition of several indicators of subjectively rated health status raised the explained variance to 2.8%. Adding several indicators of physiologic health, such as whether the insured had diabetes, hay fever, hernia, angina, hypertension, or elevated abnormalities raised the explained variance from 1.6 to 4.5%. The addition to this model of the indicator of subjective health status yielded little improvement. The measures of use in prior year were a substantial improvement to any of the health status measures in isolation. Adding prior-year use to the variables in the basic model raised the explained variance from 1.6 to 6.4%. If all available predictors were included, the explained variance went up to 9.0%, *i.e.* nearly two-thirds of the maximum explainable variance.

Van Vliet and Van de Ven (1990) found comparable results. Analyzing expenditures for hospital and specialist care of 15,000 privately insured individuals of all age-groups in the Netherlands, they estimated that at most 13.8% of the variance in these expenditures could be explained at the individual level. As predictors in the basic model they included age, gender, insurance coverage, and region. These predictors explained 2.6% of the variance. The addition to this model of factors such as unemployment status, family size, income, education level and degree of urbanization raised the explained variance to about 3%. The addition to the basic model of zip code and prior costs raised the explained variance to 7.1%, which is about half the maximum explainable variance.

Van Vliet and Van de Ven also analyzed another database, comprising some 20,000 respondents from the national Health Interview Survey. The basic model contained unemployment status and family size as well as the above mentioned basic predictors, and explained 3.2% of the variance of imputed acute care costs. The addition of the number of chronic conditions reported by the respondents, weighted with the expected costs, raised this percentage to 7.1%. The addition to this model of the number of physical impairments and the self-rated general health status raised the explained variance to 10.9%.

Thomas and Lichtenstein (1986) found similar results. Based on a sample of about 2,000 Medicare beneficiaries in Michigan they estimated several models to predict health expenditures. Their basic model included the following AAPCC-adjusters: age, gender, institutional status, and Medicare status.

This model explained only 0.3% of the variance in individual expenditures. The addition of income, years of education, and marital status raised this to 0.8%. The addition to the basic model of perceived health status and functional health status yielded 2.6 and 3.9% explained variance respectively. When prior year standardized payments and prior year utilization were added to the basic model, the explained variance increased to 5.9 and 7.2% respectively. All predictors together explained about 9% of the variance of individual expenditures (Lubitz, 1987; p. 368).

Howland *et al.* (1987) analyzed a sample of about 2700 persons aged between 60 and 65 from the Framingham Heart Study. The purpose of their study was to assess the value of risk factors for disease as predictors of hospitalization. They too came to the conclusion that demographic variables such as age, education, and marital status were relatively poor predictors. These variables explained less than 1% of the variance in the number of hospitalizations in 2 years. The following risk factors for disease appeared to have a significant effect: skinfolds (as a measure of body fat), forced expiratory volume (respiratory function), electrocardiogram (cardiac function) and blood sugar level. These risk factors explained 4.6% (men) and 1.9% (women) of the variance in the number of hospitalizations in the next 2 year. Risk factors such as the number of cigarettes per day, blood pressure, and cholesterol level, appeared to have no significant impact. By itself the number of hospitalizations in the previous 2 years explained 5.0% (men) and 1.9% (women) of the variance in the number of hospitalizations for the next 2 years. All predictors together explained 10.2% (men) and 3.2% (women). These results suggest that the two sets of variables account for different portions of the variance in hospitalization frequency.

A first conclusion from the above mentioned studies is that prior utilization, prior expenditure, and the several measures of health status are relatively good predictors of future individual expenditures; sociodemographic factors like age, gender, region, income and education appear to be relatively poor predictors.[15]

A second conclusion is that when several – but not all – potential adjusters were included, the explained variance increased to about 10%, which amounts to some two-thirds of the maximum explainable variance. Assuming that the risk-adjusters used in these studies explain to some extent different portions of the variance – which does not seem to be unrealistic – one may hope to come still closer to the maximum explainable variance. Based on these findings one may therefore be optimistic about the *technical* possibilities of finding a sufficiently refined capitation formula. However, the implementation of such a capitation payment system in practice will require a considerable research effort.

6. ADDITIONAL PROCOMPETITIVE REGULATION

In addition to the open enrollment requirement and the refinement of the capitation formula, the following forms of procompetitive regulation can be considered as tools to prevent cream skimming.

6.1 *Risk-related flat rate premium*

In section 1 it was explained that cream skimming is a result of regulation that intends to offset the loss of solidarity between the healthy and the sick that would occur in a competitive health insurance market where the insurers would be completely free to set their premiums. Probably a capitation formula that includes the suggested risk-adjustments will do a good job, although it may not yet be perfect. But one may wonder whether it needs to be perfect.[16] Does there really have to be *perfect* solidarity between the healthy and the sick? And what price is society willing to pay for it? As we have seen in section 1 the cost of achieving perfect solidarity in a competitive market – if this results in cream skimming – might be high in terms of both quality and efficiency.

As set out in section 2 the proposals of the Dutch government aim at perfect solidarity between the healthy and the sick, amongst others, by requiring the same flat rate premium for all individuals who buy the same insurance option from the same insurer. However, what would be the result if in the case of a sophisticated capitation formula the insurers were free to differentiate the flat rate premium according to what they experience to be the residual predictable risk not accounted for by the capitation payment?[17] The result will be that a part of the additional information the insurers might have about the residual predictable risk not accounted for by the capitation payment, *will not be employed for cream skimming* but for premium differentiation. Probably the resulting differences in premium will only be a small fraction of the hundred-fold differences that might occur in a completely free market as suggested in section 1. A strong argument for this is that a sophisticated capitation payment as suggested in section 5 is, as far as we know, much more refined than any risk-related premium structure that insurance companies currently employ for individual private health insurance. A reason for this might be the costs associated with risk rating, such as the cost of the actuarial calculation, the administration costs, the intransparency of the premium structure, and the transaction costs of calculating and updating the premium. Insurers make a trade-off between the costs and benefits of further refinement to their premium structure.

Socially unacceptable premium differences[18] could be mitigated by setting upper and lower bounds for the flat rate premium. Furthermore, a subsidy could be given to low income people to (partly) compensate for the above-average part of the flat rate premium. The cost of this is a lower incentive for those people to shop around for the cheapest insurer. This price, which has to be paid for a reduction in cream skimming, has to be weighted against the potential adverse effects of cream skimming.

If one would allow insurers freedom in setting their flat rate premium (possibly within boundaries), the insurers should be obliged to make explicit which risk factors they use for premium differentiation. In this way the information asymmetry between the Central Fund and the insurers – which is at the root of cream skimming – will be reduced and the Central Fund could try to include these risk factors in the capitation formula in subsequent years, which will further reduce the potential for cream skimming.

6.2 *Risk sharing between Central Fund and insurers*

Another suggestion for reducing cream skimming consists of several forms of risk sharing between the Central Fund and the insurers (Gruenberg *et al.*, 1986; Newhouse, 1986). Sharing the financial risk of deficits and/or surpluses with the Central Fund, reduces the insurers' incentive for cream skimming (as well as for efficiency). Several forms of such "partial capitation" have been suggested. For instance, the shared risk arrangement could apply to certain (groups of) insureds or to certain types of care (*e.g.* AIDS or transplants). Also the extent (*e.g.* 30% or 85%) and the form (stop losses or sliding scales) of risk sharing might differ.

An innovation to this idea of risk sharing might be the following. Let an *insurer himself* decide – within certain boundaries – for which patients, or for which types of care, or to what extent he wants to share the risk with the Central Fund. This would imply a further improvement to the procompetitive regulation that tries to simulate the freely competitive health insurance market. Such a free market would lead to the refusal of some potential high risk insureds and to exclusions because of pre-existing medical conditions. These phenomena occur if the insurer is aware of the existence of a (very) high risk, but cannot make a reliable estimate of the expected costs or does not have a risk factor at his disposal that is appropriate for premium adjustment. The refusal of potential high risks and exclusions because of pre-existing medical conditions as occurring in a free market, can be simulated by allowing an insurer to decide himself which risks he wants to insure and to what extent. An important advantage of such a flexible form of risk sharing would be that the additional information the insurers might have about the residual predictable risk that is not accounted for in the capitation payment, will *not be employed for cream skimming*, but will be reflected in the preferred form of risk sharing. Another advantage is, that again, the information asymmetry between the Central Fund and the insurers will be reduced. The information about the preferred forms of risk sharing that the insurers provide to the Central Fund, can be used to improve the risk adjustment of the capitation payment in successive years. In this way the Central Fund can make a considerable gain over the years in the ongoing game in which it attempts to incorporate in the risk-adjusted payment system as much information as the insurers have.

A disadvantage of (these flexible forms of) risk sharing may be that the insurers do not have full financial responsibility for the insureds or for the types of care to which the risk sharing arrangements apply. Therefore, risk sharing should be of a form such that it will not seriously influence the insurers' managed care activities, or the agency running the Central Fund should be involved in managing the care for the groups of patients for whom they bear the major financial responsibility.

6.3 *Qualification of insurance contracts*

Cream skimming also might be reduced if the subsidy from the Central Fund were given to insurers for qualified insurance contracts only.[19] The requirements for qualification of contracts between insurers and insureds could relate to the design of the benefit package, the copayment structure, the quality of the contracted specialty-mix, the location and accessibility of the contracted facilities, *etc*. Also, attention should be paid to the contract language. Finally, the pricing and selling of qualified health insurance should not be tied-in with other products and services.

6.4 *Enrollment procedure*

Enthoven (1978, 1986) proposed that there be no direct interaction between an insurer's sales representative and a potential insured in the enrollment process. The potential insureds deal with an agency that notifies the insurers of those who have enrolled for the coming contract-period. Every family receives a booklet, published by the administrative agency, containing meaningful, useful information on the features and merits of the presented alternatives.[20]

Furthermore, the contract period should not be too short. The shorter the contract period, the higher is the proportion of predictable episodes of costly illnesses (predictable by the insurers) during the next contract period(s). An example is the potential dumping of some patients at high risk of death (Newhouse, 1986). The one month lock-in period for a Medicare insured who chooses an HMO, provides all kinds of opportunities for cream skimming. The two year lock-in period proposed by the Dutch government seems much better. To keep competition alive the renewal dates need not to be the same for all insureds.

Finally Pauly (1988, p. 39) proposed allowing consumers to make their choice among the several insurance options a long time before the renewal date of the contract. This would lower the predictability of future costs during the new contract period and by that the potential profits of cream skimming.

6.5 *Monitoring the quality of services*

As Luft (1982, p. 299) suggested, monitoring systems might be developed by which people who change plans report the problems they experienced and whether they felt pushed out. Publication of such information could be very worthwhile for the consumer and could make the insurers more cautious about engaging in cream skimming.

The administrative agency running the Central Fund also could analyze the health care costs of those insureds who switch plans. This will give a good insight into the insurers' (and the contracted providers') behavior.

6.6 *Ethical codes for insurers*

One also could think of ethical codes for the insurers. Based on either government- or self-regulation, violation of these codes could be a punishable offence. The ethical codes could relate to things such as the quality of the contracted providers, procedures for making and handling complaints, selective advertising, golden hand-shakes, *etc*.

In our opinion, the suggestions given above are abundant solutions to cream skimming. Maybe only a few of them will prove sufficient. The choice is open to the policy-makers.

7. CONCLUSION AND DISCUSSION

In this paper we have dealt with the question of how to prevent cream skimming (or preferred risk selection) in a competitive health insurance market with a regulated premium structure. Cream skimming is caused by an information asymmetry between the insurers and the agency running the capitation payment (or voucher) system that simulates a risk-rated premium structure. The potential profits for insurers resulting from cream skimming can be significant, whilst the adverse effects of cream skimming to society in terms of reduced (incentives for) quality and efficiency of care are non-trivial. In the case of a capitation payment based exclusively on risk-adjusters such as age, gender and region, there are ample opportunities for insurers to cream skim the insureds. In this paper we have extensively dealt with two major strategies to prevent cream skimming, *i.e.* refining the capitation formula by the inclusion of more risk-adjusters and additional procompetitive regulation. In our opinion there are, in principle, enough solutions to the problem of cream skimming. However, in order to solve this problem, it deserves high priority from both policy makers and researchers.

In the late 80's, the Dutch government and parliament accepted proposals to implement a national health insurance based on regulated competition among insurers. In several other countries (*e.g.* Australia, Germany, Israel,

Switzerland and the USA) proposals for a comparable insurance system are being discussed. Therefore, the developments that are taking place in the Netherlands can be considered to be a demonstration project from which other countries can learn interesting lessons.

Some lessons that can already be learned relate to several obstinate misunderstandings that confused the discussion in the Netherlands during the last years. A first misunderstanding, especially among civil servants responsible for the design of the capitation payment system, was that "age, gender and region would explain a very large proportion of the variance of health care expenditures" (Bolhuis, 1989, p. 55). If this were true, a capitation system based on these three risk-adjusters alone would do a fairly good job. However, as we have seen in section 5 these risk factors are poor predictors and explain no more than 2 or 3% of the variance of individual health care expenditures.[21] This misunderstanding probably explains the government's decision that "for the time being the starting point is a *global* capitation formula".[22] Hopefully, the results presented in this paper will force the government to change its mind.

A second misunderstanding is that a refinement of the capitation formula (*i.e.* the extension of the capitation formula with a comprehensive set of relevant risk factors) would reduce market forces and that eventually it would lead to a system of full reimbursement of all costs, thereby removing the insurers' incentive for efficiency. This false argument has been put forward often by actuaries and representatives of the commercial insurers[23] – who have a clear financial interest in a global capitation formula because of the relatively good health status of their insureds – and by politicians and principal civil servants.[24] As we saw in section 5.1 the flaw in this reasoning is the implicit assumption that differences in individual health care expenditures can be *fully predicted*. However, by far the largest part of the difference in *individual* expenditures is unpredictable. Furthermore, a refined capitation payment would not remove the insurers' incentive for efficiency because – given a group of insureds – an insurer can influence the actual costs, but not the capitation amount.[25] Therefore, each reduction in the actual costs will be fully reflected in the insurer's surplus.

A third misunderstanding is that reinsurance could be a solution to the problem of cream skimming (Van Duuren *et al.*, 1989, p. 1235; Gerritse *et al.*, 1989, p. 32). The fallacy of this reasoning can be shown as follows. The insurer has to pay a risk-related premium to the reinsurer. Therefore, the expected costs of a "bad risk" for the insurer will be the same (or even higher because of the loading fee included in the reinsurance premium). So, reinsurance does not reduce the insurers' incentives for cream skimming.

This paper makes it clear that cream skimming, if unaddressed, forms the Achilles heel of a competitive health insurance market with a regulated premium structure. Moreover, the prevention of cream skimming is not only relevant for a competitive health insurance market, but it is also relevant with respect to competing provider groups who receive an ex-ante determined risk-adjusted capitation payment to provide a defined set of services to a defined population group (*e.g.* the GP-budget holder in Great Britain). Mutatis mutandis the same tools can be used to prevent cream skimming in these situations.

Solving the problem of cream skimming is a *necessary* condition for a successful implementation of a wide range of market oriented strategies in health care, which are being discussed these days in so many countries[26] and which offer good perspectives for both solidarity and efficiency. Therefore, research aimed at the prevention of cream skimming is the great challenge for the 90's.

NOTES

1. Cream skimming may also occur because the per capita payment per risk group is either too high or too low for otherwise homogeneous groups due to measurement error or estimation error. In this paper we will not deal with this cause of cream skimming.
2. In the case of Medicare patients in the USA who may voluntarily choose between a Health Maintenance Organization (HMO) and the traditional fee-for-service system, the losses to Medicare are twofold if the good risks "choose" an HMO, *i.e.*: Medicare has to pay the high costs of those who choose the fee-for-service sector and Medicare pays the HMOs too much because HMOs have the relatively good risks whilst the budget formula is based on the costs of the relatively bad risks (*see e.g.* Anderson *et al.*, 1986).
3. For other conditions for a successful implementation of market oriented strategies in health care, *see e.g.* Van de Ven (1991).
4. In this paper we concentrate on cream skimming (or preferred risk selection), which is just one form of selection that might take place. As Enthoven (1986, p. 107) states, biased selection may result from insurer action, consumer action or the interaction of the two as insurers manipulate consumers' choices. Selection might also occur just by chance, especially in the case of a relatively small number of insureds and because of the high skewness of the distribution of individual health care costs. However, in the case of selection which does not result from cream skimming, only one of these three problems might occur, and only to a lesser degree, *i.e.* the possibility that efficient insurers with relatively many bad risks might be driven out of the market by inefficient insurers with relatively many good risks. Furthermore, solutions to the cream skimming problem as proposed in this paper, especially the refinement of the capitation formula, include the solution to the problem of windfall profits and windfall losses in the case of other forms of selection.
5. Ministry of Welfare, Health and Cultural Affairs, the Netherlands: "Changing health care in the Netherlands", September 1988; and "Werken aan zorgvernieuwing", Tweede Kamer, 1989–1990, 21545, nr. 2, May 1990. *See* also Van de Ven (1990).
6. In this paper we will loosely use the term health status without going into details concerning either the difference between health status and need, or the various concepts of need, such as normative need, felt need, expressed need and comparative need (Bradshaw, 1972). For a discussion of the concepts morbidity, need and demand, *see e.g.* Ashley and McLachlan (1985).
7. Despite the requirement that the insurer is obliged to quote the same flat rate premium to all his insureds who choose the same insurance option, in practice this premium will be regionally differentiated. This is because an insurance company will be allowed to determine his own working area and need not (and is even not allowed) to accept insureds from outside this area. If an insurer is operating in regions with significantly different cost levels caused by, for instance, differences in supply and prices that are not reflected in the

capitation payments, he can quote regionally differentiated flat rate premiums by founding a holding company whose working companies have different working areas and quote different premiums.

8. In 1976 the mean expenditures of this group was 568 percent above the overall 1976 average expenditures. So, in a 4–year period the percentage with which this group exceeded the overall average expenditures, decreased from 568 to 119. This phenomenon of regression *towards* (but not *to*) the mean has been observed in many studies, *e.g.* McCall and Wai (1983), Anderson and Knickman (1984), Welch (1985), Beebe (1988) and Gruenberg *et al.* (1989).

9. "Werken aan zorgvernieuwing", Tweede Kamer, 1989–1990, 21545, nr. 2, May 1990, p. 60; *see* also Gerritse *et al.* (1989, p. 10).

10. This issue of adverse risk selection resulting from the choice between a high and low option is extensively dealt with in an ongoing research project within our department.

11. One may also hope that ethical considerations will prevent the physician from squeezing a patient out his practice. Newhouse (1982, p. 114), however, is skeptical that medical ethics are sufficient to make selection effects unimportant, especially as the number of competitors expands.

12. Although a refinement of the budget formula *on average* lowers the profits of cream skimming, for some individuals it might *increase* the profits (*see e.g.* Beebe *et al.*, 1985, p. 36). Therefore a more detailed exploration of the distribution of the potential profits and losses per individual insured might be necessary.

13. Prior utilization has already been successfully tested in a demonstration project (*see* Porell and Turner, 1990). .

14. It is not the intention of this paper to give a thorough analysis of the degree to which each adjuster satisfies the previously mentioned conditions for the "ideal adjuster". For this and for considerations with respect to weighing these conditions one against another *see e.g.* Thomas and Lichtenstein (1986), Newhouse (1986), Lubitz (1987) and Epstein and Cumella (1988). Note that some of the conclusions may change from one country to another, for instance, with respect to the obtainability, the administrative feasibility, the cost of collecting the data, the incentives (dependent on the existing remuneration system) and the privacy aspects.

15. This conclusion is also supported by the findings of Whitmore *et al.* (1989) and Manton *et al.* (1989).

16. *See* also the answer to the question "How far should the capitation formula be refined?" in section 5.1.

17. In order to give the insurers equal possibilities to accurately assess the risk of potential insureds they should be allowed to ask new applicants to fill out a questionnaire with questions about their health status.

18. In assessing the social acceptance one may also wonder, as Pauly (1984, p. 91) notes, about the ethical attractiveness of redistributing income from the healthy lower middle income worker to the wealthy diabetic.

19. An alternative might be certification of insurance contracts by an independent certification institute (*see* Pauly, 1988, p. 37).

20. For instance: Basic Health Plans, published by the State of California, Public Employees' Retirement System (PERS), Health Benefits Division, P.O. Box 734, Sacramento, CA 95804–0734 (August 1, 1985).

21. Of course, at the *aggregate* level age, gender and region explain a very large proportion of the variance of health care expenditures between *groups*. The fewer groups there are, the higher the proportion of explained variance. However, with respect to the problem of cream skimming the explained portion of the variance of expenditures at the *individual* level is the relevant criterium.

22. "Werken aan zorgvernieuwing", Tweede Kamer, 1989–1990, 21545, nr. 2, p. 55.

23. *See e.g.* Van Duuren *et al.* (1989), Posthuma (1990), Hammenga (1989).

24. G.B. Nijhuis, Handelingen Tweede Kamer, 4 oktober 1988, ZFW/AWBZ, p. 7–382; E.

44   W. P. M. M. de Ven and R. C. J. A. van Vliet

Veder-Smit, Handelingen Eerste Kamer, 13 december 1988, p. 11–405; D.M. Sluimers, deputy director-general, Ministry of Health, interview in INZET, nr. 11, 1988, p. III-V.
25. We implicitly make the logical assumption that the weights to be given to each risk factor in the formula, will be determined in such a way that the weighted average of these risk factors is the best predictor of the individual's cost in next year. So we exclude the (absurd) formula in which prior year cost has weight one and all other risk factors have weight zero. Even if prior year cost were the only risk factor included in the capitation formula, its weight in the best predictive formula would be at most 0.2. Such a capitation formula will generally not reduce the insurers' incentive for efficiency.
26. For instance Enthoven and Kronick (1989), Gitter et al. (1989), Launois et al. (1985) and Scotton (1989).

REFERENCES

Anderson, G.F., and J. Knickman, "Patterns of expenditure among high utilizers of medical care services: The experience of Medicare beneficiaries from 1974 to 1977", Medical Care, 22, pp. 113–119, 1984.
Anderson, G.F., E.P. Steinberg, J. Holloway, and J.C. Cantor, "Paying for HMO Care: Issues and Options in Setting Capitation Rates", Milbank Quarterly, 64, pp. 548–565, 1986.
Anderson, G.F., E.P. Steinberg, N.R. Powe, S. Antebi, J. Whittle, S. Horn, and R. Herbert, "Setting payment rates for capitated systems: a comparison of various alternatives", Inquiry, 27, pp. 225–233, 1990.
Ash, A., F. Porell, L. Gruenberg et al., "Adjusting medicare capitation payments using prior hospitalization data", Health Care Financing Review, 10-4, pp. 17–29, 1989.
Ashley, J., and G. McLachlan (eds.), " Mortal or morbid? – A diagnosis of the morbidity factor", Nuffield Provincial Hospitals Trust, London, 1985.
Beebe, J.C., "Medicare reimbursement and regression to the mean", Health Care Financing Review, 9-3, pp. 9–22, 1988.
Beebe, J.C., J. Lubitz, and P. Eggers, "Using prior utilization to determine payments of Medicare enrollees in health maintenance organizations", Health Care Financing Review, 6-3, pp. 27–38, 1985.
Bolhuis, E.A., "Normuitkeringen, de scharnier tussen doelmatigheid en solidariteit", in: Ziektekosten post Dekker, Astin Symposium, pp. 31–61, November 8. 1989.
Bradshaw, J., "A taxonomy of social need", in: G. McLachlan, Problems and progress in medical care, Oxford University Press, London, pp. 71–82, 1972.
Enthoven, A.C., "Consumer-Choice Health Plan", New England Journal of Medicine, 198, pp. 650–658 and 709–720, 1978.
Enthoven, A.C., "Managed competition in health care and the unfinished agenda", Health Care Financing Review, Annual Supplement, pp. 105–120, 1986.
Enthoven, A.C., Theory and practice of managed competition in health care finance, North Holland, Amsterdam, 1988.
Enthoven, A.C. and R. Kronick, "A consumer-choice health plan for the 1990's", New England Journal of Medicine, 320, pp. 29–37 and 94–101, 1989.
Epstein, A.M., and E.J. Cumella, "Capitation payment: using predictors of medical utilization to adjust rates", Health Care Financing Review, 10-1, pp. 51–69, 1988.
Freeborn, D.K., C.C. Pope, J.P. Mullooly, and B. McFarland, "Consistently high users of medical care among the elderly", Medical Care, 28, pp. 527–540, 1990.
Gerritse, R., R.T.J.D. Janssen, and J.D. Poelert, "Toward a budgetsystem for the Central Fund (Naar een verdeelstelsel voor de Centrale Kas)", report commissioned by the Dutch government, 1989.
Gitter, W., H. Hauser, K.D. Henke, E. Knappe, L.Menner, G. Neubauer, P. Oberender, G. Sieben, "Structural Reform of the Statutory Health Insurance System", Scientific Study Group "Health Insurance", Universität Bayreuth, June 1989.

Gruenberg, L., S.S. Wallack, and C.P. Tompkins, "Pricing strategies for capitated delivery systems", *Health Care Financing Review*, 1986 Annual Supplement, pp. 35–44, 1986.

Gruenberg, L., C. Tompkins and F. Porell, "The health status and utilization patterns of the elderly: implications for setting Medicare payments to HMO's", in: Scheffler, R.M., and L.F. Rossiter (eds.), *Advances in health economics and health services research*, Vol. 10, JAI Press, Greenwich, pp. 41–73, 1989.

Hammenga, interview, *VVP Magazine*, p. 35, August 9, 1989.

Howland, J., J. Stokes III, S.C. Crane, and A.J. Belanger, "Adjusting capitation using chronic disease risk factors: A preliminary study", *Health Care Financing Review*, 9–2, pp. 15–23, 1987.

Launois, R., B. Majnoni d'Intignano, J. Stephan, and V. Rodwin, "Les Réseaux de Soins Coordonnés (RSC): Propositions pour une Réforme Profonde du Système de Santé", *Revue Française des Affaires Sociales*, 39 (1), pp. 37–62, janvier-mars 1985.

Lubitz, J., J. Beebe, and G. Riley, "Improving the Medicare HMO payment formula to deal with biased selection", in: Scheffler, R.M., and L.F. Rossiter, (eds.), *Advances in Health Economics and Health Services Research*, Vol. 6, JAI Press, Greenwich, pp. 101–122, 1985.

Lubitz, J., "Health status adjustments for Medicare capitation". *Inquiry*, 24, pp. 362–375, 1987.

Luft, H.S., "Health Maintenance Organization and the rationing of medical care", *Milbank Memorial Fund Quarterly/Health and Society*, 60, pp. 268–306, 1982.

Luft, H.S., "Compensating for biased selection in health insurance", *Milbank Quarterly*, 64, pp. 566–591, 1986.

Manton, K.G., H.D. Tolley, and J.C. Vertrees, "Controlling risk in capitation payment". *Medical Care*, 27, pp. 259–272, 1989.

McClure, W., "On the research status of risk-adjusted capitation rates", *Inquiry* 21, pp. 205–213, 1984.

McCall, N. and H.S. Wai, "An analysis of the use of Medicare services by the continuously enrolled aged", *Medical Care* 21, pp. 567–585, 1983.

Newhouse, J.P., "Is competition the answer?", *Journal of Health Economics*, 1, pp. 109–115, 1982.

Newhouse, J.P., "Rate adjusters for Medicare capitation", *Health Care Financing Review*, Annual Supplement, pp. 45–55, 1986.

Newhouse, J.P., W.G. Manning, E.B. Keeler, and E.M. Sloss, "Adjusting capitation rates using objective health measures and prior utilization", *Health Care Financing Review*, 10–3, pp. 41–54, 1989.

Pauly, M.V., "Is cream skimming a problem for the competitive medical market?", *Journal of Health Economics*, 3, pp. 87–95, 1984.

Pauly, M.V., "Efficiency, equity and costs in the U.S. health care system", in: Havighurst C.C., et al. (eds.): *American Health Care: What are the lessons for Britain?*, London, IEA Health Unit, pp. 23–45, 1988.

Porell, F.W. and W.M. Turner, "Biased selection under the senior health plan prior use capitation formula", *Inquiry*, 27, pp. 39–50, 1990.

Posthuma, B.H., interview, *VVP Magazine*, p. 19, November 22, 1989.

Scotton, R.B., "Integrating Medicare with private health insurance: the best of both worlds?", in: Smith, C.S. (ed.), *Economics and Health: 1989; Proceedings of the eleventh Australian Conference of Health Economists*, Monash University, Clayton, Victoria, 3168, Australia, pp. 219–238, 1989.

Thomas, J.W., R. Lichtenstein, L. Wyszewianski, and S. Berki, "Increasing Medicare enrollment in HMO's: The need for capitation rates adjusted for health status", *Inquiry* 20, pp. 227–239, 1983.

Thomas, J., and R. Lichtenstein, "Including health status in Medicare's adjusted average per capita cost capitation formula", *Medical Care* 24, pp. 259–275, 1986.

Van de Ven, W.P.M.M., "From regulated cartel to regulated competition in the Dutch health care system", *European Economic Review*, 34, pp. 632–645, 1990.

Van de Ven, W.P.M.M., "Perestrojka in the Dutch health care system; a demonstration project for other European countries", *European Economic Review*, 35, pp. 430–440, 1991.

Van Duuren, R., B.H. Posthuma, and F.A.M. Ruygt, "Marktwerking, normuitkeringen en risicoselectie", *Economisch Statistische Berichten*, 74, pp. 1232–1235, 1989.

Van Vliet, R.C.J.A., and W.P.M.M. van de Ven, "Towards a budget formula for competing health insurers". Paper presented at the second World Congress on Health Economics, Zürich, September 1990 (to be published in *Social Science and Medicine.*)

Welch, W.P., "Regression towards the mean in medical care costs: Implications for biased selection in HMOs", *Medical Care*, 23, pp. 1234–1241, 1985.

Whitmore, B.W., J.E. Paul, D.A. Gibbs, and J.C. Beebe, "Using health indicators in calculating the AAPCC", in: Scheffler, R.M., and L.F. Rossiter (eds.), *Advances in Health Economics and Health Services Research*, Vol. 10, JAI Press, Greenwich, pp. 75–109, 1989.

The impact of utilization review on costs and utilization*

$G \nu \iota \quad I \mid \iota$

$\mathcal{U} S$

REZAUL K. KHANDKER

Aetna Life and Casualty, 151 Farmington Avenue, Hartford, CT 06156, U.S.A.

and WILLARD G. MANNING

School of Public Health, The University of Minnesota

ABSTRACT

This paper examines the performance of a utilization review program using data from Aetna's utilization review (UR) customers compared to a representative sample of its customers which had no utilization review during the study period. Statistical adjustments were made for the utilization management status, employee demographics, plan benefits, group size, year effects and seasonality. The study period covered from the first quarter of 1987 through the last quarter of 1988. The data suggest that UR reduces overall medical expenses by 4.4 percent, and inpatient expenses by 8.1 percent after a year of experience, largely by reducing length of stay.

INTRODUCTION

Over the past quarter of a century, the American health sector has experienced substantially higher rates of inflation than the economy as a whole. Expenditures on health care grew from 5 percent of gross national product in 1967 to almost 11 percent currently. Concerns over the overall level of health care costs and its rate of increase have spawned numerous proposals for decreasing medical care costs or reducing medical care inflation. These have included increased cost sharing, HMOs, second opinion programs, case management, and prospective payment.

Over the last few years, a literature has grown up that shows that a substantial fraction of inpatient stays may be medically unnecessary (Leape, 1989). The numbers vary from study to study, but it appears that a fifth of the hospitalizations are of dubious medical value, or that there are less expensive alternative modalities of treatment. Siu *et al.* (1986) found that cost sharing had little effect on the fraction of stays that were inappropriate.

---

*We would like to thank Howard Bailit, John Burnosky, and Thomas Gotowka of the Aetna Life and Casualty for their support and comments throughout this work.

The opinions expressed here are solely those of the authors. They are not necessarily those of either Aetna Life and Casualty or of the University of Michigan.

P. Zweifel and H. E. Frech III (eds.), Health Economics Worldwide. 47–62.
© 1992 *Kluwer Academic Publishers. Printed in the Netherlands.*

This suggests that cost sharing alone does not provide sufficient incentive to differentially reduce inappropriate inpatient use.

Given the concern about costs and a sure knowledge that some inpatient care is of little medical value, there has been a substantial interest in managed care options that will reduce hospitalizations or lengths of stay, an interest which in part reflects the success of prepaid group practices in keeping down their inpatient use rates (Luft, 1981; Manning et al., 1984). One practical form of managed care within third party fee-for-service arrangements is utilization review programs that require some type of precertification and/or concurrent review of the admission decision and length of stay.

LITERATURE REVIEW

Although case management has recently been a popular approach for insurance coverage, there have been few analyses of utilization review programs of the precertification/concurrent review variety (IOM, 1989). In a before-and-after study of Deere & Company, Kauer (1983) reported that using PSROs results in a 21 percent decrease in hospital days. However, there were a number of other changes occurring at the same time, changes that could themselves have altered the pattern of inpatient use. Getson (1987) reported the experience of Massachusetts Blue Cross Blue Shield, where utilization management (UM) had reduced inpatient days. A group with UM had 24 percent fewer days than it had earlier (1983), compared to a 12 percent change in traditional plans; this implies a net savings of 12 percent with UM. HDI (1988) reported that hospital days in a UM plan fell by 14 percent, while a conventional coverage plan exhibited a 7 percent drop; this implies a net savings of 7 percent of UM.

Using a cross-sectional design, rather than a before-and-after comparison, Zuckerman (1987) reported that Medicaid programs with prior authorization had 2.7 percent fewer beneficiaries receiving inpatient care.

In a pair of studies, Feldstein, Wheeler, and Wickizer reported on a comparison of the experiences of insurance company group customers with and without precertification, on-site review, and concurrent review (Feldstein et al., 1988; Wickizer et al., 1989). Although the group's participation was voluntary, participation was mandatory for all group members, with failures to participate subject to financial penalties. In the earlier study, the data covered 222 groups for a two year period, which did not include information on pre-UR behavior for all cases. They used least squares regression methods to control for observable demographic and insurance plan differences among the groups with various prior review options. They found that UR reduced overall expenditures by about 8.3 percent, which occurred largely by reducing inpatient admissions by 12.3 percent and inpatient days by 8.0 percent. On a subset of cases which had some pre-UR data, they found that groups that had historically higher use were more responsive to the review procedure.

In their second paper (Wickizer *et al.*, 1989), the results were only slightly different (*e.g.*, overall savings of 6 percent) after adding a third year of data. They used the LIML version of Heckman's selection model to control for possible selection biases (Heckman, 1976). However, the conclusions were not altered by the inclusion of the selection correction.

These various studies suffer from a number of possible limitations. Some are before-and-after comparisons without a contemporaneous control group. Hence, the estimated effects could reflect other ongoing changes or secular trends, as well as the effect of UR. Some are essentially cross-sectional comparisons without a direct control for possible adverse selection into the UR program. Hence, the observed differences could reflect other unobserved differences among the groups, as well as the effect of UR, if the groups that select UR are different from those who do not. The use of a selection model by Wickizer *et al.* is an attempt to correct for this.[1]

As an alternative approach, we take advantage of data on pre-UR utilization and expenditures for groups that select UR. Thus, we can use each group's pre-UR experience as a control for its unobserved propensity to consume medical services. To control for other secular changes or trends, we include a sample of non-UR cases. The difference between the pre-UR and UR experience, net of trend, provides our measure of the effect of UR. This approach assumes that there are no other choices or trends confounded with the choice of UR for the UR group only. That is, all time trends and changes are assumed to be common to both the ever- and never-UR groups.

DATA AND METHODS

This study uses data from Aetna's utilization review program for inpatient care, called Healthline. The program includes precertification and concurrent review for each medical and surgical admission. The precertification covers both the necessity of the admission and the length of stay. Failure to obtain prior approval or (in emergencies) concurrent approval results in increased cost sharing for the patient. Although Aetna operates a separate UR program for psychiatric, alcohol, and substance abuse admissions, that program is not a part of this work.

SAMPLE. The sample for this analysis included all indemnity/Major Medical customers meeting certain criteria. The customer had to have at least seven quarters of data for the two year period (including the number of covered employees), not be enrolled in other utilization review or programs during the study period, and to have more than 50 non-elderly enrollees.

UTILIZATION REVIEW. UR was introduced at different points in time during the study period. Based on the effective date, a given unit's UR and pre-UR status was determined. Because we did not know when during the quarter that a group switched from non-UR to UR, the quarter during which transition to UR took place was dropped. To act as its own control, only those UR cases which had both pre- and post-UR observations were used. Further the UR group changed composition over time. Thus, failure to use each group as its own control runs a serious risk that adverse or favorable selection effects would appreciably bias the estimates of the effect of UR.

The unit of analysis is a an account, with most employer/union groups maintaining multiple accounts. The data have been aggregated to a quarterly level because data on the number and characteristics of the insured population were available only on a quarterly basis. The data are aggregated to the account level, because of the lack of data on the age, sex, *etc.* of non-users. The period contained 828 group accounts for the UR sample with an average quarterly enrollment of 213 employees per group account. The Non-UR group had 4381 group accounts with an average quarterly enrollment of 107 covered employees per group account.

UTILIZATION DATA. Measures of utilization and expenditures were derived from claims data. The cost outcome measures included inpatient, outpatient, and total net submitted expense. The utilization outcome measures included admissions, length of stay and hospital days per 1000 covered employees. The multivariate analysis was performed excluding psychiatric and substance abuse claims because of the focus of this UR program on medical and surgical admissions.

EXPLANATORY VARIABLES. The control variables included age and sex characteristics of the insured employee population, the plan benefit information (deductibles, coinsurance rates, and stop-losses). In addition, quarterly dummy variables were used to control for seasonality, a year dummy to control for an annual effect, and interactions between the year and quarterly dummies to control for differences in seasonal patterns across years.

STATISTICAL METHODS. In this paper, we report results based on both simple analysis of variance and on multiple regression. For both, we weight each observation – an account – by the number of covered employees, because our dependent measures are rates (admissions per 1000 covered employees or dollars per covered employee). As a result of the averaging, the error for the larger accounts is less variable than that for the smaller accounts. Weighting provides efficient estimates of the coefficients and consistent estimates of the standard errors.

These data constitute a panel. We have up to eight observations on each account. We expected and found that the use and expenditure rates for each account are positively correlated over time. Failure to correct for such a correlation could yield inefficient estimates, AND inference statistics that

Table 1. Mean baseline non-UR use

Variable	Never UR	Ever UR	t	p
Expenditure per employee				
Total	539.43	562.19	2.13	0.0333
Inpatient	322.39	352.03	3.28	0.0010
Outpatient	217.04	210.16	−2.01	0.0448
Utilization per 1000 employees				
Admissions	45.45	50.39	4.76	0.0001
Hospital days	254.47	308.20	7.29	0.0001

Note: First quarter 1987. Expenses in January 1989 dollars.

are "too significant." Under certain circumstances, failure to correct could lead to biased (inconsistent) estimates of the effects of UR.

We used a fixed effects model (Maddala, 1977; Judge *et al.*, 1980) to control for the correlation. In the exploratory analysis, we conducted a Hausman test (Hausman, 1978) to see if we could use a random effects model. We could reject the random effects model at the $p < 0.001$ level. In using a fixed effects model, we use each observation as a deviation from that account's average of that dependent or independent variable over the time of the study. The resulting coefficient estimates are based on the variance in use/expenditures within an account, and do not include any variation across accounts. As a result, each account acts as its own control.

RESULTS

Table 1 reports the differences in means for each of the baseline (first quarter 1987) use and expenditure rates for the group that never acquire UR and those who eventually became UR cases. For this sample, that quarter is always a non-UR quarter, because we required that each group have at least one non-UR quarter to be included in the sample. As the table indicates, the ever UR group used significantly more inpatient services before they became UR than did the never-UR group ($p < 0.001$). However, they also used less outpatient services than the never-UR group. In a separate analysis not shown in this paper, we regressed use and expenditure values during the first quarter of 1987 on ever-UR status, employee demographics, size of group, and other insurance plan characteristics to see if these observed variables could explain the differences in baseline means for the UR and non-UR groups. For inpatient measures, the simple differences in means would be larger and more significant if we controlled for differences in employee demographics, insurance plan structure, and group size. For example, the uncontrolled difference in inpatient expenses is $30 per employee per quarter. Controlling for the available employee and plan characteristics, leaves an adjusted difference of $40 ($t = 4.08$). In contrast, these employee

Table 2. Effects of utilization review

Variable	WLS results			Fixed Effects		
	Parameter estimate	t	p	Estimate	t	p
Expenditure per employee						
Total	−71.91	−9.69	0.0001	−16.49	−2.42	0.0154
Inpatient	−51.10	−8.41	0.0001	−19.63	−3.27	0.0011
Outpatient	−20.81	−6.90	0.0001	3.13	1.27	0.2055
Utilization per 1000 employees						
Admissions	−4.53	−6.90	0.0001	−0.37	−0.63	0.5316
Hospital days	−51.62	−10.97	0.0001	−25.27	−5.67	0.0001

Note: The weighted least squares (WLS) t and p statistics are uncorrected for intertemporal correlation in the errors. An upper bound correction is to divide t statistics by 1.8.

and plan characteristics do account for the outpatient differences. The adjusted difference in outpatient expenses is $1.38 per employee per quarter, compared to $7 unadjusted.

Further, groups that picked up UR earlier in time are lower inpatient users than ones who selected it late in the period. Given this systematically higher inpatient use, direct comparisons of the UR group during their UR phase with the non-UR cases (pre-UR or never-UR) will systematically bias the estimates of the effects of UR.

Table 2 presents the UR estimates from the weighted least squares and fixed effects specifications of the multiple regression model. The first column gives the weighted least squares estimates, uncorrected for the presence of correlated responses over time. We did include an indicator variable for ever UR to try to capture the effect of the historically higher use of health care services by those accounts that subsequently use UR. The second column provides the fixed effects model estimates. Appendix A provides the full set of coefficient estimates for both the weighted least squares and fixed effect models.

The data suggest that the UR program leads to reductions in expenses of $16 per employee per quarter ($p < 0.05$). The primary source of these UR savings is the reduced length of hospital stay. Total hospital days fall by 25 per thousand covered employees per quarter, and the length of stay (LOS) falls by about half a day (both $p < 0.001$). There is an insignificant drop in the admission rates of 0.4 per thousand covered employees per quarter with UR.

The fall in inpatient use is not offset by a significant or appreciable increase in outpatient use. In our data, outpatient use increases by a $3 per employee per quarter with the introduction of the UR program net of trend ($t = 1.27$).

If we had not used the fixed effects model to control for the underlying differences between the UR and non-UR groups, we would have found substantially different estimates of the effect of UR. Typically the weighted least squares results are more than twice as large as those provided by the

Table 3. Effects of utilization review over time

	WLS results based on all CSA QTRS			
Variable	Parameter estimate	Standard error	t	p
Total expenditure per employee				
URTIME	−118.48	25.08	−4.72	0.0001
URTIME2	8.34	19.78	0.42	0.6731
Inpatient expenditure per employee				
URTIME	−98.56	20.55	−4.80	0.0001
URTIME2	23.60	16.20	1.46	0.1452
Outpatient expenditure per employee				
URTIME	−19.92	10.20	−1.95	0.508
URTIME2	−15.26	8.04	−1.90	0.0577
Admissions per 1000 employees				
URTIME	−6.33	2.22	−2.85	0.0044
URTIME2	−0.81	1.75	−0.46	0.6435
Hospital days per 1000 employees				
URTIME	−106.01	15.92	−6.66	0.0001
URTIME2	33.37	12.55	2.66	0.0079

Note: The weighted least squares (WLS) t and p statistics are uncorrected for intertemporal correlation in the errors. An upper bound correction is to divide t statistics by 1.8.

URTIME = 0 if never UR or pre-UR
= time on UR if currently UR
URTIMR2 = URTIME * URTIME

fixed effects model. We provide the weighted least squares estimates because they are more akin to the work of Feldstein *et al.* (1988) in methods. Comparison of the weighted least square and fixed effects results illustrates the need to adjust for intertemporal correlation. Given the results in both Tables 1 and 2, it is clear, that reliance on cross-sectional methods – not using the fixed effects model – can substantially bias the estimated effects of UR.

Results in Table 2 were based on a once-and-for-all UR effect, and, as such, provide an average impact of UR over time. In order to determine the pattern of UR effects over time, a quadratic specification of time on the UR program was attempted. The results, as reported in Tables 3 and 4, suggest that the effect of utilization review increases at a decreasing rate for most outcome measures. Table 3 provides weighted least square estimates and Table 4 contains fixed effects results. Results indicate that the program has its full impact after about one year. Figure 1 depicts the UR savings through time for a one year period using continuous and discrete versions of UR time variable. Although the degree of smoothness differs, both models provide estimates that are generally within 95% confidence interval of one another, and are virtually indistinguishable at one year into the program.

The fixed effects model was used to estimate the impact of the UR program. With a one year experience, the UR program generates total expendi-

Table 4. Fixed effects results based on all CSA QTRS

Variable	Parameter estimate	Standard error	t	p
Total expenditure per employee				
URTIME	−44.61	21.14	−2.11	0.0349
URTIME2	20.37	15.68	1.30	0.1939
Inpatient expenditure per employee				
URTIME	−52.59	18.63	−2.82	0.0048
URTIME2	25.52	13.82	1.85	0.0648
Outpatient expenditure per employee				
URTIME	7.99	7.68	1.04	0.2985
URTIME2	−5.16	5.70	−0.91	0.3654
Admisions per 1000 employees				
URTIME	−0.04	1.85	−0.02	0.9836
URTIME2	−0.96	1.37	−0.70	0.4841
Hospital days per 1000 employees				
URTIME	−62.85	13.85	−4.54	0.0001
URTIME2	29.13	10.27	2.84	0.0046

URTIME = 0 if never UR or pre-UR
        = time on UR if currently UR
URTIME2 = URTIME * URTIME

ture reductions of approximately $24 per employee per quarter, inpatient expenditures of $27 per employee per quarter, and reductions in inpatient days of 34 per thousand employees per quarter.

CONCLUSIONS

The data from the Aetna inpatient UR program suggest three conclusions: First, the UR option reduced inpatient costs significantly – on the order of 8 percent. These savings from UR are primarily derived from reduced length of stays, because UR lowers admissions only slightly. The combined effect on days can be substantial – on the order of a twelve percent reduction. Second, there is no discernible pattern of substitution of outpatient care for reduced inpatient activity due to UR. As a result, there is a significant reduction in overall expenditures of about 4.5 percent after a year of experience. In addition, savings from the UR option outweighs the costs of administrating the program, which runs at about $4 dollars per employee per quarter.

The qualitative pattern of our results are consistent with the literature, especially the results from Feldstein *et al.* (1988). All of the studies indicate some reductions in inpatient dollars, days, or stays. However, the specifics of the results differ. Much of the Feldstein savings is attributable to a drop of 3.3 admissions per insured person. Our results suggest a shift of less than 1 per thousand employees, let alone per 1000 persons. In contrast, they find

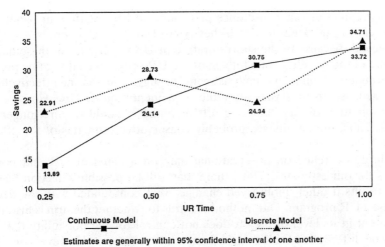

Figure 1. Effect of UR over Time.

no effect on length of stay, while we observe an 8.5 percent drop. As a result of this difference our overall dollar savings are smaller (4.5 vs 8.3 percent).

There are two likely sources of the differences. First, the UR programs run by different insurance companies will differ in their structure and effectiveness. Second, differences in statistical methods could yield different results. In our case, when we did not correct for prior utilization and expenditures, we obtained larger estimates that were more like their cross-sectional estimates. Given the significant pre-UR use differences (*e.g.*, higher use by the ever-UR group than the never-UR group) in our sample, we suspect that the failure to correct for unobserved difference may be a part of the explanation.[2]

As a cost control strategy, UR does offer some promise. It reduced use by more than enough to cover the costs of implementing and administering the program. The effect size is small but of an important magnitude – on the order of four to five percent of medical expenditures. Although this is a large sum, it is not large enough to be a primary remedy for the high level of medical care costs. Nor is it large enough to suggest that UR is largely eliminating the quarter of hospitalizations that are medically unnecessary, let alone whatever fraction is discretionary or marginal in their gains. Nevertheless, UR could be an important element in an overall cost-containment strategy.

Our conclusions, however, should be tempered by several limitations in the data. First, the estimated magnitude of UR's effect is very sensitive to which econometric model is used. The source of the difficulty is that the firms which select UR are not necessarily representative of all firms. Cross-sectional models tend to ignore this selection effect if it is not captured by demographics or other insurance plan characteristics. Different panel methods vary in the extent to which they control for this selection.

Second, because of the short duration of UR experience in these data the nature of the full effect of a fully matured UR program could not be precisely determined. Preliminary analysis seems to suggest increasing effectiveness of UR at least up to a year after the implementation of UR. However, the determination of any "tapering off" hypothesis would require longer term data. Thus, our results are probably conservative estimates of the effect of UR.

Third, we relied on observational data on a panel of UR and non-UR cases for our estimates. Thus, there may still be possible selection biases in our results if other unobserved changes were confounded with the decision to use a UR program. Our method controls for whether the firm is historically different in its level of use. It does not control for the possibility that firms may be differentially able to gain from a UR program.[3] However, our use of a fixed effects estimator in a before-and-after design with a contemporaneous control group provides greater protection against such problems than used in prior studies of UR.

Finally, we have not looked at the possibility that the UR program may have impacts on the health status of the population. This issue should be examined in future research.

NOTES

1. Although technically their model is identified by the nonlinearity in the LIML Selection model, and by exclusions of some market and plan characteristics, this particular application ignores the economic insight that variables which affect the demand for health care also affect the demand for insurance and vice versa. The form of the effects may differ between the two demands, but the same set of variables should be included. The one exception is the set of characteristics of the option not selected, which only enter the choice decision. None of the variables here seem to fall into that class; see p. 644 of Wickizer et al., 1989. Hence, most of the excluded variables should have been included in the model to begin with.
2. The use of a selection model by Wickizer et al. (1989) could in principle correct for this. However, the model is not well-behaved, and as implemented there, may not be capturing unmeasured heterogeneity.
3. We did regress the change in use on the pre-level to see if the UR effect depended on past performance. Most of the UR effect is a shift in level, and little is differential regression to the mean.

REFERENCES

Feldstein, P.J., T.M. Wickizer, and J.R. Wheeler, "The Effects of Utilization Review Programs on Health Care Use and Expenditures", *New England Journal of Medicine*, Vol. 318, pp. 1310–1314, May 19, 1988.
Getson, J., "Reforming Health Care Delivery: The Massachusetts Blues' Role", *Business and Health*, pp. 30–35, February 1987.
Hausman, J.A., "Specification Tests in Econometrics", *Econometrica*, Vol. 46, pp. 1251–1272, 1978.

Heckman, J., "The Common Structure of Statistical Models of Truncation, Sample Selection and Limited Dependent Variables and a Simple Estimator for Such Models", *Annals of Economic and Social Measurement*, Vol. 5, pp. 475–492, 1976.

Health Data Institute (HDI), "OPTIMED Managed Care Program", Lexington, MA., April 1988.

Judge, G.G., *et al.*, *Theory and Practice of Econometrics*. New York: John Wiley & Sons, Inc., 1980.

Kauer, R., "Evaluating a Corporate Health Care Utilization Review Program: The Case of Deere & Company", Health Systems Management Center, Case Western Reserve University, Working Paper No. 013, December 1983.

Leape, L.L., "Unnecessary Surgery: A Policy Synthesis", *Health Services Research*, Vol. 23, pp. 351–407, August 1989.

Luft, H.S., *Health Maintenance Organizations*, New York: John Wiley & Sons, Inc., 1981.

Maddala, G.S., *Econometrics*, New York: McGraw-Hill, 1977.

Manning, W.G., *et al.*, "A Controlled Trial of the Effect of a Prepaid Group Practice on the Use of Services", *New England Journal of Medicine*, Vol. 310, pp. 1501–1507, June 7, 1984.

Siu, A.I., F.A. Sonnenberg, W.G. Manning, *et al.*, "Inappropriate use of Hospitals in a Randomized Trial of Health Insurance Plans", *New England Journal of Medicine*, Vol. 315, pp. 1259–1266, November 13, 1986.

Wickizer, T.M., J.R. Wheeler, and P.J. Feldstein, "Does Utilization Review Reduce Unnecessary Hospital Care and Contain Costs", *Medical Care*, Vol., 27, No. 6, pp. 632–647, June 1989.

Zuckerman, S., "Commercial Insurers and All-payer Regulation: Evidence on Hospitals' Responses to Financial Need", *Journal of Health Economics*, Vol. 6, pp. 165–187, 1987.

APPENDIX A

VARIABLE DEFINITIONS

EVERHL = 1 if Healthline ever, = 0 otherwise

NOWHL = 1 if currently Healthline, = 0 otherwise

YR88 = 1 if year = 1988, = 0 otherwise

QTRi = 1 if ith quarter of the year (i = 2,3,4), = 0 otherwise

QTR88i = YR88*QTRi, year-quarter interaction (i = 2,3,4), = 0 otherwise

PERFEM = Proportion of Female

PAGE2 = Proportion of Employees below age 35

PAGE3 = Proportion of Employees age 35–49

PAGE4 = Proportion of Employees age 50–64

GT50 = 1 if number of employees > = 50, = 0 otherwise

GT100 = 1 if number of employees > = 100, = 0 otherwise

GT500 = 1 if number of employees > = 500, = 0 otherwise

GT1000 = 1 if number of employees > = 1000, = 0 otherwise

POSDED = 1 if deductible > 0, = 0 otherwise

LNDED = Log (deductible) if deductible > 0, = 0 otherwise

COINS = Average coinsurance rate: Percent paid by Actna

COINS2 = COINS*COINS

COILIM = Average coinsurance limit

Regression Coefficients Fixed Effects Results

Total Expenditure per Employee

Variable	Parameter estimate	t	p
NOWHL	−16.49	−2.42	0.0154
YR88	30.64	10.58	0.0001
QTR2	−50.94	−10.03	0.0001
QTR3	−41.57	−8.26	0.0001
QTR4	−71.13	−14.10	0.0001
QTR882	11.49	1.59	0.1127
QTR883	0.83	0.11	0.9093
QTR884	16.81	2.32	0.0202
PERFEM	−126.50	−1.86	0.0627
PAGE2	−183.28	−1.91	0.0567
PAGE3	130.15	1.26	0.2068
PAGE4	458.93	4.95	0.0001
GT50t	−30.53	−1.61	0.1082
GT100	−112.33	−6.76	0.0001
GT500	−76.91	−6.24	0.0001
GT1000	−112.19	−10.96	0.0001

Inpatient Expenditure per Employee

Variable	Parameter estimate	t	p
NOWHL	−19.63	−3.27	0.0011
YR88	6.89	2.70	0.0070
QTR2	−39.06	−8.72	0.0001
QTR3	−28.54	−6.44	0.0001
QTR4	−56.18	−12.64	0.0001
QTR882	7.60	1.19	0.2337
QTR883	−2.18	−0.34	0.7344
QTR884	11.87	1.86	0.0627
PERFEM	−87.63	−1.46	0.1434
PAGE2	−101.99	−1.20	0.2290
PAGE3	53.93	0.59	0.5528
PAGE4	307.14	3.76	0.0002
GT50	3.35	0.20	0.8413
GT100	−72.14	−4.92	0.0001
GT500	−56.16	−5.17	0.0001
GT1000	−72.22	−8.01	0.0001

Outpatient Expenditure per Employee

Variable	Parameter estimate	t	p
NOWHL	3.13	1.266	0.2055
YR88	23.75	22.564	0.0001
QTR2	−11.88	−6.439	0.0001
QTR3	−13.03	−7.129	0.0001
QTR4	−14.95	−8.160	0.0001
QTR882	3.89	1.477	0.1397
QTR883	3.01	1.137	0.2557
QTR884	4.94	1.878	0.0604
PERFEM	−38.87	−1.575	0.1154
PAGE2	−81.29	−2.326	0.0200
PAGE3	76.22	2.035	0.0419
PAGE4	151.79	4.508	0.0001
GT50	−33.88	−4.907	0.0001
GT100	−40.20	−6.655	0.0001
GT500	−20.76	−4.633	0.0001
GT1000	−39.97	−10.748	0.0001

Admission per 1000 Employees

Variable	Parameter estimate	t	p
NOWHL	−0.37	−0.63	0.5316
YR88	−1.16	−4.56	0.0001
QTR2	−2.30	−5.17	0.0001
QTR3	−1.43	−3.24	0.0012
QTR4	−3.97	−8.99	0.0001
QTR882	0.46	0.73	0.4684
QTR883	−0.37	−0.57	0.5668
QTR884	0.02	0.04	0.9718
PERFEM	−1.86	−0.31	0.7549
PAGE2	7.36	0.88	0.3817
PAGE3	12.05	1.34	0.1815
PAGE4	28.64	3.53	0.0004
GT50	−4.42	−2.66	0.0079
GT100	−4.21	−2.90	0.0038
GT500	−8.74	−8.10	0.0001
GT1000	−11.86	−13.25	0.0001

Hospital Days per 1000 Employees

Variable	Parameter estimate	t	p
NOWHL	−25.27	−5.67	0.0001
YR88	−9.21	−4.85	0.0001
QTR2	−34.52	−10.37	0.0001
QTR3	−30.18	−9.16	0.0001
QTR4	−60.81	−18.40	0.0001
QTR882	9.57	2.02	0.0438
QTR883	7.36	1.54	0.1230
QTR884	14.97	3.16	0.0016
PERFEM	14.48	0.33	0.7450
PAGE2	−30.94	−0.49	0.6235
PAGE3	82.66	1.22	0.2210
PAGE4	231.08	3.81	0.0001
GT50	−18.15	−1.46	0.1449
GT100	−31.11	−2.86	0.0043
GT500	−56.81	−7.03	0.0001
GT1000	−59.07	−8.81	0.0001

WLS Results
Total Expenditure per Employee

Variable	Parameter estimate	t	p
INTERCEP	486.46	175.47	0.0001
EVERHL	40.31	7.52	0.0001
NOWHL	−71.91	−9.69	0.0001
YR88	40.50	11.53	0.0001
QTR2	−43.67	−6.66	0.0001
QTR3	−38.00	−5.87	0.0001
QTR4	−66.82	−10.29	0.0001
QTR882	12.00	1.28	0.2005
QTR883	6.45	0.69	0.4934
QTR884	28.56	3.06	0.0022
PERFEM	−235.16	−28.00	0.0001
PAGE2	102.12	7.52	0.0001
PAGE3	391.58	28.78	0.0001
PAGE4	602.00	31.97	0.0001
GT50	3.26	0.37	0.7120
GT100	37.03	4.90	0.0001
GT500	22.87	4.09	0.0001
GT1000	−1.17	−0.24	0.8143
POSDED	−12.02	−0.49	0.6217
LNDED	−28.22	−9.61	0.0001
COINS	6.51	11.88	0.0001
COINS2	0.58	12.28	0.0001
COILIM	0.01	3.35	0.0008

Inpatient Expenditure per Employee

Variable	Parameter estimate	t	p
INTERCEP	289.04	127.31	0.0001
EVERHL	36.79	8.38	0.0001
NOWHL	−51.10	−8.41	0.0001
YR88	12.46	4.33	0.0001
QTR2	−34.10	−6.35	0.0001
QTR3	−26.63	−5.02	0.0001
QTR4	−54.07	−10.17	0.0001
QTR882	6.71	0.87	0.3825
QTR883	−0.03	−0.01	0.9964
QTR884	17.73	2.32	0.0204
PERFEM	−148.66	−21.62	0.0001
PAGE2	60.91	5.48	0.0001
PAGE3	131.71	11.82	0.0001
PAGE4	407.69	26.43	0.0001
GT50	12.38	1.71	0.0869
GT100	26.73	4.32	0.0001
GT500	8.01	1.75	0.0802
GT1000	−5.05	−1.23	0.2177
POSDED	−8.55	−0.43	0.6681
LNDED	−9.71	−4.04	0.0001
COINS	2.91	6.49	0.0001
COINS2	0.33	8.58	0.0001
COILIM	0.01	3.16	0.0016

Outpatient Expenditure per Employee

Variable	Parameter estimate	t	p
INTERCEP	197.42	175.19	0.0001
EVERHL	3.52	1.62	0.1059
NOWHL	−20.81	−6.90	0.0001
YR88	28.03	19.64	0.0001
QTR2	−9.57	−3.59	0.0003
QTR3	−11.37	−4.32	0.0001
QTR4	−12.75	−4.83	0.0001
QTR882	5.30	1.39	0.1646
QTR883	6.49	1.69	0.0903
QTR884	10.88	2.85	0.0043
PERFEM	−86.50	−25.34	0.0001
PAGE2	41.21	7.47	0.0001
PAGE3	259.87	46.99	0.0001
PAGE4	194.30	25.38	0.0001
GT50	−9.12	−2.54	0.0110
GT100	10.30	3.35	0.0008
GT500	14.86	6.54	0.0001
GT1000	3.87	1.91	0.0567
POSDED	−3.47	−0.35	0.7263
LNDED	−18.51	−15.50	0.0001
COINS	3.59	16.14	0.0001
COINS2	0.25	12.92	0.0001
COILIM	0.00	1.89	0.0588

Admissions per 1000 Employees

Variable	Parameter estimate	t	p
INTERCEP	41.74	169.93	0.0001
EVERHL	8.66	18.25	0.0001
NOWHL	−4.53	−6.90	0.0001
YR88	−0.75	−2.42	0.0157
QTR2	−1.43	−2.46	0.0140
QTR3	−0.96	−1.67	0.0951
QTR4	−3.86	−6.72	0.0001
QTR882	0.17	0.21	0.8368
QTR883	−0.10	−0.12	0.9019
QTR884	0.84	1.02	0.3093
PERFEM	−31.88	−42.85	0.0001
PAGE2	15.88	13.21	0.0001
PAGE3	26.54	22.02	0.0001
PAGE4	27.10	16.24	0.0001
GT50	−0.96	−1.23	0.2184
GT100	5.47	8.17	0.0001
GT500	3.76	7.59	0.0001
GT1000	−4.42	−9.99	0.0001
POSDED	−8.71	−4.04	0.0001
LNDED	0.37	1.42	0.1549
COINS	0.84	17.30	0.0001
COINS2	0.02	4.83	0.0001
COILIM	−0.00	−1.68	0.0922

Hospital Days per 1000 Employees

Variable	Parameter estimate	t	p
INTERCEP	224.44	127.62	0.0001
EVERHL	54.04	15.89	0.0001
NOWHL	−51.62	−10.97	0.0001
YR88	−5.34	−2.40	0.0166
QTR2	−29.15	−7.00	0.0001
QTR3	−27.48	−6.69	0.0001
QTR4	−58.81	−14.27	0.0001
QTR882	6.94	1.17	0.2431
QTR883	7.94	1.33	0.1842
QTR884	18.87	3.19	0.0014
PERFEM	−144.75	−27.17	0.0001
PAGE2	8.13	0.94	0.3452
PAGE3	55.15	6.39	0.0001
PAGE4	229.60	19.22	0.0001
GT50	8.50	1.52	0.1289
GT100	25.60	5.34	0.0001
GT500	13.45	3.79	0.0001
GT1000	−15.90	−5.01	0.0001
POSDED	−9.34	−0.60	0.5456
LNDED	−4.27	−2.29	0.0220
COINS	2.24	6.44	0.0001
COINS2	0.15	4.96	0.0001
COILIM	−0.01	−2.74	0.0062

The normative and positive economics of minimum health benefits*

MARK V. PAULY

The Wharton School of the Health Care Systems Dept., University of Pennsylvania, 3641 Locust Walk, Philadelphia, PA 19104–6218, U.S.A.

1. INTRODUCTION

Institutional structures to provide health insurance are changing. Many countries which formerly had unitary social insurance systems are looking to add elements of markets to those arrangements. In the United States, which has only provided limited social insurance for acute medical care for the elderly and the poor, there have been increasingly frequent discussions of the problem of the uninsured non-elderly and the possibility of some form of social insurance as a solution.

In both cases, the vision of the final desirable outcome seems much the same: it would combine public and private provision or financing in some way. The ideal system would not be based on a wholly market oriented arrangement; public provision would potentially touch the life of every citizen. It would not be a universal public system either; private sector supplementation would furnish a way of augmenting public resources and promoting greater efficiency.

Under either method, the configuration of public policy that is envisioned is to be one based on a privately supplementable public minimum benefit plan. The model is one in which the social insurance provides *minimum basic* insurance benefits, and people are free to purchase additional insurance beyond the basic level.

This institutional arrangement is not uncommon for other types of public goods, especially when public sector activity involves public *provision* (financing) alone, rather than public production as well. For example, the public educational system provides a certain number of hours of instruction and array of subjects to my child; I may choose to supplement that basic minimum if I wish. My township provides a certain amount of police protection; if I wish more I may install a private alarm system or hire security guards. The

---

*I am indebted to Willard Manning and Roland Eisen for very helpful comments.

P. Zweifel and H. E. Frech III (eds.), Health Economics Worldwide. 63–78.

government pays a certain amount towards veterans' college education in privately operated universities; supplementation is possible.

The purpose of this paper is to investigate the insights economic theory offers concerning such arrangements, especially as applied to health insurance. Welfare economics and positive political economy will both be used as methods of analysis. In particular, I will investigate whether a minimum benefits arrangement can offer advantages over the current institutional structures in countries with either market-based systems (as in the United States for persons under the age of 65) or fully socialized systems (as in Canada). I will show that a minimum benefit system can provide improvements, by some reasonable definitions, compared to either starting point. But I will also show that a uniform minimum insurance benefits program neither maximizes welfare nor achieves the fundamental objectives desired by those who advocate it. An optimal program is one in which minimum insurance benefits differ for different people, with the level of "minimum" benefits being lower the higher the private demand for medical care.

I also use a positive model of political economy to indicate when a country is likely to offer minimum "socialized" benefits, and what the equilibrium level of benefits will be under each of two regimes: with private supplementation forbidden, or with private supplementation possible. I show that, in contrast to a uniform insurance benefit program, permitting the level of insurance to vary with such demand indicators as the person's income may well both increase the positive likelihood that some public benefits are provided and lead to a pattern of benefits that is closer to the theoretical optimum.

2. DEFINITIONS OF MINIMUM BENEFITS

Enthoven (1988) provides what are actually two different statements of the objectives sought by a minimum benefits program. He begins by postulating that "a decent minimum standard of medical care" ought to be available to all members of society. One operationalization of the concept of a "decent minimum" he proposes is "a standard of care that equates marginal benefits and marginal costs for people of average incomes in that society." Formally speaking, this standard would represent approximately the level of use of care demanded by well informed people with average incomes who choose their level of medical care in the absence of conventional health insurance. It might also represent the level of care that would be provided by a health maintenance organization (HMO) that was preferred by people of average income.

The other approach Enthoven suggests is what he calls a "golden rule standard." The notion here is that the standard would answer the question: "if (compared to its current situation) your family were impoverished and in need of care, would you consider this standard to be fair treatment?" Each person could probably answer this question, but the level of care selected would probably vary with the respondent's income. That is, lower middle income people would probably choose a lower standard than the well-to-do. In such a case, which person's standard is to be used? One response would be to choose the standard favored by the majority – which would imply choosing the standard that represents the level of care that would be chosen by the person with the median preference in society. If one assumes a symmetric distribution of tastes at every income level, the person with the median preferences would be the person with the median income and average tastes.

Martin Weitzman (1977) also considers a general approach to a variety of goods which is similar to Enthoven's first concept. Weitzman postulates as a social objective the provision of the quantity of a good a person "needs." The amount of care a person "needs", given some indicator of need or taste, is the average quantity demanded by persons with that need or taste. Weitzman's notion applied to medical care is that the fair quantity at any illness level is the average level of consumption, which can differ from Enthoven's idea of the consumption level of the person with the average income. In what follows I will generally use Enthoven's first concept (based on average income), with recognition that other alternatives are possible and would yield different results.

There are a number of distinct forms that the process of achieving such objectives (which has been named "socialization" by Usher (1977)) might take: The first is what Usher himself meant by the term "socialization": the entire task of allocating resources to a good or service is given to the public sector; the good is publicly provided. This implies that all resources are raised via taxation, that the good is made available free of user charge, that private supplementation is impossible or illegal, and that the quantity of the good which is to be furnished is determined by political choice. Usher further assumes that the maximum possible consumption is equal for all. Public provision does not, of course, necessarily imply public production; use of private contracting or vouchers is consistent with Usher-type socialization. Usher's version of socialization does describe some health care systems: in Canada, for example, purchasing private insurance or paying doctors privately to supplement the social insurance is illegal.

Wilson and Katz (1983) pointed out a critical (and criticizable) assumption in Usher's characterization: he assumed that private supplementation of the socialized expenditure was not possible. But such prohibition is not universal, and Wilson and Katz therefore analyze the case in which socialization takes the form of a collectively chosen and tax-financed open-ended per unit subsidy to the consumption of a commodity.

There is, however, a third case possible. It is one that has not been analyzed in the literature in general, but which is especially applicable to medical care services and medical insurance. This the case in which a fixed and uniform tax-financed quantity is provided at public expense, but which one can supplement if one wishes by paying the full market price of the supplement. This approximates the case for both medical care and health insurance in a large (and growing) number of countries: a given level of care or insurance is provided free of charge, but a person is permitted to pay privately for care (or insurance which pays for that care) outside of the publicly financed system, and to finance that care with private insurance. The publicly provided level might be labelled the minimum benefits level, above which "socialization" ceases but private supplementation is permitted.

In this paper I address the normative and positive properties of both Usher's minimum benefits arrangements and of an arrangement based on fixed quantity ("closed end") provision with private supplementation. I do not deal with the Wilson-Katz subsidy case.

3. MEETING THE OBJECTIVES

The first question to be addressed is how the objective Enthoven proposes might best be achieved. Suppose that the demand curve for medical care is of the form:

$$M = M(\hat{P}, Y, S, e)$$

where $\hat{P}$ is user price, Y is income, S is the state of health, and e includes all other (unobserved) influences on demand.

Taken literally, Enthoven's characterization of a minimum standard of care requires setting $Y = \bar{Y}$ (where $\bar{Y}$ is average income), setting $\hat{P} = MC$, setting $e = 0$, and determining the value of M for a fully informed buyer for each value of S.

There are two obvious problems with this approach. First, if individuals are risk averse, insurance will be demanded against the cost of medical care, with the result that user price $\hat{P}$ will generally fall below MC even if the market price P equals MC; moral hazard can occur. We could reformulate Enthoven's objective then as defining the appropriate or fair level of care as the level of care which accompanies the level of insurance coverage that a well-informed person of average income and average tastes would demand when the price of medical care and the price of insurance both equal their respective marginal costs. Because of moral hazard, this level of care would be somewhat higher than that chosen by the same person in the absence of insurance. But it would seem to be more relevant in many settings.

One suspects that Enthoven may have had in mind instead an HMO that provided nominally full coverage but which limits the amount of medical care in each illness state to the level that satisfies the demand function (1) for $Y = \bar{Y}$ and $e = 0$. But this strategy assumes that such an HMO is feasible for all, which may well not be the case. In what follows, I will usually assume that conventional insurance will be used, and redefine minimum acceptable "benefits" as minimum acceptable insurance coverage.

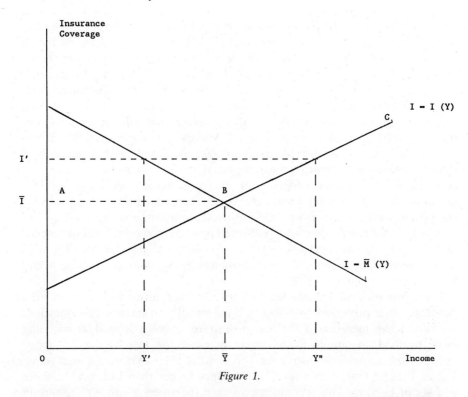

Figure 1.

Is a uniform minimum level of insurance coverage a means of achieving a uniform minimum acceptable level medical care use? If conventional insurance is used, a major paradox emerges. *Uniform insurance coverage cannot produce uniform use of medical services if there is any cost sharing and income affects the demand for medical care.* While providing the level of insurance coverage demanded by persons with $Y = \bar{Y}$ will lead to the target or minimum level of demand for person with that income level, such coverage will be too generous for persons with $Y > \bar{Y}$, and too limited for persons with $Y < \bar{Y}$.

Figure 1 illustrates. Let us assume that the demand for (nominal) insurance coverage and the demand for medical care, conditional on coverage, both vary directly with income. This relationship between income and coverage is described by the curve $I = I(Y)$. Let $\bar{M}$ be the average level of medical care consumption by persons with income $\bar{Y}$. Suppose also that $\bar{M}$ is purchased by persons with insurance level $\bar{I}$, the average level of insurance bought by persons with the average income. The line $I = \bar{M}(Y)$ then shows the levels of insurance coverage (and associated out of pocket payments) needed to induce purchase of a target level of $\bar{M}$ units of medical care at different income levels. It slopes downward, because higher levels of insurance coverage are needed to offset income effects as income falls.

If minimum coverage is set at a uniform value of $\bar{I}$ but supplementation is permitted, the line ABC shows the levels of coverage that will be purchased; it is obvious that the level of *use* M will fall below the target level M̄ for all income levels below Ȳ. If instead the level of coverage is set higher than Ī at, say, I', then use will still be below M̄ for incomes below Y'. In contrast, subsidized insurance coverage and use of care would be greater than optimal for persons with incomes between Y" and Y.

There is, in short, no level of uniform coverage that will induce consumption at level M̄ for all persons. There is not even a single level which will induce the use of at least M̄ and then permit people to buy more care than M̄ entirely with their own resources. With "minimum basic insurance" benefits, there is either underuse or overconsumption. A single level of uniform coverage at level Ī will achieve the optimum use level M̄ only for the person with income Ȳ who did not need the assistance anyway!.

A policy that used public intervention to provide income-related (a "means tested" level of coverage) will in contrast yield a uniform pattern of use. In a more general model with altruistic demands for M, the same pattern would be experienced (Pauly, 1970).

If the provision of a single level of coverage is inferior to income related coverage, is it preferred to doing nothing at all? To answer this question, we need some measure of the loss in welfare, loosely defined, from being away from M̄. A simple model might measure the loss by the difference between the actual insurance coverage and the level that would lead to M̄. Figure 1 shows that, with a level of insurance higher than Ī at, say, I', there is a set of persons with too much coverage (between Y' and Y"), and an area in which use was increased closer to the ideal by insurance (between Y = 0 and Y').

The critical question is whether gains exceed losses. The distances in figure 1 describe the gain or loss per person. The other parameter relevant to a total loss measure is the distribution of persons across various income levels. If there are relatively many very low income persons with similar incomes, and relatively few persons with incomes near the mean, there is a uniform level of socialization that gets close to the ideal. Conversely, if there are many persons with incomes close to the mean as well as those with low incomes, uniform socialization will either leave sizable numbers below or above the ideal. Some level of minimum benefits will be desirable, but no single level will be close to ideal. In this case, non-uniform benefits will have a more substantial advantage over uniform benefits. How much of a problem is associated with the uniform level of coverage, relative to income conditioned coverage, depends on the target level of out of pocket payment, on the income elasticity of demand for medical care, and on the shape of the distribution of income below the mean.

If the level of out of pocket payment which achieves M̄ is zero or nearly so, then use is likely to vary less with income than if the out of pocket payment is substantial. Roughly speaking, we could reasonably assume that demand curves for care get closer together as the user price of care approaches zero. However, it seems equally reasonable to assume that a non-negligible copayment will be chosen by persons at the average income level who have to pay the full cost of their insurance (without a tax subsidy). That is, when the quantity demanded under free care is not efficient, uniform programs have problems.

It is surprisingly difficult to determine whether and how medical care use responds to income. Feldstein (1986) summarizes a large number of studies with the conclusion that the "income elasticity for medical care expenditures is approximately unity." However, at least some of the studies he cites look not at the partial effect of income (insurance coverage and other demand variables held constant), but rather are affected by a positive income elasticity of demand for insurance. Recent work from the health insurance experiment found evidence of significant and positive income effects on the probability of using any care and on the level of outpatient use, but mixed or insignificant effects on inpatient use and total expenditure. (Manning *et al.*, 1987). Here as well as there is a difficulty in estimating a truly partial effect: the experimental insurance plans had income related upper limits on coverage, and, in any case, if lower income people are sicker for other reasons, their actual average use can be greater even if their level of use conditional on illness state is lower.

Logic alone dictates that use and expenditure must be low, given illness and insurance coverage, for some sufficiently low level of income and wealth. Exactly how spending varies over the full range of income is not known with great precision, but the assumption that medical care is a normal good with a non-trivial income elasticity seems plausible.

This fundamental message – that achieving uniformity of use requires non-uniformity of insurance coverage – appears to point out the major flaw in the minimum standards approach. While it is probably true in the United States that greater uniformity of insurance coverage than presently exists is desired, some variation of public coverage with income – or any other demand indicator – is required to achieve a minimum target use objective. Non-uniform coverage is needed to assure a minimum and uniform level of use for precisely the same reason as that which causes moral hazard to exist in health insurance: insurers cannot observe the individual's state of health precisely. In conventional health insurance, this means that pure indemnities cannot be paid, conditional on the person's state of health. In a minimum benefits arrangement, the absence of information on the state of health means that payment for just enough care to meet the minimum standard one needs in a given state of health cannot be determined. Instead, either too much or too little benefit is provided.

This is a critical difference between medical care and other commodities. For other goods whose equality of consumption is a matter of concern, providing a fixed and equal amount of that commodity is a feasible way of guaranteeing minimum consumption without inducing over consumption by the non-poor. With medical services, providing literally equal amounts (an equal number of doctor visits, an equal number of appendectomies) is obviously nonsensical. Providing equal insurance coverage will not yield a minimum level of consumption, conditional on the state of health, if coverage is incomplete. But providing complete coverage (free care) will lead to overconsumption.

However, the alternative of providing a uniform (but less than complete) level of insurance coverage leaves some with lower than the minimum level of consumption. Only making care free (full insurance coverage) comes close to assuring the minimum level of consumption for all, at all income and wealth levels. But then many people will be receiving tax financed funds that they will use to pay for care beyond the minimum level.

4. POLITICAL EQUILIBRIUM

The literature on the issue of social or national health insurance frequently asserts that "society" seems to desire minimum benefits (though sometimes this assertion is part of preaching to a society which has not yet implemented any program of the kind). It would therefore be useful to see which alternative or alternatives might be most supportable in a democratic political decision process. I begin, as did Usher, with a model with no externalities (altruistic or otherwise); I ask whether and when a majority of "selfish" individuals would tend to support some minimum benefits policy. After answering this question, I then ask how adding altruistic externalities modifies the conclusion.

The definition of political change and equilibrium here is exceedingly simplified; a policy is regarded as unlikely to be an equilibrium if a majority would support some alternative to it. I generally compare policies on a two-by-two basis; the more complex question of whether a given policy gets a majority against all other alternatives is not completely analyzed. The more realistic political world of pressure groups, parties, and unalloyed randomness is also assumed away here; the defense of the simplified single issue majority rule model is that it may, nevertheless, shed some light on tendencies, even if it is known to be incomplete. I therefore ask what level of public uniform insurance coverage (if any) will constitute an equilibrium in a simple majority voting model, and compare that equilibrium with the alternative definitions of the optimum discussed in the previous section. I also consider whether a pattern of income related subsidies can constitute a political equilibrium, compared to a single level of minimum coverage.

When will uniform insurance coverage be supported by a majority, compared to no intervention? Suppose that a level of minimum insurance benefits must be financed by a proportional income tax. It is immediately obvious that, absent altruism as a motive, all persons with incomes above the mean income will oppose "socialization", whether benefits are supplementable or not. Persons with above average income pay more in taxes than the expected cost of the insurance policy they receive. If the alternative in the non-socialized setting is to buy the same policy at its expected cost, such persons obviously lose by being forced to make a redistributive transfer. However, if the median income is less than the mean, as is usually the case, there is still a real possibility that majority may favor some positive but uniform value of the publicly provided good. When will there be a majority in favor of (non-supplementable) socialization?.

To determine how people with incomes below the average income will vote on the question of socialization, we need a more specific description of demand. Following Usher, I assume that persons have utility functions in the socialized good x and a composite good y of a Cobb-Douglas form:

$$U^i = x_i{}^{\beta i} y_i{}^{1-\beta i} \tag{1}$$

There is a distribution of income and tastes given by $f(n, \beta)$ where n is output or income and β is the "taste" parameter in the utility function. (As we will see, this function has some quite special properties, but it will be useful to shed light on some important inferences). In this discussion, I interpret x to be the level of *insurance* (*not* of medical care), and imagine that the desired goal to be provision to all persons of insurance at the level of insurance chosen by people with average incomes, financed by a proportional income tax.

If the good x is available in a (worldwide) private market at a price of p, and the price of y in the same market is normalized to one, the income constraint under the market arrangement for person i becomes:

$$n_i = px_i + y_i \tag{2}$$

where n_i is person i's total money income. The utility maximizing quantities that would be purchased in a private market are then given by:

$$x_i = \beta_i\, n_i p \tag{3a}$$

and

$$y_i = (1 - \beta_i)\, n_i \tag{3b}$$

The "ideal" quantity described by Enthoven is, in this model, that quantity of insurance x demanded in the private market by the person with average income $(n = \bar{n})$ and average tastes $(\beta = \bar{\beta})$. But note that providing this quantity requires a tax rate equal to $\bar{\beta}$. For any person, $t = px/n$, or $x = nt/p$. But from equation (3a), it follows that if $n = \bar{n}$ and $x = \bar{x}$, then, $t = \bar{\beta}$.

The question then is whether setting $t = \bar{\beta}$ is a majority rule equilibrium, in the sense that providing x at that tax rate would be preferred by a majority over market provision. If the only alternative to non-supplementable socialization is the private market level of x (as in Usher's model), we note that, for persons with income just equal to $\bar{n}$, *only* the persons with $\beta = \bar{\beta}$ will not vote against socialization (and they will be indifferent). All persons with income $\bar{n}$ and values of β different from $\bar{\beta}$ receive no net redistributive gain, and get a quantity different from their optimum. They will vote against socialization. All persons with incomes greater than ñ will also vote against socialization. However, as we reduce incomes below ñ, those with values of β close to $\bar{\beta}$ will tend to favor socialization. The closer the value of β to $\bar{\beta}$ the greater the likelihood that socialization is preferred, while those with values of β either much less than or much greater than $\bar{\beta}$ will still vote against it. Even though these "extreme taste" persons receive a transfer because they have below-average incomes, they oppose a movement away from market provision because neither group gets the quantity it wants. Some receive too much x, and others receive too little.

The proportion of persons at each income level who will favor x over market provision therefore depends on the distribution of β. If β has the same distribution at all income levels (tastes distributed independently of income), then the proportion in favor will be higher at each income level the smaller the variation in β. Conversely, given some diversity in β, a larger proportion of persons with some given value of β will prefer socialization to market provision the lower is their income relative to ñ. Hence, the outcome depends as well on the distribution of incomes below ñ.

Figure 2 illustrates. Line L shows proportions of persons at each income level in favor with low level of diversity of β, while line H shows the corresponding concept for a high level of diversity. Note that, regardless of the diversity of tastes, the percentage in favor goes to 0% at n = ñ, and must be 100% at n = 0 as long as the good has positive value to all.

This diagram therefore suggests the circumstances in which x = x̄ can at least get a majority over market provision. This will happen when the diversity in β is low, and income is unequally distributed. Conversely, as Usher noted, socialization is unlikely if tastes vary a lot and/or income varies little.

In the case where the great majority have incomes near the average income, so that there is low diversity in income levels, there would probably be little perceived gain from socialization, either form a self-interest or from an altruistic viewpoint. But in the case of large diversity in tastes, socialization will be resisted by a majority even if it might be perceived by some to be needed to bring about greater equity. If tastes vary a great deal, Enthoven's proposed objective may not be politically feasible. If, for instance, tastes for medical insurance vary less in western Europe, or in individual provinces in Canada, than they do in the U.S., the lower level of public involvement in the U.S. might be more understandable, and it might represent a political equilibrium. No socialization might be the equilibrium outcome in the U.S. even if all people are as altruistic in the U.S. as elsewhere.

Adding an altruistic motivation obviously makes socialization more likely, since altruistic benefits add to the private benefits citizens expect to achieve. An altruistic person of average income would, for example, potentially support socialization even if his or her tastes were not exactly equal to the average. However, altruism must still contend against diversity in tastes.

How is the likelihood of any socialization affected by modifying the as-

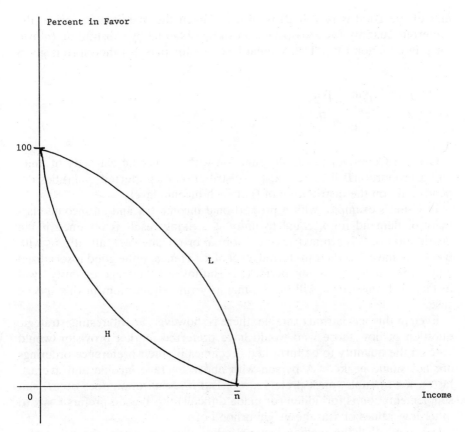

Figure 2.

sumption that supplementation is prohibited? If this modification is made, some people will change their preferred outcomes. Those with below average incomes who have values of β sufficiently high that they would demand more than x̄ units in the market now *would* favor socialization. The reason is that, although they might find public provision involves too little x, they can now supplement the x̄ amount – and they always receive a transfer. Since no one who would have supported socialization with a constraint of no supplementation would oppose it when supplementation is permitted, the conclusion is clear: permitting supplementation enhances the likelihood that any given level of provision will be preferred to the market solution.

To complete the model, however, under either assumption we need to ask about the equilibrium *level* of the good. That is, Enthoven's optimum x̄ may be preferred to market provision, but some other level of publicly provided x may be preferred to *it*.

Consider the individuals with some level of income ñ. The marginal tax price per unit of x (*i.e.*, the addition to each person's tax bill when one more unit of the good is provided) is $(\hat{n}/\bar{n})p$. Given the marginal tax price, the preferred quantity for each person i can be obtained by substituting $(n^i/\bar{n})p$ for p in equation (3a). The optimal level x^{i*} for person i therefore is given by

$$x^{i*} = \frac{\beta_i m_i}{\dfrac{n^i}{\bar{n}}p} = \frac{\beta_i \bar{n}}{p}$$

Given a Cobb-Douglas utility function with an income elasticity of unity and a proportional income tax, the distribution of preferred quantities depends only on the distribution of β at each income level.

In Usher's example, with a proportional income tax and an income elasticity of demand for x equal to unity, a striking result is obtained if the distribution of β is symmetric (*e.g.*, normal or rectangular): all citizens with $\beta = \bar{\beta}$ will have $\bar{x}$ as their preferred level of x^1. Hence, if the good is socialized and supplementation is not permitted, Enthoven's "average quantity" will in fact be furnished; it will be the majority rule equilibrium in this special case.

Even in this specialized example, there is, however, an interesting strategic question of how those who would have preferred market provision would vote on the quantity to be furnished. Technically, their preference orderings are not single peaked. A person with above average income and average tastes, for example, most prefers x = 0. But if socialization does occur, and supplementation is forbidden (or made difficult) this person prefers $x = \bar{x}$ to other low values of x in the neighborhood of $\bar{x}$.

Assuming that the median income is less than the mean, the value of x that will be a majority rule winner will differ from $\bar{x}$ under other assumptions. Different utility functions with different income and price elasticities, and different tax structures, will lead to different outcomes.

In the general case, there is no reason to expect the insurance level of the average person with the average tastes to be the majority rule winner. Sufficient conditions for the average demand to be a political equilibrium is that the person with average income pay the true cost of the insurance received, taxes be Lindahl taxes, and the distribution of tastes be symmetric.

Now suppose that supplementation is permitted. It is easy to see that this alteration will cause the quantity chosen under majority rule to be less than with no supplementation allowed. All those who would have preferred market provision now will vote for a zero level of x. This shifts the median preference to the left, and the quantity will fall. A description of the equilibrium supplementable quantity, even under Usher's assumptions, now requires knowledge of the distribution of income.

In the case of a proportional income tax and the Cobb-Douglas utility function, characterization of the equilibrium level of x with supplementation allowed requires that we know the proportion of the population with incomes below the mean income. Let this proportion be q, with ordinarily $q > 0.5$. To determine the equilibrium quantity, we need to find the value r in the expression:

$$(1 - r)q = 0.5$$

Then the equilibrium quantity is that quantity desired by the person in the $(r * 100)$ percentile of the distribution of tastes. For instance, suppose $q = 0.8$, then $r = .375$. At a level of x preferred by those at the 37.5 percentile of the distribution of tastes, half of the population (the .2 of the population above the mean and the .3 of the population with incomes below the mean but tastes below the 37.5th percentile (or .375 times .8)) would oppose, while the other half would favor. It follows that permitting supplementation reduces x by greater amounts when a smaller fraction of the population potentially receives redistributive gains and tastes are more diverse.

Permitting supplementation therefore exerts two offsetting influences. Other things equal, it increases the likelihood that some socialized quantity will be provided. But it reduces the quantity of provision that will be supported.[2]

This conclusion is relevant to an argument frequently made for social insurance, that it "forces" upper and middle income voters to provide high benefits to the poor, since cutting benefits to the poor requires that the middle income voter reduce his own benefit. Conversely, either a supplementable public program or a means-tested program is criticized because voters may then choose to provide low benefits to the low income clients of such programs.

Of course, a normative basis for accepting this argument is hard to find. If voters would choose a certain level of care for the poor, when they can make that choice explicitly and independently, a normative version of democracy would call such an outcome the *right* choice. Advocating a restrictive "tying arrangement" would be viewed as substituting for voters' preferences the analyst's personal desire for more generous support.

However, the conclusion here is that, even as a positive proposition, the argument that non-supplementable social provision necessarily maximizes the level of benefits for the poor is false. Non-supplementable socialization may well result in no support for the poor, compared to supplementable programs. The latter program is virtually guaranteed to provide at least some transfer, even if the transfer may be less than what socialization without supplementation would provide *if it survives*.

5. MEANS TESTED PROGRAMS AND POLITICAL SUPPORT

I now address informally the question of whether a means-tested program to promote greater equality of consumption of medical care services is more or less likely to garner political support than a uniform supplementable insurance. To begin to address this question at all, one needs to postulate some political support on the part of non-poor voter taxpayers for assistance for low income people. Absent such a motivation, either no assistance would be forthcoming or the problem degenerates into a zero-sum redistributional game as various income groups try to get maximum benefits and pay minimum taxes.

The literature is full of references to the notion that "we" seem to be concerned about the level of use of medical services by sick people who would otherwise go without care of high health benefit. Weitzman does not try to provide a welfare justification for the objective of rationing some goods according to needs, but simply observes that "society seems to act as if one-dimensional equity [applied to a specific commodity] is a valid principle, at least for some commodities." (Of course, since one can observe socialization as a positive equilibrium even in the absence of altruistic or motivations concerning equity, it is not obvious how Weitzman's assertion could be proved (or disproved).)

Enthoven supports his "cost-worthy minimum consumption" strategy by appeal to some ethical or moral standard, which is not justified further other than to offer the hope that many will find it acceptable. Either approach seems to imply that there are at least some individuals in society who attach value to enhancing the consumption of otherwise low using consumers.

A general solution to this problem that I have proposed in the past is to suppose that there is specific-good interdependence in utility functions, what might be called "good-specific altruism" (Pauly, 1970). I proposed generating a non-direct-user or community demand curve for care for each person from these valuations of non-users. The minimum standards approach can then be interpreted as a special case of this model, in which altruistic demand curves are both very price inelastic and all center on the same value of M.

It is easiest to analyze such issues by assuming that society can be divided into "poor" and "non-poor". If there were a gap in the distribution of income between the poverty line and the incomes of the rest of the population, the model would be more realistic. No such gap exists, but if will still be useful to develop a model of non-overlapping groups first, and then modify conclusions to fit more realistic but more complex cases.

Imagine that the income distribution falls into two groups, "poor" and "non-poor". Within each group incomes vary and there is a majority of non-poor people. Taxes are levied on the non-poor group only; the boundary between those who are taxed and those who are not is based on the division of the population into each of the two groups.

The income conditioned policy will receive majority approval over the uniform supplementable policy if it is favored by a majority that consists of both poor and non-poor voters. Relative to the policy in which there is a single supplementable level of coverage available to low income people, an income-conditioned policy may potentially provide more generous coverage for those at relatively low incomes, but less generous coverage for those at higher (but still below average) incomes.

For a given total (net) amount of taxes paid by the non-poor, one would expect non-poor persons to favor an income-conditioned program, since such a program (relative to a uniform program) allocates their taxes to those lower income, lower utilizing persons for whom marginal altruistic benefits are higher. If marginal tax rates for non-poor such voters are sufficiently well-attuned to their demand for the public good embodied in altruistic behavior, many non-poor taxpayers may favor the income-conditioned approach. In addition, the average level of consumption by the poor can well be higher under the income-conditioned program. An altruistic demand will increase the level of uniform provision that will be supported. But the level of consumption depends ultimately on the strength of altruistic demand. If such demand is sufficiently strong, it will lead to a higher level of income-conditioned support.

The more people there are with incomes closer to (but less than) the mean, the more people who would favor the uniform benefit approach over an income-conditioned one. It is obvious, however, that the number of such persons could be less than the number of very poor. Both those with high incomes and those with low incomes would then favor the income-conditioned program, and it might get a majority.

It is, however, likely to be the case that there is no unique majority rule equilibrium when any income-conditioned policy can be proposed (in addition to uniform provision with or without supplementation). Instead, cycles can occur.

6. CONCLUSION

The primary message, of course, is that the political feasibility of income-conditioned coverage or, for that matter, the feasibility of either of the other minimum benefits arrangements, cannot be determined on the basis of theory alone. The higher the extent of variation in tastes, the less likely that either of the social income programs – uniform supplementable or non-supplementable insurance – will be supported. The role of variation in income is more ambiguous, especially when above-average-income taxpayers can favor transfers *to* the poor. Nevertheless, high variation in income and tastes could increase the need for and political support of income-conditioned benefits.

NOTES

1. The elasticity of the desired publicly provided quantity with respect to income equals $\eta - \gamma \delta$, where η is the income elasticity of demand, γ is the elasticity of the tax share with

respect to income and δ is the price elasticity of demand. In the Cobb-Douglas case, with a proportional income tax, these quantities are 1, 1, and -1, respectively, so the elasticity of the desired quantity of x with respect to income, given some value of β, is zero. *See* Bergstrom and Goodman (1973).
2. This result seems quite similar to the "paradox" of federalism discussed by Bös (1979).

REFERENCES

Bergstrom, Ted, and Robert Goodman, "Private Demands for Public Goods," *American Economic Review* 63, pp. 280–296, 1973.
Bös, Dieter, "A Voting Paradox of Fiscal Federalism," *Journal of Public Economics* 11, pp. 369–382, 1979.
Enthoven, Alain, *Theory and Practice of Managed Competition in Health Care Finance*; Amsterdam: North Holland, 1988.
Feldstein, Paul, *Health Economics*. Third edition; New York: Wiley, 1986.
Manning, W.G., *et al.*, "Health Insurance and the Demand for Medical Care: Evidence from a Randomized Experiment," *The American Economic Review* 77, pp. 251–277, 1987
Pauly, Mark, *Medical Care at Public Expense*; New York: Praeger Publishers, 1970.
Usher, Dan, "The Welfare Economics of the Socialization of Commodities," *Journal of Public Economics* 8, pp. 151–169, 1977.
Weitzman, Martin, "Is the Price System or Rationing More Effective in Getting a Commodity to Those Who Need It Most?", *Bell Journal of Economics* 8, pp. 517–524, 1977.
Wilson, L.S., and M.L. Katz, "The Socialization of Commodities," *Journal of Public Economics* 20, pp. 347–357, 1983.

PART TWO

Criteria for allocating health care resources

Cost-effectiveness analysis of strategies for screening prostatic cancer

R. LAUNOIS

UFR de Bobigny, Université de Paris Nord, France

I₁₁ I₁₂

France, U S

INTRODUCTION

A screening programme is justified if it fulfils three criteria: the disease incidence is high, the natural course is known and effective treatment exists. If we confine ourselves to the first criterion, then screening for cancer of the prostate seems an absolute necessity. In 1982, 27% of the 282,660 male deaths recorded in France were due to cancer. Prostate cancer accounted for 1 in 10 cases. In other terms, 2.5% of deaths among the male population is caused by a malignant tumour of the prostate, which corresponds to a crude mortality rate in France of 27 per 100,000. On the international level, statistics show that the problem is at least as acute in the other Western countries. The rate of mortality standardized for the world population reaches 14.7 per 100,000 in the United States, versus 15 per 100,000 in France. The crude rate of incidence for the Americans is three times greater than the crude rate of mortality in the country. According to Silverberg (1987), 1 American out of 11 (8.7%) born in 1985 risks developing cancer of the prostate during the course of his life. The risk is as great as for lung cancer. On the other hand, however, it should be noted that if 90% of lung cancer patients die from their disease, death from cancer of the prostate occurs in one case out of three.

These differences between the rates of incidence and of mortality can be explained in three ways. The first is the possibility of overdiagnosing cancer of the prostate. Several lesions which are described as cancers correspond, in fact, to normal aging of the cells. The second possibility is that cancer of the prostate is mainly encountered among the elderly, who die from other concomitant diseases. The third, and more optimistic, is that two thirds of all prostate cancers are cured. Unfortunately, nothing can be found in the literature to back up this point of view.

In order to explain these differences, we need to consider the natural course of the disease. The essential variable in cancer of the prostate, as Boccon-Gibod (1988) has emphasized, is "the tumour volume which grows slowly, regularly and progressively, and this governs its potential for malignancy. Three groups of patients can be distinguished in this respect:

P. Zweifel and H. E. Frech III (eds.), Health Economics Worldwide. 81–108.
© 1992 *Kluwer Academic Publishers. Printed in the Netherlands.*

The first group includes patients who present with well-differentiated localized tumours whose kinetics are weak. Patients in this group have every
chance of dying from another intercurrent disease. This group is far more
important than would appear from the clinical series. On post-mortem,
cancer cells are found in almost 40% of all 80-year old men who were never
suspected on clinical examination of having cancer of the prostate.

The second group concerns poorly differentiated non-localized tumours
with spread to the seminal capsule at the time of diagnosis. The possibility
of metastases must be considered in such cases and early diagnosis is of little
help.

The third group, whose number represents no more than 5 to 10% of the
total, presents with a localized tumour for which early diagnosis and appropriate treatment may prove curative.

In view of these sub-populations, Whitmore's question (1988) "Is treatment necessary when it is possible, is it possible when it is necessary?" is
better understood.

The decision to screen is therefore controversial. We have not sought to
demonstrate that screening has a satisfactory cost-effectiveness ratio, but to
study the cost-effective ratio of the different programmes that are possible,
once the decision to screen has been taken.

The diagnostic methods which can be used are: digital rectal examination
(DRE), prostate specific antigen (PSA) measurement, ultrasonography (US)
and biopsy (B). We have used a decision theory model to compare and
evaluate 6 different screening protocols. Sensitivity and specificity for the
different examinations were assessed on the basis of the international literature and French series. The protocols were compared in terms of cost per
person screened and the number of cancers identified. Sensitivity was analyzed for the different rates of clinical and post-mortem prevalence. Lastly,
the different programmes were classified.

1. METHODS

1.1. *Medical issues*

1.1.1. *Tumour classification*
An ability to know the extent of the tumour and its malignant potential is
essential for estimating what might be the consequences of the various
screening programs. Numerous classification are in use to categorize prostatic
carcinoma, but none has received general agreement. We chose to elect the
ABCD and the World Health Organizations Systems. The reasons for such
a choice are very pragmatic. First the clinical staging proposed by Whitmore
and Jewett (1984) has received widespread use, especially in the US, even
if the TNM classification (Hermanek and Sobin, 1988) will probably become
more popular in the future. Second, the International Classification System

(1980) for histological grading was applied in one of the few available studies on the natural history of the disease (Johansson *et al.*, 1989), while none could be found on the Gleason system (1966).

According to the Whitmore–Jewett classification, cancer of the prostate is divided into four clinical stages depending on disease extension:

Stage A_1 non palpable, focal
Stage A_2 non palpable, diffused
Stage B_1 palpable, one lobe
Stage B_2 palpable, two lobes

Stage C local extension
Stage D metastases

These clinical parameters indicate how far the tumour has progressed along its course. Screening aims at diagnosing cancers amenable to curative therapy, i.e. stages A and B. Only palliative treatment is possible in stages C and D for the time being and it is doubtful whether palliation prolongs survival.

The WHO system is based upon pattern of glandular differenciation, and it reflects the tumour growth kinetics. Three categories are distinguished:

Well-differentiated tumour,
Moderately differentiated tumour,
Poorly differentiated tumour.

Evidence available of the tumour growth demonstrates a more aggressive behavior of the cancer with increased grade. Well-differentiated tumour grows slowly, poorly differentiated tumour grows rapidly.

1.1.2 *Testing procedures*

Prostate cancer is mainly detected by three examinations which may complement each other: digital rectal examination (DRE), trans-rectal ultrasonography (US) and prostate specific antigen (PSA).

For long, DRE was the only means of detecting the disease and it is still regarded by clinicians as an essential examination. The posterior face is palpated to seek abnormalities in shape and consistency which may be manifestations of adenocarcinoma. The information given by the examination is incomplete.

Certain anomalies are not carcinomas, whilst small tumours and lesions on the anterior surface cannot be felt. For Stamey and McNeal (1987), only cancers of the postero-lateral third can be palpated in this way. Only 45% of prostate tumours are located in this part of the gland. Another disadvantage of DRE is that only tumours that have reached a certain size are detected: in fact they have often spread beyond the capsule and curative therapy no longer possible. Thus, 95% of cancers that have reached 4 mm in size have spread beyond the gland. Despite these limitations, DRE is considered as a useful test: it is inexpensive, non-iatrogenous and its sensitivity and specificity seems to be correct.

Historically, ultrasonography (US) is the second method of detecting cancer of the prostate. Abnormalities in the consistency of the gland or in the echo are looked for. The procedure proved to have poor specificity. Many studies have shown the limitations of ultrasound in displaying signs of disease of the prostate gland and its usefulness is now questionable.

Biological markers seem more promising. Of these, the prostate specific antigen (PSA) is undoubtedly the most effective. It is not specific against tumour tissue: benign hypertrophy of the prostate also produces PSA. However, whereas BHP prostate tissue causes a rise of 0.3 nanogrammes per millilitre of PSA serum levels, tumour tissue results in an increase which is ten times greater. This explains the number of false positives when the threshold value is low: benign hypertrophy of the prostate (adenoma of the prostate) may be accompanied by a rise in the marker in the absence of any malignancy.

The value of the information provided by the diagnostic procedures used is essential in order to assess their impact on the number of tumours detected and the cost of the programmes under study. The contribution made by each type of information is evaluated through its sensitivity, specificity, the positive predictive value and the negative predictive value of each procedure.

1.1.3. *Possible protocols*
Six strategies of medico-economic interest have been assessed, and the choice approved by the main clinical specialists in the field.

The first screening strategy begins with digital-rectal examination by general practitioners (DREg). If positive, the same examination is then performed by a specialist (DREs). Positive DRE patients become candidates for US. Of the patients who undergo US, those with a positive result are biopsied. Patients with negative US receive a PSA test. If the PSA is higher than five or ten nanograms, then a biopsy is done.

The second strategy differs from the first, in that all patients have US after examination by a specialist, whether their DREs findings are normal or not. If US is positive, the patients are biopsied; if US is negative, only patients with a positive DREs undergo biopsy.

In the third strategy, PSA measurement replaces US after DREs. If PSA is elevated, a biopsy is systematically performed, whatever the results of the former tests. If PSA is normal, only patients with positive DREs undergo biopsy.

PSA is the starting point in the fourth strategy. Only patients with an elevated PSA are referred to the urologist. Patients with a positive clinical exam undergo US and if the result is positive, they are biopsied. Patients

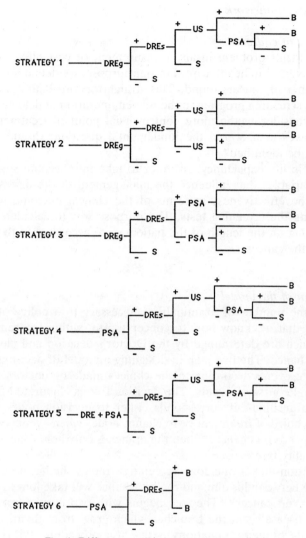

Fig. 1. Different screening programmes available.

with a negative test have only biopsy if a second PSA measure is higher than 5 or 10 nanograms.

The fifth strategy is identical to the fourth, except that DREs and PSA are associated tests carried out simultaneously during the first visit.

In the sixth strategy, all patients have only a PSA test as initial test. All positive results are referred to a specialist, both positive and negative DREs undergo biopsy.

1.2. *Analytical framework*

1.2.1. *Choice of end-points*
The most difficult problem in any measurement of cost effectiveness is to define effectiveness in health care. For our purpose, we define it in two ways:
1. The number of cancers found. This straightforward definition limits the gains of a screening program to the sole enumeration of detected tumours, without considering the more controversial point of treatment efficacy. But it leaves unanswered the fundamental question: should all cancers that exist be identified?
2. The gain in life expectancy. In order to take into account several of the clinical variables that influence the management of the disease, we also defined the effectiveness in terms of the clinical outcome for patients undergoing the screening tests. The purpose was to calculate the effect of screening on the length of the patient's life according to the stage and grade of the cancer.

1.2.2. *Design of the model*
Evaluating the number of examinations necessary to a policy of screening presupposes that we know how to conceptualize, within the same schema, elements which are determined by the Doctor's decision and elements that depend on chance. The first step in designing a model of decision-making is to schematize events according to the choices made by doctors or dictated by the natural course of events. The decision tree is elaborated from left to right. The branching-out corresponds either to decision nodes when they express the choice of treatment or to chance nodes when events occur whose outcome depends on chance. When the branches only hold chance nodes the term probability tree is used.

If the decision-maker opts for a screening strategy, he has no control over concordance between his aim and reality: chance will take him to the branch "cancer" or "no cancer". The tree begins with two master branches "disease", "no disease" and the branches which grow from them, express the aleatory results of the examinations used. Three procedures (vi) (i = 0, . . . 2) can be employed in a first round: clinical examination which includes DRE, measurement of PSA or association of the two. The rational course is to resort to one of these 3 techniques and only to propose further investigation if findings are suspect. The type of complementary examination (Ni)(i = 3, . . . 6) varies according to the programme chosen.

Once the different stages have been defined, each examination is attributed the probabilities which correspond to its diagnostic value; for each chance node, the sum of the probabilities for each eventuality, of course, equals 1. The probability or the frequency of an anomaly in a population with cancer is equal to the sensitivity of the procedure (ai): that of its absence (1–ai). The probability or frequency of the examination proving normal in a population without cancer is equal to specificity (bi) and that of a positive result within the same group of normal subjects is equal to (1–bi).

If the distribution of probabilities p and 1–p for the natural course is known, the joint probability of a positive or negative result at the end of a series of investigations can be calculated.

The frequency of positives (true or false, since the clinician limits himself to noting an anomaly without being able to distinguish between sick or non-sick subject) determines the proportion (ni) of individuals explored who must have complementary investigations. Applied to the population entered into the programme (NO), this frequency allows the number of complementary tests asked for, to be calculated: Ni = ni.NO.

The symbols used are given in Table 1 below:

Table 1. Symbols

Type of Exploration	Proportion of R+ in previous tests	N° Exams	Se	Sp
Initial Vis.				
DREg (i=0)	0	v0	a0	b0
PSA (i=1)	0	v1	a1	b1
DREg+PSA (i=2)	0	v2	a2	b2
Compl. Exams				
DREs (i=3)	n3	N3 = n3 N0	a3	b3
Echo (i=4)	n4	N4 = n4 N0	a4	b4
PSA (i=5)	n5	N5 = n5 N0	a5	b5
Biop (i=6)	n6	N6 = n6 N0	a6	b6
Biop+ (i=7)	n7	N7 = n7 N0	–	–
Number of Individuals sampled		N0		

DREg : DRE general practitioner, DREs : DRE specialist, R+ : positive result
Se : Sensitivity, Sp : Specificity

If the cost (c_i) of the first examinations and of the complementary investigations (p_k) are considered as known, the total cost (C_t) of a strategy depends exclusively on the number of initial examinations (v_i) and complementary (N_i) examinations used.

$$C_t = c_i v_i + \sum_{k=3}^{6} p_k N_k \quad (i = 0, \ldots, 2)$$

The numbers vary for each programme (j) (j = 0, ... 6), depending on the investigations carried out previously and their classification. The above equation can then be rewritten as:

$$C_t^j = c_i v_i^j + \sum_{k=3}^{6} p_k n_k^j No \quad (i = 0, \ldots, 2)(j = 0, \ldots, 6)$$

The frequency of detection of cancer in the population that has accepted to take part in the screening programme (j) is equal to the proportion of biopsies that turn out to be positive. The number of tumours detected therefore amounts to:

$$Ca^j = n_7{}^j No \quad (j = 0, \ldots, 6)$$

1.2.3. Decision rules

Establishing the cost and effectiveness of a screening programme is of little sense in absolute terms. What is more important is to define the cost and effect of one decision in relation to another. All positive and negative effects are studied in relation to a standard situation. Two approaches can be considered: either the cost and effectiveness of screening are assessed in relation to a policy of no screening or the additional cost and advantages of each screening programmes are evaluated differentially from the simplest to the most elaborated. The second solution reflects better the choices available and is the one that has been selected. The programmes were first classified according to the number of tumours detected. When results were equal or inferior, the more costly programme in absolute terms was excluded from the analysis. The remaining programmes were analyzed solely in terms of their incremental cost-effectiveness. The additional cost of a programme that was more aggressive than another (incremental cost) was then divided by the additional advantage that it brought in terms of the number of additional tumours detected (incremental effectiveness). The programmes, whose cost-effectiveness ratio was dominated, were eliminated and the others classified according to the increase in cost that they required for each new tumour detected.

1.3. Available data

1.3.1. Characterization of the pretest likelihood

Estimates of the prostatic cancer prevalence is complicated because the adenocarcinoma may be identified in three different settings. First, it can be clinically diagnosed by physical exams or symptoms. Second, it can be discovered when the prostate is removed for other reasons than prostatic cancer, for instance during a radical cystoprostatectomy for bladder cancer. In such a case, the term "incidental cancer" is used. Third, the tumour can be discovered at autopsy; it is then called "latent cancer". Estimates of clinical prevalence are derived from American tumour registeries or from clinical series. They vary from 0.3% in the Connecticut (Feldman et al., 1986) to 3% reported by Teillac et al. (1990) in a screening context and 14% in a French hospital setting (Vallancien et al. 1990). The clinical prevalence increases dramatically with age −0.9% of men 60–69 years' old, compared with 3.7% of men over 70.

It has long been recognized that the clinical prevalence represents only

Table 2. Prevalence of clinical cancers.

	30-49	50-59	60-69	> 70	Average
Feldman 1986	0.002	0.1	0.9	3.6	0.372

Table 3. Prevalence of incidental cancers.

Patients	40-49	50-59	60-69	70-79	80 +	Average
Sheldon Survey 1981 Stad A	6.3	10.4	18.5	28.7	37.1	10
Pritchett 195 1988	11	14	36	28	50	27 (45/165)
Kabalin 66 1989						38 (25/66)
Montie 84 1989	< 60 26 (7/27)		60-75 61 (23/28)	> 75 43 (3/7)		46.0 (33/72)

the top of the iceberg, reported rates of incidental cancer by Kabalin *et al.* (1989) or Montie *et al.* (1989) reach respectively 38% and 46% (Table 3).

Franks (1954) found a 30% prevalence in 180 men over 50 year old examined at autopsy. The prevalence of latent cancer reaches even 40% for the 70–79 group (Table 4).

The high prevalence of silent cancers poses a unique problem, some of them will never present clinically during the lifetime of men in whom they

Table 4. Prevalence of latent cancers.

Patients	40-49	50-59	60-69	70-79	80 +	Average
Edwards 173 1953	3.4 (1/23)	9.7 (3/31)	18.5 (10/54)	25 (12/48)	17.6 (3/17)	16.7 (29/173)
Franks 210 1954	0 (0/18)	29.0 (11/38)	30.2 (16/53)	40.0 (28/70)	73.0 (14/19)	37.6 (69/210)
Hudson 261 1954	4.2 (2/48)	12.9 (17/133)	16.1 (17/99)	16.9 (3/17)	0	13.0 (39/300)
Scott 158 1969	-	-	-	41.0 (41/1)	57.0 (33/58)	46.0 (74/158)
Wynder Survey 1971	4	5-14	8-30	20-40		
Holund 223 1980	12.5 (1/8)	8.6 (2/23)	12.5 (7/56)	25.8 (24/93)	40.0 (16/4)	22.4 (50/223)

Table 5. Results of DRE studies.

Authors	Patients	Biopsies	False+	True+	False-	True-	Total	Se	Sp
Systematic Biopsy									
Guinan 1980	300	300	ND	63		ND	300	0.69	0.89
Perrin 1989	481	481	24	59	24	342	481	0.71	0.95
Vallancien 1989	167	167	12	32	7	116	167	0.82	0.90
Work-up Bias									
Devonec 1990	666	226	30	34	11	151	226	0.75	0.83
Perrin 1989	1,147	354	157	87	7	103	354	0.92	0.39
Teillac 1990	600	93	18	8	11	56	93	0.42	0.75
Statistical Bias DRE- = True negative									
Vihko 1985	771	66	21	6	3	741	771	0.66	0.97
Lee 1988	784	77	19	10	12	743	784	0.45	0.97

occur. If methods for early diagnoses are introduced, how do we know that only dangerous lesions are identified and treated?

1.3.2. *Characterization of screening tests*

The series are infrequent and often biased (tables 5,6,7). For example, with regard to DRE, only three investigators (Guinan, 1980; Vallancien *et al.*, 1989; Perrin and Maquet, 1989) have applied the gold standard biopsy to the whole population included in the studies. Other authors contented themselves with exploring only patients whose DRE was positive.

The key parameters are then calculated either for the biopsied sub-population, which is not representative of the population in general, and the results suffer from a work-up bias[1] (Devonec *et al.*, 1990; Perrin and Maquet, 1989; Teillac *et al.*, 1990), or they are based on all the patients in the study at the cost of an unacceptable hypothesis; negative DREs are assimilated to true negatives without any proof. Vihko's series (Vihko *et al.*, 1985) is a typical example. He studied 771 patients and 66 biopsies were conducted. The number of true negatives reached 741. The 705 apparently normal DREs were obviously reintegrated into the final result along with the 36 negative DREs where biopsies had been performed. The statistical bias is obvious.

1.3.3. *Survival assumptions*

A key factor in estimating the benefit of screening is the distribution of survival by stages and grades. Our estimates were derived from a population-based study published by Johansson *et al.* (1989). The following distribution was observed: stages A and B, 47%, stages C and D, 53%. If we combine all B_1, well-differentiated B_2 and A_2 into a low-risk group that we consider the most important target group for prostatic screening and radical prostatec-

Table 6. Results of US studies.

Authors	Patients	Biopsies	False+	True+	False-	True-	Total	Se	Sp
Systematic Biopsy									
Perrin 1989	481	481	168	65	18	230	481	0.78	0.57
Vallancien 1989	167	167	21	27	12	107	167	0.69	0.83
Work-up Bias									
Teillac 1990	600	93	74	9	10	35	93	0.47	0.43
Statistical Bias									
Cooner 1989	1,035	275	221	54		760	1,035	0.10	0.76
Lee 1988	784	77	44	20	2	718	784	0.91	0.94

tomy, we found only 17.3% of the detected patients. This subgroup was chosen as a treatable population. The survival rate of treated patients was derived from a retrospective survival analysis conducted by Lepor *et al.* (1989) for patients with clinical stage B_1 who underwent radical prostatectomy at the Johns Hopkins hospital. In both cases, the survival has been ascertained, using a cause-specific survival curve. The corrected ten years survival for patients who were left untreated in the Swedish series until progression occurred was approximately equal to 89%. The ten-year corrected survival following radical prostatectomy for men with B_1 carcinoma was approximately 92.5%. For calculating the corresponding life expectancy, we used the DEALE method elaborated by Beck *et al.* (1982). The curative potential of the intervention has been expressed as the increment in life expectancy following treatment, compared with no treatment. We calculated

Table 7. Results of PSA studies.

Authors	Patients	Biopsies	False+	True+	False-	True-	Total	Se	Sp
Systematic Biopsy									
Lee 1989 (> 2.5 ng)	248	248	87	94	8	59	248	0.92	0.40
Work-up Bias									
Teillac 1990 (> 5 ng)	600	93	42	18	1	32	93	0.94	0.43
Statistical Bias									
Cooner 1989 (> 4 ng)	1,035	275	nd	nd	nd	nd	1,035	0.68	0.83

the net expected gain per detected cancer to be 0.18 years for the 50 year-old, 0.09 years for the 65 year-old and 0.04 for the 75 year-old.

1.4. *Quality of the data*

1.4.1. *An imperative: deciphering information*
Some of the series published in France give consolidated results and the authors prefer to use straightforward parameters such as the positive predictive value and the detection rate rather than to reason in terms of sensitivity and specificity. This approach deprives the scientific community of data which could be very helpful and it impedes reasoning of a sequential type based on likelihood ratio. Perrin and Maquet's (1989) prospective study including 481 patients is exemplary. All patients who had a positive DRE or a positive ultrasound scan were biopsied. The authors' findings are presented in the following table:

Table 8. DRE and US results.

DRE	US	D+	D−	Total
+	+	57	41	98
+	−	2	15	17
−	+	8	127	135
−	−	16	215	231
		83	398	481

D+ : cancer present   D- : cancer absent

It is possible, from the results for the association DRE + US, to determine the number of positive or negative results for DRE alone: all positive DRE results are added together (whatever the US result) and the same is done for all the negative results. For DRE alone, the results are:

Table 9. Results of DRE alone.

	D+	D−	Total
DRE+	59	56	115
DRE−	24	342	366
Total	83	398	481

If the disease can only be considered as present if both examinations are positive, then 57 tumours were detected. If DRE alone is positive, then 59 cancers were found: US has consequently ruled out 2 lesions, which become false positives.

It may legitimately be argued (Perrin and Maquet 1989), that a positive US scan and a positive DRE increase the predictive value from 11% (2/17) to 58% (57/98) in comparison with what would have been found in the event of a normal scan following a suspect DRE.

Table 10. Comparing the results of US + DRE and DRE alone.

10a First test (DRE)

	D+	D–
DRE+ DRE–	59 24	56 342

10b Second test (US/DRE)

	D+	D–
US+/DRE+ US–/DRE+	57 2	41 15
	59	56

	D+	D–
US+/DRE– US–/DRE–	8 16	127 215
	24	342

But the efficacy of combining the two positive tests could have been assessed by comparison with a positive DRE alone. The increase in information would then have been much smaller, 7 points only (58% versus 51%), since the positive predictive value of the DRE alone immediately reached this last value (59/115).

Moreover, to be really precise, the probability of a negative error and the probability of a positive finding cannot be reduced to a common dimension.

1.4.2. *Conditional sensitivity and specificity*

Table 8 not only allows calculation of overall sensitivity for DRE and US, but it also shows that the sensitivity of US differs according to whether DRE is positive or negative. The overall sensitivity of each examination taken separately can be calculated from the data it contains (Table 11a), as can the conditional sensitivity of an ultrasound scan which depends on the positive or negative findings of the prior DRE (Table 11b).

Overall US sensitivity can be calculated from Table 11a: 65 of the 83 patients have an anomaly on scanning. Overall US sensitivity is 65/83, i.e. 0.783.

Table 11b supplies the information needed to calculate the conditional sensitivity of US when its results depend on those obtained by DRE. In the sub-population of 59 patients with a positive DRE, scan findings were abnormal in 57 cases. Of all 83 patients, only 65 had a positive US scan. Only 8

Table 11a. Overall sensitivity.

D+	US+	US–	
DRE+ DRE–			59 24
	65	18	83

Table 11b. Conditional sensitivity.

D+	US+	US–	Total
DRE+ DRE–	57 8	2 16	59 24
	65	18	83

Table 12a. Overall specificity.

D-	US+	US-	
DRE+ DRE-			56 342
	168	230	398

Table 12b. Conditional specificity.

D-	US+	US-	Total
DRE+ DRE-	41 127	15 215	56 342
	168	230	398

patients, therefore, of the 24 with a negative DRE correspond to a positive scan.

If sensitivity for the whole of the patient population is 0.783 (65/83), it rises to 0.96 (57/59) in the group of positive DREs and drops to 0.33 (8/24) in the patients with a negative DRE.

Conditional sensitivity is rarely published in the literature, and it is to the credit of Perrin and of Vallancien that their work draws attention to it. The numbers in the 4 cells in the above four way tables can only be obtained by scrupulous clinical examination which demonstrates the non-independence of the examinations.

Specificity for the two examinations in the group of subjects without disease (D-) can be analysed in the same fashion.

1.4.3. Queries about the gold standard

Last and by no means least, the gold standard chosen may be queried. Biopsy fails to detect tumours located beyond the area considered suspect on clinical examination. Three biopsies are now advocated for each lobe in order to prove the presence or absence of a cancer. This modification in diagnostic criteria means earlier series are out of date. But we have even doubts on the ability of this new procedure to discriminate between the presence or the absence of cancer. In the basic model, we assume that biopsy is a perfect test, but in the sensitivity analysis, we consider the possibility of errors, in particular confronting clinical series (Vallancien et al., 1990) and autopsy data (Franks, 1954), we assume that a procedure fails to identify the disease 30% of the time, but we keep the perfect specificity assumption.

1.5. An example of costing

The model is elaborated to assess the effects of a more or less intensive screening policy when the clinical prevalence is equal to 3%, the latest data available for France (Teillac et al., 1990) (cf Decision tree, Fig 2).

The tree begins with the decision node with which the decision-maker is immediately confronted: Which screening programme (Prj) (j = 0 . . . 6) does he intend to apply? Whatever his decision, a tumour may or may not be present. The prevalence of the disease defines the first random choice node of each branch. If screening is decided on, a DRE is performed by a general practitioner (GP): the results may be positive or negative. In the first in-

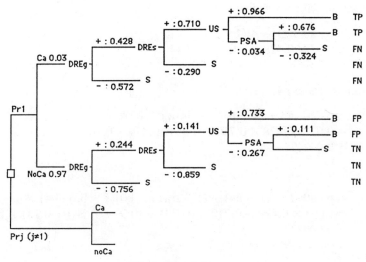

Fig. 2. Decision tree.

stance, referral to a specialist is mandatory; in the second, follow-up (S) is recommended. DRE by a specialist (SP) can confirm or refute the first findings of the first examination. If the opinion of the two physicians concords, then a US scan is obtained and if this is positive a biopsy is performed. If the scan is negative, then biological examination is requested. When the PSA value exceeds the normal upper limit, a biopsy is carried out. If the PSA value is normal, the patient is followed-up regularly. If the opinions of the GP and the specialist do not concord, then it is the absence of an anomaly noted by the specialist that prevails and he prescribes simple surveillance.

When the main branches of the chart have been identified, the tree is completed by adding above each branch the frequency of positive and negative results observed in the French series after each examination:

Table 13. Frequency of positive and negative results in French series.

		TP Rates ai	FN Rates 1 − ai	FP Rates 1 − bi	TN Rates bi
DREg	Teillac 1990	0.428	0.572	0.244	0.756
PSA 1st round	Teillac 1990	0.947	0.053	0.568	0.432
DREg + PSA	Teillac 1990	0.971	0.029	0.673	0.327
DREs	Perrin 1989	0.710	0.290	0.141	0.859
US/DRE+	Perrin 1989	0.966	0.034	0.733	0.267
US/DRE−	Perrin 1989	0.335	0.665	0.372	0.628
PSA 2nd round	Cooner 1989	0.685	0.315	0.169	0.831
" "	Teillac corrected	0.676	0.324	0.111	0.889

By definition, $n0 = n1 = n2 = 1$ since each person screened had at least one of the three examinations. The frequency with which the other examinations are applied has been established as follows:

Consultation with a specialist: n3,

$$= p \cdot a0 + (1 - p)(1 - b0)$$
$$= 0.03 \times 0.428 + 0.097 \times 0.244$$
$$= 0.24952$$

Ultrasound scans: n4,

$$= p \cdot a0 \cdot a3 + (1 - p)((1 - b0)(1 - b3))$$
$$= 0.03 \times 0.428 \times 0.710 + 0.97 \times 0.244 \times 0.141$$
$$= 0.04249$$

PSA: n5,

$$= p \cdot a0 \cdot a3 \cdot (1 - a4) + (1 - p)((1 - b0)(1 - b3) \cdot b4)$$
$$= (0.03 \times 0.428 \times 0.710 \times 0.034) + (0.97 \times 0.244 \times 0.141 \times 0.267)$$
$$= 0.00922$$

Biopsies: n6,

$$= p(a0 \cdot a3 \cdot a4 + a0 \cdot a3 \cdot (1 - a4) \cdot a5)$$

$$+ (1 - p)((1 - b0)(1 - b3)(1 - b4) + (1 - b0)(1 - b3)b4(1 - b5))$$
$$= 0.03 (0.428 \times 0.710 \times 0.966 + 0.428 \times 0.710 \times 0.034 \times 0.676) +$$
$$0.97 (0.244 \times 0.141 \times 0.732 + 0.244 \times 0.141 \times 0.267 \times 0.111)$$
$$= 0.03447$$

Positive biopsies: n7,

$$= p(a0 \cdot a3 \cdot a4 + a0 \cdot a3 \cdot (1 - a4) \cdot a5)$$
$$= 0.03(0.428 \times 0.710 \times 0.966 + 0.428 \times 0.710 \times 0.034 \times 0.676)$$
$$= 0.00902$$

The number of examinations applied to a population of 100,000 persons at risk amounts to:

Consultation with GP	:v0	= 100,000
Consultation with specialist	:N3	= 0.24952 × 100,000 = 24,952
US scans	:N4	= 0.04249 × 100,000 = 4,249
PSA	:N5	= 0.00922 × 100,000 = 922
Biopsies	:N6	= 0.03447 × 100,000 = 3,447

The cost of each item, from the National Health Insurance point of view, is calculated according to Relative scale value laid down by the Department of Public Health.

Expenses for programme 1 amount to 16,560,825 FF per 100 000 screenees, when the G.P., S.P., US, PSA and biopsy costs are respectively estimated to be 85, 125, 360, 123 and 957 FF and when the prevalence is supposed to be 0.03 (Central assumption).

Table 14. Current cost data in France, in FF.

Consultation with GP			85
Consultation with specialist			125
PSA	BM 70		123
US	K 30		360
Biopsy			
+ Tests	E C B U	B70	123
	hemostasis	B40	70
+ Antibio-prophylaxy			
	Noxorine 400 mg box of 10		68
	Peflacine 400 mg box of 2		139
	Bactrine box of 10		19
	Flagyl 500 mg box of 15		62
+ Surgery	K 30 + K 20/2		520
+ Histological examination B 100			176

Total cost to the National Health insurance of biopsy between 957 FF and 1300 FF according to the type of antibiotic used

II. RESULTS

The search for the best programme is divided into two stages. The first selects those programmes that are efficient according to the principle of dominance. The second determines the value judgment that must be made to select one efficient strategy over its alternatives. The search for an optimal allocation aims to achieve the maximum consistency possible and takes the

Table 15. Volume of consumption.
$Pv = 0.03$

Medical Acts	Programmes					
	(1)	(2)	(3)	(4)	(5)	(6)
Consultation with GP	100,000	100,000	100,000	100,000	100,000	100,000
Consultation with specialist	24,952	24,952	24,952	57,937	68,194	57,937
US Scan	4,249	24,952	0	9,786	11,272	0
PSA 1st round	0	0	24,952	100,000	100,000	100,000
PSA 2nd round	922	0	0	2,142	2,528	0
Total no PSA	922	0	24,952	102,142	102,528	100,000
Biopsies	3,447	11,937	16,150	7,919	'9,066	57,937
Tumours detected	902	1,037	1,264	1,995	2,046	2,841
False positives	2,545	10,900	14,886	5,924	7,020	55,096

Table 16. Value of consumption, in FF.

Pv = 0.03

Medical Acts	Programmes					
	(1) (F)	(2) (F)	(3) (F)	(4) (F)	(5) (F)	(6) (F)
Consultation with GP	8,500,000	8,500,000	8,500,000	8,500,000	8,500,000	8,500,000
Consultation with specialist	3,119,000	3,119,000	3,119,000	7,242,125	8,524,250	7,242,125
US Scan	1,529,640	8,982,720	0	3,522,960	4,057,920	0
PSA	113,406	0	3,069,096	12,563,466	12,610,944	12,300,000
Biopsies	3,298,779	11,423,709	15,455,550	7,578,483	8,676,162	55,445,709
Total	16,560,825	32,025,429	30,143,646	39,407,034	42,369,276	83,487,834

place of empirical quest for efficiency. The purpose of such procedure is to prevent more sickness for a given budget. This can be done by equalizing the marginal health return between preventative actions, no matter the illness being considered.

The axiom of dominance enables a number of possible choices to be ruled out. A situation dominates another when the cost per unit of effectiveness is less than or equal to that of the reference situation (average cost-effectiveness ratio). If the different programmes are classified according to this criterion, the programme Pr2 will never be used, since all the other programmes detected more cancers for a lower expenditure per unit (Table 18a).

By extension, when several programmes are *mutually exclusive*, it is agreed that one option is dominated by another when the incremental cost of moving from one option to the next is less than the one before (incremental cost

Table 17. Synthesis of results.

	Total Cost Ct	Total no tumours Ca
Pr0 : nothing	0	0
Pr1 : DREx2->USE->PSA2	16,560,825	902
Pr2 : DREx2->USS	32,025,429	1,037
Pr3 : DREx2->PSA2->Biop	30,143,646	1,264
Pr4 : PSA1->DRE->USE->PSA2	39,407,034	1,995
Pr5 : PSA1->DREx2->USE->PSA2	42,369,276	2,046
Pr6 : PSA1->DRE->Biop	83,487,834	2,841

Note :

DREx2 = two DREs   US E = elective US
US S = systematic US   PSA1 = PSA 1st round
PSA2 = PSA 2nd round

Table 18a. Feasible programmes: average cost-effectiveness ratio.

	Pr0	Pr1	Pr2	Pr3	Pr4	Pr5	Pr6
Ca	0	902	1,037	1,264	1,995	2,046	2,841
Ct (kf)	0	16,560	32,025	30,143	39,407	42,369	83,487
Ct/Ca (f)	0	18,360	30,883 (dominated)	23,848	19,753	20,708	29,387

(kf) : thousands of French Francs   (f) : French Francs

Table 18b. Feasible programmes: marginal cost-effectiveness ratio.

		Pr1-Pr0	Pr3-Pr1	Pr4-Pr3	Pr5-Pr4	Pr6-Pr5
Δ Ca	0	902	362	731	51	795
Δ Ct (kf)	0	16,560	13,582	9,263	2,962	41,118
Δ Ct/ΔCa (f)	0	18,360	37,521 (dominated)	12,672	58,083 (dominated)	51,721

(kf) : thousands of French Francs   (f) : French Francs

effectiveness ratio). The rule to apply is simple: a programme can be eliminated if, and only if, the incremental cost entailed in its replacement by another is lower than the incremental cost per cancer detected which would have been associated with its implementation. On the basis of this criterion, programme Pr3 is dominated by programme Pr4. The same applies to Pr5 in relation to Pr6 (Table 18b).

Intuitive reasoning is as follows (supposing that returns are constant to scale); if (Table 18b) the country believes that it is justified in spending an

Table 19a. Efficient programmes: average cost-effectiveness ratio.

	Pr0	Pr1	Pr4	Pr6
Ca	0	902	1,995	2,841
Ct (kf)	0	16,560	39,407	83,487
Ct/Ca (f)	0	18,360	19,753	29,387

(kf) : thousands of French Francs   (f) : French Francs

Table 19b. Efficient programmes: marginal cost-effectiveness ratio.

	Pr1-Pr0	Pr4-Pr1	Pr6-Pr4
Δ Ca	902	1,093	846
Δ Ct (kf)	16,560	22,846	44,080
Δ Ct/ΔCa (f)	18,360	20,902	52,104

(kf) : thousands of French Francs   (f) : French Francs

additional 13.5 million francs to detect 362 new cancers at a marginal cost of 37,521 F per cancer discovered, it will be willing, in the absence of any financial constraint, to adopt programme Pr4, for which an additional expense of 9,263,000 F has to be paid for finding 731 new cancers at a lesser incremental cost of 12,672 F. Programme Pr3 will therefore never be used, for it will always be possible to do better by using programme Pr4.

One may query the soundness of possibly replacing programme 1 by programme 4 on the effectiveness interval of 0–902 of detected cancers. This choice cannot be advocated, since the marginal cost per cancer discovered by programme 1 is less than that of programme 4 on this interval.

Efficient programmes are those for which health outcome cannot be improved without an increase in cost. The one that society will prefer remains to be defined. This supposes that society will adopt a criterion for assessment by deciding the maximum amount of money it is prepared to spend per additional cancer discovered. Choice in this field is mainly arbitrary, since the marginal cost of each new tumour detected ranges from 18,360 to 52,104:

$$\frac{\Delta Ct}{\Delta Ca} = \begin{cases} 0 & Ca = 0 \\ 18{,}360, & Ca < 902 \\ 20{,}902, & 902 \leqslant Ca < 1{,}995 \\ 52{,}104, & 1{,}995 \leqslant Ca < 2{,}841 \end{cases}$$

Society has no means of choosing between the different options on the basis of truly scientific criteria. The choice is a political one. The same reasoning applies when the results are presented in terms of cost per life year saved, which varies between 102,230 FF for strategy 1 to 115,970 FF for strategy 4 and 288,110 FF for strategy 6. There is no theoretical justification for asserting that the efficient strategy with a higher cost per life year is least desirable. The crucial value judgment is left to decision makers.

The ranking of the mutually exclusive programmes can also be described in terms of extra units of outcomes per extra franc spent. The procedure adopted is symmetric to the one previously described. First, the best initial increment is selected, using the point with the maximum incremental effectiveness cost ratio. Second, the best programme from the list of the next possible increments is entered into the solution. The procedure is repeated until all programmes under consideration are exhausted. At each step, one cautiously checks that the additional outcome per extra franc is less than it was after choosing the previous best alternative. When the criterion is not satisfied, the programme previously entered into the solution is dominated and should be discarded. Finally, the incremental effectiveness cost ratio of the selected option has to be recalculated with the dominated variant excluded.

The non dominated programmes are on the boundary of the set of the production possibilities. Interior points, which are obviously inefficient, are dominated by options on the "frontier": a greater outcome can be obtained for the same cost or the same outcome can be produced for a lower cost.

Resources are employed in a wasteful manner, and the corresponding options should be ruled out. Options on the boundary are cost effective in the sense that there are no other options that are both more effective and less expensive. Programme Pr1, Pr4 and Pr6 are the only efficient ones. However, because the willingness of the society to pay is unknown, it is not possible to identify a single strategy as being the most cost-effective.

III. SENSITIVITY ANALYSIS

The central analysis was performed with the clinical prevalence equal to 3% and based upon clinical estimates of sensitivity and specificity. But it is known that incidental and latent prevalence might be much higher than the clinical one. Furthermore, it might be erroneous to extrapolate findings of the biopsied group of patients to the general population. We tried to check whether our results were robust by varying those parameters.

3.1. *Variability according to prevalence rate*

The prevalence of adenocarcinoma varies widely according to age subgroups (50–59, 60–69 and over 70) and the criteria used to assess the pretest likelihood of prostatic cancer: clinical exam (Feldman *et al.*, 1986), randomized biopsy (Vallancien *et al.*, 1990) and autopsy study (Franks 1954). Alteration in prevalence has no effect on the relative ranking of the strategies when the end-point chosen is the number of cancers found. Strategies 1, 4, 6 are still the dominating strategies. However, the magnitude of the cost-effectiveness ratios decreases dramatically. The cost per cancer found is divided by 3 for the 50–59 year group when prevalence increases from 0.13% to 29%, by 4 for the 60–69 year old when prevalence varies from 0.9 to 30%, and by 16 for the over 70 year old when the prevalence range is between 3.6% and 40%.

3.2. *Correcting for work-up bias*

Two decisions have to be taken for the fourway tables to be filled in: was the result of the examination positive or negative and was disease present or not according to the reference diagnostic gold standard (biopsy). When these two aspects are not investigated independently, statistical bias is introduced into the analysis. This is mainly the case when the physician is reluctant to perform a reference examination, which may be expensive or hazardous, on all patients. For example, in the study conducted by Teillac *et al.* in 1989, of 600 patients entered into the study, 11 had inassessable DRE. Of the remaining 589 patients, 33 had a positive DRE and 556 a negative DRE. Biopsy was requested for all positive DREs, but some patients refused and only 26 biopsies were carried out. For the 556 negative DREs, only 67

Table 20. Incremental cost per cancer detected for different age-groups and prevalence assumptions ("naive" Se, Sp, B)*

Age	Strategy	Feldman	Vallancien	Franks
50-59 years		0.13%	8.5%	29%
	1	396,478	7,305	3,042
	4	458,201	8,127	3,287
	6	1,224,660	17,479	4,027
60-69 years		0.90%	11%	30%
	1	57,857	5,955	2,983
	4	66,403	6,609	3,145
	6	175,694	13,104	3,842
> 70 years		3.6%	24%	40%
	1	15,258	3,409	D
	4	17,104	3,707	D
	6	42,057	5,182	2,605

French Francs

* Se : sensitivity,   Sp : specificity,   B : biopsy

biopsies were performed following abnormally elevated PSA levels or positive US scans. The biopsy rate is therefore 78% for positive DREs versus 12% for negative DREs. The positive results are therefore over-represented in patients who had complementary examinations and this increases the sensitivity of DRE. On the other hand, negative DREs are under-represented which reduces the specificity of the test.

In the sub-population that had biopsies, classification of subjects as normal or not is unequivocal, since the corresponding procedure is considered as the criterion according to which cancer is or is not present. On the other hand, allocating people taken from the population in general to one or the other of these two groups is not possible, since the negative clinical examination has not been histologically confirmed. Clinical estimates of sensitivity and specificity are therefore highly distorted. Fortunately, it is possible to correct the bias. To extrapolate the results for the biopsied population to the population in general, it must be assumed that the disease is totally independent of the verification procedure selected (Begg *et al.*, 1983, 1986, 1988). To eliminate the work-up bias, it is therefore accepted that biopsy is only requested when an anomaly is found on clinical examination, independently of any a priori idea as to whether cancer is present or not in the patients under consideration. In this case, the positivity of the sign alone determines the suspect population, whatever the true underlying pathological condition may be. Therefore:

$$P(V/R) = P(V/R, D)$$

where:

R = R +   disease found

R = R −   findings normal
V = V +   suspect case chosen for histological confirmation
V = V −   case not suspect, no biopsy
D = D +   patients
D = D −   normal subjects

The probability of having the disease when the sign is present is therefore the same whether there has been histological confirmation or not:

$$P(D+/R+, V+) = P(D+/R+)$$

When Bayes' theorem is applied to the results of the examination rather than to the presence or absence of the disease, it can be rewritten as follows:

$$P(R+/D+) = \frac{P(R+) \times P(D+/R+, V+)}{P(R+) \times P(D+/R+, V+) + P(R-) \times P(D+/R-, V+)}$$

The probability of a positive DRE among all patients with cancer $P(R+/D+)$, i.e. the corrected sensitivity Se, is equal to the product of the frequency with which an anomaly is detected by DRE $P(R+)$ in the population at large and the frequency of cancer in the sub-population of biopsied subjects who had a positive DRE $P(D+/R+, V+)$. The result is divided by the probability for the whole of the subjects studied of having cancer, whether their DRE was normal or not. The probability of a negative DRE among normal subjects $P(R-/D-)$ i.e. specificity Sp, is calculated in the same way.

The following table illustrates these calculations using the figures taken from Teillac's study (Teillac *et al.*, 1990):

Table 21a. Verfication sample.

V+	D+	D−	Total
R+	8	18	26
R−	11	56	67
	19	74	93

Table 21b. Source population.

Pop	D+	D−	Total
R+			33
R−			556
			589

P(R+)	=33/589	=0.056
P(D+/R+, V+)	=8/26	=0.307
P(R−)	=556/589	=0.944
P(D+/R−, V+)	=11/67	=0.164

$$Se = \frac{0.056 \times 0.307}{0.056 \times 0.307 + 0.944 \times 0.164} = 0.099$$

$$P(R-/D-) = \frac{P(R-) \times P(D-/R-, V+)}{P(R-) \times P(D-/R-, V+) + P(R+) \times P(D-/R+, V+)}$$

P(R−)	=556/589	=0.943
P(D−/R−, V+)	=56/67	=0.835

$$P(R+) \qquad\qquad = 33/589 \qquad = 0.056$$
$$P(D-/R+, V+) \quad = 18/26 \qquad = 0.692$$

$$Sp = \frac{0.943 \times 0.835}{0.943 \times 0.835 + 0.0560 \times 0.692} = 0.953$$

When the corrected values of the coefficients of sensitivity and a specificity are taken to calculate the positive likelihood ratio, the probability of detecting a tumour by DRE, when disease prevalence is about the same as for Connecticut, USA (0.38%, all ages taken together), is about 1%. This theoretical result seems to concord with the rates of detection (R of D) effectively found in most studies on the effectiveness of mass screening (Table 22).

Changing sensitivity and specificity (Table 23) of the test alters substantially the strategy ranking (Table 24).

Strategy 6 is dominating all the other strategies, whatever the criteria chosen, i.e. number of cancers found or of life-years saved. The cost effectiveness ratios per life saved become acceptable: 243,500 FF for the 70 year-old versus 196,500 FF for the 60–69 age bracket and 122,600 FF for the 50–59 when the prevalence is respectively 24%, 11% and 8.5%. When the probability of prostatic cancer is so high, even invasive testing might be desirable. PSA + biopsy appears to be more efficient, because the greater cost is offset by the lower incidence of false positives. In the event that PSA + biopsy is used in asymptomatic patients, it is more cost-effective to perform biopsy in patients with positive PSA rather than proceeding directly to DRE or US. Strategy 6 is the dominating strategy.

CONCLUSION

The advantages and costs of a case finding program could have been compared with those that could be expected from a mass screening program. But this aspect has not been studied. We have limited our analysis to calculating the financial cost to society and to refer it back to the theoretical effectiveness of screening examinations in order to bring out the dominant programs. When key parameters are not corrected for work-up bias, a range of strategies are efficient. When the bias is corrected, it appears that strategy 6 is the dominant one. In both cases, the implementation of the strategies depends on the collective marginal willingness to pay. No particular technique has been used to propose a choice, decisions taken in other areas could be used as guidelines: values observed a posteriori in other fields of prevention (marginal cost for colorectal cancer or carcinoma of the breast) can be applied a priori. But this would suppose that the previous decisions had been optimal. In reality, only the authorities can select one particular value in the screened case. The work of the assessor is to make explicit the scale of values on which their decisions are based and make it transparent. But as Marc Guil-

Table 22. Results of DRE prostate Cancer screening studies.

	Follow up	Patients	Age	Nodules (DRE+)	cancers	PPV %	R of D %
Screening exams							
Gilbertson 1971 (USA)	1948-1964 (5 years)	5 856	48-72	ND	75	ND	1,2
Faul 1982 (RFA)	1978 (1 year)	1 500 000	> 45	21308	1951	9,1	1,28
Thompson 1984 (USA)	1978-1983 (4 years)	2 005	40-92	65	19	29,2	0,85
Vihko 1985 (Finland)	1979-1984 (5 years)	771	54-76	27	9	39,3	1,16
Lee 1988 (USA)	1985-1987 (19 months)	784	60-86	29	10	34,0	1,20
Mueller 1988 (USA)	1979-1985 (6 years)	4 883	40-79	312	122	39,1	2,49
Imai 1988 (Japon)	1981-1985 (4 years)	5 770	> 50	202	54	26,7	0,93
Chodak 1989 (USA)	1981-1987 (6 years)	2 131	45-80	144	37	25,6	1,73
Perrin 1989 (France)	1988 (6 months)	863	50-60	19	3	15,7	0,34
Perrin 1989 (France)	01.87/04/89 (28 months)	530	X = 67	59	6	10,1	1,6
Teillac 1989 (France)	ND	600	> 50	26	8	30,7	1,3
Hospital visits							
Devonec 1989 (France)	01.87/01/88 (12 months)	666	X = 67	64	34	53,0	5,10
Perrin 1989 (France)	10.88/04.89 (6 months)	481	X = 67	115	59	51,3	13,5
Vallancien 1989 (France)	ND	167	46-89	44	32	72,7	19,1

PPV : Positive predictive value defined as the ratio of the number of true positive to the total number of positive tests.
R of D : rate of detection defined as the ratio of the number of cancers found to the total number of people screened

Table 23. Assessing the sensitivity and specificity of tests subject to work-up bias.

	DRE	PSA	DRE + PSA
"naive" sensibility	0.428	0.947	0.969
corrected sensibility	0.100	0.676	0.708
"naive" specificity	0.757	0.432	0.326
corrected specificity	0.950	0.889	0.847

Table 24. Incremental cost per cancer detected, in FF (Se, Sp, B, corrected for bias).

Age	Strategy	Feldman	Vallancien	Franks
50-59 years		0.13%	8.5%	29%
	1	D	D	D
	4	D	D	D
	6	1,264,984	22,058	8,594
60-69 years		0.90%	11%	30%
	1	D	D	D
	4	D	D	D
	6	182,317	17,729	8,407
> 70 years		3.6%	24%	40%
	1	D	D	D
	4	D	D	D
	6	46,823	9,756	7,059

laume (1971) underlined twenty years ago "one cannot propose anything without transforming oneself into a political advisor".

BIBLIOGRAPHY

Beck, R., Kassirer, J., Pauker, S., (1982). A convenient approximation of life expectancy (The Deale) used in decision-making. Am J Med, 73: 889–897.

Begg, C., Greenes, R., (1983) Assesment of diagnostic test when disease verification is subject to selection bias. Biometrics, 39: 207–215.

Begg, C., Greenes, R., Iglewicz, B., (1986) The influence of uninterpretability on the assessment of diagnostic tests. J Chron Dis, 39, 8: 575–584.

Begg, C., McNeil, B., (1988) Assessment of radiologic tests: control of bias and other design considerations. Radiology, 167: 565–569.

Boccon-Gibod, L., (1988) Le dépistage du cancer de la prostate, défi de la décennie 1990. An Urol 22 6: 385–387.

Chodak, G., Keller, P., Schoenberg, H., (1989) Assessment of screening for prostate cancer using the digital rectal examination. The J of Urol, 141: 1136–1138.

Cooner, W., Mosley, B., Rutherford, C. et al. (1989) Coordination of urosonography and prostate-specific antigen in the diagnosis of non-palpable prostate cancer. J of Endour, 3: 19–25.

Devonec, M., Fendler, J.P., Monsalier, M., et al. (1990) The significance of the prostatic hypoechoic area: results in 226 ultrasonically guided prostatic biopsies. *J of Urol*, 143: 316–319.

Edwards, C., Steinthorsson, E., Nicholson, D., (1952) An autopsy study of latent prostatic cancer. Cancer, 6: 531–554.

England, W., Halls, J., Hunt, V., (1989) Strategies for screening for colorectal carcinoma. *Med Decis making*, 9: 3–13.

Faul, P., (1982) Experience of a German annual preventive check-up examination. *International Perspectives in Urology* 3 Prostate Cancer. Ed. Jacobi, G. and Hohenfellner R., Williams and Wilkins, Baltimore.

Feldman, A., Kessler, L., Myers, M., and al. (1986) The prevalence of cancer: estimates based on the Connecticut tumour registry. *N Engl J of Med*, 315: 1394–1397.

Franks, L.M., (1954) Latent carcinoma of the prostate. *J Path Bact* v, 8: 603–6166.

Gilbertsen, V., (1971) Cancer of the prostate gland. *Jama*, 215: 81–84.

Gleason, D.J., (1966) Classification of prostatic carcinomas. *Cancer chimiotherapy reports*, 50: 125–128.

Guinan, P., (1980) The accuracy of the rectal examination in the diagnosis of prostate carcinoma. *N Eng J Med*, 303: 499–503.

Guillaume, M., (1971) La valeur de la vie humaine dans le choix des investissements routiers. *Revue Rationnalisation des choix budgétaires*, (septembre): 48–58.

Hermanek, P., Sobin, L., (1988) TNM classification des tumeurs malignes. Springer-Verlag, Ed. France.

Holund, B., (1980) Latent prostatic cancer in a consecutive autopsy series. *Scand J Urol Nephrol*, 14: 29–35.

Hudson, P., Finkle, A., Hopkins, J., et al. (1954) Early prostatic cancer diagnosed by arbitrary open perineal biopsy among 300 unselected patients. *Cancer*, 7: 690–703.

International Histological Classification of Tumours (1980) n° 22, Histological typing of prostate tumours, Geneva: WHO.

Imai, K., Zimbo, K., Shimizu, K., and al. (1988) Clinical Characteristics of prostatic cancer detected by mass screening. *The prostate*, 12: 199–207.

Johansson, J., Andersson, S., Krusemo, U., et al. (1989) Natural History of localized prostatic cancers. A population based study in 223 untreated patients *Lancet*, **i** 15: 799–803.

Kabalin, J., McNeal, J., Price, H., et al. (1989) Unsuspected adenocarcinoma of the prostate in patients undergoing cystoprostatectomy for other causes: incidence, histology and morphometrics observations. *The J of Urol*, 141: 1093–1094.

Lee, F., Littrup, P., Torp-Pedersen, S., (1988) Prostate cancer: comparison of transrectal US and digital rectal examination for screening. *Radiology*, 168: 389–394.

Lee, F., Torp-Pedersen, S., Littrup, P., et al. (1989) Hypoechoic lesions of the prostate: clinical relevance of tumor size, digital rectal examination and prostate-specific antigen. *Radiology*, 170: 29–32.

Lepor, H., Kimball, A., Walsh, P., (1989) Cause-specific actuarial survival analysis: a useful method for reporting survival data in men with clinically localized carcinoma of the prostate. *The J of Urol*, 141: 82–84.

Montie, E., Wood, P., Pontes, J., (1989) Adenocarcinoma of the prostate in cystoprostatectomy specimens removed for bladder cancer. *Cancer*, 63: 381–385.

Mueller, E., Craint, T., Thompson, I., et al. (1988) An evaluation of serial digital examination in screening for prostate cancer *The J of Urol*, 141: 1445–1447.

Perrin, P., Maquet, J.H., (1989) Screening for prostate cancer, a European experience. Research paper accepted for publication in *Br J of Urol*.

Pritchett, T., Moreno, J., Warner, N., et al. (1988) Unsuspected prostatic adenocarcinoma in patients who have undergone radical cystoprostatectomy for transitional cell carcinoma of the bladder. *The J of Urol*, 139: 1214–1216.

Ransohoff, D., Feinstein, A., (1978) Problems of spectrum and bias in evaluating the efficacy of diagnostic tests. *N Engl J of Med*, 299: 906–930.

Scott, R., Mutchnick, D., Laskowski, T., (1969) Carcinoma of the prostate in elderly men: incidence, growth, characteristics and clinical significance. *The J of Urol*, 101: 603–607.

Sheldon, C., Williams, R.D., Fraley, E.E. (1980) Incidental carcinoma of the prostate: review of literature and critical reappraisal of classification. *The J of Urol*, 124: 626–631.

Silverberg, E., (1987) Statistical and epidemiologic data on urologic cancer. *Cancer*, 60: 692–716.

Stamey, T.A., McNeal, J.E., (1987) Prostate specific antigen as a serum marker for adenocarcinoma of the prostate. *N Engl J Med*, 317: 909–16.

Teillac, P., Bron, J., Tobolski, F., et al. (1990) Dépistage du cancer de la prostate: étude de 600 cas. *Ann Urol*, 24: 37–41.

Thompson, I., Ernst, J., Gangai, M., et al. (1984) Adenocarcinoma of the prostate: results of routine urological screening. *The J of Urol*, 132: 690–692.

Vallancien, G., Prapotnich, D., Sibert, L., (1989) Comparison of the efficacy of digital rectal examination and transrectal ultrasonography in the diagnosis of prostatic cancer. *European Urol*, 16: 321–324.

Vallancien, G., Prapotnich, D., Veillon, B., (1990) Systematic prostatic biopsies in 100 men with no suspicion of cancer on digital rectal examination. Accepted for publication in the *J of Urol*.

Vihko, P., Kontturi, M., Lukkarinen, O., et al. (1985) Screening for carcinoma of the prostate. *Cancer*, 56: 173–177.

Whitmore, W., (1984) Natural history and staging of prostate cancer. *Urology clinics of North-America*, 11: 205–220.

Whitmore, W., (1988) Overview: historical and contemporary in Consensus Development Conference on the Management of Clinically Localized Prostate Cancer. National NCI monographs n° 7: 7–11.

Winder, E., Mabuchi, K., Whitmore, W., (1971) Epidemiology of cancer of the prostate. *Cancer*, 28 2: 344–359.

The validity of the MIMIC health index – some empirical evidence*

ROBERT E. LEU, MICHAEL GERFIN and STEFAN SPYCHER

Economics Institute, University of Bern, Vereinsweg 23, CH-3012 Bern, Switzerland.

I10 I12

Germany

1. INTRODUCTION

The rise of medical care expenditure over the last few decades has made the economic evaluation of medical services increasingly important. However, economic appraisal of specific medical therapies is a complex issue, particularly with respect to the benefit side of the analysis. Previous studies often have ignored treatment benefits, restricting analysis to cost differentials between treatment alternatives or have focused exclusively on improvements in patients' earnings capacity through reductions of morbidity or mortality. Both approaches are clearly unsatisfactory if (i) a new therapy constitutes significant therapeutic progress without reducing treatment costs, (ii) the major effect of a new therapy is to improve patients' well-being, enjoyment of life, or life quality rather than to increase longevity or earnings capacity and (iii) the benefits of a new therapy accrue mainly to patients who are not part of the labor force, *i.e.* persons working in the household or retired people. In all these situations, economic evaluation requires assessment of the direct and immediate treatment benefits: the improvement in patients' well-being (life quality).

One promising approach which seems to offer considerable potential for measuring patients' well-being (health or health impairment, respectively) is the use of latent variable models. In recent years, such models have been employed repeatedly for that purpose (compare, for example, Robinson & Ferrara 1977, Lee 1979, Van de Ven & Van der Gaag 1982, Zweifel 1982, Hoijmans & Van de Ven 1983, Wolfe & Behrman 1984, Leu 1985, Haveman

*The research presented here was in the first phase financed by Thomae AG, Biberach, in the second by the Swiss National Science Foundation (Project No. 3.927–0.85). It draws on earlier work of other people who have been engaged in this project at some point: dipl. psych. Rosemarie Deutschmann (Deutschmann & Co., Basel) designed the patient questionnaire and did the interviews, Dr. Thomas Keller provided the two physician scales used in Section 7. The authors would like to thank Peter Zweifel for helpful comments.

P. Zweifel and H. E. Frech III (eds.), Health Economics Worldwide. 109–142.
© 1992 *Kluwer Academic Publishers. Printed in the Netherlands.*

& Wolfe 1985, Wagstaff 1986, Leu & Schaub 1990). However, little attention has been devoted so far to the question of how valid health indices estimated in this way are. The purpose of this paper is to provide some empirical evidence on this issue. We use a MIMIC model (MIMIC = *M*ultiple *I*ndicators *M*ult*I*ple *C*auses) for measuring health impairment/disability (hereafter referred to as disability) caused by a specific disease, chronic bronchitis. The disability index derived from that model is then subjected to a number of validity tests. First, we look at construct validity. Second, we compare the MIMIC index to an evaluation of the same patients by a group of physicians. The physicians provide a direct rating scale as well as a risk index derived from a Torrance (1976) Standard Gamble approach. Comparison to the latter provides some information on whether the MIMIC index can be interpreted to reflect utility units directly.

The paper contains ten sections. In section 2, a MIMIC model for measuring bronchitis-related disability (impairment of life quality) is developed, treating disability as a latent (unobservable) variable which is characterized fully by its causes and indicators (effects). The data are described in section 3 and the estimation results are displayed in section 4. In section 5, we derive the disability index from the estimated model using the approach developed by Van Vliet & Van Praag (1987). Construct validity of this index is investigated in section 6. In section 7, the relative validity of the MIMIC index as compared to the direct rating scale and the Torrance Standard Gamble index provided by the physicians is assessed. The results are discussed in section 8. Section 9 contains some reflections on the potential of the MIMIC index as an outcome measure in the economic appraisal of medical services. Finally, section 10 provides a summary and the major conclusions.

2. A MIMIC MODEL FOR BRONCHITIS-RELATED DISABILITY

The MIMIC model is a special case of the more general LISREL model (LISREL = *Li*near *S*tructural *Rel*ations), containing only one unobservable endogenous variable. The formal structure of the MIMIC model is as follows (*see* Jöreskog & Goldberger 1975):

$$\eta = \Gamma'X + \zeta \tag{1}$$
$$Y = \Lambda\eta + \epsilon \tag{2}$$

where
η = the latent variable,
X = a vector of k exogenous causes, k = 1,. . . ,i,
Γ' = a vector of parameters to be estimated,
ζ = an error term,
Y = a vector of m endogenous indicators, m = 1,. . . ,j,
Λ = a vector of parameters to be estimated, and
ϵ = a vector of measurement errors.

Equation (1) represents the structural model, equation (2) the measurement model. The error term ζ and the measurement errors ϵ are assumed to be mutually independent and to have a multivariate normal distribution. To remove the indeterminacy in the structural parameters of this model, a normalization has to be adopted. This can be accomplished either by restricting one of the λ's or by restricting the variance of the latent variable η. In this paper, we chose the former possibility, arbitrarily setting one of the λ's equal to one. We thereby define a zero point and a unit of measurement for the latent variable η which is determined up to a linear transformation in the model.

Estimation of the model entails searching values of the free parameters which will fit the predicted moment matrix to the observed moment matrix of the data (Schoenberg & Arminger 1989). The GAUSS subprogram LINCS is used to obtain full-information maximum-likelihood estimates of the structural parameters. Details of the estimation procedure used as well as of the computation of the various descriptive and test statistics are provided by Schoenberg *et al.* (1987) and Schoenberg & Arminger (1989).

The overall fit of the model is measured by the Adjusted Goodness of Fit Index (AGFI, where $0 < AGFI < 1$) which is corrected for degrees of freedom and measures how closely the predicted moment matrix fits the observed moment matrix. The familiar R^2 is computed for each equation in both the structural and the measurement model. The specification of the model can be checked using a likelihood-ratio (χ^2) statistic and the Hausman (1978) test.

Using a MIMIC model for measuring disability caused by chronic bronchitis is based on three assumptions: (1) Disability caused by chronic bronchitis is a multidimensional qualitative variable. (2) What can be observed directly are "causes" and "indicators" (effects) of bronchitis-related disability. (3) Bronchitis-related disability can be characterized sufficiently by these observable causes and effects.

The first two assumptions can be asserted by analogy to the literature on general health status measurement on a conceptual level (compare Van de Ven & Hoijmans 1982). Whether assumption (3) holds depends obviously on how accurate the information contained in the data used for estimating such a model is. Since the data in the present study are based on patients' perceptions of the causes for and effects of their bronchitis-related disability (see below), the third assumption is likely to be fulfilled also. This was confirmed by the reaction of the interviewees to the questionnaire (*see* Deutschmann 1984).

Having established that the structure of the MIMIC model lends itself readily to measurement of bronchitis-related disability, two further questions arise: (1) Which variables should be included in the model, and (2) which of these variables constitute causes and which represent indicators (effects) of bronchitis-related disability? The literature does not offer a comprehensive theoretical model that would be readily applicable to these two questions.

Instead, we had to rely on patients' perceptions regarding their disease as well as on opinions and viewpoints expressed by medical and psychological experts in this field.

The first question was solved by interviewing both physicians and selected persons suffering from chronic bronchitis. In particular, in-depth interviews with a dozen bronchitis subjects were carried out by a psychologist. The results of these interviews, supplemented with the information obtained from health professionals in the field, provided the relevant variables (dimensions) which were included in the questionnaire used for interviewing the entire sample. Since our aim is to measure self-rated disability caused by the disease, this seemed to be the most appropriate approach.

With respect to the second question of how to partition the variables collected in oral interviews into causes and indicators we rely heavily on what appears to be the predominant view among physicians and psychologists in this field (see, for example, McSweeney & Labuhn 1990, Morgan et al. 1983, Hanson 1982, Cegla 1982, Lebovitz 1977, Fehrlinz 1974). Following this view, we use three groups of variables as causes of bronchitis-related disability: (1) Symptoms of the disease (including functional limitations), (2) attitudes towards and coping strategies with the disease, and (3) age and gender. The remaining variables in the data set either describe the effects of bronchitis-related disability or provide a self-assessment of the severity of the disease-related disability. Therefore, they are included as indicators in the model. Five groups of indicators are distinguished: (1) Effects on the time budget (time costs), (2) financial effects, (3) effects on social life, (4) psychological impairment as a result of the disease, and (5) self-assessment of severity of the disability.

Groupwise principal components analysis using Varimax-Rotation was employed to reduce the number of variables (items) with respect to both causes and indicators. Definitions and summary statistics are displayed in Table 1 for the 13 variables included as causes and in Table 2 for the 13 variables included as indicators in the model. Appendices A and B provide detailed descriptions of the principal components serving as causes or indicators, respectively.

On first sight it may seem astonishing that the symptoms of the disease – cough, expectoration, functional limitations etc. – should be used as causes of bronchitis-related disability. Figure 1 clarifies this point. There are two separate latent constructs that should be distinguished: One is "Chronic Bronchitis", the disease (left half), the other is "Disability" caused by the disease (right half). Although neither is directly observable, observable causes and indicators (symptoms, effects) exist for both. Chronic bronchitis – like most diseases – has a multiple etiology (left half). The causal (risk) factors of the disease are represented by $W_1, \ldots, W_k$. Some of them are known (genetic factors, smoking etc.), others are not. Presence of the disease is manifested by its symptoms $X_1, \ldots, X_i$ (cough, expectoration etc.). In the language of the MIMIC model these symptoms are indicators for the presence

Table 1. Causes of disability due to chronic bronchitis (N = 145)

Abbreviation	Definition of variables	Mean	Standard deviation	Mini- mum	Maxi- mum
PCCOUGH	Principal component for cough	0	1	-2.31	2.34
PCEXPECT	Principal component for expectoration	0	1	-2.47	2.37
PCSHORBR	Principal component for shortness of breath	0	1	-1.51	3.37
DURCHRBR	Duration of chronic bronchitis in years	9.63	10.34	0	30
DURCHRB2	Duration of chronic bronchitis in years squared	19.89	31.32	0	90
CONCDIS	Number of concomitant diseases	1.30	1.19	0	5
PCPHYSIM	Principal component for physical impairment	0	1	-1.47	2.34
PCRESIGN	Principal component for attitude of resignation (fatalism) towards the disease	0	1	-1.59	2.64
PCINDIFF	Principal component for dismissal of the disease	0	1	-2.05	2.67
PCENVIRO	Principal component for lack of symptoms in clean air	0	1	-2.21	2.02
SELFINFL	Feelings that the disease is self-inflicted (0 = no; 1 = yes)	0.41	0.49	0	1
AGE	Age in years	48.35	14.73	18	80
GENDER	Gender (Male = 1)	0.52	0.50	0	1

Table 2. Indicators of disability due to chronic bronchitis (N = 145)

Abbreviation	Definition of variables	Mean	Standard deviation	Mini- mum	Maxi- mum
TREATDUR	Duration of daily treatment in minutes	32.08	98.32	0	720
ACUTEDUR	Duration of treatment in acute phases in minutes	53.69	121.09	0	860
TIMEBURD	Perceived burden of time cost of treatment (2 = none; 8 = very stressful)	3.19	1.51	2	8
FINBURD	Perceived financial burden of treatment (1 = none; 4 = a great deal)	1.36	0.68	1	4
PCCONTAC	Principal component for general social contact problems	0	1	-1.08	4.92
PCFAMILY	Principal component for family problems	0.	1	-1.55	4.08
PCPARTNE	Principal component for problems with partner	0	1	-2.33	1.71
PCWILLIV	Principal component for lost will to live as a result of the disease	0	1	-2.02	3.92
PCINTROV	Principal component for introversion as a result of the disease	0	1	-1.61	3.00
PCINFERI	Principal component for feeling insecure and inferior because of the disease	0	1	-2.40	3.43
PCMIND	Principal component for feeling all right despite the disease	0	1	-3.23	1.73
SRDIS	Self-rated degree of bronchitis-related impairment/disability (0 = not disabled at all; 10 = seriously disabled)	4.40	2.51	0	10
SRBRON	Self-rated degree of bronchitis (1=none ; 5=serious)	2.66	1.03	1	5

of the disease. At the same time, however, these symptoms clearly constitute (along with other variables) causes for the latent construct "bronchitis-related disability" as perceived by those suffering from the disease (right half of the figure). Since our aim is to measure the latter construct, the symptoms of the disease are included as causes in the model.

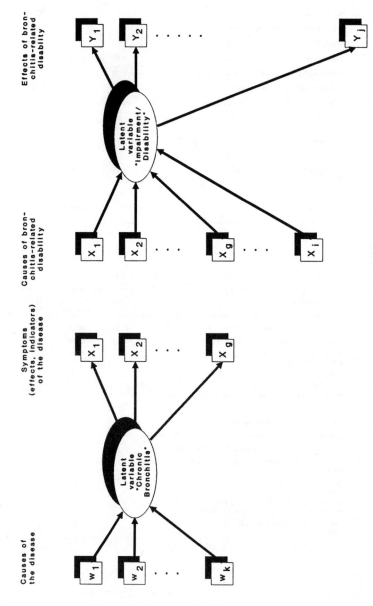

Fig. 1. "Chronic Bronchitis" and "Bronchitis-Related Health Impairment/Disability" as two separate latent constructs.

The second group of variables included among the causes of bronchitis-related disability describes attitudes towards and coping strategies with the disease. The underlying psychological model postulates a simple hypothesis (*see* Muthny 1989): Certain attitudes towards the disease as well as certain ways of coping with the disease will - other things being equal - make a person feel more or less disabled depending on what these attitudes and ways of coping are. Both types of variables - those expressing attitudes as well as those expressing ways of coping with the disease - are supposed to influence causally how disabled someone is in his/her own judgement (self-rating), other things being equal. On a theoretical level, therefore, both types of variables can be viewed only as causes of bronchitis-related disability in the MIMIC model.

Age and gender constitute the third group of causes for bronchitis-related disability. They are included to control for their possible influence although we do not have any specific hypotheses with respect to the expected direction of this influence. In the context of our model both variables can only be thought of as causes of bronchitis-related disability for obvious reasons.

As mentioned above the remaining variables either describe the effects stemming from the disability caused by the disease along various dimensions or indicate a self-assessment of the severity of the disease-related disability. They are therefore included as indicators in our model ($Y_1, \ldots, Y_j$ in Figure 1).

Previous studies using latent variable models for measuring disability have, with few exceptions, included medical care utilization in the structural part of the model, specifying the demand for health care explicitly as a function of the latent variable, prices, income, health insurance and sociodemographic characteristics. The results of Van Vliet & Van Praag (1987) as well as our own results in previous studies (Leu & Schaub 1990) indicate, however, that incorporating medical care utilization combined with a structural model explaining utilization does not provide much relevant information if the purpose of the study is to measure health or disability. Therefore, we confine the structural part of our model to the equation for the latent variable η, *i.e.* bronchitis-related disability.

MIMIC health/disability indices have five major advantages over traditionally constructed indices (compare Leu & Schaub 1990 for a more detailed discussion): (1) The weights of the variables included in the index do not have to be determined arbitrarily but can be estimated from the data using an adequate estimation method. (2) Measurement errors for the indicators are explicitly allowed for. Using the more general LISREL model would, in addition, provide the possibility of allowing for measurement errors in the exogenous causes of the model. (3) The number of variables (disease dimensions) which can be included in the index is limited only by computer capacity, *i.e.* is unlimited for practical purposes. This constitutes a major advantage with respect to measurement of multi-attribute health states. (4) If deemed appropriate, the information for estimating such an index can be gathered from those most directly involved: the persons (patients) suffering from it. This is important since patients' perceptions are taken increasingly seriously in the health field. It also eliminates the need for arbitrarily selecting a group of experts who then determine the dimensions of the index and the weights for each dimension. (5) Estimating a MIMIC index is much less cumbersome and less costly than producing a comparable index using psychometric methods.

3. DATA

The subjects studied in this paper were drawn from the population in West Germany excepting Berlin in the course of a general population survey carried out by INFRATEST-Gesundheitsforschung (1985). They were identified as persons suffering from chronic bronchitis using the standard WHO questions defining that disease (*see* Leu & Schaub 1990, Chapter 6, for a more detailed description). The sample is restricted to adults between 18 and 80 years of age. Structured interviews which are based on a number of in-depth interviews were conducted with 150 persons suffering from chronic bronchitis in 1985, 145 of which could be included in the analysis.

4. ESTIMATION RESULTS

The maximum-likelihood estimation results for the structural parameters of the MIMIC bronchitis model are displayed in Tables 3 and 4. The Adjusted Goodness of Fit Index (AGFI), indicating the overall fit of the model, is 0.74. The R^2 of the structural equation is 0.86 while the corresponding values for the equations of the measurement model vary between 0.55 and 0.02. Most of the estimated parameters are statistically significant and all but one ("Dismissal of the disease") have the expected sign.

According to Table 3, all of the variables in the first group (symptoms of the disease) except "Other concomitant diseases" are statistically significant. Cough, expectoration and shortness of breath all have a disability-increasing effect, with expectoration being the most important variable of these three. The relationship to "Duration of chronic bronchitis" is hill-shaped, indicating that disability caused by the disease first increases and then decreases with duration of chronic bronchitis. One possible interpretation is that persons suffering from the disease learn to live with it. The negative sign on "Lack of symptoms in clean air" indicates that overall disability is less severe for those who do not feel the symptoms of bronchitis unless exposed to a polluted environment. A strong disability-increasing effect - as expected - is exerted by "Impaired physical performance" caused by the disease. That "Other concomitant diseases" are not significant indicates that the latent variable in

Table 3. Estimated coefficients of the causes of disability due to chronic bronchitis (structural model)[a]

Cause	Estimated parameter
Symptoms of the disease	
Cough	0.30 (2.86)
Expectoration	0.54 (4.79)
Shortness of breath	0.21 (1.89)
Duration of chronic bronchitis	0.06 (1.72))
Duration of chronic bronchitis (squared)	- 0.27 (- 2.34)
Lack of disease symptoms in clean air	- 0.27 (- 2.60)
Impaired physical performance due to chronic bronchitis	0.46 (3.17)
Other concomitant diseases	- 0.03 (- 0.34)
Attitudes towards and coping strategies with the disease	
Attitude of resignation (fatalism) towards the disease	0.96 (6.84)
Dismissal of the disease	0.04 (0.39)
Conviction that the disease is self-inflicted	- 0.20 (- 0.85)
Socioeconomic variables	
Age	0.05 (0.56)
Gender	- 0.01 (- 0.05)
R^2	0.86
N	145
AGFI	0.74
Likelihood ratio statistic[b]	464.53

[a] Full-Information Maximum-Likelihood Estimation; t-values in parentheses (two-tailed test).

[b] The degrees of freedom equal 221.

our model really measures the specific health impairment caused by chronic bronchitis rather than general well-being.

Only one of the three variables in the second group of causes is statistically significant. "Attitude of resignation" (fatalism) increases bronchitis-related disability. "Dismissal of the disease" and "Conviction that the disease is self-inflicted" lack significance with the former exhibiting the "wrong" sign. Age and gender, the two variables included in the last group of causes, do not have a significant influence, *i.e.* bronchitis-related disability does not depend on these demographic characteristics, other things being equal.

As is shown in Table 4, all of the indicators have the expected sign and all but one of the coefficients ("Introversion because of the disease") are statistically significant. The coefficients are largest for "Self-rated degree of disability", "Perceived burden of time cost" and "Self-rated degree of bronchitis" in this order. The coefficient on "Self-rated degree of disability

Table 4. Estimated coefficients of the indicators (effects) of disability due to chronic bronchitis (measurement model)[a]

Indicator (effect)	Estimated parameter	R^2
Effects on the time budget		
Duration of daily treatment	0.21 (4.56)	0.16
Duration of treatment in acute phases	0.26 (4.54)	0.16
Perceived burden of time cost	0.43 (6.20)	0.29
Financial effects		
Perceived financial burden	0.17 (5.27)	0.20
Effects on social life		
General social contact problems	0.23 (4.84)	0.18
Family problems	0.22 (4.79)	0.18
Problems with partner	0.11 (2.30)	0.06
Psychological effects of the disease		
Lost will to live as a result of the disease	0.19 (4.01)	0.13
Introversion as a result of the disease	0.04 (0.86)	0.02
Feeling insecure and inferior because of the disease	0.12 (2.53)	0.05
Feeling all right despite the disease	-0.23 (-4.94)	0.19
Self-assessment of severity of disease		
Self-rated degree of impairment/disability	1.00	0.55
Self-rated degree of bronchitis	0.40 (8.45)	0.51

[a] Full-Information Maximum-Likelihood Estimation; t-values in Parentheses.

is arbitrarily set to one, thus defining a zero point and a unit of measurement for the latent variable. The disability index derived in the next section is independent of this normalization. Using a different restriction (*i.e.* choosing another variable or another numerical value for the restricted coefficient) would change the estimated structural parameters of the model proportionally, but would leave the index unaffected.

The R^2-values on the right hand side of Table 4 indicate how well the individual indicators mirror the latent concept. "Self-rated degree of disability", "Self-rated degree of bronchitis" and "Perceived burden of time cost" in this order represent the latent concept most accurately. By contrast, some of the indicators ("Introversion as a result of the disease" *etc.*) are related only marginally to the latent disability concept and could be dismissed with little loss of information.

A Hausman (1978) specification test is used to determine whether the model is sufficiently well specified to yield consistent estimates. The Hausman test statistic has an asymptotically central χ^2 distribution with degrees of freedom equal to the number of parameters (*see* Schoenberg & Arminger 1989 for a more detailed description of the test procedure). For all 39 parameters of the model the test statistic is 250.72. We therefore reject the hypothesis that the entire model is correctly specified. However, restricting the test to the structural parameters only (*i.e.* Λ and Γ) produces a test statistic of 0.79, indicating that the structural parameters are estimated consistently. These results suggest that the misspecification is located in the assumed distribution of the error terms. This is also reflected in the high value of the likelihood ratio test statistic which is very sensitive to misspecification of this kind (*e.g.* heteroscedasticity in the data). It appears that this is a common problem in practically all empirical applications of latent variable models.

5. DERIVATION OF THE DISABILITY INDEX

A disability index can be derived from the estimated model using the approach developed by Van Vliet & Van Praag (1987). Following their procedure we compute 14 proxies for the latent variable η from the estimated coefficients: one from each equation in the measurement model and one from the structural equation. Each of these proxies has an error variance. The index is then defined as the weighted sum of these proxies, where the weights are calculated so as to minimize the variance of the difference between the true value and the index and add up to one.

Consider, for example, an equation for a specific indicator m, as derived from (2):

$$\eta = \frac{1}{\lambda_m} (y_m - \epsilon_m), \quad m = 1 - 13, \tag{3}$$

where $\hat{\lambda}_m$ is the m-th element of $\hat{\Lambda}$. Ignoring ϵ_m, we obtain for each m a proxy

$$\hat{\eta}_m = \frac{1}{\hat{\lambda}_m} y_m. \tag{4}$$

The difference between the true value η and $\hat{\eta}_m$ is

$$\hat{\eta}_m - \eta = \frac{\epsilon_m}{\hat{\lambda}_m}. \tag{5}$$

With 13 indicators we use a weighted sum

$$\hat{H} = \sum_{m=1}^{13} p_m \hat{\eta}_m, \tag{6}$$

where the weights p_m add up to one. The optimal choice of the weights is that which minimizes the variance of

$$\hat{H} - \eta = \sum_{m=1}^{13} p_m(\hat{\eta}_m - \eta)$$

$$= \sum_{m=1}^{13} p_m \frac{\epsilon_m}{\hat{\lambda}_m}, \tag{7}$$

i.e. to derive these weights the following expression has to be minimized:

$$\min[\text{var}(\hat{H} - \eta)] = p'[\delta^{-1}(I - B)^{-1}\Sigma_{\epsilon\epsilon}(I - B)^{-1}\delta^{-1}]p$$

$$= p'Ap, \tag{8}$$

where

  δ = diagonal matrix containing the estimated coefficients $\hat{\lambda}_m$,

  B = the correlation matrix of the data,

$\Sigma_{\epsilon\epsilon}$ = diagonal matrix with the variances of the residuals, and

  A = the expression in square brackets.

The optimal weights can be generated by minimizing the Lagrangian equation

$$L = p'Ap + \mu(p'\iota - 1), \tag{9}$$

where μ is the Lagrange multiplier and ι is a vector of ones.

From the first order conditions of (9) one can derive

$$p^* = A^{-1}\iota \frac{1}{\iota'A^{-1}\iota}, \tag{10}$$

where p^* is the vector of optimal weights.

The proxy for the structural part of the model can be integrated by adding one row and one column of zeros to A except for the diagonal element where the estimated variance of the residual of the structural equation is placed (*c.f.* Van Vliet & Van Praag 1987, footnote 7).

Table 5 shows the computed weights for the individual indicators and the structural equation. The highest weights are obtained for "Self-rated degree of disability", the proxy of the structural equation, "Perceived burden of time costs" and "Self-rated degree of bronchitis". The sum of the weights for the proxies computed from the measurement model is 0.81, the weight for the structural equation proxy is 0.19.

Previous studies have usually computed the index using the estimated parameter values of equation (1) only. In our case, calculating the index from the structural equation alone explains 86% of the variation of η. Computing the index from both the structural and the measurement model according to the method of Van Vliet & Van Praag increases the share of explained variance to 97%. Since the index is determined only up to a linear transforma-

Table 5. Computed weights for the individual indicators and the structural equation

Equation	Weights
Indicators of the measurement model	
Duration of daily treatment	0.04
Duration of treatment in acute phases	0.05
Perceived burden of time cost of treatment	0.12
Perceived financial burden	0.03
General social contact problems	0.04
Family problems	0.04
Problems with partner	0.01
Lost will to live	0.02
Introversion as a result of the disease	0.002
Feeling insecure and inferior because of the disease	0.01
Feeling all right despite the disease	0.04
Self-rated degree of impairment/disability	0.32
Self-rated degree of bronchitis	0.08
Structural equation	0.19

Table 6. The disability index according to selected variables included in the model

Variable / Prinicipal Component	Category/ Group	MIMIC Index	Number of Persons
Symptoms			
Cough[a]	slight	29	36
	extensive	39*	36
Expectoration[a]	slight	20	36
	extensive	44*	36
Shortness of breath[a]	slight	29	36
	extensive	41*	36
Duration of chronic bronchitis	1 - 4 years	25	22
	5 - 9 years	36*	29
	10 - 19 years	32	28
	20 years or over	31	37
Lack of disease symptoms in clean air[a]	slight	35	36
	extensive	29	36
Impaired physical performance[a]	slight	17	36
	extensive	49*	36
Attitudes towards and coping strategies with the disease			
Attitude of resignation[a]	slight	18	36
	extensive	50*	36
My bronchitis does not bother me	true	23	69
	not true	38*	76
I am worried about a deterioration	true	33	93
	not true	26*	52
Dismissal of the disease[a]	slight	32	36
	extensive	32	36

Table 6. Cont.

Variable / Prinicipal Component	Category/ Group	MIMIC Index	Number of Persons
Demographic characteristics			
Age	- 30	21[b]	24
	31 - 40	25[c]	17
	41 - 50	28[d]	33
	51 - 60	35*	37
	61 or over	38	34
Gender	male	33	75
	female	28	70
Restrictions in activity			
Restricted career possibilities (men only) [e]	true	49	12
	not true	30*	63
Restricted housework (women only) [f]	true	43	13
	not true	25*	57
Social problems due to the disease			
General social contact problems[a]	slight	28	36
	extensive	42*	36
Family problems[a]	slight	26	36
	extensive	37*	36
Problems with partner[a]	slight	25	36
	extensive	33*	36
Psychological effects of the disease			
Lost will to live[a]	slight	27	36
	extensive	43*	36
Introversion as a result of the disease[a]	slight	31	36
	extensive	35	36
Feeling insecure and inferior because of the disease[a]	slight	27	36
	extensive	42*	36
Feeling all right despite the disease[a]	slight	43	36
	extensive	20*	36
Self-assesment of severity of disease			
Self-rated degree of impairment/disability	none / a little	10	28
	medium	28*	74
	serious	45*	33
	very serious	62*	10
Self-rated degree of bronchitis:	none	16	19
	a little	20	45
	medium	35*	54
	serious	45*	20
	very serious	69*	7

*) This index value differs significantly from that of the previous group.

a) This variable is a principal component. We compare the lowest with the highest quartile.

b) This index value differs significantly from the group "41–50", "51–60" and "61 and more".

c) This index value differs significantly from the group "51–60" and "61 and more".

d) This index value differs significantly from the group "61 and more".

e) There were not enough career women to warrant a separate comparison.

f) There were not enough men working at home to warrant a separate comparison.

tion, the zero point and the unit of measurement can be chosen arbitrarily. We compute the index in such a way that it runs from 0 to 100. The index value zero indicates the degree of impairment of the best off person in the sample (the least disabled person), the index value 100 that of the worst off person.

6. TESTING FOR CONSTRUCT VALIDITY

In this section, the MIMIC disability index is compared to selected single variables (or principal components, respectively) which partly are and partly are not included in the model. We test whether the mean values of the index for subsequent subcategories of these variables differ significantly. The mean values for which this holds are marked with a star. In this way, we can check whether the index performs to a priori expectations. The results of these tests are purely descriptive in nature. As opposed to the estimated parameters of the variables in the model, they indicate simple correlations between the MIMIC index and these variables. By contrast, the parameters in the MIMIC model are partial derivatives, indicating the effect of these variables keeping constant all other variables included in the model.

Tables 6 and 7 show the MIMIC disability index according to selected variables which partly are (Table 6) and partly are not (Table 7) included in the model. In all those cases where a clear a priori hypothesis exists the index behaves consistently with this a priori expectation. Hence we conclude that the index has considerable construct validity.

In addition to the groupwise comparisons in Tables 6 and 7 we have carried out extensive sensitivity analysis with respect to the specification of the model. In particular, we have estimated an alternative version of the model containing only "Self-rated degree of disability" and "Self-rated degree of bronchitis" as indicators, including all other variables as causes. Despite this major change in specification, the resulting disability index is highly correlated with the one computed from the main version of the model ($r = 0.92$). Minor changes in specification hardly showed any influence at all with respect to the index derived from the model. Hence we conclude that the results are fairly robust with respect to changes in model specification.

That the MIMIC index computed in this way really measures bronchitis-related disability as perceived by the patients is further confirmed by simple correlations between the index and the two variables "Self-rated degree of disability" and "Self-rated degree of chronic bronchitis". The correlation coefficient is $r = 0.83$ in the former and $r = 0.70$ in the latter case.

Table 7. The MIMIC disability index according to selected variables not included in the model

Variable	Category/ Group	MIMIC Index	Number of Persons
Socioeconomic variables			
Income	< 1000	36[a]	10
	1000 - 3000	33[a]	88
	3000 - 5000	26*	32
	> 5000	22	15
Degree of education	Primary school / secondary school	31	111
	Colleges / University	29	34
Employment status	working / in professional training	26	85
	not working / unemployed	38*	60
Medical care utilization			
Physician visits (past six months)	none	19	40
	1 to 3	25*	35
	4 or over	40*	69
Hospital spells (past 12 months)	yes	51	15
	no	28*	130
Spells in sanatorium	yes	38	20
	no	30*	125
Self-rated general health status			
Present health status	excellent	12	6
	good	28*	95
	fair	37*	38
	poor	53*	6

*[*] This index value differs significantly from that of the previous group.
[a] The index value differs significantly from the group ">5000".

7. RELATIVE VALIDITY WITH RESPECT TO PHYSICIANS' EVALUATIONS

In this section, we compare the MIMIC index with an evaluation of selected patients by a group of physicians. First, we describe the study design used for deriving the physicians' ratings (section 7.1). In section 7.2 we compare the MIMIC index to the direct rating scale, in section 7.3 to the Torrance (1976) Standard Gamble index provided by these physicians.

7.1. *Study design*

The physician investigation was carried out by Keller (1987) using the following study design: From the total of 145 persons in the sample, 10 were selected to be evaluated by the physicians. They were chosen arbitrarily according to their index value in an earlier version of the MIMIC model (Leu *et al.* 1986). Keller picked those persons whose index value was closest to 0, 10, 20, . . . , 90, respectively. Since we now use a slightly different model and compute the index in a different way, the index values of these test persons are different. The person with the highest value (highest disability) was described to the physicians as a point of reference (person X). The physicians were given the bulk of information obtained through the interview. Therefore, they had the same information available that is used to estimate the MIMIC model. They then had to fill out the response sheet shown in appendix C for the 10 subjects labelled A to K.

The physicians were asked to do the following:

1. Read the patient sheet for each patient A to K carefully. Try to imagine these patients and to judge how severely sick (disabled) they are relative to each other.
2. Mark each patient (A to K) with a dash on the scale provided by the answer sheet. Person X is already marked on the scale; this is the worst case.
3. Imagine that there is a hypothetical new therapy for these patients. In some cases, the therapy can improve the patient's situation substantially. However, there is also a risk that the therapy fails. In this case, the patient's status worsens dramatically, deteriorating to the level of patient X for the rest of his/her lifetime.
4. Consider now for each patient: What would be the maximum risk of failure at which you would apply the therapy and above which you would not? Please note this percentage in the answer sheet.

The first two steps of this procedure provide the direct rating scale S, steps 3 and 4 the Standard Gamble risk index Q (*see* Torrance 1976, 1986; Card *et al.* 1977). We use a slightly modified version of the Standard Gamble method as developed by Torrance (1976) and implemented by Card *et al.* (1977) since we do not ask for the minimal rate of success which is required for the physicians to be willing to apply the therapy but rather for the maximum risk of failure that they are willing to accept. The reason is that chronic bronchitis cannot presently be cured. A pilot study had revealed that presenting a scenario to the physicians in which the patients can be properly cured was too hypothetical.

The medical team consisted of 21 physicians with various medical backgrounds working in the region of Basel. Table 8 displays for each of the ten patients A to K the values of the MIMIC index M_i and the mean values of the direct rating scale $\bar{S}_i$ as well as those of the Standard Gamble risk index $\bar{Q}_i$ provided by the 21 physicians together with their standard deviations, where i denotes the i-th patient.

Comparison of the scales M and $\bar{S}$ in Table 8 shows that persons B and C, F and G as well as I and K have switched places. Not unexpectedly, the differences are more pronounced between the scales M and $\bar{Q}$ since the latter includes a risk assessment of the experts as well.

7.2. *MIMIC index and direct rating scale*

To investigate further the relationship between the MIMIC index M and the direct rating scale S, we use a descriptive regression estimation framework:

Table 8. MIMIC index, direct rating scale and standard gamble index

Individual	Age	M_i	$\bar{\bar{S}}_i$	std. dv.	$\bar{O}_i$	std. dv.
A	35	3.11	1.33	0.92	3.28	6.15
B	26	9.77	2.57	1.18	9.56	20.58
C	47	15.96	1.67	1.29	4.82	7.94
D	42	23.08	3.65	1.41	14.79	16.60
E	68	30.92	3.68	1.37	15.97	17.48
F	66	35.49	4.71	1.56	26.67	24.95
G	36	41.58	3.72	2.12	10.74	15.49
H	44	45.39	5.45	1.84	23.00	19.53
I	54	59.48	7.85	1.37	48.57	24.96
K	56	80.00	7.50	1.70	46.31	30.70
Mean	47.4	34.48	4,21		20.37	
Std.dv.	12.96	22.30		2.57		24.62

$$S_{ij} = \alpha_0 + \alpha_1 M_i + \epsilon, \tag{11}$$

where i denotes the i-th person with chronic bronchitis ($i = 1, \ldots, 10$) and j is the subscript for the 21 physicians.

To examine the appropriate form of this equation, a Box-Cox (1962) transformation is applied to the data (*see* Maddala 1977, p. 314ff). This involves using a general form of (11):

$$S_{ij}^* = \alpha_0 + \alpha_1 M_i^* + \epsilon, \tag{12}$$

where

$$S_{ij}^* = (S_{ij}^\lambda - 1)/\lambda, \quad M_i^* = (M_i^\gamma - 1)/\gamma \quad \text{for } \lambda \neq 0, \gamma \neq 0$$
$$S_{ij}^* = \ln(S_{ij}), \quad M_i^* = \ln(M_i) \quad \text{for } \lambda = 0, \gamma = 0. \tag{13}$$

λ and γ represent transformation parameters to be estimated.

If $\lambda = \gamma$, equation (12) contains the linear and the log linear form as special cases:

$$S_{ij} = \alpha_0 + \alpha_1 M_i + \epsilon \qquad \text{for } \lambda = \gamma = 1 \tag{14}$$

$$\ln(S_{ij}) = \beta_0 + \beta_1 \ln(M_i) + \epsilon \quad \text{for } \lambda = \gamma = 0. \tag{15}$$

Estimation of the unrestricted equation (12) produces a maximum-likelihood estimate of γ, $\hat{\gamma} = 0.75$ (estimated standard error $= 0.14$), which is not significantly different from one at the 0.025 level. Therefore, transformation of the right-hand variable M can be dispensed with. The estimated value of λ, $\hat{\lambda}$, is 0.68 (0.06) and differs significantly from both zero and one ($p \leqq 0.05$). Estimating equation (12) using $\gamma = 1$ provides the estimation results displayed

Table 9. Maximum-likelihood estimation results of equations (11) and (17)[a)]

Dependent Variable	S^*	Q^*
Constant	0.28	- 0.66
	(2.00)	(- 1.71)
MIMIC index	0.06	0.09
	(10.13)	(9.48)
$\hat{\lambda}$	0.70	0.25
	(11.60)	(9.27)
N	210	210
t-values (H_0: λ = 1)	- 5.01	- 28.49

[a)] Estimated using $\gamma = 1.0$. t-values in parentheses.

in the left column of Table 9. The likelihood ratio test statistic of 1.44 confirms that the restriction $\gamma = 1$ cannot be rejected at the 0.05 level ($\chi^2_1 = 3.84$). The coefficient on the MIMIC index is positive and highly significant. Hence, we conclude that there is a systematic, but nonlinear relationship between the physicians' direct rating scale S and the MIMIC disability index M.

7.3. Relationship between the MIMIC index and the Standard Gamble risk index

In this section, we investigate whether the MIMIC index can be interpreted directly in terms of utility. In principle, this can be accomplished by comparing the MIMIC index to a utility function over all levels of bronchitis-related disability. Formally, this involves investigating a relationship of the following form:

$$U = \alpha_0 + \alpha_1 M^b, \qquad (16)$$

where

U $\quad$ = a utility function over all levels of bronchitis-related disability,
α_0, α_1, b = unknown parameters, and
M $\quad$ = the MIMIC index.
The question is whether $b \gtreqless 1$. If $b = 1$, (16) reduces to

$$U = \alpha_0 + \alpha_1 M. \qquad (17)$$

In this case, the units of the MIMIC index could be interpreted directly as ratio-scaled utility units with a dimension of their own and the MIMIC index would provide a directly applicable outcome measure for cost-utility analysis (*see* Torrance 1986 for a description of cost-utility analysis).

In the present study, the Standard Gamble risk index Q provided by the group of physicians is used as an empirical approximation of U. On the proviso that a function like Q provided by a group of physicians indeed reflects utility associated with different degrees of disability as perceived by those suffering from the disease (*see* section 8), we can test whether the MIMIC index reflects utility by simply comparing it to the risk index Q.

As in section 7.2, we employ the Box-Cox transformation procedure to determine the adequate form of the equation

$$Q_{ij}^* = \beta_0 + \beta_1 M_i^* + v, \tag{18}$$

where the variables with an asterisk have the same meaning as in equation (13), β_0 and β_1 are parameters to be estimated and v is an error term.

The maximum-likelihood estimate of γ, $\hat{\gamma} = 0.67$ (0.22), is not significantly different from one, rendering transformation of M unnecessary. The estimated value of the transformation parameter for the Standard Gamble risk index Q amounts to $\hat{\lambda} = 0.24$ (0.03) and is significantly different from both zero and one at the 0.05 level. Estimating equation (17) using $\gamma = 1$ yields a highly significant relationship between Q^* and M (*see* Table 9, right column). The likelihood ratio test statistic of 1.03 indicates that the imposed restriction $\gamma = 1$ cannot be rejected at the 0.05 level. As in the case of the direct rating scale S we conclude, therefore, that there is a systematic, but nonlinear relationship between the Standard Gamble risk index Q and the MIMIC disability index M.

8. DISCUSSION

In this section, we will discuss some of the problems associated with validating the MIMIC bronchitis index as estimated in this paper. Our case study indicates that the MIMIC disability index satisfies two criteria: (1) It has high construct validity, and (2) it is related in a systematic, but nonlinear way to both a direct rating scale as well as a Standard Gamble risk index provided by a group of 21 physicians with various medical backgrounds. To state the obvious first it should be clear that these results apply only to the bronchitis disability index as estimated here and do not carry over to any other application of the MIMIC model to health status measurement. The validity of a disability index computed from such a model depends primarily on the accuracy of the data used to describe the latent construct. Since this will vary from study to study no general conclusion regarding validity can be drawn from a single case study.

One of the difficulties which we encountered specifically in this case study was the lack of a comprehensive theoretical model for the measurement of disability caused by chronic bronchitis. This problem would have been less severe in the case of other chronic diseases or general health status measurement where more work on measurement issues has a been done and published. We have dealt with this lack of a comprehensive theory by drawing on different strands of the medical and psychology literature and by carrying out in-depth interviews with both selected persons suffering from the disease as well as with health professionals in the field. Despite these efforts, our estimation model remains somewhat *ad hoc* in the sense that we cannot assume that another research team, tackling the same question, would come up with exactly the same model specification. However, this problem is specifically associated with the case of chronic bronchitis and is in no way related to the MIMIC approach for measuring disability. The same problem would hamper any other method of constructing a disability index for chronic bronchitis. A mitigating factor is that the results are fairly robust with respect to changes in model specification according to the sensitivity analyses.

In estimating the MIMIC disability index we have taken the viewpoint of the patients and have measured bronchitis-related disability as perceived by those suffering from the disease. This does not mean, however, that we would consider only patients' preferences to be relevant. Rather, we regard patients' and physicians' preferences as two complementary points of view for the evaluation of the same unobservable phenomenon. The appropriateness of these viewpoints depends primarily on the purpose of the study (*see* the discussion on economic appraisal in section 9). Nor does the approach taken in this paper imply that the MIMIC model is confined to measuring disability from the patients' points of view. Analogous models could be estimated, based either entirely on information obtained from health professionals (provided a sufficiently large number of them could be persuaded to participate) or including information gained from both physicians and patients.

The validation approach chosen in this paper raises the question of whether it is possible to validate a disability index based on patients' preferences by comparing it to a direct rating scale and a Standard Gamble risk index provided by a group of health providers, reflecting the preferences of the latter. The question has been discussed in the literature in general terms (*i.e.* not related to the MIMIC index) and has generated controversy. One line of argument is that physicians, due to superior knowledge and experience, have better judgment and therefore should constitute the ultimate authority when it comes to evaluating health or chronic states. That view is increasingly challenged by those who argue that patients' preferences should be decisive since the ultimate goal of medical care is improving patients' well-being. On a more technical level, some researchers have claimed that the Standard Gamble risk index obtained from a group of experts (physicians) permits "objective" measurement of the patients' "subjective" utility (*see*, for example, Card *et al.* 1977). If their argument were correct, the Standard Gamble risk index obtained from a group of experts would provide the most appropriate criterion for testing whether the MIMIC index directly reflects utility.

However, this view has been rejected fervently by those who argue that a Standard Gamble risk index provided by experts primarily measures the degree of risk aversion of these experts rather than patients' utility (see the discussion in Keller 1987, p. 107f.). Whether one considers it appropriate to validate a patient based index with an index provided by health professionals thus depends on which of the above positions one is willing to accept.

That large differences in risk aversion may exist among experts (physicians) and that such differences may influence the Standard Gamble risk values is confirmed by the present study. The mean value of the maximum acceptable risk reported by the surgeons in the group was roughly three times higher than that reported by the other physicians (with twice the standard deviation), and the difference was significant statistically (see Keller 1987, p. 153). Surgeons seem to have a lower degree of risk aversion and, correspondingly, are willing to apply the therapy in question at significantly higher risk. This observation sheds considerable doubt on the proposition that patients' utility can be measured properly using a Standard Gamble approach no matter who the experts are. It also raises the question of who the experts should be and how they should be selected. That replacing one expert by another can change the outcome of such evaluations significantly is a well-known observation in the literature on psychometric scales (see Ware et al. 1981, p. 623 f.).

Since it is not clear whether a Standard Gamble risk index provided by a group of health professionals properly reflects patients' utility, our results should be interpreted carefully. What the results do imply is that the MIMIC index does not measure utility as derived from the preferences of the physicians employed as experts. Whether the index reflects utility as derived from patients' preferences remains an open question. One way of tackling this question would be to replicate the Standard Gamble procedure with a group of bronchitis subjects. However, this could be criticized on the grounds that the risk values reported by these subjects might depend on their own state of chronic bronchitis. In addition, there is doubt how well laypersons would be able to handle the hypothetical scenarios of such a procedure.

Further problems of measuring utility are discussed extensively in the literature. For example, one issue concerns the validity of the Von Neumann-Morgenstern (1953) utility theory itself upon which the Standard Gamble approach is based (compare, for example, Bell et al. 1988; Richardson 1990). Another is the question of aggregation and its validity (see Torrance 1986, p. 17). Overall, it seems fair to summarize the literature as far as it concerns validation of the MIMIC index in the following way: (1) There is no unchallenged and unambiguous reference scale available against which the MIMIC index could be validated. (2) The Standard Gamble risk index represents by far the best criterion for such a test because of its theoretical merits. (3) Whether the "experts" in a Standard Gamble approach used for validating a patient-based MIMIC index should be health professionals or patients/diseased subjects is an open question. Since we have compared the MIMIC disability index as estimated here only to a Standard Gamble risk index provided by a group of physicians, no definite conclusion can be drawn concerning whether this index measures utility and, hence, could be employed directly as an outcome measure in cost-utility analysis.

9. POTENTIAL AS OUTCOME MEASURE FOR ECONOMIC APPRAISAL

This section contains some reflections on the potential of the MIMIC index for economic appraisal. In particular, we will briefly discuss its applicability as an outcome measure in cost-effectiveness, cost-utility and cost-benefit analysis.

Cost-effectiveness analysis (CEA): The most obvious application of the MIMIC index is in cost-effectiveness analysis. CEA determines a cost-effectiveness ratio whose denominator represents a measure of the health effects of the therapy (program) under study. Since CEA does not require that the health measure reflect utility the MIMIC index clearly provides a potential outcome measure for that type of evaluation.

The MIMIC index allows proper assessment of the impact of a disease on patients' well-being (life-quality) at a given moment in time, as the preceding sections of this paper have demonstrated. By the same token, the index allows for measurement of improvements in patients' well-being due to the application of a new treatment method over time. However, this requires a prospective study design, *i.e.* patients have to be interviewed at least twice, along with a control group, once before and once (or several times) after the onset of the new therapy (for example, in the course of a clinical trial). The index can then be computed for successive stages of the new therapy. In the case of treatment success, the mean value of the index (scaled as above) will go down, in the case of failure, it will remain unchanged or go up. The index expresses the effectiveness of the new therapy in improving patients' well-being (life quality) taking possible side effects into account.

In a prospective study, it is possible to compute the cost-effectiveness ratio $\Delta\text{MDI}/C$ of the new therapy where ΔMDI denotes the change of the MIMIC disability index over time due to the therapy and C represents the therapy costs. The ratio $\Delta\text{MDI}/C$ gives the reduction of the index per unit of treatment cost. If two (or more) treatment alternatives are available, one can determine which one is more cost effective: $\Delta\text{MDI}_1/C_1 \gtreqless \Delta\text{MDI}_2/C_2$ where subscripts 1 and 2 refer to the respective treatment methods.

CEA is restricted to comparisons of alternative treatment methods for the same disease (diagnosis) whose outcomes (health effects) are measured in the same units. This is typically the case when a new treatment method such as a new chemical substance has to be evaluated against existing therapies. By contrast, CEA cannot be employed when a single program has to be assessed or when disparate alternatives, *i.e.* treatments for different diseases, have to be compared.

Cost-utility analysis: Cost-utility analysis is more widely applicable than CEA. At least in principle, it lends itself to evaluations of disparate alternatives, *i.e.* treatments (programs) for different diseases, across the entire health sector. Whether a MIMIC index as estimated in this paper may be employed as an outcome measure in cost-utility analysis depends on its validity as a measure of utility and the purpose of the study.

Validity of the MIMIC bronchitis index was discussed in section 8. If one considers physicians' preferences as the ultimate yardstick, the index is not a valid measure of utility associated with different states of chronic bronchitis. By contrast, if one considers patients' preferences as being decisive, the question of whether the MIMIC index is a valid measure of utility remains open.

CUA can be employed for two types of evaluations: (1) A comparison of two or more alternative treatment methods for the same disease, and (2) a comparison of disparate treatments for different diseases. If the purpose of CUA is comparison of alternative treatment methods for the same disease, patients' utilities are appropriate. By contrast, if treatments across different diseases are to be assessed, the appropriate utilities are those of an informed member of society (*see* Torrance 1986, p. 5), *i.e.* a random sample of the general public or a group of health professionals on the grounds that they are the appointed proxies of the public in the health field. In the latter case the MIMIC index as measured in this paper, *i.e.* based on patients' preferences, is not applicable. However, as pointed out in section 8, alternative MIMIC models could be specified and estimated based on evaluations of health professionals.

Another possible application consists of combining a patient-based MIMIC index with a Standard Gamble risk index provided by a group of health professionals. Since we found a systematic relationship between the two indices, the former can be transformed and expressed in utility units (as derived from the experts' preferences) using the estimated regression coefficients. This, in turn, opens up the possibility of employing the so-transformed MIMIC index for evaluation of medical treatments across different diseases, provided that all these treatments are subjected to a prospective evaluation and that the same group of experts provides a ranking of chronic states for these other diseases as well. The advantage of such an approach would be that the evaluation using experts would need to be carried out only once and could then be combined with patient-based MIMIC indices estimated whenever a new treatment alternative were to appear or a new evaluation of an existing treatment were carried out. While a procedure of this type may seem desirable in principle, there is clearly a long way to go until resources in health care will be allocated according to such a scheme.

Cost-benefit analysis (CBA): CBA, at least in principle, is even more widely applicable than CUA because (1) it allows comparisons of investment alternatives across the entire economy and not just in the health field, and (2) it permits assessment of a single program. Obviously, the MIMIC index does not lend itself directly as an outcome measure in CBA. However, as in CUA, it could be combined with a direct or indirect assessment of the willingness-to-pay of patients, community representatives or informed members of the general public, respectively (depending on the purpose of the study), for improvements across chronic states associated with each of the diseases to be evaluated. Again, the advantage would be that willingness-to-pay for improvements in chronic states would have to be assessed only once and that it could then be used in successive evaluations of (new) medical therapies involving new patient-based MIMIC index estimates. In the present study, no attempt has been made to assess patients' or society's willingness-to-pay for improvements in chronic states of bronchitis which would allow changes in the MIMIC index to be expressed in monetary units.

10. SUMMARY AND CONCLUSIONS

This study evaluates the potential of econometric models with latent (unobservable) variables for measuring health or health impairment due to a specific disease. A MIMIC disability index is estimated for a sample of 145 adults with chronic bronchitis, expressing their self-reported disability caused by the disease on a one-dimensional scale. The index is determined up to a linear transformation. Disability is thus measured on an interval scale. The data were collected by interviews. The questionnaire used for this purpose is based on a number of in-depth interviews with selected bronchitis patients conducted beforehand. The study therefore focuses directly on the patients' perceptions of their disease.

The validity of the index is evaluated in three different ways. First, construct validity is assessed performing groupwise analysis and testing for differences in the index values by subgroup. To a large extent, the index is consistent with a priori expectations. Therefore, we conclude that it has high construct validity.

Second, validity of the index is assessed by comparing its results to a direct rating scale produced by 21 physicians with various medical backgrounds. The MIMIC index turns out to be related in a systematic, but nonlinear way to this direct rating scale. This can be interpreted in two different ways. If one accepts the preferences of health providers as the ultimate yardstick when it comes to ranking health or chronic states the result suggests that the MIMIC index estimated in this way is not a valid measure of treatment success. By contrast, if patients' preferences are considered to be decisive, it suggests that physician-based ratings should be substituted for or at least complemented with patient-based indices (such as the MIMIC disability index estimated here) when evaluating medical services in terms of cost-effectiveness.

Third we explore the extent to which the MIMIC index reflects utility associated with different states of disability, using a modified Torrance Standard Gamble approach. The above-mentioned physicians are used as experts in this procedure. The results indicate that the MIMIC index as estimated here is related in a systematic, but nonlinear way to the Standard Gamble risk index as well. The fact that this relationship is nonlinear indicates that the MIMIC index does not measure utility as derived from the experts' preferences directly. How this index would fare compared to a Standard Gamble risk index provided by patients (bronchitis subjects) is a question which remains open. Therefore, no definite conclusion can be drawn concerning whether the MIMIC index as estimated here could be used directly as an outcome measure in cost-utility analysis.

Overall, our results indicate that the MIMIC index warrants further attention as a potential outcome measure for economic appraisal of medical services.

REFERENCES

Bell, D.E., H. Raiffa, and A. Tversky, *Decision Making: Descriptive Normative and Positive Interactions*, Cambridge: Cambridge University Press, 1988.
Box, G.E.P. and D.R. Cox, "An analysis of transformations", *Journal of the Royal Statistical Society*, series B, pp. 211–243, 1962.
Card, W.I., M. Rusinkiewicz, and C.I. Phillips, "Utility Estimation of a Set of States of Health", *Methods of Information in Medicine* 16, pp. 168–175, 1977.
Cegla, U.H., "Atmungserkrankungen - chronische Bronchitis", *Fortschritte der Medizin* 4, pp. 97–100, 1982.
Deutschmann, R., *Psychosoziale und wirtschaftliche Auswirkungen der chronischen Bronchitis*, Pilotstudie, Deutschmann & Co., Forschungskreis für Gesundheit und Gesellschaft, Basel, 1984.
Fehrlinz, R., "Erkrankungen der Atemwege: chronische Bronchitis", in: Fehrlinz, R., *Lungen- und Bronchialerkrankungen. Ein Lehrbuch der Pneumologie*, Thieme, 1974.
Hanson, E., "Effects of chronic lung disease on life in general and on sexuality: perceptions of adult patients", *Heart and Lung* 11, pp. 435–441, 1982.
Hausman, J.A., "Specification tests in Econometrics", *Econometrica* 46, pp. 1251–1272, 1978.
Haveman, R. and L. Wolfe, "Disability Status as an Unobservable: Estimates from a Structural Model", *Discussion Paper No 775–85*, University of Madison, Wisconsin, 1985.
Hooijmans, E.M. and W.P.M.M. Van de Ven, "A Multiple Indicator Multiple Causes Health Status Index", in: *Actes du Xe Coloque International d'Econometrie Appliqué*, Lion, 1983.
Infratestforschung (ed.), *Gesundheitsforschung – Chronische Bronchitis in der Bundesrepublik Deutschland*, München, 1985.
Jöreskog, K.G. and S. Goldberger, "Estimation of a Model with Multiple Indicators and Multiple Causes of a Single Latent Variable", *Journal of the American Statistical Association* 70, pp. 631–639, 1975.
Keller, T., *Gesundheitszustandsmessung in der ökonomischen Therapieevaluation*, Diss. Basel, 1987.
Lebovitz, M.D., "The Relationship of Socio-Environmental Factors to the Prevalence of Ob-

structive Lung Diseases and other Chronic Conditions", *Journal of Chronic Diseases* 30, pp. 599–611, 1977.

Lee, F.L., "Health and wages: A simultaneous equation model with multiple discrete indicators", *Discussion paper* 79–197, University of Minnesota, 1979.

Leu, R.E., "Economic Evaluation of New Drug Therapies in Terms of Improved Life Quality", *Social Science and Medicine* 21, pp. 1153–1161, 1985.

Leu, R.E., T. Schaub, und R. Deutschmann, "Chronische Bronchitis: Lebensqualität der Betroffenen und volkswirtschaftliche Kosten", *Praxis und Klinik der Pneumologie* 40, pp. 367–371, 1986.

Leu, R.E. und T. Schaub, "Gesundheit, Behinderung und Lebensqualität: der Patient hat das Wort", *Gesundheitsökonomische Beiträge*, Baden-Baden: Nomos, 1990.

Maddala, G.S., *Econometrics*, Tokyo: McGraw-Hill, 1977.

McSweeney, A.J. and K.T. Labuhn, "Chronic Obstructive Pulmonary Disease", in: Spilker, B. (ed), *Quality of Life Assessments in Clinical Trials*, Raven Press, 1990.

Morgan, A.D., D.F. Peck, D.R. Buchanan and G.J. McHardy, "Effect of attitudes and beliefs on exercise tolerance in chronic bronchitis", *British Medical Journal* 286, pp. 171–173, 1983.

Muthny, F., "Wege der Krankheitsverarbeitung und Verarbeitungserfolg im Vergleich verschiedener chronischer Erkrankungen", in: Speidel, H. and A. Strauss (eds.), *Zukunftsaufgaben der psychosomatischen Medizin*, Berlin: Springer, 1989.

Von Neumann, J. and O. Morgenstern, *Theory of Games and Economic Behavior*, Third Edition, Princeton: Princeton University Press, 1953.

Richardson, J., "Cost-Utility Analysis: What Should be Measured – Utility, Value or Health Year Equivalents?", Paper presented at the 2nd World Conference on Health Economics, Zürich, September 1990.

Robinson, P.M. and M.C. Ferrara, "The Estimation of a Model for an Unobservable with Exogenous Causes", in: D.J. Aigner and A.S. Goldberger (eds.), *Latent Variables in Socio-Economic Models*, Amsterdam: North Holland, 1977.

Schoenberg, R., G. Arminger, and L. Edlefsen, *Linear Covariance Structures Version* 1.1, User Guide, RJS Software, Kensington, Maryland, 1987.

Schoenberg, R. and G. Arminger, *Linear Covariance Structures Version* 2.0, User Guide, RJS Software, Kensington, Maryland, 1989.

Torrance, G.W., "Social Preferences for Health Status: An Empirical Evaluation of Three Measurement Techniques", *Socio-Economic Planning Science* 10, pp. 129–136, 1976.

Torrance, G.W., "Measurement of Health State Utilities for Economic Appraisal", *Journal of Health Economics* 5, pp. 1–30, 1986.

Van de Ven, W.P.M.M. and J. van der Gaag, "Health as an Unobservable – A MIMIC-Model of the Demand for Health Care", *Journal of Health Economics* 1, pp. 157–183, 1982.

Van de Ven, W.P.M.M. and E.M. Hooijmans, *The MIMIC-Health Status Index – What it is and How to Use it*, Leyden: Center for Research in Public Economics, 1982.

Van Vliet, R.C.J.A. and B.M.S. van Praag, "Health Status Estimation on the Basis of MIMIC Health Care Models", *Journal of Health Economics* 6, pp. 27–42, 1987.

Wagstaff, A., "The demand for Health – Some new empirical evidence", *Journal of Health Economics* 5, pp. 195–233, 1986.

Ware, J.E. Jr., *et al.*, "Choosing Measures of Health Status for individuals in general populations", *American Journal of Public Health* 71, pp. 620–625, 1981.

Wolfe, B. and J. Behrman, "Determinants of women's health status and health care utilization in a developing country: A latent variable approach", *The Review of Economics and Statistics*, pp. 696–703, 1984.

Zweifel, P., *Ein ökonomisches Modell des Arztverhaltens*, Berlin: Springer, 1982.

APPENDIX A

Principal component analysis (Varimax-Rotation) of variables in the structural model

The principal components are displayed according to their Eigenvalue. Only the most significant variables with a factor loading of at least 30.0% are displayed.

Number of variables analyzed	Principal components (Eigenvalue)	Share of variance explained by the principal components relative to the total variance of the analyzed variables
13	PCSHORBR (4.26) PCCOUGH (1.79) PCEXPECT (1.23)	56.0%
6	PCPHYSIM (4.63)	77.0%
16	PCRESIGN (3.79) PCINDIFF (1.91) PCENVIRO (1.57)	45.4%

Principal component for shortness of breath (PCSHORBR)

Question	Factor loading
- Do you wake up during the night due to shortness of breath?	0.83
- Do you sometimes feel you are suffocating?	0.75
- Are you sometimes short of breath while resting?	0.73
- Do you sometimes get a feeling of tightness or pressure in the chest?	0.61

Principal component for cough (PCCOUGH)

Question	Factor loading
- Do you have coughing attacks during the day?	0.87
- Is coughing unavoidable?	0.82
- Do you have coughing attacks during the night?	0.65

Principal component for expectoration (PCEXPECT)

Question	Factor loading
- Do you have any expectoration in the morning?	0.86
- Do you have persistent phlegm?	0.78
- Do you feel a rumbling, whistling or whining in your bronchial tract?	0.59

Principal component for physical impairment (PCPHYSIM)

Question	Factor loading
- Compared with earlier healthy days, to what extent do you feel physically impaired when walking up hill?	0.92
- Compared with earlier healthy days, to what extent do you feel physically impaired when carrying light or medium loads (e.g. shopping basket)?	0.91
- Compared with earlier healthy days, to what extent do you feel physically impaired when carrying heavy loads (e.g. a bucket of water)?	0.90
- Compared with earlier healthy days, to what extent do you feel physically impaired when climbing stairs?	0.88
- Compared with earlier healthy days, to what extent do you feel physically impaired when walking on the level?	0.84
- Compared with earlier healthy days, to what extent do you feel physically impaired when carrying out your daily routine (undressing/dressing, getting up, having a bath/shower)?	0.79

Principal component for lack of symptoms in clean air (PCENVIRO)

Question	Factor loading
- My problems disappear in clean air.	0.82
- The environment affects my health (harmful substances in the workplace, pollution).	0.74

Principal component for attitude of resignation (fatalism) towards the disease (PCRESIGN)

Question	Factor loading
- Chronic bronchitis limits my activities.	0.88
- Chronic bronchitis determines my way of life.	0.87
- If I didn't suffer from chronic bronchitis, I would be a completely different person.	0.82
- Compared to other persons with chronic bronchitis I am relatively well off.	- 0.64
- The thought of suffocating worries me.	0.59
- My experience with chronic bronchitis has taught me to take more care of my body and health.	0.52

Principal component for dismissal of the disease (PCINDIFF)

Question	Factor loading
- You don't take chronic bronchitis seriously until it is too late.	0.67
- I grew up in a family where physical ailments were ignored.	0.65
- My illness does not bother me at all.	0.34

APPENDIX B

Principal component analysis (Varimax-Rotation) of variables in the measurement model

The principal components are displayed according to their Eigenvalue. Only the most significant variables with a factor loading of at least 30.0% are displayed.

Number of variables analyzed	Principal components (Eigenvalue)	Share of variance explained by the principal components relative to the total variance of the analyzed variables
14	PCCONTAC (3.17) PCFAMILY (1.91) PCPARTNE (1.42)	46.4%
26	PCWILLIV (5.39) PCINTROV (2.15) PCINFERI (1.88) PCMIND (1.49)	45.4%

Principal component for general social contact problems (PCKONTAC)

Question	Factor loading
- Due to my illness I find it difficult to make new friends.	0.84
- Despite my illness I can have as many contacts with relatives and friends as I wish.	- 0.80
- Since I have been ill I have had fewer contacts with relatives and friends.	0.74

Principal component for family problems (PCFAMILY)

Question	Factor loading
- Coughing attacks at night annoy my partner.	0.81
- It is unpleasant for other people to hear me cough and expectorate frequently.	0.68
- Due to my illness I am restricted in fulfilling my family duties.	0.43

Principal component for problems with partner (PCPARTNE)

Question	Factor loading
- My partner is very understanding and helps me cope with my illness.	0.82
- My partner is not at all bothered by my illness.	0.82

Principal component for lost will to live (PCWILLIV)

Question	Factor loading
- There are times when the disease eradicates my will to live.	0.85
- Sometimes I wish I were dead and far away from everything because of my disease.	0.83
- Looking back over the years I feel I have reached quite a number of my goals despite my disease.	- 0.48
- I have suffered more setbacks than others because of my disease.	0.40

Principal component for introversion as a result of the disease (PCINTROV)

Question	Factor loading
Because of the disease:	
- I am somewhat introverted.	0.81
- I have created my own world into which I like to withdraw.	0.77
Despite the disease:	
- I am an optimist.	0.52
Because of the disease:	
- I am often depressed and sad.	0.50

Principal component for feeling insecure and inferior because of the disease (PCINFERI)

Question	Factor loading
Because of the disease:	
- I need a lot of reassuring.	0.71
- I have psychological problems, feelings of inferiority .	0.69

Principal component for feeling all right despite the disease (PCMIND)

Question	Factor loading
- I keep telling myself that I am all right despite the disease.	0.76
- I would not be any different even without my illness.	0.60
- I feel just as happy now as before the onset of my illness.	0.53

Welfare economics and cost-utility analysis*

J.R.G. BUTLER

*National Centre for Epidemiology and Population Health
and Division of Economics and Politics, RSSS, Australian National University, GPO
Box 4, Canberra ACT 2601, Australia.*

I 1 2   I 3 1

INTRODUCTION

It is generally agreed that the final output of the health care system is expected to be an improvement in health status. The various components of the health care system produce a wide variety of intermediate outputs which are almost invariably used as inputs into another production function which may again produce intermediate outputs and so on, but eventually the final output of the health care system appears as an input, along with other inputs such as the environment and life-style, into the health production function itself. And although the presumption that the marginal product of health care in terms of improvements in health status is positive has been questioned by some (*e.g.* Illich 1976), there is little dispute that conceptually this is what the health care system aims to achieve.[1]

Broadly, health status can be considered as having two dimensions – quantity of life (or longevity) and quality of life – and health care programs can potentially affect either or both of these. Of these two dimensions, quantity of life is more amenable to measurement because death is a readily identifiable event, and estimates of the number of life-years gained as a result of a program can often be obtained from epidemiological evidence on the effectiveness of the program. Measuring quality of life, however, is somewhat more problematic and yet can be critical in the economic evaluation of programs which have differential effects on the quality of life-years gained. Perhaps the earliest recognition of this in the domain of economic evaluation was in a study of the cost-effectiveness of alternative treatments for end-stage renal disease by Klarman *et al.* (1968). Since patients on dialysis generally have a lower quality of life than the recipients of a kidney transplant,

---

*I am grateful to the participants in a seminar held at The Australian National University, and to two anonymous referees, for their helpful comments on this paper. The usual caveat applies.

P. Zweifel and H. E. Frech III (eds.), Health Economics Worldwide. 143–157.
© 1992 *Kluwer Academic Publishers. Printed in the Netherlands.*

the authors applied a weight of 1.25 to the life-years saved through the use of transplantation as compared with dialysis.[2]

Over thirty years have now elapsed since the study by Klarman *et al.* and that time period has witnessed a prolific growth in the development of quality-of-life measurement instruments.[3] From an economic perspective, the concern with developing quality-of-life weights to be applied to life-years gained arises out of the problem that a life-year gained is not a homogeneous unit of output. Such weights can be used to capture the heterogeneity of life-years gained from different programs and render them comparable. The generic name given to this weighted unit of output is the 'quality-adjusted life-year' (QALY).

Framed in this way, the problem appears to be one of *objective* measurement. Given that the crude unit of output 'life-year gained' is heterogeneous, how can this measurement unit be refined to reduce this heterogeneity? This is logically distinct from the *subjective* measurement of the value which consumers/patients place on such life-years gained. Indeed, the distinction between the objective measurement of the output of a program and the subjective valuation of that program lies at the heart of the distinction between cost-effectiveness and cost-benefit analysis. The former technique is concerned with comparing the cost per unit of output of different technologies used to produce similar types of output (or outputs which can be rendered similar by the use of weights). Consumers' valuations of these outputs do not enter into the calculation. In cost-benefit analysis, however, the measurement of 'benefit' is, at least theoretically, based upon individuals' valuations of the outputs produced as expressed by their willingness-to-pay (or compensating variations). It is this which enables cost-benefit analysis to answer the question 'Should the output be produced?' rather than the more limited question 'What is the relative cost of producing the output by various means?' which is addressed by cost-effectiveness analysis.

Related to the development of quality adjustment weights is the emergence of a third technique of economic appraisal of health care programs, *viz.* cost-utility analysis. The distinguishing feature of this technique is that "the quality adjustment is based on a set of values or weights called utilities, one for each possible health state, that reflect the relative desirability of the health state" (Drummond *et al.* 1987, p. 113). These utility weights are then used to render the disparate life-years saved commensurate and allow comparisons between the cost per QALY gained from various programs. Interest has now developed in constructing a 'league table' which ranks health care programs in terms of their cost per QALY.[4]

Given the theoretical foundations of cost-benefit analysis in welfare economics and the basis of the concept of benefit in utility theory, it is pertinent to ask why cost-utility analysis as a third type of economic appraisal is necessary. What is it which this technique achieves which cost-effectiveness and cost-benefit analysis do not achieve? Does the technique rest upon a different theoretical foundation to the existing techniques? In discussing these matters, the paper falls into two main sections. The first of these addresses the question as to whether health status is objectively measurable. The second then considers the welfare foundations of cost-utility analysis.

OBJECTIVE *VS* SUBJECTIVE MEASUREMENT OF HEALTH STATUS

The distinction between objective and subjective rates of substitution in consumption and production lies at the core of the economic theory of production and exchange. Objective rates of substitution in production, both between inputs and between outputs, are technologically determined and embodied in the concepts of the production function and the transformation frontier. Conversely, subjective rates of substitution between commodities are based upon individuals' preferences as reflected in their indifference maps. Equality between these objective and subjective rates of substitution at the margin is a familiar requirement for the achievement of the first-best optimality conditions.

Health as a commodity can be integrated into this theoretical analysis (Grossman 1972). In some cases, increased health will be consumed as a by-product of the consumption of health-generating activities (*e.g.* regular physical exercise). In other cases, health will be traded off in favour of increased consumption of health-reducing activities (*e.g.* smoking). In the latter case utility-maximising individuals will equate their marginal rate of substitution of health for other health-reducing activities with the relevant objective rate of transformation between the two.[5]

This analysis, of course, is predicated on the notion that health states are objectively measurable, *i.e.* that they can be measured in a way that does not depend upon individuals' subjective valuations of them. It views health as being the output of a production function in the same way that motor vehicles and other commodities are outputs of production functions, and although health may be more difficult to measure, in principle at least it can be done.

A contrary, and commonly held, view is that health status and quality of life are inherently subjective magnitudes. Siegrist and Junge (1989, p. 464) state: "Information on quality of life always refers to some extent to subjective evaluation by those suffering from disease and treatment. It defines reality in subjective terms . . ." And a group of sociologists from the University of York and elsewhere state, as part of a contrived dialogue: "Your faith in the possibility of devising 'objective' measures of quality of life is touching, but I think misplaced" (Ashmore *et al.* 1989, p. 95). But this view is not confined to disciplines other than economics. Mooney (1986), for example, argues quite forcefully that an important aspect of health status measurement is "that it is value-laden. . . Let us consider an example. Someone with a cold, *ceteris paribus*, has a lower/poorer health status than someone without a cold. Someone with pneumonia, *ceteris paribus*, has a lower health status

Table 1. Dimensions of handicap, levels of disability and index scores for each combination

Dimension	Levels of Disability(a)			
	A,a	B,b	C,c	D,d
	No difficulty	Some difficulty but can do own	Not on own	Never because too difficult
Getting to or using WC	0	4	6	6
Getting in and out of bed	0	2	3	3

Notes: (a) Upper case letters (A,B,C,D) refer to level of disability on the dimension 'Getting to or using WC' while lower case letters refer to 'Getting in and out of bed'.

Source: Culyer (1976, p.37).

than *either* someone without either pneumonia or a cold *or* someone with a cold. These statements both involve value and technical judgments" (pp. 35–8). Culyer (1978) emphasises this point also, focusing on three kinds of value judgment necessary in health status measurement: "the choice of dimensions in which health status is to be measured; the choice of weights by which various dimensions are to be 'traded off', and the choice of numbers to be assigned to the dimensions that have, in this way, been combined" (p.11).

To illustrate this argument, consider the following example taken from Culyer (1976) and based upon an earlier study aimed at measuring handicap. Table 1 lists two of the ten dimensions of handicap included in that study (getting to or using WC; getting in and out of bed) together with the four levels of disability for each dimension (No difficulty, *etc.*) and the index scores of handicap for each dimension (0,2,4,). The index of disability for each individual is obtained as the sum of the relevant scores from Table 1 for each dimension. The resulting 16 index numbers, which range in value from zero to nine, are plotted in Figure 1.

Leaving aside the issue of whether the numbers in Figure 1 are cardinal or ordinal, Culyer argues that, in constructing the numbers, "value judgements have been utilised to make the 'trade-off' between different combinations of measures" (Culyer 1976, p. 38). Thus the combination (B,b) is equally bad as the combination (D,a) since each receives a score of six.

Without discussing the argument whether there are, or are not, value judgments involved in constructing the index scores, it is argued here that the kinds of decisions which have to be taken in constructing this index are no different in principle to the kinds of decisions involved in constructing an index of output for any commodity which possesses multiple attributes. For example, suppose instead the commodity under consideration were motor vehicles and the two dimensions of interest were fuel economy and comfort. The axes in Figure 1 could be re-labelled accordingly and the resulting index

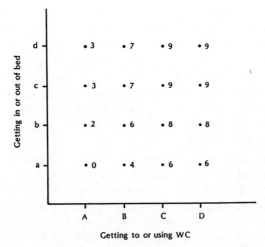

Fig. 1. Disability scores using two dimensions of disability.

numbers plotted. But does this process involve any judgements which differ *in kind* from the judgements exercised in constructing the health status measure? The position taken here is that it does not. Either value judgments are involved in both or they are involved in neither, but it would seem difficult to sustain an argument that they are involved in one and not the other. The problems which must be confronted in dealing with quality varia-tions across similar types of output are of the same genre whether the output is health or motor vehicles.

Commodities with multiple attributes can be analysed in terms of the new theory of consumer behaviour developed by Lancaster (1966a, 1966b, 1971). Arguing that it is not goods themselves but the characteristics of goods which are the objects of utility, he introduces the concept of a consumption technology which embodies the relationship between goods (the inputs) and characteristics (the outputs). In the context of the present paper, what is important about this consumption technology is that the relationship which it embodies is an objective one – "The objective nature of the goods-charac-teristics relationship plays a crucial role in the analysis . . ." (Lancaster 1966a, p. 134). The subjective element in consumer behaviour enters only with respect to choices between sets of characteristics. The relationship between goods and the characteristics which they possess is a purely technical one.[6]

It might be argued, however, that the characteristics of goods can be measured independently of who owns them whereas this is not the case with health. It is certainly not being denied here that consumers/patients are integral to the process of measuring health state characteristics. What is being questioned is whether this *necessarily* introduces subjective value considerations. For individuals in identical initial health states, the reduction in mobility occasioned by a broken leg can presumably be assessed independently of the welfare loss which each of the individuals suffers as a result of it (and hence independently of their willingness-to-pay to avoid it).[7] A knowledge of the resource costs involved in restoring mobility by repairing a broken leg relative to the costs of improving other dimensions of health would provide the basis for establishing the objective trade-offs between various dimensions of health.

The argument here, then, is that the distinction between objective and subjective measures of health status is as sustainable as it is with respect to any other commodity. Hence it is not necessary to rely on utility weights (the construction of which will be discussed below) as the weights to apply to life-years gained in the search for a homogeneous output measure.

An implication of this argument for cost-utility analysis is that the analyst must then decide whether objective or subjective measures of health status are being sought. If a cost-effectiveness analysis is being undertaken, objective measures are required. If, on the other hand, subjective measures are sought then consumers'/patients' valuations of health states enter the analysis. Does this then change the analysis to cost-benefit analysis, or is there still room for something called cost-utility analysis which differs in principle from cost-benefit analysis? This question will be addressed in the following section.

THE WELFARE FOUNDATIONS OF COST-UTILITY ANALYSIS

Given the use of subjective utility weights in assessing quality of life, do the welfare foundations of cost-utility analysis then differ from cost-benefit analysis? This question will be addressed by considering first, the technique for soliciting an individual's utility weights and second, the aggregation procedure and its implications for the underlying social welfare function.

Eliciting individual utility weights

Cost-utility analysts employ a number of different techniques for obtaining utility weights: rating scale, standard gamble, time trade-off, equivalence, and ratio scaling (Torrance 1986). A description of each of these will not be provided here. Rather, our attention will be concentrated on the standard gamble approach which has its basis in expected utility theory and the axioms first developed by von Neumann and Morgenstern (1953). In this respect it is based on the classic method for the measurement of cardinal utility. As such, any search for the welfare foundations of cost-utility analysis seems most likely to bear fruit by concentrating on this approach.[8]

The standard gamble approach is based upon obtaining the certainty

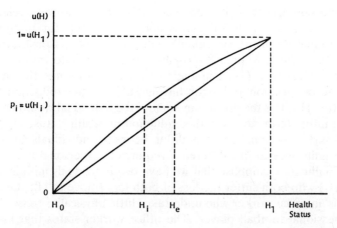

Fig. 2. The standard gamble approach to obtaining utility weights.

equivalent of an uncertain prospect facing an individual. In the present context, the prospect consists of two possible health states (H_1 and H_0) with probabilities of occurrence p and $1 - p$ respectively ($1 > p > 0$). Let H_1 represent 'perfect health' and H_0 represent death. The utility of perfect health $u(H_1)$ is arbitrarily set at unity and the utility of death $u(H_0)$ at zero.[9] Now suppose the health program results in the attainment of a single-attribute, intermediate health state H_i which lies somewhere between perfect health and death.[10] The standard gamble asks the individual to indicate the value of p which yields the expected utility of the prospect equal to the utility of the intermediate health state H_i. This value of p, the certainty equivalent, is then that individual's utility weight.

A diagrammatic exposition of this procedure is provided in Figure 2. Health status (H) is measured on the horizontal axis and utility on the vertical axis. The linear expected utility function connects the points (H_1,1) and (H_0, 0). Given the certain health state H_i, probability p is varied until the expected utility of the prospect is equal to the utility of H_i. This occurs where the expected value of health status is H_e. The resulting probability p_i is then a measure of the utility of the health state H_i.[11]

It should be stressed that although this measure of utility is a cardinal one because the resulting utility function is unique only up to a positive linear transformation (Gravelle and Rees 1981, pp. 555–7 provide a nice proof of this), it does not measure 'satisfaction' or 'pleasure' as usually connoted by the term 'utility'. Rather, the utility number is a numerical representation of a preference ordering. When constructed for a series of possible health outcomes for the individual, these utilities allow a ranking of the relative desirability of those outcomes for that individual.[12]

An important aspect of the above analysis for our purposes relates to the interpretation of the individual's certainty equivalent, for it provides the basis of a measure of the individual's willingness-to-pay to avoid the health state H_i. In fact, the willingness-to-pay in utility terms to avoid this state is precisely the distance (1–p) in Figure 2. This constitutes the individual's compensating variation (CV) for having suffered the reduction in health status $(H_1 - H_i)$. It is the maximum amount the individual would be prepared to pay in utility terms to avoid this reduction in health status.

Needless to say, this CV can differ between individuals but attaching welfare significance to this difference requires interpersonal comparisons of utility. To illustrate, suppose that we have two individuals initially in perfect health (H_1) who both suffer the loss of both legs (move to H_i). One of these persons is an office worker who undertakes little physical exercise. The other is a professional football player. The office worker states that his/her certainty equivalent (p) is 0.5 while the professional football player's is 0.3. Alternatively, the CV (1–p) for the football player is 0.7 while that for the office worker is 0.5, indicating that the football player's willingness-to-pay to avoid the condition (or his/her benefit from avoiding the condition) is greater than that of the office worker. If we assume that the welfare significance of the unit of measurement of the CVs is identical for the two persons (so that a CV of 0.1 for each means that the welfare loss for each is identical) then the football player is worse off than the office worker in health state H_i.

A requirement that cost-utility analysts usually argue should be imposed on the CVs obtained by the above approach is that they be unaffected by individuals' income/wealth positions. Torrance (1986, p. 18) states that "the utility measurement should be unconfounded by the subject's economic wellbeing. Thus, it is important to assure the subject that all treatment and all outcomes will be costless to him and to his family - that is, the subject is to assume full-coverage health insurance and salary continuation insurance". Williams (1981, p. 273) puts the same argument specifically in a welfare economic context:

> The benefit measure sought is one which embodies the ethical principle that any interpersonal comparison of the value of health shall not depend upon the wealth or economic value of the people concerned. This reflects not only the ostensible ethic of the medical profession itself, but also the putative political principle on which health services are organized in many countries, and is one of the major reasons why the provision of health services has not been left to the market, but treated more as a "citizen's entitlement" than as part of society's "reward system" (Donabedian 1971). In that context, measures of the value of health which reflect people's ability to pay will be irrelevant. The interest lies in seeing how far we can get in establishing an "uncontaminated" set of values which give as much rein as possible to differences in the *relative* values they attach to different

attributes of health, while pursuing some kind of egalitarian principle between the weight given to one person's valuations compared with another's.

For this requirement to be fulfilled, the CVs obtained from the standard gamble must be 'uncontaminated' by individual's income/wealth positions. In considering whether this is the case, the first point to be made is that abstracting from the effects of health costs and income loss ensures only that the pre-illness income/wealth distribution is maintained. Therefore, whatever inequalities existed in the pre-illness income/wealth distribution will be present in the post-illness income/wealth distribution. It must then be considered whether the CVs elicited by the standard gamble reflect that income/wealth distribution.

The influence of the income/wealth distribution on CVs arises directly in conventional cost-benefit analysis because a money metric is adopted as the unit of measurement of willingness-to-pay. The greater a person's income /wealth, the larger can be the willingness-to-pay expressed in terms of money. Cost-utility analysis seeks to break this nexus by employing a different metric altogether for measuring CVs, *viz.* a 0–1 measurement scale. Individuals are restricted to possessing a maximal initial endowment of unity on this scale (the utility weight corresponding to 'perfect health') and are then asked to express their willingness-to-pay in terms of the proportion of this initial endowment which they would be prepared to forgo to avoid a particular health state. Since this alternative metric is not expressed in monetary terms, or in terms of any commodities which individuals may possess, their initial endowments of income/wealth or specific commodities should not then influence their CVs expressed in terms of this metric.[13] But do they?

The employment of the 0–1 metric certainly breaks any *direct* connection between income/wealth and the CVs in that more units of the former do not directly enable individuals to indicate higher CVs (as in conventional cost-benefit analysis). But this leaves open the question as to whether there may be an *indirect* effect. If higher CVs measured on the 0–1 scale are correlated with greater income/wealth this may be pure chance but it may also be evidence of a systematic relationship between income/wealth and the ability of people to 'enjoy life'. A systematic relationship would arise if wealthier individuals had 'more to lose' by being moved from perfect health to any given inferior health state. If greater income/wealth endows people with a greater capacity for enjoyment of life than those with lesser wealth, then wealthier individuals could be expected to consistently indicate higher CVs in comparing any given health states, even when expressed in terms of the alternative 0–1 metric.[14] Returning to our previous example, the football player's higher CV reflects a greater psychic loss as a result of losing both legs, and this psychic loss may in turn be a reflection of the effects of greater income/wealth on that individual's innate capacity for enjoyment.

A systematic relationship between income/wealth and the CVs may also arise if income/wealth is correlated with risk-aversion. For example, if individuals demonstrate decreasing risk-aversion with respect to health as income /wealth increases, this will result in wealthier individuals having lower certainty equivalents (*i.e.* lower p values) and hence higher CVs for any given health state. Whether these indirect effects of income/wealth on CVs actually exist is an empirical question worthy of further research.

Leaving aside these possible indirect effects, it is the case that the 0–1 metric purges the CVs of the effects of income/wealth. But while the use of this metric would allow comparisons of the costs and benefits of projects *within* the health sector (assuming it is employed in the evaluation of all such projects), it precludes comparisons of the results of these evaluations with projects evaluated *outside* the health sector where the conventional money metric is employed. As a result, it is not possible to determine whether devoting additional resources to health enhances or reduces efficiency in resource allocation compared with, for example, devoting additional resources to education. This is potentially most serious for non-health sector projects which result in life-years gained (*e.g.* road safety programs). The situation may then arise where the same type of output is valued using different metrics in the health and non-health sectors. For example, Jones-Lee (1989, p. 293) reports that the UK Department of Transport has recently proposed adoption of a willingness-to-pay approach to valuing the avoidance of road accident fatalities with the value of a statistical life for transport risks being taken as £500,000. Clearly, such an approach employs the money metric and hence the results are non-comparable with those obtained from cost-utility analysis which employs the 0–1 metric.

The aggregation of preferences

Applied work in economic evaluation requires that the problems of interpersonal comparability of utility, an aggregation rule and an objective function be addressed. In applied cost-benefit analysis, it is conventionally assumed that the marginal utility of income is equal for all persons affected by the project so that an extra dollar of benefit has the same social significance to whomsoever it accrues. Alternatively assumptions can be made about the marginal utility of income for different individuals and built into the analysis by weighting benefits to reflect the marginal utility of income (Eckstein 1961; Sugden and Williams 1978).[15] The aggregation rule is the summation of the CVs (weighted or unweighted, positive and negative) across individuals. The objective function is the maximisation of this sum.

Cost-utility analysts conventionally assume that the difference in utility between the best health outcome (defined as a normal healthy life from birth to age 70) and the worst health outcome (defined as death in hospital shortly after birth) is equal for each individual (Torrance *et al.* 1982, p. 1054). Utilities are weighted equally – "a year of healthy life is to be regarded as of equal intrinsic value to everyone, irrespective of age, sex, *etc.*" (Williams

1981, p. 276). The aggregation rule is the arithmetic mean, which gives the utility weight to be applied to life-years gained from the program. The objective function is the maximisation of the weighted sum of life-years gained for any given budget constraint.

Leaving aside for the moment the aggregation rule, the assumptions made concerning interpersonal comparability of utility are identical in both cost-benefit analysis and cost-utility analysis. Under cost-utility analysis, an assumption must be made concerning the interpersonal comparability of the certainty equivalents or CVs in exactly the same way as for cost-benefit analysis. However, the metrics adopted for measuring these CVs differ between the two techniques. The objective function in cost-utility analysis is also the same as for cost-effectiveness analysis but differs from that for cost-benefit analysis in that the utility weights are applied to the physical output measure and summed whereas under cost-benefit analysis the objective is the maximisation of the sum of the CVs themselves.

The aggregation rule differs between cost-benefit and cost-utility analysis, but it is debatable if this is of any consequence in the present context. Indeed, Harsanyi (1955) has presented an argument for defining social utility as the arithmetic mean rather than the sum of individual utilities. If the objective function in cost-utility analysis were the maximisation of the arithmetic mean of utilities, then for a given population this would be formally equivalent to maximising the sum of utilities (Harsanyi 1987). But cost-utility stops short of this, using the mean of individuals' certainty equivalents to weight physical output rather than as the basis of a measure of social utility. Were it to do so, it would be formally equivalent to cost-benefit analysis with the exception of the metric employed for measuring the CVs.

As it stands, however, applications of cost-utility analysis are more akin to cost-effectiveness analysis, in which case the use of subjective rather than objective weights for obtaining QALYs seems to be misplaced. Since cost-effectiveness analysis does not purport to value output, it is methodologically questionable to use a set of weights which do incorporate individuals' subjective valuations of various health states in weighting physical output. This paper has attempted to show that the weights which are employed are directly related to individuals' CVs which form the basis of benefit estimation in cost-benefit analysis although a different metric is employed. If the weights were used to calculate the compensating variations, and if the objective function were to maximise the mean of these variations, cost-utility analysis would be formally equivalent to cost-benefit analysis.

Finally, there is an avenue not explored in this paper which may provide a theoretical foundation for the use of subjective quality adjustment weights. As discussed earlier, in Lancaster's characteristics theory of consumer demand, the consumption technology is an objective relationship between goods and characteristics. But is it possible to interpret the utility weights as estimates of the elements in that consumption technology matrix? Can they be interpreted as hedonic prices, the ratios of which, under certain conditions, might be equal to the characteristics transformation ratio? If so, then the utility weights might be taken as estimates of the relative shadow marginal costs of producing the health characteristics. This could be a fruitful avenue for further theoretical research.[16]

CONCLUSION

Cost-utility analysis has arisen out of attempts to attach weights to life-years gained to reflect the quality dimension of the output of health care programs as well as the quantity dimension. The estimation of such weights based upon individuals' utilities of different health states has lead to the development of the QALY as a quality-adjusted unit of output.

It is undoubtedly important to recognise that taking unweighted life-years gained as the output of health care programs ignores the crucial quality-of-life dimension. However, this paper has argued that the attempt to derive a set of utility weights for this purpose has resulted in a technique which seems to have a questionable methodological status. If the purpose of the exercise is to refine cost-effectiveness analysis then objective measurement of health status is what is required. If the purpose is to obtain estimates of the *value* of different health states, one moves into the domain of cost-benefit analysis. Apart from employing a different metric, cost-utility analysis has the potential to do the latter but for its use of the mean certainty equivalents as subjective weights to apply to physical output measures rather than as a basis for expressing compensating variations. It is for this reason that its results appear to be a modified form of cost-effectiveness analysis when it is actually employing most of the theoretical framework of cost-benefit analysis.

As Arrow (1983) has said with respect to a "new kind of benefit-cost analysis", *viz*. risk-benefit analysis: "At a fundamental level, the issues in benefit-risk analysis are not different from those in more familiar welfare comparisons" (p. 20). The same may be said of cost-utility analysis.

NOTES

1. This is not to deny that there are formidable difficulties in empirically estimating a health production function and the associated productivity of health care.
2. This procedure was also adopted by Doessel (1978) in his Australian study of end-stage renal disease.
3. A recent survey of these can be found in McDowell and Newell (1987).
4. For an example of this kind of 'league table' see Maynard (1987, p. 190).
5. This argument implicitly assumes that health and utility (in the sense of well-being) are distinct concepts. But if health is defined broadly to include both physical *and* mental health, the distinction becomes blurred.
6. Lancaster (1966b, pp. 21–2; 1971, Ch.10) specifically uses motor vehicles as an applied example of the new theory. For an application of Lancaster's theory to the quality of health care, *see* Doessel and Marshall (1985).

7. There is a difference between asking consumers/patients to *describe* health states and to *value* health states. The statements 'A broken leg reduces my mobility by 50 per cent' and 'On a utility scale with a value of zero for a state of death and unity for perfect health, I would value a health state with a broken leg at 0.9' are quite different in kind. But this is anticipating later discussion.

8. A critical evaluation of these other approaches and the standard gamble approach can be found in Carr-Hill (1989). See also Loomes and McKenzie (1989) (1990).

9. Note that this precludes any utility being gained from bequests. It does not, however, rule out the possibility that some living states will be considered worse than death and hence yield negative utility.

10. Multi-attribute health states can also be handled in this framework. *See* Torrance *et al.* (1982).

11. Being based upon expected utility theory, the standard gamble approach is subject to all the criticisms which can be levelled at that theory (Pope 1988; Schoemaker 1982). Our purpose here, however, is not to criticise this approach on these grounds. For the purpose of our argument, expected utility theory is accepted as a legitimate basis for eliciting utility weights.

12. It is interesting to note that the illustration of the standard gamble approach in Figure 2 highlights the underlying assumption that health status can be measured objectively on the horizontal axis and is independent of the individual's subjective valuation of that health status.

13. The alternative metric must be completely unrelated to any endowments of individuals which are capable of being enhanced by the possession of greater income/wealth else the problem which the technique is attempting to overcome simply reappears in another form. For example, if the metric adopted were apples, the CVs would continue to be 'contaminated' by the initial endowments of income/wealth since income/wealth can be converted into apples.

14. Under these circumstances the 0–1 and money metrics may give measures of CVs which are proportional transformations of each other.

15. For arguments against the weighting of benefits *see* Mishan (1982) and Ng (1984).

16. For theoretical analyses of hedonic functions without specific reference to health, *see* Muellbauer (1974) and Triplett (1987).

REFERENCES

Arrow, K.J., "Behavior under uncertainty and its implications for policy", in: B.P. Stigum and F. Wenstop (eds.), *Foundations of Utility and Risk Theory with Applications*, D. Reidel Publishing Company, Dordrecht, pp. 19–32, 1983.

Ashmore, M., M. Mulkay, and T. Pinch, *Health and Efficiency: A Sociology of Health Economics*, Open University Press, Milton Keynes, 1989.

Carr-Hill, R.A., "Assumptions of the QALY procedure", *Social Science and Medicine*, Vol. 29 No. 3, pp. 469–477, 1989.

Culyer, A.J., *Need and the National Health Service*, Martin Robertson, London, 1976.

Culyer, A.J., "Need, values and health status measurement" in: A.J. Culyer and K.G. Wright (eds.) *Economic Aspects of Health Services*, Martin Robertson, London, pp. 9–31, 1978.

Doessel, D.P., "Economic analysis and end-stage renal disease", *Economic Analysis and Policy*, Vol. 8 No. 2, 1978; reprinted in: J.R.G. Butler and D.P. Doessel (eds.) *Health Economics: Australian Readings*, Australian Professional Publications, Sydney, pp. 278–290, 1989.

Doessel, D.P., and J.V. Marshall, "A rehabilitation of health outcome in quality assessment", *Social Science and Medicine*, Vol.21 No. 12, pp. 1319–1328, 1985.

Donabedian, A., "Social responsibility for personal health services: an examination of basic values", *Inquiry*, Vol. 8 No. 2, pp. 3–19, 1971.

Drummond, M.F., G.L. Stoddart, and G.W. Torrance, *Methods for the Economic Evaluation of Health Care Programmes*, Oxford University Press, Oxford, 1987.

Eckstein, O., "A survey of the theory of public expenditure criteria" in: National Bureau of Economic Research, *Public Finances: Needs, Sources and Utilization*, Princeton University Press, Princeton, pp. 439–494, 1961.

Gravelle, H., and R. Rees, *Microeconomics*, Longman, London, 1981.

Grossman, M., *The Demand for Health: A Theoretical and Empirical Investigation*, Occasional Paper No. 119, National Bureau of Economic Research, New York, 1972.

Harsanyi, J., "Cardinal welfare, individualistic ethics, and interpersonal comparisons of utility", *Journal of Political Economy*, Vol. 63 No. 4, pp. 309–321, 1955.

Harsanyi, J., "Interpersonal utility comparisons" in: J. Eatwell, M. Milgate and P. Newman (eds.) *The New Palgrave: A Dictionary of Economics*, Macmillan, London, Vol.2, pp. 955–958, 1987.

Illich, I., *Medical Nemesis: The Expropriation of Health*, Pantheon Books, New York, 1976.

Jones-Lee, M.W., *The Economics of Safety and Physical Risk*, Blackwell, Oxford, 1989.

Klarman, H.E., J.O'S. Francis, and G.D. Rosenthal, "Cost effectiveness analysis applied to treatment of chronic renal disease", *Medical Care*, Vol. 6, 1968; reprinted in: M.H. Cooper and A.J. Culyer (eds.), *Health Economics*, Penguin, Harmondsworth, pp. 230–240, 1973.

Lancaster, K.J., "A new approach to consumer theory", *Journal of Political Economy*, Vol. 74 No. 2, pp. 132–157, 1966a.

Lancaster, K.J., "Change and innovation in the technology of consumption", *American Economic Review*, Vol. 56 No. 2, pp. 14–23, 1966b.

Lancaster, K.J., *Consumer Demand: A New Approach*, Columbia University Press, New York, 1971.

Loomes, G., and L. McKenzie, "The use of QALYs in health care decision making", *Social Science and Medicine*, Vol. 28 No. 4, pp. 299–308, 1989.

Loomes, G., and L. McKenzie, "The scope and limitations of QALY measures", in: S. Baldwin, C. Godfrey and C. Propper (eds.) *Quality of Life: Perspectives and Policies*, Routledge, London, pp. 84–102, 1990.

Maynard, A., "Markets and health care", in: A. Williams (ed.) *Health and Economics*, Macmillan, London, pp. 187–200, 1987.

McDowell, I., and C. Newell, *Measuring Health: A Guide to Rating Scales and Questionnaires*, Oxford University Press, New York, 1987.

Mishan, E.J., "The new controversy about the rationale of economic evaluation", *Journal of Economic Issues*, Vol. 16 No. 1, pp. 29–47, 1982.

Mooney, G.H., *Economics, Medicine and Health Care*, Wheatsheaf Books Ltd., Sussex, 1986.

Muellbauer, J., "Household production theory, quality, and the 'hedonic technique'", *American Economic Review*, Vol. 64 No. 6, pp. 977–994, 1974.

Ng, Y-K., "Quasi-Pareto social improvements", *American Economic Review*, Vol. 74 No. 5, pp. 1033–1049, 1984.

Pope, R.E., "Additional perspectives on modelling health insurance decisions: a discussion arising from the Burrows-Brown paper", in: C. Selby Smith (ed.) *Economics and Health: 1988 Proceedings of the Tenth Australian Conference of Health Economists*, Public Sector Management Institute, Monash University, Melbourne, pp. 189–205, 1988.

Schoemaker, P.J.H., "The expected utility model: its variants, purposes, evidence and limitations", *Journal of Economic Literature*, Vol. 20 No. 2, pp. 529–563, 1982.

Siegrist, J., and A. Junge, "Conceptual and methodological problems in research on the quality of life in clinical medicine", *Social Science and Medicine*, Vol. 29 No. 3, pp. 463–468, 1989.

Sugden, R., and A. Williams, *The Principles of Practical Cost-Benefit Analysis*, Oxford University Press, Oxford, 1978.

Torrance, G.W., M.H. Boyle, and S.P. Horwood, "Application of multi-attribute utility theory to measure social preferences for health states", *Operations Research*, Vol. 30 No. 6, pp. 1043–1069, 1982.

Torrance, G.W., "Measurement of health state utilities for economic appraisal", *Journal of Health Economics*, Vol. 5, pp. 1–30, 1986.

Triplett, J.E., "Hedonic functions and hedonic indexes", in: J. Eatwell, M. Milgate and P. Newman (eds.) *The New Palgrave*: *A Dictionary of Economics*, Macmillan, London, Vol.2, pp. 630–634, 1987.

Von Neumann, J., and O. Morgenstern, *Theory of Games and Economic Behavior*, 3rd edn, Princeton University Press, Princeton, 1953.

Williams, A., "Welfare economics and health status measurement", in: J. van der Gaag and M. Perlman (eds.) *Health*, *Economics*, *and Health Economics*, North-Holland, Amsterdam, pp. 271–281, 1981.

PART THREE

Administrative and market allocation in health care

Excess demand and patient selection for heart and liver transplantation*

BERNARD FRIEDMAN, RONALD J. OZMINKOWSKI and
ZACHARY TAYLOR

*Division of Provider Studies, Agency for Health Care Policy and Research, 5600
Fishers Lane, Rockville, MD 20857, U.S.A.*

A. INTRODUCTION

The number of transplantations of major organs and tissues (OTs) grew dramatically in the mid-1980s in the U.S. and Europe, despite their very high cost, as technological improvements led to increased survival rates.[1] Follow-up studies using patient registries have clarified the survival rates of grafts and patients in relation to underlying diseases, complications, tissue matching and drug therapy, leading to publication of recommended "indications" and "contraindications" for specific OT procedures (*e.g.*, for the complicated case of liver transplantation, *see* Foster and Burton, 1989; Agency for Health Care Policy and Research, 1990). However, the actual allocation of organs might differ from outcome-based medical guidelines for a number of reasons such as variation in third-party coverage and patient ability-to-pay, competition among health care organizations, or experimental investigations.

Public programs such as Medicare and Medicaid in the U.S., as well as private insurers have expanded their coverage and payment for kidney, heart, and liver transplantation. The expansion of coverage has been accompanied by regulations addressing patient outcome standards, cost, and fairness of allocation of transplantable organs. Concerns about the effects of insurance coverage on the growth of demand and expenses for OT, at least for solid organs, have been relatively mild, due mainly to the limited availability of cadaver organs (*e.g.*, DeLissovoy, 1988).

*The authors wish to thank Drs. Rosanna Coffey, Donald Goldstone, and Judy Ball for much helpful advice, Hermann Liau for computer programming, and Craig Spirka of Systemetrics for expert and timely assistance with the database for this project.

The views expressed in this paper are those of the authors and no official endorsement by AHCPR or the U.S. Department of Health and Human Services is intended or should be inferred.

P. Zweifel and H. E. Frech III (eds.), Health Economics Worldwide. 161–186.
© 1992 *Kluwer Academic Publishers. Printed in the Netherlands.*

Motivating Questions and Plan of the Paper

The goals of the paper are both analytical and descriptive. In view of excess demand for both heart transplants (HT) and liver transplants (LT), we presume that supplier behavior, shaped in part by regulations, is the crucial determinant of the pattern of rationing. Therefore we plan to develop and test several null hypotheses about selection of patients. In addition, we will offer descriptive trends for both recipients and non-recipients of transplants to help a wider audience develop and weigh their own theoretical perspectives. Therefore, we begin by posing some empirical questions that could be interesting to a broad audience.

1. How do the characteristics of transplant recipients compare with published guidelines regarding indications and contraindications? As the number of procedures expanded greatly, what changes in the profile of recipients (diagnoses, age, insurance coverage) occurred over time?
2. How large is the "potential candidate pool" for heart and liver transplants as determined from hospital discharge abstracts?
3. What are the contrasting characteristics of patients receiving transplants vs. other treatments of similar underlying health problems (diagnostic and severity factors, payment source, income)?
4. While the number of transplantations was increasing and waiting lists were growing, were there significant changes in the treatments and charges for potential candidates who did *not* receive transplants?

This paper will offer some tentative answers to these questions. Eventually, intensive research following patients over time who have received transplants or alternative treatments would permit a definitive evaluation of the benefits and costs of transplantation. Important results from that type of research have been demonstrated in the case of kidney transplantation.[2]

We proceed first to develop testable hypotheses about patient selection and supplier behavior. We then provide a brief synopsis of recent growth of OT in the U.S. and Europe, improvements in outcomes, expansion of insurance coverage, and evidence of lengthening waiting lists. The background section also notes the regulations and guidelines for medical practice that have accompanied public financing. Previous studies are reviewed, based on their relevance to questions of potential demand for OT, actual allocation among candidates, and economic implications.

The empirical part of the paper follows the order of the motivating questions listed above and tests the null hypotheses using a large national database of patient and hospital characteristics maintained at the Agency for Health Care Policy and Research. In some respects, the results of the analysis to date are reassuring about the consequences of excess demand for OT, although some lingering concerns about "queue-jumping" and the fairness of rationing remain. There are important measurement and evaluation issues that cannot be solved with present data resources. The concluding section offers some evidence and thoughts about cross-national differences in treatment patterns, payment policies and the effects of budget constraints.

B. THEORETICAL CONSIDERATIONS AND HYPOTHESES[3]

Transplant centers could be assumed to follow one of two broadly contrasting models: either a "social health benefit" model of maximizing total expected health benefits subject to a breakeven constraint, or a "private business" model of maximizing their net income subject to consumer demands and regulations. Regulations and professional literature concentrate on patient survival rates (for a 1–year, 3–year or 5–year period) as a health outcome of greatest concern. The basic model of "social health benefit" maximization can best be operationalized for now as the selection of patients with the best predicted survival rates. It is still desirable to keep a sharp watch for financial incentives and market forces that may intervene.[4]

Suppose that a particular transplant team has Q available organs over some time interval, but a larger number of candidates are seeking treatment. Let all candidates be ranked in descending order according to expected health benefit, B_i. Then total health benefit is maximized by moving down the B_i scale until all of Q are allocated at some cutoff level B_q. Whether this solution can be supported by a pricing system that raises sufficient revenue to cover the total costs of a transplantation center depends on several additional considerations.

Suppose the maximum that each candidate is willing to pay is W_i, where i corresponds to the ordering of B_i. Availability of insurance reimbursement is included in W. The level of W is presumably correlated with the level of B, but with a random component depending on financial resources that is independent of the level of B. Let the cost of providing Q procedures be $C[Q]$. If the hospital charges the same price to every recipient, $P = C[Q]/Q$, the benefit-maximizing solution may not be feasible, because W_i might frequently be less than P for the top candidates. In that event, price discrimination – charging a higher price P* but discounting to W_i for those unable to pay more – may still maximize total benefit while generating sufficient total revenue for the program. Moreover, an institution may wish to cross-subsidize the cost of transplants from revenues derived from other services or grants. A transplant program might be deemed worthy of some cross-subsidy for social purposes of advance in knowledge or training. But neither the subsidies nor the price discrimination may be a stable situation.

Since there is a randomly distributed element in W that is independent of B, some of the candidates below the B_q level will be willing to pay more than subsidized patients above that level. These unsatisfied demands will tend to seek some means of outbidding or "queue-jumping" for the limited organs. Institutions may consider acceding to these demands in order to either lower P^*, reduce operating losses, or use the extra revenue to subsidize other worthwhile activities. Patients with substantial resources choosing among competing centers would encourage new centers to open who are willing to cater to those demands. In addition, third-party payers may resist paying a price greater than average cost for their covered patients in order to subsidize poorer patients, or paying different prices to different centers. These competitive forces, unless outweighed by regulatory pressures, may prevent centers from using price discrimination to cover their costs.

How does the situation change with expanded insurance coverage or improved outcomes for all patients due to technological improvements? Expanded insurance coverage would reduce the need for price discrimination to cover costs, and hence would reduce the incentive for institutions to allow queue-jumping. Improving outcomes could work in the opposite direction. Improved outcomes may not only increase the number of candidates but make all candidates more equal in expected benefit. The sacrifice of total health benefit from queue-jumping would decrease relative to the rewards to the institution for shifting some of the limited number of organs available. The impact of competitive forces should therefore be greater in this case.

The full effects of excess demand and frustrated candidates extend beyond the question of who receives the limited supply of organs. The treatments and costs for non-recipients may be affected by the existence of the OT technology with hopeful outcomes. One would expect extra resources to be used at transplant centers in weighing the possible benefits of a transplant for each candidate. If outcomes of transplantation improve relative to alternative treatment, and if insurance coverage improves, one expects a greater number of potential candidates to be referred to transplant centers. With this rise in effective demand for care, centers would be able to ask higher prices for their services of screening, evaluation, and prolonging life in the hope of receiving a transplant.

This possibility is more than a cynical view of how fearful patients might be exploited. Physicians in the role of agents may go beyond simply supplying information and make decisions that they believe maximize the subjective well-being of patients. (The agency literature was recently summarized by Mooney, 1990, in a paper for this conference.) The subjective utility of the terminally ill patient and his/her family might be substantially higher by keeping alive the hope of a transplant until the last moment, involving the supply of continuing services, rather than simply conveying the information early on that a transplant was extremely unlikely. It is not clear, however, whether keeping alive the possibility of a transplant would lead to much more expenses for health care than would ordinarily be incurred for any terminally ill patient.

Hypotheses

(H1) The advance and dissemination of knowledge about outcomes of transplants should have led by 1987 to an allocation of organs that strongly favors those with the highest expected health benefits, regardless of ability to pay. The improvement in potential outcomes for all candidates and the expansion in third-party insurance coverage have theoretically offsetting effects regarding the relationship between ability-to-pay and the receipt of a transplant. Therefore, no *a priori* hypothesis is offered about whether the importance of ability to pay has changed over time.

(H2) The null hypothesis of health benefit maximization implies that ability-to-pay would affect the probability of receiving a transplant only within a group of candidates of roughly equal health status and expected benefit. An indication of queue-jumping would be if many candidates of relatively high expected benefit are not being served, but among those with relatively lower expected benefit, there is a correlation between ability to pay and receipt of a transplant.

(H3) Improvement in outcomes for transplants should raise demand for screening, evaluation and life-prolonging services by all potential candidates. This could lead to higher costs and prices for non-recipients over time – more so at hospitals with transplant programs than at other hospitals.

C. BACKGROUND

The numbers of transplants and persons on waiting lists in the U.S., as well as improvements in survival, are abstracted from a variety of public and private agencies and disseminated in annual reports from the U.S. Health Resources and Services Administration (the 1988 report is used below, unless another source is cited). In the cases of heart and liver transplants, survival rates of cadaver organs and patients receiving them improved enough, particularly since 1982, to win wide acceptance by the medical profession, private insurers and public reimbursement programs.

Before 1970, fewer than half of heart transplant patients survived one year. In the early 1980s, one-year survival rates of 60–65% were reported, and by 1986 the rate was approximately 80%. For liver transplants, the most technically difficult of solid organ transplants, with the broadest range of diseases treated, one-year survival rates were about 33% at the pioneering center in the 1960s and early 1970s. One-year survival rates have improved dramatically, but because of the disparate patient types, published results vary from 54–85% (AHCPR, 1990).

The recent surge in utilization is seen in the following table. Information about kidney transplantation is provided for comparison because it was already well established and funded before this period.

Growth of utilization also occurred in Europe. Between these two years, growth in the number of kidney transplantations reported to the European Dialysis and Transplant Association Registry was similar to the U.S. –

Table 1. Transplants performed in the U.S.

	1983	1987	Increase
Kidney	6,112	8,967	47%
Heart	172	1,438	736%
Liver	164	1,199	631%

about 50%, from 6,869 to 10,301 (Kramer, *et al.*, 1984; Brunner *et al.*, 1988). It appears that the number of heart transplants grew more rapidly in the U.S. than in Europe (totals for the international registry are reported in Heck, Shumway and Kaye, 1989).

The registry system established in the U.S. for sharing of information and donor organs provides national data on the number of registered persons awaiting transplants. At the end of 1987, nearly 12,000 persons were awaiting kidney transplants, 450 were awaiting hearts, and over 400 were awaiting livers. Since that time, it is reported that waiting lists for hearts and livers have grown faster than the number of actual operations (*e.g.*, a waiting list of 1,280 heart patients in 1989). Such clear evidence of long waiting lists is rare in the U.S. health care system.

Insurance Coverage

Private insurance coverage expanded more rapidly than public reimbursement for heart, liver and other transplant procedures. Already by 1985, a survey of 65 major group insurers by the Health Insurance Association of America reported that 55 plans covered heart transplants (Task Force on Organ Transplantation, 1986). At that time also, "well over half" of total Blue Cross and Blue Shield plan enrollees were covered for heart and liver transplants, using a new national risk-pooling arrangement (Mayers, 1987).

Coverage of transplants in state Medicaid programs for the indigent expanded in parallel with private insurance. By 1986, liver transplants were covered in 33 states and heart transplants in 24 states. Federal Medicare coverage of heart transplantation for the disabled and elderly was formally adopted in 1987, liver transplantation for certain diagnoses in children in 1983, and liver transplantation for adults in 1990. Because of the limitations on eligibility for Medicare based on age and length of time with a disability, the Medicare coverage is more significant for its regulatory criteria than for the incremental increase in the number of transplants reimbursed. For example, after Medicare included liver transplantation for children as "reasonable and necessary", no child needing the procedure has been eligible for reimbursement.

Private insurers rely primarily on medical peer review to determine when a procedure is an "accepted treatment", and whether a particular claim fits with explicit or judgmental criteria of safety, efficacy, and accepted practice. State Medicaid programs have tended to cover transplants on a pre-approval basis without formal explicit criteria. The Medicare coverage decisions have involved increasingly rigorous studies of safety and effectiveness and have been issued with regulations about patient selection, outcome standards, and other eligibility criteria for participating centers.

Medicare regulations for coverage of heart transplants (Federal Register, 4/6/87, p. 10935–10951) may be called a "centers of excellence" approach. The criteria for patient selection based on medical conditions describe some specific contraindications associated with poorer outcomes. Facilities are indirectly accountable for adhering to such guidelines by a requirement that high patient survival rates be demonstrated in order to retain approval for payments. A high level of staff capabilities and experience in cardiology and cardiac surgery is required, together with an expectation of at least 12 transplants per year. There is a requirement to participate in the national Organ Procurement and Transplantation Network, an activity funded in part by the federal government. Participation in the network involves the announcement of characteristics of patients on waiting lists, rapid notice of available donor organs, and some rules of "sharing" available organs. Together, these regulatory criteria encourage rationing on the basis of potential health benefit.[5]

The Medicare regulations for coverage of liver transplants in adults (Federal Register, 3/8/90, p. 8547–8553) make the coverage dependent on the reason for liver failure. In addition, the extent to which other physiological problems would interfere with survival or recovery are specifically addressed in the regulations. As in the case of heart transplants, the risks of the procedure itself are taken into account. The surgical teams must have a history of performing at least 12 transplants over a two-year period to qualify for Medicare reimbursement. It was estimated that only about 10–20 of 73 liver transplant programs would qualify for Medicare participation within the next several years.

Previous Empirical Studies of Organ Allocation

The U.S. General Accounting Office (1989) conducted a study of patient selection for heart transplants in 18 hospitals with Medicare-approved transplant programs (only 23 of 131 hospitals performing heart transplants had Medicare approval). These hospitals performed 674 transplants in 1987, with several hundred additional candidates accepted for waiting lists. The study found "relatively standardized" medical criteria for selecting transplant candidates. Of 507 patients screened but not accepted, only 7% were rejected on the basis of financial criteria. Fourteen of the 18 hospitals were willing to accept non-paying patients; however, in the sample of records studied, only 21 non-paying patients were accepted. Thirty-six patients who could not pay for care were rejected for surgery. However, it was not clear whether ability-to-pay was the criterion used to reject these applicants. It is important to note that even prior to the evaluations for surgery at a medical center, financial considerations could affect the potential pool of candidates. Referring physicians and patients at the time of the initial contact with institutions may be screened on the basis of ability-to-pay and told of down-payment requirements.

Studies of outcomes of liver transplantation in relation to underlying diseases have become important as a basis for patient selection. Starzl *et al.* (1989) begins his review of the wide-ranging experience at University of Pittsburgh with the following observation: "The conceptual appeal of liver transplantation is so great that the procedure may come to mind as a last resort for virtually every patient with lethal hepatic disease." The AHCPR (1990) assessment found that as of 1987, "no program yet has based candidate selection on diagnosis as a primary significant predictive variable." There was evidence, for example, that survival results for recipients with the diagnoses of cancer were quite low (5-year survival less than 30% compared to 70% for diagnostic groupings such as primary biliary cirrhosis). Yet until such survival results were known, the percentage of liver recipients who had been diagnosed with cancer was reported as high as 33% by the European Liver Transplant Registry.

In the unusual case of kidney transplantation, with uniform and nearly complete reimbursement coverage of all patients, the allocation of scarce organs should have minimal dependence on ability-to-pay. Held, *et al.* (1988) used a proportional hazards model to estimate the likelihood of patients registered in the End Stage Renal Disease Program receiving a cadaveric transplant (through 1985). Median income in the county of the "coordinating dialysis unit" for the patient was a significant factor (0.02 level) after controlling for age, sex, race, primary diagnosis and form of dialysis therapy. A 20% difference in median income was associated with a 10% increase in the likelihood of receiving a transplant. The association however was not large in comparison to the effects of the other variables. Non-whites had a significantly lower (about 60% lower) relative likelihood of receiving transplants. This may have been due in part to lesser availability of voluntary live donors in the non-white populations. The authors suggest that out-of-pocket costs such as transportation and drugs may continue to limit access to transplants even when insurance pays most of the costs of the procedures, and that the referral process may have subtle discriminatory tendencies that are impervious to regulation.

Previous Studies to Estimate the Candidate Pool and Costs

Several authors and reports have grappled with the problems of estimating how many persons with "end-stage" organ failure would be suitable candidates for transplant at a steady state rate. The 1986 Final Report of the Task Force on Organ Transplantation estimated an annual "need" for 3,864 heart transplants and 2,448 liver transplants (excluding alcoholic cirrhosis or hepatic cancer). The origin of the assumptions in the Task Force report of 60 hearts per million population and 40 livers per million is not given. Because of constraints on donor availability, the "high" estimates of transplants likely to be performed were 355 for hearts and 648 for livers. Actual transplants exceeded these estimates by 300% and 50% respectively in 1986.

An influential work on potential use and cost of heart transplants (HT) in the early 1980s was a large study by Evans, *et al.* (1984). After considering a wide range of estimated needs for cardiac replacement in various reports, they concluded that 1932 hearts would be needed to meet demand based on physiological criteria. They reached this conclusion by first assuming 14,100 persons aged 10–54 died in 1980 with a condition that warranted a heart transplant. Then they used the Stanford University experience to estimate that 13.7% of the candidates would have been accepted for surgery.

Death certificates often do not provide sufficient information either to determine underlying diseases that may have been appropriately treated by a transplant, or to determine contraindications to transplant. And clearly, death certificates cannot clarify what alternative treatments were employed, especially for people who survived. When hospital discharge data were considered by Evans *et al.*, the estimate of potential demand for transplants was over 250,000. Clearly, many patients with cardiovascular disease were included who might benefit from coronary artery bypass surgery and other treatments now accepted as the treatments of first choice.

Medicare covered 50 heart transplants in its first year, 1987, compared to its forecast of 65. However, among the recipients, half were above the age of 55, which was assumed to be an upper age limit in Medicare forecasting models. Therefore, deLissovoy (1988) reestimated that Medicare would cover about 300 HTs in 1991, rather than the 143 officially forecasted. He suggests that continued broadening of patient selection criteria by practicing physicians will continue to increase Medicare expenses beyond forecasts, but that transplantation will still not take more than a small share of expenses.

The technology assessment by AHCPR (1990) led to an estimate that about 4,600 persons who die each year from end-stage liver disease may be acceptable candidates for LT (a range of 4,000 to 10,000 is used for cost forecasting). Van Thiel *et al.* (1988) provide a unique comparative estimate of the cost of care for "end-stage" liver disease patients who did and did not receive LTs at the University of Pittsburgh during 1981 to 1984. The mean one-year cost of hospitalization was estimated at $45,643 for non-recipients, compared to $92,866 for recipients. Follow-up care, including immunosuppressive drugs and professional fees, added another $32,000 to the cost for LT.

Summary of Some Weak Points in Previous Research

A large part of the literature of OT and the issues raised for regulation and social policy are not germane to the present study, *e.g.*, legal aspects of the recruitment and sharing of donor organs. We found one major study for HT in the U.S. comparing the allocation of organs in relation to published medical guidelines and ability-to-pay (GAO, 1989). That study, however, does not deal quantitatively with prevalence of contraindications in recipients, and appears to severely underestimate the role of ability-to-pay in referrals for treatment. The major study of actual practice and outcome variations for LT (AHCPR, 1990) did not find evidence of the effects of financing on patient selection in the current allocation of livers. However, issues of financing have been prominent in the many press reports, philanthropic appeals, and policy debates on the subject. In general, one would expect ability-to-pay to be a more critical determinant of the allocation of HT and LT than for kidneys.

D. SOURCES AND LIMITATIONS OF DATA

The Division of Provider Studies (DPS) is an intramural research unit within the Agency for Health Care Policy and Research. One major hospital database developed at DPS contains patient discharge abstracts for approximately 500 hospitals over the period 1980–87. Hospitals in the sample were randomly selected from a universe of short-term general, non-Federal hospitals with at least 30 beds. The sample was designed on a stratified basis to achieve national representation. In general, differences between the sample and the universe are as follows: hospitals in the southern census region are somewhat under-represented and the sample hospitals are somewhat larger, more likely to be teaching facilities, and less likely to be investor-owned. More details about the sampling design and background are provided in Coffey and Farley (1988).

Hospital characteristics are compiled from the American Hospital Association's Annual Survey of Hospitals. This survey provides information on the characteristics of hospitals such as size, ownership, teaching status, location, utilization, finances, and personnel. Unlike the two other major data systems used to study hospital discharges and facility operations in the U.S., the Medicare data system and the discharge survey of the National Center for Health Statistics, all age groups and all discharges from sample hospitals are included in the DPS database. Since the data are contributed voluntarily, confidentiality of patient and hospital identities have been protected.

Distinct Patients vs Episodes of Care

Analyses here are affected by the lack of a patient-specific identifier. Due to this problem, we are not able to determine if a particular patient was registered on an official waiting list for a transplant (this would clarify patient selection results). Moreover, the number of candidate *episodes* where a transplant may have been appropriate will overestimate the number of candidate *patients* during a period of time, since a patient may have had more than one hospital stay. For example, in the elderly and disabled populations covered by Medicare, the number of hospital admissions per distinct person served was about 1.5 in 1984. Finally, transplant recipients may have had one or more stays prior to the transplant for the same illness. On the earlier stays, their care may have been different from candidates who never received a transplant.

We have taken two steps to make the data useful despite the above problems. First, we drop all non-recipient candidate cases transferred to another hospital (where they may have received a transplant) or with stays of two or fewer days (to avoid some preoperative and postoperative episodes). Second, we restrict analysis of non-recipients to those with a high severity level.

Diagnosis Codes, Disease Categories, and Disease Stage

Patient discharge abstracts contain a "principal" and several "secondary" diagnoses, coded using the ICD-9–CM criteria. While the principal discharge diagnosis is meant to represent the main reason for the admission and should be listed first, in practice the ordering of listed diagnoses is variable (*e.g.*, for reimbursement purposes), and not necessarily reflective of the patient's health status or the rationale for treatment decisions. To deal with this problem and to systematically assign a score for "severity of illness," we use the classification system known as Disease Staging. This system is now available in a commercial software product used in a number of research studies (*see* Gonnella, Hornbrook and Louis, 1984; Coffey and Goldfarb, 1986; Prospective Payment Assessment Commission, 1989).

In the Disease Staging system, an underlying disease most critical to the patient's life expectancy is identified after a review of all the listed diagnoses and other patient information. Diagnoses not relevant to the underlying principal disease are flagged as secondary diseases. These consistently-applied concepts of underlying principal and secondary disease are helpful in analyzing potential candidates for transplants.

The "Disease Stage level" for each disease is a value along a scale of 0 to 4. A stage of 1 to 1.9 indicates a single impaired organ system with no complications with other organ systems. A stage of 2 to 2.9 indicates significantly increased risk of complications. A stage of 3 or more indicates poor prognosis with multiple sites of organ impairment or generalized systemic disease. (A stage of 4 is reserved for death, but, in this study, all patients who died have been recoded as if that fact were unknown.) The Disease Stage of the underlying medical problem is an indicator that systematically uses all the diagnostic information. Moreover, the stage of secondary diseases is a convenient way to assess the complexity of the patient's condition. We create a variable to measure the highest stage among secondary diseases.

Other Variables

Hospital charges are recorded on a majority of records in the DPS database, but such data must be cautiously interpreted to allow for the considerable variation of billed charges in relation to full cost of resources used across hospitals and across treatments. Professional fees and the growing use of outpatient services can make hospital charges a substantial underestimate of total episode costs, particularly for those hospitals that have responded most strongly to the payment incentives to shift billings to outpatient care.

The payer category for each patient is based on the expected primary source of payment. Errors can arise if a person is not covered by the private insurance that they expected to have or if a person becomes eligible for Medicaid as a result of the episode of treatment. An estimate of the patient's financial resources is made from the median household income in the patient's zipcode of residence. This imputation from Census data is affected by changes over time in zipcode boundaries, particularly the addition of new zipcodes in growing areas – which are believed to be areas of above-average income. About one-third of patient zipcodes in 1986–87 did not match census files based on 1980 boundaries. Therefore, the statistical analysis of income data will use categories rather than a continuous variable, and a separate category will be used for non-matching zipcodes.

E. RECIPIENT CHARACTERISTICS FROM 1984 TO 1987

The diagnoses for which a transplant may be indicated are described in various publications with enough specificity for coding in the ICD-9–CM system. For HT, we used the Medicare regulations as well as the 1984 report by Evans, *et al.*, and journal articles such as Shimon *et al.* (1989). Diagnostic specifications pertaining to LT were taken from the federal Medicare legislation and from the NIH synthesis article of outcome studies (Foster and Burton, 1989).[6]

Contraindications are typically divided in the literature into "absolute" and "relative" categories, where the latter depend on the clinical assessment of severity of the secondary problems, using measures that are typically not available for research, except directly from the full medical record. Alcoholic cirrhosis is considered a relative contraindication, since the clinical judgment about the ability of the patient to carry out follow-up regimens and lifestyle restrictions is an important factor. A diagnosis of viral or chronic hepatitis is not considered to be a relative contraindication for LT, although some patients may still have had positive antibody or antigen tests that would deter some surgeons from carrying out the procedure.[7]

Less than 5% of cases coded as receiving HT or LT were dropped from analysis because of unreconcilable diagnoses. Some of these were retransplant cases and others were probable coding errors. This left a total of 346

Table 2. Prevalence of contraindications for transplant recipients

Contraindication Status	Heart Transplants 1984-85	1986-87	Liver Transplants 1984-85	1986-87
No Contraindications	59 79.7%	218 80.1%	54 85.7%	175 87.5%
Absolute contras	9 12.2%	38 14.0%	5 7.9%	9 4.5%
Relative contras only	6 8.1%	16 5.9%	4 6.4%	16 8.0%
Total	74 100.0%	272 100.0%	63 100.0%	200 100.0%

Source: Division of Provider Studies, Agency for Health Care Policy and Research

Notes: The distributions shown in the table did not change significantly over time (Chi-square test, p > 0.05 for both heart and liver OT).

cases receiving HT and 263 cases receiving LT from 1984 through 1987. The recipients were characterized by contraindications as reported in Table 2. Years are combined into pairs to permit larger counts for statistical comparisons.

The table indicates that about 14% of LT recipients and 20% of HT recipients had some contraindications. There was no change over time in the overall rate of contraindications. The most prevalent contraindications for HT recipients were pulmonary hypertension, chronic airway obstruction and diabetes. An increase in the number of pulmonary problems was associated with an increase in the simultaneous transplantation of heart and lung (such procedures are currently regarded as experimental). A quite small number of LT recipients are reported with a diagnosis of cancer – 2 cases in the earlier period and 5 cases in the later period. The relative contraindications for LT were scattered among cardiac, pulmonary and kidney impairments.

The high proportion of patients with no contraindications gives some confirmation to hypothesis H1. It is also noteworthy that there were insignificant changes over time in rate of contraindications during this period of rapid growth in the number of procedures. This finding reflects the continued existence of a pool of candidates without contraindications, and that neither expanded insurance coverage nor improved technology were dominant over other influences by shifting the criteria for patient selection. It would be very difficult to determine the maximum feasible proportion of organs that could be allocated to patients without contraindications, which would depend on (a) randomness in arrival of organs and patients, and (b) other aspects of tissue matching that have not been addressed here.

To further describe the characteristics of recipients and the hospitals where they were treated, we prepared tables and chi-square tests for changes in distribution of the following measures: primary diagnosis, age, payer class, teaching status of the hospital and size of the transplant program. Since the sample contained 15 HT centers but only 5 LT centers, there is much lower power for statistical testing of LT center characteristics. A full set of tables

Table 3. Distribution of liver and heart transplant patients by age group, 1984–85 vs. 1986–87

Age Group	Liver Transplant		Heart Transplant	
	1984-85 Number (%)	1986-87 Number (%)	1984-85 Number (%)	1986-87 Number (%)
0-10	32 (50.8)	78 (39.0)	0 (0.0)	8 (2.9)
11-20	5 (7.9)	11 (5.5)	5 (6.8)	15 (5.5)
21-30	3 (4.8)	14 (7.0)	6 (8.1)	17 (6.3)
31-40	6 (9.5)	30 (15.0)	18 (24.3)	30 (11.0)
41-50	14 (22.2)	39 (19.5)	24 (32.4)	65 (23.9)
51-60	3 (4.8)	26 (13.0)	21 (28.4)	105 (38.6)
61-70	0 (0.0)	2 (1.0)	0 (0.0)	32 (11.8)
Total	63 (100.0)	200 (100.0)	74 (100.0)	272 (100.0)
Mean age	19.1	25.2	41.2	45.3

Source: Division of Provider Studies, Agency for Health Care Policy and Research.

Notes: For liver transplant patients, a Chi-square test did not find significant differences in the age distribution over time (p = .32), but this could be due to low power. Several of the age category cells in the Chi-square test had expected values less than 5.

A t-test of the difference in mean age over time does show a significant difference (p = 0.04) for the liver patients.

Differences in mean age appear to be due to a lower proportion of children and a higher proportion of those over age 50 who get liver OT in later years.

For heart transplant patients, the mean age is not significantly different over time (t-test, p > .05), but the age distributions are significantly different (Chi-square, p < .01).

Differences in the age distributions of heart OT patients are striking. Note the lower proportions of patients aged 31–40 and 41–50 in 1983–84, and the higher proportions aged 51–60 and 61–70 in the later years.

is available in the longer report from the authors. Highlights of the descriptive comparisons are as follows.

- For HT recipients there has been a significant (P < .01) shift in age distribution to persons in their 50's and 60's, and a much reduced share for persons aged 20–40. This has not been accompanied by changes in the distribution of primary diagnoses. The proportion of LT recipients who are children with biliary atresia has declined, while the proportion of older recipients increased (Table 3).

- There was no significant change over this period in the distribution of transplants across third-party payer classes of government programs, private insurance and self-pay or no charge. Private insurance coverage is about 70%, government programs about 24%, and self-pay about 6%.

Table 4. Distribution of liver and heart transplant patients by primary payer, 1984–85 vs. 1986–87

Payer	Liver Transplant		Heart Transplant	
	1984-85 Number (%)	1986-87 Number (%)	1984-85 Number (%)	1986-87 Number (%)
Missing	0 (0.0)	4 (2.0)	0 (0.0)	5 (0.0)
Medicare	1 (1.6)	6 (3.0)	8 (10.8)	44 (16.5)
Medicaid	7 (11.1)	24 (12.0)	6 (8.1)	17 (6.4)
Other govt.	0 (0.0)	6 (3.0)	1 (1.4)	7 (2.6)
Private	52 (82.5)	147 (73.5)	54 (73.0)	182 (68.1)
Self	3 (4.8)	13 (6.5)	5 (6.7)	17 (6.4)
Total	63 (100.0)	200 (100.0)	74 (100.0)	272 (100.0)

Source: Division of Provider Studies, Agency for Health Care Policy and Research.

Notes: While the percent of heart and liver OT patients with private insurance declined over time, the payer distributions do not differ significantly (Chi-square, $p > 0.10$). Note that low power may be a problem in these Chi-square tests.

For both heart and liver OT patients, there is no significant difference in the proportions of self-pay or government-pay patients over time (Chi-square p-value > 0.10). Government-pay = Medicare + Medicaid + Other government payors.

This proportion of self-pay and no charge is somewhat smaller than for all hospital admissions or for a leading DRG with only non-elderly patients (Table 4).[8]

- The mean of hospital charges for the stay that included the transplant did not change significantly during the period for either LT or HT (a relatively high variance makes such comparisons imprecise). In 1986–87, mean hospital charges were about $138,000 and $59,000 for liver and heart, respectively (Table 5).

F. POTENTIAL CANDIDATES WHO DID NOT RECEIVE TRANSPLANTS

To select potential candidate discharges for HT for this analysis, we began with all cases in the database having a diagnosis of cardiomyopathy as one of the listed diagnoses. This approach will eliminate a fairly small number of accepted candidates for transplant (perhaps 10% of recipients), but excludes as well a vast number of patients with cardiovascular diseases who have more promising alternative treatment options. We applied the Disease

Table 5. Length of stay and total charges for liver and heart transplant discharges, 1984–85 vs. 1986–87*

Variable	Liver Transplants		Heart Transplants	
	1984-85	1986-87	1984-85	1986-87
	Mean (Std.dev.) [Number]	Mean (Std.dev.) [Number]	Mean (Std.dev.) [Number]	Mean (Std.dev.) [Number]
Length of stay	44.6 (29.2) [56]	53.2 (42.6) [194]	45.0 (32.4) [71]	37.6 (28.0) [266]
Total charge per stay	128,905 (79,276) [33]	137,692 (106,366) [58]	55,220 (36,547) [41]	58,924 (47,542) [158]

*Questionable values for length of stay and total charges have been omitted from the calculations.

Source: Division of Provider Studies, Agency for Health Care Policy and Research.

Notes: For heart transplants, the difference in mean length of stay is statistically significant (t-test, p = 0.05). None of the remaining differences in means are significant.

Staging software to select those cases where cardiomyopathy was judged to be the most important underlying disease. Each year there were over 7,200 discharges for persons under age 70 in this disease category. We dropped all cases with absolute contraindications for HT, despite the fact that some actual recipients (14%) suffered from these same diseases. In addition discharges were excluded if the patient was discharged to another hospital or the hospital stay was less than 3 days.

These exclusions still left about 5,000 discharges per year for further analysis, nearly 40 discharges for every transplant recipient. While this number is an underestimate for the reasons given above, it might well exceed the number of distinct patients due to the inclusion of multiple stays within a year for the same individual (in the Medicare data system, there are about 1.5 admissions per distinct person admitted during a year).

A similar approach was employed in selecting potential candidate discharges for LT, except that the range of diagnoses for which transplantation is a reasonable therapy was larger. All patients with cancer were excluded. A screen for a Disease Stage level of 2 or higher was used to drop several thousand discharges with the least risk of death – specifically, most viral hepatitis cases. It is possible that some of these cases involved such extensive organ damage, with no remaining active infection, that a transplant would have been considered. About 5,500 discharges per year remained, more than 40 per transplant recipient.

Reducing these estimates further by one-third to allow for multiple admissions, and considering that our sample hospitals had slightly less than 10% of all HT and LT performed in the U.S., we estimated the following numbers of non-recipient potential candidates per year: 34,500 for hearts, and 39,000 for livers. These numbers are still more than twice as large as estimates published in the major previous reports (*e.g.*, Task Force on Organ Transplantation, 1986). One reason for the higher estimates is the upward shift in the age distribution of current recipients.

G. COMPARISONS BETWEEN RECIPIENTS AND NON-RECIEPIENTS

The central issues here are the effects of medical condition (prospects for benefit of transplant) and ability-to-pay on the probability of receiving a transplant. The recipients from 1986–87 are used in this analysis. Due to the much larger number of non-recipients, we use only 1987 non-recipients to reduce some possible problems of computation with low probability events. Over much of the income distribution, ability-to-pay depends critically on insurance coverage. An estimate of household income or assets is imputed from average values in the zipcode of the patient's residence. For hypothesis testing, income or assets is divided at the national median into higher and lower categories, reserving an extra category for "new" zipcodes with no income data available – these zipcodes are presumed to reflect high growth areas.

The method used for testing hypothesis H2 is logistic regression analysis with a standard maximum likelihood technique to fit the dependent variable which takes the value 1 if a transplant was received. Not only do we want to determine the statistical importance of differences in ability to pay, but also to test for interactions with the presence of contraindications. All the variables used in the regression are dichotomous classifications and the most frequent group for each variable was usually taken as the default with a dummy value of zero. Therefore, the effect of each variable can readily be converted to a relative odds for receiving a transplant compared, usually, to the modal case in the sample. Table 6 gives results of the tests.

It is clear that the independent effect of the presence of contraindications is to drastically reduce the relative odds of receiving a transplant of either organ. In the case of HT, the odds of receiving a transplant were doubled for those from high income areas. For both organs, those people in new zipcodes and believed to be wealthier than average had significantly higher odds of receiving a transplant. It is noteworthy that the interaction between income and contraindications was not significant in either case. This verdict was not changed by including insurance coverage, age, or severity levels in the regression. Due to the relatively small numbers of people receiving transplants, it is not possible to allow as many interaction effects as might be useful for testing the hypothesis of queue-jumping.

To further explore these issues, Table 7 provides a more detailed breakdown of the probability of receiving a transplant within classes of patients with and without contraindications. If we focus on the columns for patients with contraindications, there are significant chi-square tests of ability to pay that suggest queue-jumping for hearts, but not for livers. The probability of receiving a heart despite contraindications appears to be significantly higher

178   *B. Friedman, R. J. Ozminkowski, and Z. Taylor*

Table 6. Results from logistic regression analysis of the probability of receiving a heart or liver transplant

Dependent Variable = 1 if received a heart or liver transplant

Variable	Heart (n=6999)			Liver (n=5377)		
	Mean	Coeff.	Relative Odds	Mean	Coeff.	Relative Odds
Intercept	1.00	-3.51*		1.00	-3.10*	
Has at least one relative contraindication	0.30	-2.55*	0.08	0.46	-2.17*	0.11
High income	0.62	0.69*	2.00	0.62	0.28	.NS
New zipcode**	0.18	0.50*	1.65	0.19	0.74*	2.10
Has at least one relative contra and high income	0.18	0.79	.NS	0.28	-0.17	.NS
Model χ^2	152.74			172.86		
Model p-value	< 0.01			< 0.01		

*p < 0.01
**Income information is not available for discharges who lived in areas that changed zipcodes after 1980. The "New zipcode" dummy indicates discharges for whom income information is missing.
NS = Relative odds are not significantly different from 1.0.
Source: Division of Provider Studies, Agency for Health Care Policy and Research.

for those with private insurance or in areas with higher income or new zipcodes. This result differs from the results of the logistic regression, presumably due to the more detailed breakdown of ability to pay classes. We therefore suggest that queue-jumping may be a significant, even if relatively small, factor in selection of recipients for hearts.

H. EFFECTS OF EXCESS DEMAND ON SERVICES AND CHARGES TO NON-RECIPIENTS

In order to test hypothesis H3 that an increase in demand would affect the intensity of care and charges for potential candidates who did not receive transplants, we first pooled data on non-recipient discharges for 1984 and 1987. After inspecting the detailed information on treatment received (up to 10 procedures are coded on the discharge summaries), we did not find major changes over time in the number of procedures per case.

The average number of procedures recorded for cases in the LT non-recipient group rose slightly over time from 2.33 to 2.51; the average number for the HT non-recipient group was roughly constant at about 1.70. For all hospital discharges, the average number of recorded procedures was essentially constant between 1984 and 1987. Considering only the "principal"

Table 7. Number and percent of discharges receiving heart or liver transplants, by contraindication status, payor, and income level

Variable	Heart				Liver			
	Contras (n=3246)		No contras (n=3753)		Contras (n=2613)		No Contras (n=2764)	
Payor:	No.	%	No.	%	No.	%	No.	%
All discharges	54	1.68	218	5.81	25	0.96	175	6.33
Medicare	9	0.60	35	2.67	1	0.16	5	1.11
Medicaid	4	1.08	13	3.53	6	1.18	18	4.14
Other government	0	0.00	7	7.78	1	1.12	5	4.07
Private	41	3.74	141	8.57	15	1.48	132	9.47
Self-pay / No-charge	0	0.00	17	5.70	1	0.32	12	3.65
Missing	0	0.00	5	11.90	1	2.04	3	9.38
x^2 p-value*	< 0.01		< 0.01		0.09		< 0.01	
Income:	No.	%	No.	%	No.	%	No.	%
All discharges	54	1.68	218	5.81	25	0.96	175	6.33
Below median**	11	0.84	44	3.23	8	0.79	45	4.23
Above median	25	1.79	106	6.27	11	0.94	63	5.65
Missing***	18	3.37	68	9.70	6	1.39	67	11.47
x^2 p-value*	< 0.01		0.03		0.56		< 0.01	

*Indicates significance level for x^2 test of independence of the proportions of discharges receiving transplants between the payor and income groups.
**Median 1987 income = $26,000
***Income information is not available for discharges who lived in areas that changed zipcodes after 1980.
Source: Division of Provider Studies, Agency for Health Care Policy and Research.

procedure and the first additional procedure, the most common procedures for the HT group were diagnostic ultrasound and cardiac catheterization (each of these was recorded in about 14% of cases). The rate of recording of these procedures and most others did not change to a substantial degree during the period. For the LT group, ligation of esophageal varices (12% of cases in 1987), small bowel endoscopies (17%) and abdominal paracentesis (15%) were the most common procedures, all increasing noticeably over time. However, many other procedures declined over time, notably percutaneous biopsy, and nuclear isotope scans. The procedure rates do not indicate substantial change in the intensity of inpatient treatment.

The use of intensive care bed units as a proportion of days increased by a small but statistically significant amount over the period. For HT candidates, while less than half of stays used any intensive care days, the average use of intensive care rose from 16% to 18% of total days. For LT candidates the average rose from 5% to 8% of total days. The total days of stay per case fell by 7% for the HT group but rose by 2% for the LT group. The

Table 8. Regression of charges, hospital stays for non-recipient potential candidates for HEART TRANSPLANT, 1984 and 1987

```
DEPENDENT VARIABLE:  Log of Hospital Charge

METHOD:  Ordinary Least Squares
         (Coefficients with t-value for no effect, not reported if P>.05)
```

Independent Variables	Coefficient	t-value
Age group by decade (0/1)		
0- 9	-0.221	-2.19
10-19	n.s.	
20-29	n.s.	
30-39	-0.092	-2.04
40-49	n.s.	
50-59	n.s.	
default: 60-69		
Stage level of primary disease	0.453	2.77
Highest stage of secondary diseases	0.051	3.03
Source of admission (0/1)		
Emergency department	0.119	5.54
Outpatient department	0.372	7.32
Another hospital	0.503	5.90
default: all other sources		
Female (0/1)	0.043	2.05
Non-white ethnic code (0/1)	n.s.	
Payor category (0/1)		
Medicare	n.s.	
Medicaid	n.s.	
Other governmental	0.159	2.06
Private insurance	n.s.	
default: self-pay or no charge		
Census region (0/1)		
East	-0.225	-6.76
South	-0.263	-8.46
Central	-0.311	-9.73
default: West		
Hospital costliness (log)	0.639	15.74
Major teaching hospital (0/1)	n.s.	
Presence of transplant program (0/1)	0.096	2.38
Number of transplants 1986/87	-0.002	-2.45
Year 1987 (0/1)	-0.116	-5.69
Intercept	1.677	2.75
Adjusted R-squared	0.148	
Residual degrees of freedom	5325	

NOTES:
1. Charges in 1987 are deflated by the natural average increase from 1984.
2. Transplant recipients are excluded from the analysis.

overall picture is one of rather modest change in resource intensity of treatment.

The null hypothesis is principally concerned about the change in services and charges over time, but we should control for patient characteristics and possible change in the distribution of patients across hospitals with different practices and costliness. Table 8 gives results of an OLS regression of the log of deflated hospital charges on patient characteristics and hospital characteristics for HT non-recipients. An analogous approach to the LT non-recipient charges is available but not presented. Charges in 1987 are deflated by an increase that would expected for all hospital admissions, independent of changes related to transplantation. The deflator is 1.286 which reflects the

28% cumulative growth of inpatient revenue per admission between the two years for all community hospitals.

A dummy variable for the year of 1987 is included in the regression, along with a dummy variable for whether the case was treated at a hospital with a transplant program. Several other variables control for differences between hospitals in overall costliness of care and/or style of practice: the geographic region, whether the hospital is member of the Council of Teaching Hospitals, and the log of total cost per adjusted admission using data from the American Hospital Association survey.

Severity levels (from Disease Staging) of the primary disease, as well as secondary diseases, were significant determinants of charges. There was no consistent pattern by age. Charges were slightly higher for females, but they were not significantly different by race. By comparison to self-pay patients, charges were not significantly different for those with private insurance, Medicare or Medicaid.

Allowing for the patient characteristics, overall hospital costliness and growth of charges, we find a mixed verdict on hypothesis H3. Charges did not appear to increase over time despite evidence of excess demand revealed in lengthening waiting lists for transplants. However, charges were higher at transplant centers as hypothesized, and fell with the number of transplants per year.

The apparent absence of growth in charges over time might be clarified by study of the following influences:
(a) the controlled growth of services and expenses for each inpatient stay may be offset by an increased number of stays, outpatient services and physician bills that increase total expenses at a faster rate than found here; or
(b) increased expertise in dealing with these serious diseases, combined with financial incentives for more conservative practices may have reduced the use of ineffective or unnecessary services.

I. CONCLUDING DISCUSSION

The findings with regard to the null hypotheses can be summarized as follows.
(H1) In basic accord with expectations, the rate of contraindications among recipients of hearts or livers in 1987 was quite low – 20% and 14% respectively. The rate did not change during the period of rapid growth between 1984 and 1987.
(H2) The evidence for a substantial amount of queue-jumping was mixed. The proportion of potential candidates who received a transplant despite contraindications was significantly related to income or to private insurance coverage in the case of hearts. There were not analogous significant effects in the case of livers. Logistic regressions to test the interaction of ability-to-pay and presence of contraindications found

insignificant results. The higher cost of LT, or perhaps the smaller number of centers may account for the lesser apparent degree of queue-jumping in that case.

(H3) The hypothesized effects of excess demand on services and charges to non-recipients were not found. Allowing for the severity of illness, other patient characteristics and overall hospital costliness, deflated hospital charges to non-recipients of hearts or livers did not appear to increase between 1984 and 1987. For HT non-recipients, hospital charges were higher at transplant centers as hypothesized and declined with the total number of transplants.

This paper has been limited to the analysis of hospital use and charges; it would be desirable to follow both recipients and non-recipients of hearts, livers and other tissues over time to obtain better comparisons than now exist of total resource use, length and quality of life.

Complacency About Growth of OT and Costs in the U.S.

The economic impact of OT, judging from experience with heart and liver transplantation, may continue to be modest for the following reasons: (a) the fairly small available supply of cadaveric organs, (b) tentative findings about relatively low and steady contraindication rates and only mild evidence about queue-jumping, (c) tentative findings that the expense of treating non-recipients has not grown in response to excess demand, and (d) a continuing presumption (not thoroughly tested) that selective contracting with a limited number of transplant centers of substantial size is advantageous.

This situation could be strongly altered by further technological change – in the use of live donor tissues (*e.g.*, the case of bone marrow transplants), better retrieval and storage of cadaveric organs, mechanical implants or "bridges" to await transplants, *etc.* Given the widespread and increasing efforts to restrain total spending on health care in the U.S., the costs of open-ended commitments to OT will warrant more research.

Payment and regulatory policies for OT in the U.S. have not been based on a methodology of comparing net benefits of OT versus other uses of social resources. (In the interesting case of the state of Oregon, surveys of professional and voter attitudes are being used, together with other data, to prioritize services for Medicaid coverage, and OT is judged as relatively low in priority.) There is presently no quantitative basis for "accepted medical treatment", *i.e.*, a process to resolve how large a 1–year or 5–year survival rate should be to justify the extremely high costs of OT, and the exclusion of particular patients. It would seem desirable to focus some research on consumer valuations. Changes in private insurance will likely continue to be a major determinant of the growth of OT, and insurance coverage decisions do provide opportunities to test consumer valuation of risks.

Comparative Studies of Health Systems

It is interesting to ask whether systems with total budget constraints for facilities or districts tend to spend a higher or lower proportion of resources on OT. Aaron and Schwartz (1984), compared the use of selected technologies for the U.K. versus the U.S. Some of their major observations were:

1. a much lower rate per capita of use of kidney dialysis in the U.K., but a nearly equal rate of kidney transplantation;
2. much lower rates in the U.K. for coronary artery bypass surgery, CT scanning, use of intensive care units, and a somewhat lower rate of hip replacement;
3. roughly equal rates in cancer radiologic therapy, chemotherapy, bone marrow transplantation, and treatment of hemophilia.

The authors suggest that the evidence tends to support a view that decisions in a fixed budget system would tend to favor (a) visibly saving lives, (b) treatments not requiring specific new capital investments, (c) treatment of "dread" diseases where the public is relatively well informed and vocal, (d) services that offer indirect savings of other social resources such as long-term care, and (e) favoring the young versus the old. The authors point out that it would take many more data points to discriminate among the separate hypothetical influences.

The high likelihood of visible saving of lives (at least for 1–3 years) when there is no hopeful alternative treatment could favor OT in any payment system. The contributing possibility that OT is favored due to less requirement for new investment is not clear, since OT has a relatively high requirement for intensive care bed units.[9]

Rublee (1989) compared the availability of several technologies between Canada and the U.S. and found that organ transplantation units per million population were roughly equal while cardiac catheterization, radiation therapy, shock wave lithotripsy, and magnetic resonance imaging were available in Canada at only one-third to one-eighth the rate in the U.S. A comparison between Germany and the U.S. did not find the same pattern – relative availability in Germany of cardiac catheterization, radiation therapy, lithotripsy and magnetic resonance imaging were the same or greater than OT. But such comparisons of units per capita are very rough in view of possible variations in the size and number of procedures per unit.

Rublee's report joins with Aaron and Schwartz in observing that requirements for new capital investment would strongly influence the adoption of new health technologies in a system with fixed budgets. Whether or not this is economically efficient or just a peculiar type of bias in political decision-making could be an interesting question.

Interpretations of how resources tend to be rationed in a fixed budget system will vary with the disciplinary background of the viewer. For economists, it is not very difficult to model most of the "political" influences suggested by Aaron and Schwartz within a framework of consumer-oriented evaluation of benefits versus social costs of health care. The chance of preserving life in rare circumstances may indeed be more valuable to voters everywhere, as well as to purchasers of health insurance, than (say) an equal amount of premiums going for reimbursement of expenses for chronic disease.

NOTES

1. As an illustration of the growth of OT, the Registry of the International Society for Heart Transplantation reported a rise from 300 heart transplants in 1983 to nearly 2,500 in 1988. Mortality within 30 days of operation fell by about half during this period, and long-term survival curves are shown to be significantly improved by the new drug regimens introduced in the mid-1980s (Heck, Shumway and Kaye, 1989). In the Medicare prospective pricing system, heart transplants in 1988 carried the highest relative hospital payment "weight" of 11.9, compared to the most common diagnostic group "heart failure and shock" at 1.0. The cost of physician services would substantially enlarge the relative cost comparison.
2. In the case of kidney transplantation, there is the life-saving alternative treatment of dialysis, so that research has been targeted to the relative cost-effectiveness of transplantation. For a review of evidence, *see* Evans, *et al.* (1987). For most candidates for heart or liver transplantation, there is currently no analogous life-preserving alternative treatment. Moreover, research on kidney transplantation is aided by a unique data system, arising from the End Stage Renal Disease program which provides uniform payment and administrative coverage for virtually all persons with chronic kidney failure.
3. A more fully developed theoretical discussion is available from the authors, with reference to a substantial body of past literature on non-price rationing and applications in health care.
4. In order to develop the main ideas expeditiously, we do not consider some aspects of the allocation of organs such as the possibility of using volunteer donors (this is important for kidneys and bone marrow), tissue matching problems, and geographic distances affecting organ availability to particular patients. We assume that all available organs are used and only one per recipient.
5. Some authors (*e.g.*, Blumstein, 1989) have argued that current regulations restrict donor recruitment and access to OT procedures. Federal law requires that transplant programs must meet the certification requirements of the United Network for Organ Sharing (UNOS). Failure to do this jeopardizes the Medicare and Medicaid funding for all hospital care, even that which is not provided by the OT program. Officials do not believe that UNOS imposes significant restrictions on organ acquisition or donor recruitment. A quite different issue is whether payment of compensation to donors would sharply increase total supply.
6. The ICD-9 codes for indications for HT were as follows (leading digits of 5–digit codes): 2127, 391, 393–398, 402, 410, 411, 413–416, 421, 422, 424–429, 745–746. The ICD-9 codes for indications for LT were as follows: 070, 1550–1552, 2710, 2720, 2727, 2751, 2770–2776, 2860, 2861, 2115, 2308, 2353, 2390, 4530, 570, 5710, 5712, 5714, 5715, 5716, 5718, 5719, 5728, 5758, 5761, 5762, 75161, 75169, 7744, 7778, and 864. Multiple transplants and retransplants can be a source of confusion. In our data for 1986–87, of the 272 heart recipients, 8 also received a lung and one received a kidney. Four of 200 liver recipients also received a kidney.
7. The ICD-9-CM codes (leading digits of 5–digit codes) used for absolute contraindications were as follows: for HT they were 416, 140–208, 290–292, 295–299, 303–304, 4010, 4020, 4030, 4040, 4050, 491–492, 496, 500–508, and 570–572; for LT they were 140–195, 3483, 34982, and 452. The codes used for relative contraindications were as follows: for HT they were 250, 278, 443, 531–533, and 562; for LT they were 4030, 4040, 4050, 414, 416, 425, 428, 491, 492, 5712, 5714, 582 and 585.

8. In our sample of hospitals, about 11% of all cases were in the self-pay or no charge categories. A leading DRG with a high proportion of elderly such as #127, heart failure and shock, has only about 2.5% self-pay, while another leading DRG with mostly non-elderly such as #183, gastroenteritis and miscellaneous digestive disorders, had 12.6% self-pay or no charge.
9. In our sample, the average number of ICU days was 12.7 for LT patients and 5.3 days for HT patients. By contrast, the average number of ICU days for other expensive and more frequent DRGs were the following: 3 days for coronary artery bypass surgery, 1 day for major cerebrovascular diseases, 0.2 days for major joint reattachment, and 0.7 days for major bowel procedures.

REFERENCES

Aaron, H.J., and W.B. Schwartz, "The Painful Prescription: Rationing Hospital Care", Washington, DC: Brookings, 1984.

Blumstein, J.F., "Government's Role in Organ Transplantation Policy", in: Blumstein, J. and F. Sloan (eds.) *Organ Transplantation Policy – Issues and Prospects*, Durham, NC: Duke University Press, 1989.

Brunner, F.P. *et al.*, "Combined Report on Regular Dialysis and Transplantation in Europe, XVII, 1987" for European Dialysis and Transplant Association- European Renal Association; London, Springer-Verlag, 1988.

Coffey, R., D. Farley, "HCUP-2 Project Overview", *Hospital Studies Program Research Note* 10, Agency for Health Care Policy and Research (DHHS Publication No. (PHS) 88–3428), 1988.

Coffey, R.M., and M.G. Goldfarb, "DRGs and Disease Staging for Reimbursing Medicare Patients", *Medical Care*, 24:814–829, 1986.

DeLissovoy, G., "Medicare and heart transplants: will lightning strike twice?", *Health Affairs* 7: 61–72, 1988.

Evans, R.W. *et al.*, "National Health Transplantation Study", Final Report to the Health Care Financing Administration; Seattle: Battelle Human Affairs Research Centers, 1984.

Evans, R.W., D.L. Manninen, L.P. Garrison, L.G. Hart, "Findings from the National Kidney Dialysis and Kidney Transplantation Study", Office of Research and Demonstrations, Health Care Financing Administration Special Report, Baltimore, MD: U.S. Dept. of Health and Human Services, 1987.

Foster, W., and B. Burton, "Technology Assessment Applied to Liver Transplantation in Adults", *Intl. J. of Technology Assessment in Health Care*, 5:173–182, 1989.

Gonnella, J.S, M.C. Hornbrook, D.Z. Louis, "Staging of Disease: a Case-Mix Measurement", *JAMA*, 251:637, 1984.

Heck, C.F., S.J. Shumway, M.P. Kaye, "Registry of the International Society for Heart Transplantation: Sixth Official Report – 1989", *Journal of Heart Transplantation*, 8:271–276, 1989.

Held, P., M. Pauly, R. Bovbjberg, J. Newmann and O. Salvatierra, "Access to Kidney Transplantation: Has the United States Eliminated Income and Racial Differences?", *Archives of Internal Medicine*, 148:2594–2600, December 1988.

Kramer, P. *et al.*, "Combined Report on Regular Dialysis and Transplantation in Europe, XIV, 1983", *Proceedings of the European Dialysis and Transplant Association – European Renal Association*, 21:5–65, 1984.

Lindsey, P.A., E.A. McGlinn, "State coverage for organ transplantation: a framework for decision making", *Health Services Research* 22: 881–922, 1988.

Mayers, B.W., "Blue Cross and Blue Shield Coverage for Major Organ Transplants", in: Cowan, D.H. *et al.* (eds.), *Human Organ Transplantation: Societal, Medical-Legal, Regulatory and Reimbursement Issues*, Ann Arbor: Health Administration Press, 1987.

Mooney, G., "The Agency Relationship: An Empty Box?", presented at Second World Congress of Health Economics, Zürich, Switzerland, September, 1990.

Prospective Payment Assessment Commission, "Report and Recommendations to the Secretary, U.S. Department of Health and Human Services, March 1989.

Rublee, D.A., "Medical Technology in Canada, Germany, and the United States", *Health Affairs*, 8:178–181, 1989.

Shimon, D.V. *et al.*, "Heart Transplantation – State of the Art", *Israel Journal of Medical Sciences*, 25:575–582, 1989.

Starzl, T.E., A.J. Demetrius, D. van Thiel, "Liver Transplantation (part 1)", *New England Journal of Medicine*, 321:1014–1022, 1989.

Task Force on Organ Transplantation, "Organ Transplantation: Issues and Recommendations", U.S. Health Resources and Services Administration, April, 1986.

U.S. Agency for Health Care Policy and Research (AHCPR), "Assessment of Liver Transplantation", *Health Technology Assessment Reports*, 1990, *Number* 1.

U.S. General Accounting Office (GAO) *Heart Transplants*: *Concerns About Cost, Access, and Availability of Donor Organs*, Washington, D.C.: 1989.

U.S. Health Resources and Services Administration, Division of Organ Transplantation, "Scientific and Clinical Status of Organ Transplantation: Report for 1987 as required by section 376 of the Public Health Service Act", October, 1988.

Van Thiel, D.H., L. Makowka, T. Starzl *et al.*, "Liver Transplantation: Where it's been and Where it's Going", *Gastroenterologic Clinics of North America*, 17:1–18, 1988.

Non-price allocative procedures: Scottish solutions to a National Health Service problem*

ROBIN G. MILNE AND BEN TORSNEY

University of Glasgow, Dept. of Political Economy, Adam Smith Building, Glasgow, G12 8RT, Scotland

$$I \, 18$$

$$\Gamma \, 11$$

$$uK$$

ABSTRACT

Except for a few NHS services, the allocation of resources depends on administrative-cum-medical decision-making. At one level the Scottish Home and Health Department allocates funds between the fifteen health boards, at another level clinicians allocate resources between patients. We examine experience at a level intermediate between these two, and focus on the provision of two services – diagnostic radiology and ECG – at health centres.

A benefit: cost framework is used to test three hypotheses about how the two services have been allocated. The three hypotheses relate to the benefits from provision and are characterised as 'medical excellence', 'equity' and 'market' orientated. Data on health centre list size and distance to alternative provision are used to test the hypotheses. The conclusions are as follows.

The equity and market models are equally valid descriptions for ECG, a service provided by general practitioners. A combination of the equity and/or market model *with* the medical model is a valid description for diagnostic radiology, a service provided by health boards and the Scottish Home and Health Department.

1. INTRODUCTION

Resources are allocated in the National Health Service (NHS), largely without information on prices as a measure of value as a consequence of deliberate government policy to ensure that the best medical care is equally available to all. This policy was expressed in the National Government's White Paper on the National Health Service in the following terms:

*We should like to thank the Scottish Home and Health Department for giving access to the survey of health centres it conducted in 1976, and to all the health boards for providing supplementary information. Dr Berkeley kindly provided similar access to the raw data of his survey of the use made of diagnostic radiology services. Finally, this paper benefitted from comments and advice from the two editors and from Hugh Gravelle, Don McCreadie, David McLaren, Sandy Neilson, John Parr and David Vines (none of whom should be held responsible for the contents of this draft) and from presentations to colleagues at the University of Glasgow and at the Scottish Economists Conference at the Burn in September 1987.

P. Zweifel and H. E. Frech III (eds.), Health Economics Worldwide. 187–202.

... everyone in the country – irrespective of means, age, sex or occupation – shall have equal
opportunity to benefit from the best and most up-to-date medical and allied services available.
(Ministry of Health, Department of Health for Scotland, 1944, p. 47.)

The enabling legislation introduced three years later, in 1947, also indicated
that "area of residence" and "insurance qualification" should not be a dis-
qualification to access.

Published research on the allocation of NHS resources has tended to focus
on the outcome either at the macro level, being the regional distribution of
national revenue funding (see for example Maynard and Ludbrook, 1980),
or at the micro level, being the study of health service use by individuals
(see for example Le Grand, 1978 and Townsend and Davidson, 1982; and
more recently Wilkinson, 1986). Little research has been done on the outcome between the macro and micro levels. Two exceptions are Hunter (1980)
and Ham (1986) which use the case study approach for two health boards[1]
(in Scotland) and two district health authorities[2] in England), respectively.

Access to a survey (Macgregor et al., 1980) of all health centres[3] in
Scotland, by the Scottish Home and Health Department (SHHD)[4], supplemented by a further survey of our own allows us to analyse outcomes without
recourse to the case study approach. No attempt is made to establish a
general positive theory of which health centres will have facilities: rather we
use the benefit: cost framework, within this general theory, to predict which
ones should have facilities. We then compare the actual distribution of
facilities with the predictions made using the benefit: cost framework. Predictions are based on three different hypotheses of the benefit to patients
from health centres duplicating facilities already provided in hospitals. These
predictions are tested for two services: diagnostic radiology (X-ray), and
(diagnostic) electrocardiology (ECG). The decision to provide X-ray facilities
is made by the SHHD and health boards; the decision for ECG is made by
GPs, except where it is support for consultant out-patient sessions in general
medicine in which case provision is usually automatic and made by health
boards.

The data set refers to all health centres in operation at least one year in
1981. It identifies which health centres had each of the two services, and also
includes information on the number of patients on the GPs' lists at each
health centre (P) and the distance, for each service, to the nearest alternative
facility (D) measured in miles. Scatter diagrams relating to P and D and to
the presence and absence of provision are given in Figure 1 for the two
services. It will be noted that some health centres with very large lists (i.e.
P large) had no facility; whereas some others no distance to alternative
provision had one.

In Section 2 and the Mathematical Appendix we derive the benefits from,
costs of, and conditions (i.e. benefits exceeding costs) for a health centre to
have a facility, in terms of P and D. The rest of the paper is given over to
showing how the hypotheses may be tested and the results of doing so. Other

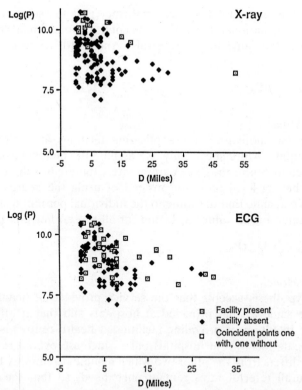

Fig. 1. The observed provision of facilities at Health Centres by Population (P), Distance (D) and Service.

factors will impinge on the decision without necessarily conflicting with the efficiency criterion, but we assume they are uncorrelated with P or D.

2. THE MODELS

The Benefit Function

The three hypotheses focus on the benefits from the duplication of services at health centres. They are characterised as being motivated by considerations of 'medical excellence', 'equity' and 'market' forces. The derivation of the benefits from provision at any given health centre is expressed in terms of P and D, as is now described in turn for the three hypotheses.

H1: Medical Excellence
In this case provision at health centres is perceived as distinctly different from that already existing in hospitals. The benefits from any given health centre m, ($B_{1,m}$) will depend on the health centre list size (P_m). Three

assumptions are made. First, the referral rate (r) is the same for all health centres, being the national referral rate. Second, the individual's benefit from referral (b_1) is the same for all referrals. And third, there is no resource constraint. Thus:

$$B_{1,m} = b_1 r P_m$$

H2: Equity Model

In this case the motivation for duplicating facilities at health centres is geographic equity. More specifically, we assume the benefits from provision at a given health centre m, ($B_{2,m}$) are greater, the greater the distance, D_m saved from having local provision instead of using the nearest alternative provision. We assume that the value to the individual per unit distance saved, (b_2), is the same for all values of D and for all those referred. Thus:

$$B_{2,m} = b_2 D_m r P_m$$

H3: Market Model

The third hypothesis accepts that the service provided at health centres is basically the same as that provided at hospitals and that it offers medical benefit. The intention of providing facilities at health centres is, therefore, not to duplicate facilities at hospitals but to increase overall referral rates. This service differs from the other two which assume, to simplify the analysis, that the overall referral rates remain unchanged, so that the addition to referrals from a health centre acquiring a facility is matched by a reduction in referrals elsewhere.

The benefits from providing a facility at any given health centre m, ($B_{3,m}$) depend on the number of those referred. We assume, again, that the benefits for those referred are the same for each individual (b_3). The number referred will depend on the health centre's size (P_m) and on the health centre's referral rate (r_m). In this case, however, the referral rate is *not* the national referral rate, r, but depends on the distance patients must travel to obtain access. Schultz (1970) has argued that referral (r_D) depends on distance in the following functional form:

$$r_D = r_0 \exp(-\theta D) \quad \text{where } r_0 \text{ is the referral rate close to the point of access, and } \theta \text{ is a parameter to be estimated.}$$

Data drawn from sources other than the sample of 130 health centres studied allow us to obtain independent estimates of r_0 and θ for diagnostic radiology. The data for are drawn from 81 general medical practices in the Grampian region in 1973, and refer to rates per annum. r_0 is allowed to take different values for group practices as against single-handed practices, and θ is constrained to take the same value. Using this specification $\hat{\theta} = 0.045$. Further information on this source may be found in Mair et al (1974).

There is no source apart from our sample of health centres to indicate

Table 1. Benefit, Cost and Boundary Functions, by Hypothesis

Hypothesis	Benefits (B)	Costs (C)	Boundary (B > C)
H_1	$B = b_1 r P$	$C = K$	$P > K/(b_1 r)$
H_2	$B = b_2 D r P$	$C = K$	$DP > K/(b_2 r)$
H_3	$B = b_3 r_0$ $\times \{1 - \exp(-\theta D)\} P$	$C = K + c r_0$ $\times \{1 - \exp(-\theta D)\} P$	$\times \{1 - \exp(-\theta D)\}$ $\times P > \dfrac{K}{r_0(b_3 - c)}$

Key:

(i) The terms b_1, b_2, b_3, c, K, r_0, θ are service specific parameters. All are assumed to be the same for each health centre.

(ii) b_1, b_2, b_3 refer to the benefits, per person referred, associated with hypotheses H1, H2 and H3 respectively.

(iii) K is the capital outlay per health centre.

(iv) c is the recurrent outlay per referred person.

(v) r is the national referral rate and is assumed to apply to each health centre.

(vii) θ is defined by the relationship $r_D = r_0 \exp(-\theta D)$, where r_D is the referral rate at distance D from the point of access.

what values r_0 and θ have for ECG. Evidence *internal* to the data set suggest $\hat{\theta} < 0.00951$ (see sub-section 5.2), which is quite consistent with the value found for diagnostic radiology.

Whatever the values of r_0 and θ:

$$B_{3,m} = b_3 \Delta r_m P_m$$

where Δr_m is the increase in the overall referral rate due to the effective reduction of D_m to approximately zero, namely

$$\Delta r_m = r_0 \{1 - \exp(-\theta D_m)\}.$$

Therefore:

$$B_{3,m} = b_3 r_0 \{1 - \exp(-\theta D_m)\} P_m.$$

The benefit functions are summarised in Table 1

b) The Cost Function

The rule for deciding which health centres should have facilities is an efficiency one: namely, that the benefits from provision exceed its cost. We have just derived the benefit functions (for the three hypotheses) in terms of P and D for each health centre. We now do the same for the costs of each of the two services. The relevant costs identified are those generated as a result of the decision to provide facilities at health centres. In a benefit: cost framework focussed on patients it is not important who bears the cost; but in terms of the actual outcome this may be very important. In the case of diagnostic radiology the capital costs would be borne by the SHHD and the recurrent costs by the health boards. In the case of ECG the costs would be borne by GPs, unless raised by charity.

In the cases of the first two hypotheses (H1 and H2) we make the simplifying assumption that the overall referral rate remains unchanged. Thus any increase in referrals (at the health centre) is balanced by a corresponding reduction elsewhere (in the hospitals). We further assume that resources associated with these recurrent expenditures, such as staff time and materials, are freely transferable, so that expenditure on them does not increase. The only additional outlays are: capital expenditures, K, for equipment and accommodation for diagnostic radiology, and for equipment for ECG.

Thus for diagnostic radiology and ECG the cost functions for hypotheses 1 and 2, respectively are:

$$C_{1,m} = K$$
$$C_{2,m} = K$$

In the case of the third hypothesis (H3), we allow the provision of facilities to increase referrals. In this case there will be recurrent costs, c per referral, in addition to those already identified. The cost function for diagnostic radiology and ECG is therefore:

$$C_{3,m} = K + cr_0\{1 - \exp(-\theta D_m)\}P_m$$

This concludes our derivation of the cost functions in terms of P and D. The results are also summarised in Table 1.

c) *The Boundary Function*

The decision rule for an efficient allocation of resources is that the benefits from provision exceed its costs. The benefit and cost functions have both been expressed in terms of P and D. The locus of points, then, on which benefits equal costs define a key boundary. Health centres on one side should possess a facility, while those on the other side should not. These boundaries, however, do not indicate the *extent* to which facilities are or should be used.

We derive general formulae for these boundaries in the Mathematical Appendix, and the results are summarised in Table 1 and given visual representation in Figure 2. A variety of assumptions were made to derive these results. In particular that b_1, b_2, b_3 and c were the same for all individuals and, therefore, for all health centres, and that K, r_0 and θ were the same for all health centres. These assumptions are hardly likely to be correct. For example, young and old benefit differently from the provision of ECG. Unfortunately we do not have information on the age and sex composition of health centre populations. But so long as that age/sex composition is not correlated with P and D our results can be interpreted without qualification. We assume there is no such correlation. By the same reasoning we assume

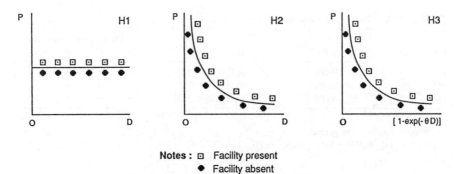

Notes : ☐ Facility present
          ● Facility absent

Fig. 2. Boundary functions by Hypothesis.

that if b_1, b_2, b_3, c, K, r_0, and θ varied, as they almost certainly did, they did so independently of P and D.

The implications are that the boundaries for diagnostic radiology and ECG are rectangular hyperbola for hypotheses 2 and 3, in P and D, and in P and $\{1 - \exp(-\theta D)\}$, respectively. Note that $\{1 - \exp(-\theta D)\}$ is an increasing function of D. All other boundaries are horizontal.

An inspection of Figure 1 shows that none of the services exhibit a clear cut boundary where, on one side, all health centres have facilities and, on the other, none of them have any. This fuzzy boundary is not unexpected. A variety of assumptions were made to derive the results in Table 1 and Figure 2. However, the general shape of the boundaries derived may still prevail and one could compare the actual distribution of facilities between health centres with the distributions predicted by the benefit: cost framework. This is the subject of the rest of this paper.

3. STOCHASTIC EXTENSIONS OF THE MODELS

In the previous section the contrast between Figures 1 and 2 suggested that 'fuzzy' boundaries are a more realistic proposition than a deterministic boundary. We therefore propose the notion that a health centre has a probability of possessing a service given its value of P and D (and possibly other factors). Contours in (P, D)-space of constant value of this probability are stochastic boundaries. Accepting this, the shapes suggested above by the three hypotheses for the original boundaries can then be viewed as conjectured shapes for these iso-probability contours. It is possible to test for the feasibility of these shapes.

In order to do so we adopt a key assumption or probability model. We will suppose that a contour of iso-probability value q is given by the equation

$$F(L) = q,$$

Table 2. Model Parameter Predictions by Hypothesis

Hypothesis	g(P)	h(D)	Parameter Predictions			
			α	β	γ	ρ
H2	ln(P)	$h_a(D)$	$-$	$+$	$+$	1
H3	ln(P)	$h_b(D)$	$-$	$+$	$+$	1
H1	ln(P)	$h_a(D)$ or $h_b(D)$	$-$	$+$	0	0

Key:
'+' = positive, '−' = negative,
$h_a(D) = \ln(D)$, $h_b(D) = \ln\{1 - \exp(-\theta D)\}$.

where

  (i) $L = \alpha + \beta g(P) + \gamma h(D)$,

  (ii) $g(P)$, $h(D)$ are functions to be chosen,

  (iii) α, β, γ are unknown parameters to be estimated, and

  (iv) $F(L) = e^L/(1 + e^L)$.

There are three features of the equation $F(L) = q$ which merit comment:
  (i) the lack of dependence on variables other than P and D;
  (ii) the form of dependence on P and D; and
  (iii) the presence of the function $F(L)$.
  We take these in turn.
  (i) The lack of dependence on other variables is in keeping with our earlier stated assumption that the effects of other variables are uncorrelated with P and D – an orthogonality assumption.
  (ii) The form of dependence on P and D is restrictive in that we assume first that the argument L depends on them only through a function g of P and a function h of D, and second that L depends linearly on g and h. However, α,β,γ, are free parameters and a wide class of contours are possible for a given choice of the pair (g,h). Moreover, two choices of the pair are considered for each service. These are such that the conjectured contour(s) under a particular hypothesis for a particular service is/are a possibility under at least one choice of (g,h) with some conditions on β and γ. Moreover the latter conditions have a very simple formulation, namely they propose unique values for the ratio $\rho = \gamma/\beta$: namely 0 or 1. Illustration is given in the Mathematical Appendix, while details are listed in Table 2 for each facility and hypothesis: namely the choice of (g,h) and the conditions on α,β,γ,ρ.
  That ρ proves to be such a key parameter becomes clear from an alternative equation, under our general model, for contours: namely $g(P) = \delta - \rho h(D)$, where $\delta = [\ln\{q/(1 - q)\} - \alpha]/\beta$. This reveals that ρ is an index of shape. We focus particular attention on assessing whether our data support the numerical values for ρ listed in Table 2.
  (iii) The function $F(L)$ is the logistic distribution function and is used because the value of the variable to be explained – the presence/absence of a

Table 3. Model Fitting of Provision: X-Ray and ECG

	X-Ray		ECG	
	Model 1	Model 2	Model 1	Model 2
g(p)	ln(P)	ln(P)	ln(P)	ln(P)
h(D)	ln(D)	ln$\{1 - e^{-\theta D}\}$	ln(D)	ln$\{1 - e^{-\theta D}\}$
		$\hat{\theta} = 0.045$		$\theta = 0.00951$
				$(\hat{\theta} \leqslant \theta)$
SD	54.00	55.07	140.04	140.04
DF	127	127	113	112
P-value	1.0000	1.0000	0.0431	0.0375
$\hat{\alpha}$	−29.64	−25.87	−7.726	−5.862
	(7.235)	(6.206)	(2.684)	(2.471)
$\hat{\beta}$	2.782	2.644	0.7446	0.7460
	(0.6955)	(0.6708)	(0.2865)	(0.2892)
$\hat{\gamma}$	0.7977	0.6991	0.4023	0.4547
	(0.4865)	(0.5250)	(0.1516)	(0.1688)
$\hat{\rho}$	0.287	0.264	0.5403	0.5952
IE for ρ	(0.005, 0.600)	(0.003, 0.641)	(0.187, 1.834)	(0.211, 1.911)

Key:
SD denotes standard deviation
DF denotes degrees of freedom
IE denotes interval estimate

facility – is either zero or unity. We could have used some other distribution function F(L), which is increasing in L and satisfies the condition for a probability, $0 \leqslant F(L) \leqslant 1$. Other options include taking F(L) = Φ(L), the normal distribution function – a probit model. However these functions take similar values for non-extreme values of L, so that results should be robust with respect to choice of F(L).

4. METHODS OF ANALYSIS

A first step is to estimate the unknown parameters α,β,γ from the data we have on health centres in operation at least one year in 1981. There are 130 of these and all of them are included in the analysis of diagnostic radiology. In the case of ECG 14 of the health centres were excluded. They are the centres that had out-patient clinics in general medicine, and in all but two had backup ECG facilities (provided by the health board). One of the two that did not have ECG was sited in hospital grounds with alternative provision.

Maximum likelihood estimates of α,β and γ are reported in Table 3: namely the values $\hat{\alpha},\hat{\beta},\hat{\gamma}$ which jointly maximise the likelihood of the data under the relevant model. The likelihood is the function

$$\prod_{m=1}^{N} F(L_m)^{Z_m} [1 - F(L_m)]^{1-Z_m},$$

where

(i) N is the number of health centres considered (130 for diagnostic radiology and 116 for ECG),

(ii) $L_m = \alpha + \beta g(P_m) + \gamma h(D_m)$,

(iii) m identifies the health centre,

P_m is its list size (population),

D_m is the distance from health centre m to the nearest alternative facility (in miles), and

$$Z_m = \begin{cases} 1 & \text{if health centre m has the facility,} \\ 0 & \text{otherwise.} \end{cases}$$

Estimated standard errors are also quoted in parentheses. However the logarithm of our likelihood function is a nonquadratic function of α, β, γ, whereas the latter errors are calculated on the assumption that the log-likelihood is approximately quadratic in the region of $\hat{\alpha}, \hat{\beta}, \hat{\gamma}$. The evidence is that this is not always reasonable, particularly in the case of γ and hence of ρ. For this reason an estimated standard error is not reported for ρ. Instead an interval estimate for ρ with a confidence of about 0.95, calculated using the profile likelihood method, is recorded. Typically this is not centred on $\hat{\rho}$, as it would be if the log-likelihood were approximately quadratic.

The remaining terms – SD, DF and P-value – quoted in Table 3 can be used to judge the adequacy of the relevant logistic model. Under the model the scaled deviance (SD) should follow a chi-square distribution with DF degrees of freedom. Too large a value suggests that the model is not a good fit to the data. A significance test at a 5% level rejects the model if SD exceeds the upper 5% point of the $\chi^2(DF)$ distribution, or equivalently if its P-value is less than 0.05.

Note that we can now be more precise about our orthogonality assumption. It is that, if extra variables were included in the formula for L_m the estimates of their coefficients would be uncorrelated with $\hat{\beta}$ and $\hat{\gamma}$.

5. MODEL FITTING OF PROVISION BY SERVICE

We now consider the two services separately, and we take them in the order: diagnostic radiology, and ECG.

5.1. *Diagnostic Radiology*

(i) Two choices for the pair {g(P), h(D)} are listed in Table 3. These are prompted for consideration by Table 2. The scaled-deviance values are markedly small and the P-values approximately 1 for both models, a phenomenon which is probably due to the small overall proportion of health centres with this service.

(ii) Results are very similar for both models especially in respect of $\hat{\beta}, \hat{\gamma}$ and $\hat{\rho}$. This is because the independent estimate of θ obtained from the Aberdeen data is small ($\hat{\theta} = 0.045$). As a result the following are true:

$$\ln\{1 - \exp(-\theta D)\} \cong \ln(\theta D) = \ln(\theta) + \ln(D),$$

$$\alpha + \beta g(P) + \gamma \ln\{1 - \exp(-\theta D)\} \cong \alpha' + \beta g(P) + \gamma \ln(D),$$

where $\alpha' = \alpha + \gamma \ln(\theta)$.

Thus one model is in effect a reparameterisation of the other, the two differing in the definition of the 'constant' term α. In our earlier terminology, the equity and market models are equivalent, given the functions $\{g(P), h(D)\}$.

(iii) The estimated standard errors of $\hat{\gamma}$ are particularly unreliable here. Taken at face value they would suggest that γ is not significantly different from zero. This conflicts with conclusions suggested by the interval estimate for ρ, and would conflict with an interval estimate for γ calculated by the profile likelihood method.

(iv) Under both (probability) models the interval estimates for ρ are contained within the range $(0,1)$. This implies that we can reject the possibilities of $\rho = 0$ (hypothesis 1) and of $\rho = 1$ (hypotheses 2 or 3).

(v) Similar results were obtained when the models were fitted to variations of the data set based on both excluding one health centre (considered an outlier) and reclassifying two health centres as not having diagnostic radiology. The latter consisted of one health centre which used mobile equipment and one which did not staff its equipment. Interval estimates for ρ were always contained within the range $(0,1)$.

5.2. *ECG*

(i) Again two choices prompted by Table 2 for the pair $\{g(P), h(D)\}$ are considered. The scaled deviances reported in Table 3 for both models share a large common value whose P-value is just less than 0.05. Thus the data do not particularly favour these models. However the tests are just significant at the 5% level. So we proceed tentatively with parameter inference.

(ii) For ECG there is not an independent estimate of θ. In theory it is possible to determine a maximum likelihood estimate $\hat{\theta}$ which, with $\hat{\alpha}, \hat{\beta}, \hat{\gamma}$, jointly maximises the likelihood. However our data imply that $\hat{\theta}$ is small in which case it is difficult to determine $\hat{\theta}$ precisely. As in the case of diagnostic radiology (5.1(ii)), one probability model is approximately a reparameterisation of the other with β, γ and ρ – but not (or nearly not) θ – uniquely estimable. In view of this we have identified the small value of θ (namely $\theta = 0.00951$) under which the scaled deviance of the model with $h(D) = \ln\{1 - \exp(-\theta D)\}$ is the same as that for $h(D) = \ln(D)$. The value of $\hat{\theta}$ is smaller than this and produces a smaller scaled deviance. Both probability models produce similar estimates of β and γ, and the implication is again that our equity and market models are equivalent.

(iii) Under both (probability) models the interval estimate for ρ is an interval of positive values containing 1. Hence we reject the possibility of $\rho = 0$ (hypothesis 1) but it is possible that $\rho = 1$. The data lends credance to hypothesis 2 and to hypothesis 3.

6. RANK CORRELATIONS, SYNTHESIS AND DISCUSSION

The purpose of this paper has been to use a benefit: cost framework to predict which health centres would be most likely to have two particular services, and to compare predictions with actual distribution. In so far as these correspond, then the system of allocating resources can be described as efficient in terms of one of the three hypotheses about the benefits from health centres having the services, or possibly in terms of a combination of them. We formulate conclusions in these terms for each service. Additional confirmation for them is to be found in a simple rank correlation analysis.

It is possible to rank health centres in respect of the amount by which benefits exceed costs under a given hypothesis. These rankings are equivalent to rankings according to known specific functions of P and D with the qualification that they depend on θ in the case of H3. Motivations for these functions are given in the Mathematical Appendix. Since we cannot estimate θ precisely in the case of ECG, it is not strictly possible to produce a ranking for this service under H3. However we can make inferences about correlations with H3.

In Table 4 we report a set of such correlations which excludes any involving H3 for ECG. Consider first correlations between the hypotheses. With one exception these correlations are less than 0.400. The exception is the extremely high correlation (0.991) between H2 and H3 for diagnostic radiology. This is consistent with the approximate equivalence (noted in paragraph 5.1(ii)) of the fits of the models under which H2 and H3 could be assessed, which in turn is a consequence of the small value of $\hat{\theta}$. The comparable values of the correlations of both H2 and H3 with H1 are also in keeping with such an equivalence. If we reject one of H2 or H3 we would expect to reject the other.

In respect of ECG we have one calculated correlation, between H1 and H2. However we have observed an equivalence between H2 and H3 for this service too (See paragraph 5.2(ii)). We suggest that the correlation between these two hypotheses is high. If the data support one of them, it is possible that they would support the other; further, given the low correlation between H1 and H2, we would then expect H1 to be rejected.

Table 4. Rank Correlations by Service

Hypothesis (Function)	X-Ray H1 (P)	H2 (PD)	H3 (P{1 − exp(−θD)})	ECG H1 (P)	H2 (PD)	H3 (P{1 − exp(−θD)})
H1	1			1		
H2	0.324	1		0.326	1	
H3	0.399	0.991	1	a	b	1
Pred.	0.785	0.788	0.827	0.590	0.936	c

Key:
Pred = Predicted ordering under adopted model
a = unobtainable but should be close to that between H1 and H2
b = unobtainable but should be close to 1
c = unobtainable but should be close to that between H2 and Pred.
Note:
The ranking under a hypothesis (H_i) is identical to that under the function recorded below H_i in parentheses. The parameter θ in the function for H3 is such that $\hat{\theta} = 0.045$ for diagnostic radiology while for ECG θ is not accurately estimable.

Consider now rankings with fitted models. In our earlier analysis we considered more than one model for each service in order to accommodate the three hypotheses. In the interests of simplicity and because they gave at least as good a fit to the data as the others, we limit discussion to the following model: $h(D) = \ln(D)$ and $g(P) = \ln(P)$. It is rank correlations between the predicted rankings of the health centres under the fits of these selected models and the rankings under the hypotheses which are reported in Table 4.

The interval estimates for ρ under these selected models imply the following summary conclusion about the hypotheses: there is some support for hypotheses 2 and 3 but not for hypothesis 1 in the case of ECG; and there is no formal support for any single hypothesis in the case of diagnostic radiology. These statements can be seen to be in keeping with the rank correlations just mentioned.

Consider first diagnostic radiology. We have a small but moderate estimate $\hat{\rho} = 0.287$ of ρ and an interval estimate which excludes 0 and 1. Thus the conjectured contours of all three hypotheses are rejected. Instead, since the interval estimate comprises slightly more than the left half of the interval $(0,1)$, contours under the model must be moderately decreasing, and so are something of a combination of the horizontal contours of hypothesis 1 and the more sharply decreasing rectangular hyperbolic contours of hypotheses 2 and 3. This conclusion is consistent with the near equality of the three moderately high correlations reported for this service between the predicted and each of the three hypothesised rankings (0.785 to 0.827). An implication would seem to be that the distribution of this service has been governed by a combination of all three hypotheses: that is, of the medical and the equity and/or market models. Hence we might argue that the distribution of diagnostic radiology is consistent with an efficient allocation of resources, where efficiency is measured by some composite of the benefits envisaged by the three hypotheses, with that of the medical model possibly dominating in view of the interval estimate for ρ.

Consider now ECG. We have $\hat{\rho} = 0.540$, and the interval estimate for ρ contains 1 but not 0. This implies support for hypotheses 2 and 3 (in view of their equivalence) but not for hypothesis 1. This scenario is in keeping with the correlations between the model and the two hypotheses. The correlation of the model with hypothesis 2 is strong (0.936). We would expect a correlation with hypothesis 3 to be similarly strong. Contours could be rectangular hyperbolic as conjectured under hypotheses 2 and 3. We conclude that the equity and market models are possibly valid descriptions for this service. Hence the distribution of ECG facilities is consistent with an efficient allocation of resources, as defined by hypotheses 2 or 3.

In conclusion, it would seem that despite the very varied experience of health centres having diagnostic radiography and ECG services, it is possible that provision is consistent with an efficient allocation of resources. One way or another the decision-making process – involving GPs, health boards and the Scottish Home and Health Department – has achieved this result without resort to the use of charges to patients as a device for eliciting the values of these services. However, experience of a third service not included in this paper, consultant outpatient services, suggests that this outcome might well have been fortuitous. But that is a topic for another paper.

MATHEMATICAL APPENDIX

(I) Boundary Identification

In Table 1 the benefit and cost functions, in terms of P and D, are defined. In this section we derive the boundaries, on which the benefits from provision would begin to exceed its cost. They have the same form for both services, but with different values for b_1, b_2, b_3, c, K, r_0 and θ. The term $\Delta r_m = r_0 \{1 - \exp(-\theta D_m)\}$.

Benefits exceed costs at health centre m under the following respective conditions for the three hypotheses:

H1: if $b_1 r P_m > K$, i.e. $P_m > K/(b_1 r)$.
H2: if $b_2 D_m r P_m > K$, i.e. $D_m P_m > K/(b_2 r)$.
H3: if $b_3 \Delta r_m P_m > K + c \Delta r_m P_m$,

$$\text{i.e. } \Delta r_m P_m (b_3 - c) > K$$

therefore

$$r_0 \{1 - \exp(-\theta D_m)\} P_m (b_3 - c) > K,$$
$$\text{i.e. } \{1 - \exp(-\theta D_m)\} P_m > K/(r_0(b_3 - c)).$$

(II) Choice of ranking functions and the functions g(P) and h(D)

We have identified conditions under which benefits (B) exceed costs (C). Motivation for the choice of functions g(P) and h(D) in Table 2 can now be given. It is that the curve defined by the equation F(L) = q, with L = $\alpha + \beta g(P) + \gamma h(D)$ (defining a contour of probability-value q), should have the same 'formula' as that defined by the equation B = C for at least one value of $\rho = \gamma/\beta$.

For example, consider the case g(P) = ln(P) and h(D) = ln(D), under which both hypotheses 1 and 2 can be tested.

Now the following is true:

$$F(L) = q$$
$$\Rightarrow L = f, \text{ where } f = F^{-1}(q)$$
$$\Rightarrow \alpha + \beta\ln(P) + \gamma\ln(D) = f$$
$$\Rightarrow \ln(P^\beta D^\gamma) = f - \alpha$$
$$\Rightarrow P^\beta D^\gamma = \exp(f - \alpha).$$

The latter becomes PD = constant if $\beta = \gamma$, i.e. $\rho = 1$, and becomes P = constant if $\gamma = 0$, i.e. $\rho = 0$.

Now note that the forms of the equation B = C are: $P_m D_m = K/(b_2 r)$, i.e. $P_m D_m$ = constant, in the case of hypothesis 2; and $P_m = K/(b_1 r)$, i.e. P_m = constant, in the case of hypothesis 1. Note also in Table 4 that the functions P and PD determined the initial deterministic model. Health centres above and to the right of the relevant figures in Figure 2 are expected to have diagnostic radiology or ECG equipment. In the case of our probability model these rules correspond to expecting the probability of possessing equipment to increase with P in the case of hypothesis 1, or PD in the case of hypothesis 2. The rules also lead to the predictions about α, β and γ in Table 2 and, in particular, predictions regarding signs.

NOTES

1. Health boards are the public bodies, in Scotland, responsible for the running of the hospital and community health services. Their performances would be monitored by the Scottish Home and Health Department. Central government funds for the Scottish NHS are channelled through the Scottish Home and Health Department.
2. District health authorities, in England, correspond to health boards in Scotland. They are responsible to their designated regional health authority which monitors their performance.
3. Health centres are a device created to bring together, into the community, various health services. Typically their creation depends on the support of general medical practitioners (GPs). Health centres often accommodate community health and hospital outpatient services.
4. See footnote 1 for the role of the SHHD.

REFERENCES

Ham, C. (1986), *Managing Health Services: Health Authority Members in Search of a Role*. Bristol: School for Advanced Urban Studies.

Hunter, D.J. (1980), *Coping with Uncertainty: Policy and Politics in the National Health Service*. Chichester: Research Studies Press.

Le Grand, J. (1978), "The distribution of public expenditure: the case of health care" *Economica* 45, pp. 125–142.

Macgregor, I.M., J.S. Patterson, D.C. Drummond and B.C.S. Slater (1980), "Health centre practice in Scotland: Part 2" *Health Bulletin* 38, pp. 5–22.

Mair, W.J., J.S. Berkeley, L.A. Gillanders and W.M.C. Allen (1974), "Use of radiological facilities by general practitioners" *British Medical Journal*, 21 September, pp. 732-734.

Maynard, A. and A. Ludbrook (1980), "Budget allocation in the National Health Service" *Journal of Social Policy* 9(3) pp. 289–312.

Ministry of Health and Department of Health for Scotland (1944), *A National Health Service* Cmd. 6502 London: HMSO.

Schultz, G.P. (1970), "The logic of health care facility planning" *Socio-Economic Planning Sciences* 4, pp. 383–393.

Townsend, P. and N. Davidson (eds.) (1982), *Inequalities in Health* Harmondsworth: Penguin Books. A more readily available source of the Black Report published in 1980 by the DHSS.

Wilkinson, R.G. (ed.) (1986), *Class and Health* London: Tavistock Publications.

Priorities among waiting list patients[1]

TOR IVERSEN and ERIK NORD

Unit for Health Services Research, National Institute of Public Health, Geitmyrsveien 75, N-0462 Oslo 4, Norway

1. INTRODUCTION

Scarce goods can be rationed by various mechanisms. In modern societies the common rationing mechanisms are ability and willingness to pay, waiting time to obtain a good and rationing by administrative means. In national health services administrative rationing plays a dominant role. This role is taken care of by health personnel, especially physicians. In the literature this is often referred to as physicians as gatekeepers.

Rationing by administrative means has both normative and descriptive aspects:
1. The normative question, "what criteria should priority decisions in the health services be based on ?
2. The descriptive question, "what kind of criteria do actually guide priority decisions and do health personnel really apply the criteria they claim to apply?

This article addresses the second question and draws attention to the setting of priorities among patients enrolled on hospital waiting lists. As far as we know, priority setting in hospitals is a "black box" where little systematic knowledge is available.

In national health services, like the Norwegian, a referral from a general practitioner or a specialist is necessary to obtain treatment in a hospital. For elective treatments patients often experience a considerable time on the waiting list before they are admitted. The waiting time can be considered as an important aspect of the access and hence the quality of medical care provided. The relative waiting times of the various patient groups, therefore, reveal important aspects of the rationing of medical care. The scope of our study is limited to priorities among waiting list patients waiting for a consultation at the hospital outpatient clinic. Often patients with an identical diagnosis experience unequal waiting times in the same hospital. How can this be explained? Are the unequal waits the outcome of a consistent process of setting priorities? We approached this problem by asking the consultants of two Norwegian hospitals about the criteria they used when they made priori-

P. Zweifel and H. E. Frech III (eds.), Health Economics Worldwide. 203–216.

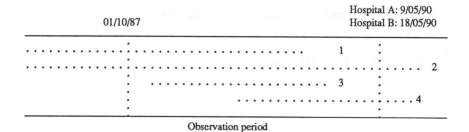

Figure 1. Types of observed waiting times.

ties within two specific groups of patients. The first diagnosis was "Various and unspecified back diseases (ICD 9: 724.)" and the second diagnosis was "Primary arthrosis (715.1)". It is known from other studies (Elstein *et al.*,1986, Lomas *et al.*, 1989) that the outcome of doctors' decisions often deviate from their statements in general terms. Accordingly, to analyse the problem properly we had to collect data about the patients' episodes of waiting. The consultants' stated criteria were confronted with these data. The empirical analysis was done by means of the Cox proportional hazard model. It turned out that few of the factors that were said to be important by the clinicians, were statistically significant. The stated priority criteria were quite similar in both hospitals. The estimated contributions from the various factors differed, however, among the hospitals.

Section 2 of the paper describes the data and the method of analysis. In section 3 the results are presented. Section 4 gives some concluding remarks.

2. DATA AND METHODS

2.1. *Sample*

We used data about waiting list patients waiting for a visit to the hospital outpatient clinic. The data were collected in the period 1 October 1987 until the beginning of May 1990 and cover two hospitals, Hospital A and Hospital B. Within the observation period all the entries to and exits from the chosen waiting lists were reported. The data collected on 1 October 1987 also include patients already on the list at that date. Accordingly, we observed four types of waiting times, shown in figure 1.

Patient 1 entered the waiting list before the observation period started (our data set includes information about the date he was admitted on the waiting list) and was examined at the outpatient department within the observation period. Patient 2 also entered before the start of our observation period and was still on the list when our observation period ended. We do not know when he will get his consultation. In statistical terms he was censored because we were not able to observe the event that completes the waiting time. Patient 3 entered as well as left the waiting list within the observation period. Patient 4 entered the list within the observation period, but is censored similar to patient 2. In the analysis of the data, it is important to distinguish between these categories of patients.

2.2. *Variables*

The patients were referred from a general practitioner or a private specialist. A referral form gave medical and personal information about the individual patient. When the hospital receives a referral, the consultant decides on the priority, classified into: ought to be treated within 1 week, 3–4 weeks, 2 months, 6 months and more than 6 months. The patient's medical record is sent to the head nurse of the department, who assigns a date for the consultation. The first three categories of patients are treated separately. These patients are immediately assigned a specific date. The referral forms of the last two categories are filed and reviewed regularly in order to pick up patients for consultations. Accordingly, the observed relative waiting times are the results of a joint decision where both doctors and nurses are involved.

We decided to concentrate on diagnoses where the clinicians agreed that our data were fundamental to their priority decisions. These diagnoses comprise mainly diseases in the muscles and skeleton where no malignity is suspected. We picked out two groups of diagnoses (ICD-9 codes in parenthesis):
1. Various and unspecified back diseases (724.)
2. Primary arthrosis (715.1)

The first group consists of various four digit diagnoses, most of them very vaguely defined. The bulk of the patients have dorsalgi – unspecified back pain – as their diagnosis from their referring doctor. The second group consists mainly of patients with hip arthrosis, but also a few patients with knee arthrosis are present.

All waits were involuntary. The data about patient characteristics were collected from the referral form sent from the general practitioner to the outpatient department. Table 1 summarizes our information about the individual patient.

In hospital B a considerable proportion of the patients had entered the waiting list before our observation period started. The characteristics of these patients were not known to the hospital staff at the date of their referral to the hospital. At the start of the observation period each of these patients received a letter from the hospital. They were asked to confirm whether they still would like to have an appointment. Those who were still interested, were asked to complete a form corresponding to the form sent by the general practitioners on behalf of the patients referred within the observation period. It may be that the consultants did not trust these self reports to the same extent as the reports from their colleagues. If this is true, to be enrolled on

Table 1. Variable specification

Variable	Specification
Male	1 for male gender, 0 otherwise.
Older than x years	The age of the patients dichotomized as described in table 2 and table 3.
Diagnosis	The preliminary diagnosis reported by the general practitioner.
In the workforce	1 if the patient belonged to the active workforce, 0 otherwise.
High socioeconomic status	1 if professionals and selfemployed except for farmers and fishermen, 0 otherwise.
No information about socioeconomic status	1 if the referral form had no information about socioeconomic status, 0 otherwise.
Strong pain	1 if the patient suffered from strong pain because of the disease, 0 otherwise.
Sleeplessness	1 if the patient suffered from sleeplessness because of the disease, 0 otherwise.
Walkproblems	1 if the patient found it difficult to walk 100 meters, 0 otherwise.
Finds it difficult to do housework	1 if the patient found it difficult to do ordinary housework, 0 otherwise.
On sick leave	1 if the patient was on sick leave because of the disease, 0 otherwise.
Selfadministered report	1 if the patient by a self report gave the information contained in the explanatory variables, 0 otherwise.

the waiting list before the start of the observation period, should contribute negatively to the probability of having an appointment. We therefore introduced the dummy variable called "selfadministered report" in table 1.

When the data were collected, the present analysis was not planned yet. Accordingly, neither the referring physicians nor the hospital staff were aware of the application of the data for this purpose. It is therefore unlikely that the present study had any influence upon the decisions about priorities.

2.3. *Method of analysis*

The data set consists of observations of finished as well as unfinished (censored) waits. Survival analysis is an appropriate statistical method for the analysis of these data. We applied the Cox proportional hazard model. The computations were done by the computer program BMDPPC 2L. A brief introduction to survival analysis and the estimation procedure is given below.[2]

Consider a positive random variable W with the value of its continuous distribution function $F(w) = P(W \leq w)$ and density function $f(W) = F'(W)$. W represents the survival time in a certain condition. In our study, the survival time is the waiting time between referral and consultation at the hospital outpatient department.

Two important concepts in survival analysis are the survival distribution and the hazard rate. The survival distribution is:

$$S(w) = 1 - F(w) = P(W > w)$$

In the waiting list context the survival distribution expresses the probability of waiting at least w time units. Another important concept is the hazard rate function (or transition intensity). The hazard rate function is defined as: $\lambda(w) = f(w)/S(w)$. The interpretation of the hazard rate is the probability of a transition in the next moment for an individual who is still waiting at time w. In our context this means the probability of having a consultation tomorrow if you are among today's names on the waiting list.

The Cox proportional hazard model (Cox, 1972) is a specific kind of survival analysis. It is assumed that certain explanatory variables contribute to the explanation of the hazard rate and the functional relationship between the hazard rate and the explanatory variables is exponential:

$$\lambda(w) = \lambda_0(w)e^{B'Z(w)} \tag{1}$$

where $B'Z(w) = \beta_1 z_1(w) + \beta_2 z_2(w) + \cdots + \beta_n z_n(w)$. $\lambda(w)$ is an arbitary basis hazard function, $z_i(w)$ $(i = 1, 2, \ldots, n)$ are explanatory variables and β_i $(i = 1, 2, \ldots, n)$ are unknown parameters. $B = [\beta_1, \ldots \ldots, \beta_n]$ and $Z(w) = [z_1(w), \ldots \ldots, z_n(w)]$ are vectors.

Consider the model with one fixed covariate taking the values zero or one. The hazard of a person with $z = 1$ relative to a person with $z = 0$ is then:

$$\lambda(w; z = 1)/\lambda(w; z = 0) = e^\beta$$

The two hazard functions are proportional independent of the value of the time variable. That is why the model is called the proportional hazard model. This property is attractive because it simplifies the estimation of the coefficients as well as the interpretation of the results. It is, however, restrictive, because it forces the data into a simple functional relationship. In the application of the model it is therefore important to check that the data fulfil the proportionality assumption of the model.

Estimates of the coefficients are obtained along the following mode of reasoning. Let $W_1 < W_2 < \cdots < W_k$ be the distinct times of admissions to the outpatient department in the observation period. Let Z_j be the vector of explanatory variables for the person who is admitted at time W_j. From the definition of a conditional probability we find that the conditional probability that a person with a vector Z_j is admitted at time W_j given that a single admission takes place, can be expressed as:

$$L_j(B) = \frac{\lambda_0(W_j)\exp(B'Z_j)}{\Sigma_{r\in R_j}\lambda_0(W_j)\exp(B'Z_r)}$$

where R_j includes the individuals on the waiting list (the risk set) just prior to W_j. The denominator accordingly expresses the probability that one transition takes place. $L_j(B)$ may be simplified to:

$$L_j(B) = \frac{\exp(B'Z_j)}{\Sigma_{r\in R_j}\exp(B'Z_r)}$$

The partial (because the baseline hazard function disappeared) likelihood function (the partial likelihood of obtaining the observed pattern of admissions) may then be expressed as:

$$L(B) = \prod_{j=1}^{k} L_j(B) = \prod_{j=1}^{k} \frac{\exp(B'Z_j)}{\Sigma_{r\in R_j}\exp(B'Z_r)} \tag{2}$$

The maximum partial likelihood estimators of B is found numerically by the computer program.

The choice of time variable was not straightforward in this study. There are two alternative candidates, waiting time or calendar time. Let us first consider the waiting time as a time variable. The patients experienced their waiting episodes at various calendar times. Both the departments' capacity and the flow of referrals increased during the observation period. Accordingly, the patients' waiting times were not independent of the date of their referral. A patient with strong pain referred to the hospital in a period with small capacity may experience a longer wait than a patient with moderate pain referred in a period with large capacity. From this, however, we cannot conclude that the patients' level of pain is not taken into account. It may well be that if the two patients were referred to the hospital at an identical calendar time, the patient with strong pain would have experienced a shorter wait than the patient with moderate pain. When we use waiting time as the time variable, we therefore have to take this potential bias into account. One possible way of doing this is to calculate for each patient the waiting time they would have experienced if the service mechanism "First in – first out" (FIFO) were simulated. Since we know all the referral dates as well as the consultation dates, we can to each patient assign the first available consultation date and calculate the implied waiting time. This simulated waiting time for a patient under the FIFO service mechanism is an indicator of the size of the waiting list relative to the department's future capacity at the date when the individual referrals were received. This variable may enter the regression in the same way as the other explanatory variables.

The second alternative is to use the calendar time as a time variable. Then we automatically take into account that the patients may enter the waiting list under various circumstances with respect to waiting list and capacity size. Methodologically this approach therefore seems to have a sounder basis. The disadvantage with this approach is that estimation of survival time and survival curves is not very meaningful in our context.

We have tried both of the two alternatives. Generally (there were a few exceptions), the estimated effects from the explanatory variables on the hazard rate did not depend upon the alternative we chose. In this article calendar time will be the time variable. Referring to figure 1 each patient entered the risk set (R_j in (2)) on the calendar time the hospital received his referral and left the risk set when he had his appointment or was censored. Some of the patients, for instance no. 1 and no. 2 in figure 1, were referred to the hospital before the start of the observation period. In the analysis a person who entered the waiting list t weeks before the observation period started, will be in the risk set from the t'th week of his wait.

3. THE RESULTS

3.1. *Various and unspecified back disease*

In Hospital A there were 199 patients with the diagnosis "various and unspecified back disease". 24 of them were still waiting at the end of the observation period. To establish an hypothesis about the explanatory variables we asked one of the hospital's consultants[3] about patients' characteristics that are taken into account when degree of urgency is considered. He was asked to specify what factors are of great importance, minor importance and no importance. He stated that the patient's level of pain and whether or not the disease disturbs the sleep are of great importance. Age, workforce participation, whether or not the patient has difficulties with walking 100 meters, whether or not the patient has difficulties with doing housework and whether or not the patient is on sick leave were all considered to be factors of minor importance. Of no importance was the patient's sex.

In hospital B there were 122 patients with the diagnosis "Various and unspecified back disease". Only 9 patients were still waiting when our observation period ended. The consultant in hospital B told us that pain, sleeplessness and problems with walking 100 meters were very important for the priorities, the patient's occupation and whether or not he is on sick leave are factors of minor importance and sex, age, activity in the workforce and ability to do housework were all of no importance.

The criteria stated to have great importance or minor importance were used as explanatory variables in the Cox proportional hazard model. One may suspect that the explanatory variables were linearly dependent. For instance, a person with strong pain can also be expected to experience sleeplessness. We therefore examined whether there was multicollinearity among the explanatory variables. For each of the explanatory variables we did an ordinary linear regression with the other explanatory variables as independent variables. The multiple correlation coefficients of these regressions gave information about the strength of the multicollinearity. The squared multiple correlation coefficients varied between 0.1 and 0.5. Accordingly, the problem of multicollinearity was not important.

Properties of the explanatory variables and the results of running the Cox proportional hazard model are shown in Table 2.

The descriptive statistics column shows the mean of the various dummy variables. For instance among the patients in hospital A 50 per cent are older than 45 years and about 23 percent have strong pain because of the disease. We also note that as much as 35 percent of the patients in hospital A and 30 percent of the patients in hospital B were on sick leave at the date they were referred to the hospital.

The variable "Waiting time" in table 2 is a time dependent variable. Each time a transition from the waiting state takes place this variable measures the experienced waiting time for all the patients on the waiting list. In a "First in – first out" priority system (FIFO) the experienced waiting time is the only relevant variable for deciding who is going to have the next appointment. We therefore introduced this variable to examine to what extent the FIFO system could be traced in the two hospitals. The variable "Waiting time" is a continuous variable.

The estimated coefficients are maximum likelihood estimates of the B-vector with calendar time as the time variable. A positive coefficient tells that the explanatory variable contributes positively to the probability of getting out of the waiting state and having the appointment.[4] Only the variables marked by a "+" in table 2 are statistically significantly different from zero. The likelihood ratio test is applied. A coefficient is said to be significantly different from zero if the explanatory variable z_i makes "a sufficient contribution" to the likelihood. Under H_0 ($\beta_i = 0$) the likelihood ratio $L_{zi} = -2\ln$ [likelihood without z_i/likelihood with z_i] is $\chi^2(1)$. A small L_{zi} means that the variable z_i does not increase the likelihood much. In this article a coefficient is significantly different from zero if the probability of rejecting H_0 when H_0 is true, is less than 0.1.[5]

From table 2 we see that in hospital A being on sick leave, socioeconomic status and experienced waiting time all have statistically significant effects different from zero. The results imply that a patient on sick leave has a probability of being admitted that is 1,59 times the probability of a patient who is not on sick leave. We also calculated that a patient who is not on sick leave has to experience an extra waiting time of 290 days to have an identical probability of being admitted as a patient on sick leave. Somewhat surprising is it that patients with high socioeconomic status, contrary to what the consultant stated, in fact had priority. Theoretically, the possible effect of socioeconomic status is quite open. On the one hand, occupations with low socioeconomic status are often manual occupations where a back disease

Table 2. Various and unspecified back disease: Descriptive statistics of the variables and estimated coefficients (standard errors in parentheses) in the Cox proportional hazard model.

Explanatory variables	The consultants' priority statements		Descriptive statistics. Mean		Estimated coefficients with std. deviation	
	Hospital A	Hospital B	Hospital A	Hospital B	Hospital A	Hospital B
Selfadministered report			0.4590			-0.8969 + (0.4126)
Waiting time					0.0016 + (0.0009)	0.0043 + (0.0007)
Older than 45 years	*		0.5025	0.3443	-0.2860 (0.1732)	
In the workforce	*		0.5175	0.5328	-0.3377 (0.2056)	
High socioeconomic status		*	0.0603	0.0902	0.7958 + (0.3569)	-0.2406 (0.3598)
Strong pain	**	**	0.2362	0.2541	0.3674 (0.2224)	0.4054 (0.2454)
Sleeplessness	**	**	0.4774	0.4262	0.0160 (0.2284)	-0.1423 (0.2108)
Walkproblems	*	**	0.3417	0.4672	0.0916 (0.2137)	-0.1147 (0.2175)
Finds it difficult to do housework	*		0.3769	0.5082	-0.1824 (0.2268)	
On sick leave	*	*	0.3568	0.3033	0.4660 + (0.2319)	0.1552 (0.2418)
Male			0.5075	0.4180		

** indicates factors stated by the consultant to be of great importance
* indicates factors stated by the consultant to be of minor importance
+ indicates coefficients statistically significant at 10 percent level

is more disruptive than in occupations with high socioeconomic status. On the other hand, various social mechanisms pull in the direction of priority if a high socioeconomic status is present. Our empirical analysis supported the second hypothesis in the case back disease, showing that a high socioeconomic status contributed to a high probability of getting out of the waiting state. None of the factors stated to have great importance were significant, although "Strong pain " was close to the significance level.

In hospital B none of the three factors stated by the consultant to be of great importance were significant, although "Strong pain" also now was close to the significance level. Both the effect of self administered report and the effect of experienced waiting time had the expected signs and were statistically significant. A patient with his personal characteristics reported by his general practitioner had a probability of getting out of the waiting state 2.5 times larger than the patient with a self administered report.

It is also of interest to know whether an hypothesis of a FIFO system is as compatible with the data as the systems stated by the consultants. A likelihood ratio test can also give us some information about this question. We tested whether all the n variables stated by the consultants (including experienced waiting time) gave "big enough" contribution to the likelihood function compared to a system with experienced waiting time as the single explanatory variable (the FIFO system). Under H_0 (the inclusion of the variables stated by the consultants does not make a sufficient contribution to the likelihood) the likelihood ratio $L = 2 \ln$ (likelihood with all n variables/likelihood with only waiting time) is $X^2(n - 1)$. In both hospitals we found that the effect of introducing the stated variables was significantly different from zero at a 10 per cent level.

3.2. *Primary arthrosis*

In hospital A there was information about 93 waiting list patients with the diagnosis primary arthrosis. 13 of them were still waiting at the end of the observation period. The consultant expressed similar criteria of prioritising as with the previous diagnosis. In Hospital B there were 189 patients. Only 5 of them had censored waits. The consultant stated that pain and sleeplessness were the important criteria for the prioritising of these patients. Of less importance were age and difficulty of walking. The other factors were of no importance.

For this diagnosis we had information about the occupation only for a few of the patients. We therefore had to drop the variable from the analysis. The results of the analysis are summarized in table 3.

From the column of descriptive statistics we can see that old people no longer active in the workforce are the dominant group among these patients. In hospital A two variables had a statistically significant effect different from zero: the experienced waiting time and the presence of a strong pain. None of the variables stated by the consultant in hospital B had a statistically significant effect on the probability of getting out of the waiting state. The only significant effect was experienced waiting time.

We also now tested for the total effect of the variables stated by the consultants compared to the assumption of a FIFO priority scheme. We found that for neither of the hospitals the introduction of the consultants' stated priority system made a significant contribution to the likelihood compared to experienced waiting time as the only explanatory variable.

Table 3. Primary arthrosis: Descriptive statistics of the variables and estimated coefficients (standard errors in parentheses) in the Cox proportional hazard model.

Explanatory variables	The consultants' priority statements		Descriptive statistics. Mean		Estimated coefficients with std. deviation	
	Hospital A	Hospital B	Hospital A	Hospital B	Hospital A	Hospital B
Self administered report				0.1164		0.0466 (0.3728)
Waiting time					0.0060+ (0.0014)	0.0017+ (0.0005)
Older than 70 years	*	*	0.4194	0.3704	−0.1836 (0.2850)	0.2323 (0.1624)
In the workforce	*		0.1720	0.2698	0.2319 (0.4288)	
Strong pain	**	**	0.3441	0.4127	0.6121+ (0.2936)	0.1755 (0.1780)
Sleeplessness	**	**	0.6129	0.4603	−0.2342 (0.3232)	0.0652 (0.1694)
Walking problems	*	*	0.6774	0.6878	0.0673 (0.3768)	−0.1913 (0.1761)
Finds it difficult to do housework	*		0.5699	0.5450	0.1238 (0.3147)	
On sick leave	*		0.0538	0.1534	0.1307 (0.6012)	
Male			0.3548	0.3915		

** indicates factors stated by the consultant to be of great importance
* indicates factors stated by the consultant to be of minor importance
+ indicates coefficients statistically significant at 10 percent level

Table 4. Summary of the results.

Explanatory variable	Stated degree of importance				Estimated coefficients measured in std. deviation in expected direction			
	Back pain		Arthrosis		Back pain		Arthrosis	
	A	B	A	B	A	B	A	B
Strong pain	**	**	**	**	1.65	1.65	2.08	0.98
Sleeplessness	**	**	**	**	0.06	−0.67	−0.72	0.38
Walking problems	*	**	*	*	0.42	−0.52	0.17	−1.08
On sick leave	*	*	*		2.00	0.64	0.21	
Age	*		*	*	−1.65		−0.64	1.43
Experienced waiting time					1.82	5.95	4.22	3.78

** indicates factors stated by the consultant to be of great importance
* indicates factors stated by the consultant to be of minor importance

4. CONCLUDING REMARKS

In this study we have analysed factors contributing to the priorities among patients on a waiting list for a visit to the hospital outpatient clinic. We analysed separately two different diagnoses in two different hospitals. Hypotheses about what factors contributed to the probability of getting out of the waiting state were formed by asking consultants about their priority criteria. The hypotheses were tested with patient data from both hospitals. The influence of the various factors were estimated by the Cox proportional hazard model as it is computed in the program BMDPPC 2L.

Table 4 brings the main results from the analysis of both of the diagnoses in both of the hospitals together. If we consider each hospital as a part of a common medical culture, we may compare the stated criteria with the estimated coefficients measured in standard deviation in the expected direction. From table 4 we see that the comparison shows a good correspondence for the variable "Strong pain" and a weaker correspondence for the variable "On sick leave". For the other variables declared to be of importance, no relationship can be traced from the table. It is, however, interesting to notice the strong influence the patients' experienced waits have on the probability of getting out of the waiting state.

A few comments should be made with respect to the data quality and completeness. It is well known that calls from a patient or his general practitioner may shorten the wait. We have no data about these calls. If any relationship between the frequency of calls and our explanatory variables exists, it seems reasonable that the patients in great pain are more likely to call. The exclusion of calls would then overestimate the contributions from the other variables. We find it unlikely, therefore, that the inclusion of calls would strengthen the estimated contributions from those explanatory variables we have taken into consideration.

Some doctors may exaggerate the problems of their patients in order to shorten their waits. To the extent that hospitals see through such exaggeration, variables like pain, sleeplessness etc. will lose their explanatory power in our analysis. To distinguish between types of general practitioners may therefore be important. However, our data did not allow us to do that.

From (2) we see that the individual transitions from the waiting state are assumed to be independent of each other. Strictly speaking, this assumption is not fulfilled in our context. Since the capacity is limited, the event of one patient having an appointment prevents another patient from having the same appointment. We must admit that we have not found any method of taking this interdependency into account. It was also assumed that the censoring mechanism was independent of the explanatory variables. This assumption seems to be fulfilled.

An interesting question is whether we can address a poor correspondence between stated and effective criteria to the doctors or to the nurses involved in the decision process. As reported in the data section each patient is classified by the consultant into one out of five priority groups. Considering these priority groups, the head nurse of the department assigns a date to the patients. The head nurse, accordingly, must see to it that waiting times correspond to patients' priorities. We checked whether this was properly done by running Cox proportional hazard models with priority groups as the explanatory variables. It turned out that the estimated coefficients had the expected sign and were statistically significant for both diagnoses in both hospitals. Accordingly, it looks like the nurses did what was expected. Two possible hypotheses then emerge. Firstly, the priority groups may have been too broad to catch the individual characteristics of the patients. For instance in hospital B about 75 per cent of the patients were in priority group no. 5. Secondly, the patients may have been placed in a priority group not consistent with the consultants' stated criteria. We have not yet examined the relative merit of these hypotheses. There has been a considerable decrease in the expected waiting time during and after our observation period. If the first hypothesis is true, it is reasonable to expect a better correspondence between stated and effective priority criteria now compared to what we found.

Clinicians often strongly oppose that studies of populations may have applications in their clinical practice. The reason is that every patient is claimed to be very special. In this study we have in fact taken as our point of departure that every patient is different. The study suggests that consultants' declared criteria for prioritising waiting list patients are only to a very limited extent supported by the empirical outcome. This is probably not surprising. It is well known from other sectors that the macro consequences of microbehaviour often is unintended. The human capacity for handling information is limited. In a modern hospital resource allocation is influenced by the focus of the massmedia and the public. Priorities of patients are not open to public scrutiny and accordingly, there is no outside pressure on allocating resources to the activity of prioritising patients.

The question comes up whether it might be rewarding to apply more formal rules when prioritising patients. A more formalized system has, however, its costs. A few patients have reasons for a short wait that are not easy to quantify. There may be a trade-off between considering these patients and the structure of priorities for all the patients. Imposing a system from outside may cause strong reactions from the hospital staff. A better idea would probably be to launch a discussion among health personnel about how to improve the quality of their priority decisions. As the reader may have noticed, there seems to be a strong tie between this debate and the general debate about clinical freedom.

NOTES

1. Comments from Vidar Christiansen, Jostein Grytten, Sven Ove Samuelsen and the editors of this volume are highly acknowledged. The usual disclaimers apply.
2. Standard references to survival analysis are Cox and Oakes (1984) and Kalbfleisch and Prentice (1980). Hopkins (1988) described the details of the estimation procedure in the computer program we made use of.
3. We found it difficult to address more than one consultant in each hospital. In hospital A the deputy chief consultant of the surgical department answered our questions. In hospital B the chief consultant of the orthopedic section answered our questions.
4. In more technical terms this corresponds to the hazard rate or the intensity of transition.
5. We also tested the proportionality assumption by introducing interaction terms between the explanatory variables and the time variable (see for instance Hopkins, 1988, pp.726–727). Applying the likelihood ratio test as explained above, we did not find the interaction effects significantly different from zero.

REFERENCES

Cox, D.R., 1972, Regression models and life tables (with discussion), *Journal of Royal Statistical Society B*, 34, 187–220.
Cox, D.R. and D. Oakes, 1984, *Analysis of survival data*, London: Chapman and Hall.
Elstein, A.S. et al., 1986, "Comparisons of physicians' decisions regarding estrogen replacement therapy for menopausal women and decisions derived from a decision analytic model", *The American Journal of Medicine*, 80, 246–258.
Hopkins, Alan, 1988, "Survival analysis with covariates – Cox models", pp. 719–744, in: *BMDP statistical software manual, volume 2*, Berkeley: University of California Press.
Kalbfleisch J.D. and R.L. Prentice, 1980, *The statistical analysis of failure time data*, New York: John Wiley & Sons.
Lomas, J. et al., 1989, "Do practice guidelines guide practice? The effect of a consensus statement on the practice of physicians", *The New England Journal of Medicine*, 321, 1306–1311.

Consumer information, price, and nonprice competition among hospitals*

H. E. FRECH III

University of California, Dept. of Economics, Santa Barbara CA 93106, U.S.A.

and

J. MICHAEL WOOLLEY

University of Southern California, Los Angeles 90089, U.S.A.

I. INTRODUCTION

As the cost of health care has soared, policymakers have begun to lose faith in planning and regulation as a means of controlling expenditures. Partly as a result, competition among hospitals has received increasing attention as a cost-cutting measure. According to the traditional antitrust view, more hospital competition improves market performance and lead to lower prices. Thus antitrust enforcement officials have become more active in health care, and more hospital mergers have been challenged by the U.S. Federal Trade Commission and the U.S. Department of Justice. In the United Kingdom as well, the government is promoting hospital competition (*Working For Patients*, [1989]).

Some observers have argued that competition among hospitals increases hospital costs (Salkever [1978], Joskow [1982], Farley [1985], and Robinson and Luft [1985]). Furthermore, a recent paper using Medicare data has shown that total charges rise in more competitive markets (Noether [1988]). Many believe that because of health insurance, quality (broadly defined to include hospital amenities, range of services, convenience, *etc.*) is generally too high (Mancur Olson [1985]), that is, quality is higher than consumers would choose if they were well informed and faced the true prices. Competition on the basis of price would help resolve the problem, but nonprice

*We would like to thank Monica Noether, Frank Sloan, Richard Steinberg, and Peter Zweifel for their helpful comments. We would also like to thank seminar participants at the University of Chicago, the Claremont Graduate Center, The University of California at Berkeley, UCLA, and at the annual meetings of the Western Economic Association and the American Economic Association. Data was kindly provided to us by Louise Russell of the Brookings Institution, Paul Joskow of MIT, and James Ramsey of New York University. Thanks are due to the Academic Senate and the Community Organization Research Institute, both at the University of California at Santa Barbara, for research support. Tom Barrera and James Lipking provided helpful research assistance.

P. Zweifel and H. E. Frech III (eds.), Health Economics Worldwide. 217–241.

competition, especially in the form of costly technology and more services, might only worsen it.

The outline of the paper is as follows: first, a discussion of the peculiarities of health care markets; second, the dominant theoretical models of hospital competition; third, a brief review of the literature; fourth, the empirical model and the data; fifth, the results and interpretations; and finally our conclusions.

We use cross-sectional data with more detail on consumer information and prices than past studies. We find that less concentrated markets have higher costs and provide more services, suggesting substantial nonprice competition. In the same markets, daily room charges are higher (but by a smaller percentage than costs) and laboratory charges are actually lower. This suggests more price competition also in these markets, and therefore lower hospital margins.

The consumer information variables were empirically important in determining lab prices, but less so in determining daily room charges and average costs.

II. THE NATURE OF HEALTH CARE COMPETITION

A. Consumer information

The high cost of consumer information is one of the causes of imperfect competition in health care. Health care can be fully evaluated only through extended experience over a significant length of time, thus classifying it as what Phillip Nelson (1970) calls an experience good. A consumer searching for an experience good depends upon the recommendations of family, friends and associates.[1] Because information is so costly, consumers are typically informed about only a small subset of the possible physicians or hospitals. Common forms of health insurance both exacerbate the information problems and weaken incentives to respond to known differences in prices.

B. Health insurance

Insurance reduces consumer sensitivity to price differences. Heavily insured consumers have a reduced incentive to search for lower prices and, even if they know of a lower priced hospital, they have little incentive to switch hospitals in response. As a result, hospitals realize that they can raise prices above the competitive level without losing all or even most of their customers.[2] Consequently, individual hospitals, even where there are many hospitals, have a degree of market or monopoly power.[3]

Recent reforms in health insurance encouraged price competition in two ways. First, higher coinsurance has encouraged consumers to more actively search and choose partially on price. Second, Preferred Provider Organizations (PPOs) and Health Maintenance Organizations (HMOs) have directly negotiated with hospitals over price and utilization.[4] Our data is purposely taken from a time predating these reforms. Thus it is biased against finding price competition to be important.

III. THEORIES OF HOSPITAL COMPETITION

A. Traditional antitrust theory

Essentially, there are three theories of hospital competition. The first is the traditional antitrust model where increased market concentration (decreased competition) leads to higher quality-adjusted prices. Several standard oligopoly theories give this result including Stigler's theory stressing collusion, and theories stressing oligopolistic interaction without collusion, such as Cournot or Bertrand.

However, the antitrust theory does not predict whether increased concentration will be accompanied by higher or lower quality. In either case, increased concentration is correlated with a widening of the price-cost margin, leading to higher profits. If price competition dominates, then prices rise more quickly than costs, while if nonprice competition dominates, prices fall, but more slowly than costs.

B. The redundant resources theory

The redundant resources theory, well described by David Salkever (1978), stresses the physician's influence over the highly insured, passive patients. Hospitals compete to attract physicians through increased equipment and technology, and excess personnel. Increased concentration among hospitals leads to less intense nonprice competition, reducing quality and costs.

Patients passively follow their physician's orders and hospital pricing is not given explicit attention. It appears that hospitals are assumed to raise prices to maintain profits at some target level as increased nonprice competition raises their costs. Thus, this theory says that fewer competitors or higher concentration would cause quality to fall, perhaps towards optimality, but there would be no change in price competition. Thus the price of a constant-quality hospital day would not change, nor would price-cost margins.

C. The increasing monopoly theory

The third theory considers the importance of patient information and search in markets where consumers have imperfect information about alternatives.[5] One version (Stiglitz, 1987) demonstrates that if consumers have convex (increasing) search costs, then there is a possibility that prices could rise with an increase in the number of sellers in the market. This is because the cost

Table 1. The effect of an increase in concentration on

	Price	Cost	Price-Cost Margin	Quality
Traditional Antitrust	?	?	+	?
Redundant Resources	–	–	0	–
Increasing Monopoly	?	?	–	?

of searching for a discounting firm rises with an increase in the number of firms, reducing consumer search effort and lowering elasticity of demand at the level of the individual firm.

Another version, an application of Mark Satterthwaite's (1979) analysis to the hospital market, models consumers as exchanging information about their own experiences at hospitals. Assuming that overlap in recommendations (or increasing returns to information) is necessary for the consumer to have confidence in his information, it follows that information can be worse where there are more hospitals, due to the dilution of information about each hospital. Thus the presence of more sellers can reduce competition, driving the price of a constant-quality hospital day up and increasing profits.

In either case, the increasing monopoly model implies that increased concentration (a decrease in the number of hospitals) leads to increased search efficiency, more consumer search, more hospital competition, lower quality-adjusted prices, and narrower price-cost margins.

IV. PAST EMPIRICAL RESEARCH[6]

Roger Feldman and Bryan Dowd (1986) found individual hospital demand elasticities to range from -0.799 to -3.94.[7] While these elasticities are small enough (in absolute value) to decisively reject perfect competition, they are also large enough to reject the hypothesis of no competition just as decisively.[8] Thus, we can say that while hospital competition is imperfect, the market is also far from a perfect monopoly.

Studies regarding hospital nonprice competition have had mixed results. Cross-sectional analyses of costs (Noether [1988], Robinson and Luft [1985]), hospital bed reservation margins (Joskow [1982]), and nursing staff per patient (Hersch [1984]), have consistently found decreased nonprice competition in more concentrated markets. Analyses of nonprice competition in the form of technological diffusion have differed. Russell (1979) found conflicting relationships between concentration and elapsed time for hospital adoption of new technologies. Similar studies have found conflicting results with some concluding that technology diffused more slowly in more concentrated markets (Rappaport [1978], Robinson, Garnick, and McPhee [1987]), some finding varied relationships (Romeo, Wagner, and Lee [1984], Lee and Waldman [1985], Luft et al. [1986]), and some finding more diffusion in more concentrated markets (Sloan et al. [1986]). A recent study by David Dranove,

Mark Shanley, and Carol Simon (1990) finds that concentration has only a small effect on reducing the number of hospitals offering specialized services.

Other studies have analyzed the effects of concentration on hospital revenue.[9] Examining California markets and correcting concentration measures to account for multi-hospital ownership and management, Henry Zaretsky (1984) found a weakly negative effect of concentration on revenue per patient day.[10] Dean Farley (1985) found that hospitals in markets with more competitors produce significantly higher gross revenues and operating expenses (per adjusted admission) than those in single hospital markets. Monica Noether (1987, 1988) found that lower concentration had a positive, but small and statistically insignificant effect on revenue per patient in ten of eleven different disease categories.

Research using data since 1982 shows a somewhat different picture. As had been predicted based on insurance reforms over the past decade (Frech and Ginsburg [1978], price competition has become more important. Jack Zwanziger and Glenn Melnick (1988) found that hospital costs, measured either per day or per discharge, rose more slowly from 1982 to 1985 in less concentrated hospital markets within California. James Robinson and Harold Luft (1988) found similar results for hospitals nation-wide.

Accounting data are subject to systematic errors, rendering exclusive reliance on them suspect. Michael Woolley (1989) has utilized financial market data in order to circumvent these limitations. Examining stock returns to the competitors of merging hospital chains, he finds that mergers raise the rates of return on the stocks of the competing hospital firms. Furthermore, the greater the local market impact of the merger, the higher the rate of return to competitors. These results are consistent with the theory that mergers raise profits by reducing price and nonprice competition among hospitals.

None of these past studies have explicitly examined actual prices. At best they used total charges per Medicare admission. Additionally, past studies have considered only one or a small number of hospital attributes separately. Finally, past researchers have largely ignored the role of consumer information and search.

V. THE MODEL

A. Hospital behavior

For simplicity, we model the hospitals as monopolistic competitors who maximize profits. This implies that price (for a constant quality output) is a function of the marginal cost and the individual firm's price elasticity of demand, ξ

$$P = MC\left(1 + \frac{1}{\xi}\right)$$

The price is increasing in the marginal cost and decreasing in the elasticity of demand.

The determinants of elasticity of demand are

$$\xi = \xi(HERF, INF, DEM, SOC)$$

where,

HERF = concentration of the hospital market,[11]

INF = consumer information variables,

DEM = demand variables,

SOC = socio-demographic variables

The determinants of marginal cost are as follows

$$MC = MC (HERF, PI, OWN),$$

where,

PI = price of inputs,

OWN = the type of ownership or property rights.

After including some other variables, the price and quality model in its reduced form is given by

$$CHG = CHG (HERF, INF, DEM, SOC, OWN, PI, OTHER)$$

where,

CHG = charge for hospital services.

Furthermore, the level of quality is presumably a function of the same variables,

$$QUAL = QUAL (HERF, INF, DEM, SOC, OWN, PI, OTHER)$$

where,

QUAL = quality (broadly defined[12]) of hospital services.

B. The data

The data are market or SMSA level averages for 1970. The year was selected to bias against finding price competition and a role for consumers. Insurance was close to its maximum completeness in 1970 and direct negotiation with hospitals was still rare. Data definitions, their sources, and descriptive statistics are presented in the appendix. Most of the hospital variables are built up from individual non-federal, short-term general hospital data taken from the American Hospital Association Annual Survey. The individual hospitals do not report every variable. Thus, the averages are based on a set of hospitals from which some nonreporting ones have been dropped. The average proportion of hospital bed-days dropped is 16 percent.

All the variables are aggregated from the hospitals that reported all variables except for the measure of concentration, which represents the concentration of adjusted bed days among hospitals reporting adjusted bed days. Hospitals reporting adjusted bed days are more numerous than hospitals reporting revenues and costs. Since the hospitals that have been dropped may be atypical, a variable for the proportion of beds in the SMSA accounted for by the dropped hospitals in each regression is included. Any SMSA in which PROPDROP exceeded 0.5 (more than half of the hospital bed-days in the SMSA were not accounted for) were deleted from the sample. Of the 193 observations, 18 were deleted for this reason.

This study uses actual hospital charges for a hospital day and for several specific ancillary laboratory services. Hospital charges are the actual prices paid by those with no insurance or with certain types of insurance. Commercial insurance, at the time of our study, paid full hospital charges, as did most Blue Cross plans in the West and the South. Some other insurers paid something less than charges, based on accounting costs, particularly Medicare, Medicaid and Blue Cross plans outside of the West and South. Paying a negotiated fee or a negotiated discount on charges was very rare then, though it has become more common in recent years. In 1970, hospital charges were the prices faced by most consumers.

Hospital prices were taken from the American Hospital Association Survey of Hospital Charges and consist of daily charges for ordinary accommodations, CHGDR, as well as those for X-ray and lab charges (including professional fees) including chest X-ray, CHGCXR, complete blood count, CHGCBC, electrocardiogram, CHGEC, pap smear, CHGPS, upper gastrointestinal series, CHGUGI, and urinalysis, CHGU. All charges are weighted averages of government and non-government hospital data. These values, along with all other dollar denominated variables, were adjusted for the cost of living within the SMSA.[13]

Measures of hospital quality (broadly defined) include hospital costs, an index of the services and technology available, and a measure of hospital personnel per adjusted patient-day. Hospital costs, AVGCOST, were found by dividing total hospital expenses by the number of adjusted patient days

The range of services available is an element of quality itself, highly valued by both consumers and physicians. Feldman and Dowd (1986: p. 291), found that demand for hospital admissions was directly related to the number of different services offered. Additionally, consumer survey evidence shows that breadth of services, especially technologically advanced ones, is important to consumers in their choice of hospital. For example, a 1986 survey of Eugene, Oregon consumers found 89 percent agreeing with the statement "The best hospitals have the widest range of services," and 81 percent agreed with the

statement "The best hospitals have the latest technology." No other aspect
of hospital price or nonprice competition commanded assent by more than
49 percent of consumers (Lucas-Roberts 1986, p. 4).

This leads to a second measure of quality, an index of the services and
technology provided by the hospital, INDEXS&T. This variable was constructed by first regressing average daily room charge on all of the services
and technology offered. The coefficients from this regression provide a dollar-
denominated measure of the value that patients place on the availability of
such services. Second, the coefficients were multiplied by the SMSA variable
values to construct this measure of hospital quality.

The third measure of nonprice competition is an index of nursing intensity,
INDEXN.[14] This variable is defined as the number of registered nurses,
licensed practical nurses, and aides and orderlies, each weighted by their
average salary, per adjusted patient day.

Hospital concentration is measured by the Herfindahl index of adjusted
patient days, HERF. The adjustment increases measures of patient days to
take account of hospital costs for outpatient care. It is done by the AHA
using standard procedures. This index is the sum of squared market shares
of all sellers in the market and ranges in value between zero and one. Thus,
the Herfindahl index weights mergers between larger firms more heavily than
smaller ones.

As consumer information, INF, improves, competition should increase,
causing prices to decline for a constant-quality hospital day. Enhanced information also might lead to more nonprice competition for consumers, thus
raising quality (broadly defined). Consumer information variables, taken
from U.S. Census data, include some of the measures used by Pauly and
Satterthwaite (1981), as well as one additional measure. The variables are
the proportion of female headed households, FEMH, the proportion of
housing units moved into between 1965 and 1970, MOVED, and the proportion of households with telephone available, PHONE. FEMH is a proxy
for households with less time for search. A higher value for MOVED would
imply that people have less experience with the market area and therefore
presumably less information. PHONE represents technology that reduces
search costs.

For demand (DEM), the income, INCOME, and population variables,
POP and POPCHNG, are from the Census. POP is important because large
cities attract more complex cases. The insurance variable, INSUR, is taken
from Louise Russell's data set, which she kindly provided to us. INSUR is
the proportion of hospital costs paid by all third parties. It is constructed
from the state data available from the Health Insurance Association of
American (HIAA) on private insurance and from the Department of Health
and Human Services data on Medicare and Medicaid. Unfortunately, INSUR
is measured with a fairly high degree of error.[15]

The socio-demographic variables include the proportion of the population over age 65, under age 14, female, white, college graduates, and of those receiving aid to families with dependent children. These values are taken from the Census and perform two roles here. They proxy for the casemix in the city's hospitals and they pick up some information relevant to demand. In particular, one could think of some of these variables as measuring aspects of the size distribution of income that are relevant to demand.

The property rights variables, OWN, refer to the market shares of nonprofit (excluded in the regressions), profit-seeking (PROFIT), or nonfederal government owned hospitals (GOVT), and are taken from the AHA survey. If one were to measure the exogenous impact of property rights on the pricing (given costs) of individual hospitals, profit-seekers would be expected to have higher prices than nonprofit hospitals, and both would have higher prices than government hospitals. However, there are two complications.

First, the measures of prices is a market average. Since profit-seeking hospitals are widely thought to be more aggressively competitive, their presence may reduce the overall price level in the market, even if their own prices are higher than comparable nonprofit firms in the same market.[16] The second complication cuts the other way. The model treats the proportion of nonprofit and profit-seeking hospitals as exogenous. However, Ross Mullner and Jack Hadley (1984) have empirically confirmed that profit-seeking hospitals seek out less competitive markets. Quality, costs, and prices are all expected to be lower for governmental hospitals. Indeed, many government hospitals cater to Medicaid and nonpaying indigent consumers almost exclusively. Thus, the effect of property rights on hospital charges is ambiguous.

The input price variables include an index of nursing wages, WNURSE, based on Census figures for the SMSA wages of registered nurses, licensed practical nurses and nurses' aids and orderlies. The index is formed using expenditure weights (.51 for RNs, .16 for LPNs, and .32 for aides and orderlies) based on national employment statistics for the three occupations. A measure of hospital input costs, the average housing cost, PHOUSE, is taken from the Census. PHOUSE is used to measure construction and land costs.

The other standardizing variables, OTHER, include the average length of stay, medical school affiliation, employee unionization, local government health expenditures and the proportion of the hospital beds in the market for which all variables are not available. The average length of stay is important since the cost of hospital days declines very steeply with increases in the length of stay. Thus, in markets where stays tend to be long for any reason, the costs and prices per day will tend to be lower from this purely mechanical effect. Hospitals affiliated with medical schools typically offer more services and higher technology (imperfectly captured by our other variables) due to their teaching and research roles. Hospitals with a high proportion of employee union membership would be expected to pay higher wages and hire fewer personnel.

C. Geographical market definition

When one considers the importance of convenience for the patient, his doctor, and his friends and relatives, the local nature of hospital markets is clear. Thus, the SMSA will be used as the hospital market area. In the typical small or medium sized city, isolated from other metropolitan areas by farmland or other geographical barriers, the SMSA is the relevant shopping market for many goods and services, including hospital care. Indeed, SMSAs are defined to make them economically self-contained for shopping and commuting.[17]

It is unlikely that the SMSA could ever be seriously too small. But, at the other extreme, the largest SMSAs are clearly larger than hospital markets. In a large SMSA travel can take far too long for distant hospitals to be seriously considered. Further, ethnic and class differences may make consumers unwilling to patronize some geographically close hospitals. Thus, concentration measured over the largest SMSAs is understated. Use of the Herfindahl index as a measure of concentration diminishes this bias somewhat because the inclusion of an additional firm has a smaller effect as the number of firms in the market increase.

VI. EMPIRICAL RESULTS

The model is estimated by ordinary least squares, OLS, which is unbiased. It might appear that the technique of seemingly-unrelated-regressions might be used to improve efficiency. However, seemingly-unrelated-equations collapses to OLS when the independent variables are identical across equations, as is the case here (Pyndyck and Rubinfeld [1976], p. 303–304).

A. Price estimates

The regression estimates for prices are presented in Table 2. Most of the variables have the expected influences. The results are described below.[18]

1. Concentration
Concentration is negatively related to daily charges, although not significantly so. To study the quantitative effect, consider a market initially comprised of three equal sized firms. A merger between two firms would cause the Herfindahl index to rise by 0.22 (about one standard deviation for HERF). This "standard merger" would reduce daily charges by $0.72 or 1.8 percent. This relationship is statistically significant at only the 22 percent level, based on a two-tailed test.

In contrast increased concentration raises prices for the majority of laboratory charges. The most precise of these estimates, that for pap smear lab

Table 2. The effect of selected variables on hospital daily room and laboratory charges[1]

DEP VAR	CHGDR Daily Room	CHGU Urin- alysis	CHGCBC Blood Count	CHGEC Electro- cardiogram	CHGCXR Chest X-ray	CHGPS Pap Smear	CHGUGI Upper GI
HERF	-3.283 (2.687)	0.388 (0.363)	0.209 (0.342)	1.799 (0.845)	1.300 (0.814)	1.072 (0.407)	3.863 (2.14)
FEMH	93.265 (46.362)	9.749 (6.655)	-0.057 (6.271)	15.274 (15.472)	14.789 (14.860)	-1.606 (7.461)	62.372 (39.094)
MOVED	-9.717 (12.916)	-1.317 (1.825)	-4.824 (1.719)	-15.088 (15.492)	-13.320 (4.064)	-4.764 (2.046)	-37.200 (10.691)
PHONE	-2.922 (14.951)	0.523 (2.14)	0.276 (2.019)	-18.964 (4.98)	-8.063 (4.786)	-4.099 (2.402)	-12.811 (12.591)
GOVT	-2.349 (2.512)	-0.230 (0.304)	0.101 (0.286)	1.226 (0.707)	0.976 (0.678)	0.348 (0.341)	1.835 (1.783)
PROFIT	-0.476 (7.095)	-0.049 (1.017)	-0.542 (0.958)	5.889 (2.365)	2.490 (2.276)	1.825 (1.140)	4.229 (5.987)
CON	-0.033 (0.188)	0.007 (0.027)	0.061 (0.025)	0.294 (0.062)	0.297 (0.060)	0.123 (0.030)	1.321 (0.157)
GOVHEALTH	-5.115 (20.454)	6.536 (2.957)	10.781 (2.786)	15.503 (6.874)	32.391 (6.616)	11.464 (3.315)	63.613 (17.406)

Equation

R^2	0.499	0.317	0.435	0.599	0.593	0.507	0.604
Adj R^2	0.412	0.201	0.339	0.531	0.522	0.423	0.536
N	170	173	173	173	171	173	171

[1]Standard errors in parenthesis.

charges, is significant at the 1 percent level. The standard merger leads to a rise in the pap smear lab charge of about 4.1 percent of the mean (as compared to −1.8 percent for CHGDR). Concentration also plays a significant role in explaining price variation for electrocardiograms and upper gastrointestinal series. The coefficient on concentration was positive and significant at the 10 percent level in each of these regressions.

Daily room charges seem to be negatively related to concentration, while lab prices are positively related. One explanation may be that laboratory procedures are relatively well-defined so that patients are relatively unresponsive to quality variation in the consumption of these goods. Furthermore, many of these procedures can be done on an outpatient basis so that the consumer can shop amongst hospitals more readily. Thus, hospitals cannot increase the demand for laboratory procedures much by increasing quality

Table 3. The statistical significance of selected blocks

Block F-Test P-Values

	Independent Variable Blocks	
Dependent Variable	Information	Property Rights
Daily Room Price[1]		
CHGDR	0.16	0.64
Lab Prices		
CHGCXR	0.006	0.19
CHGCBC	0.0000001	0.31
CHGEC	0.00002	0.01
CHGPS	0.09	0.16
CHGUGI	0.003	0.45
CHGU	0.47	0.75
Nonprice Competition[2]		
AVGCOST	0.32	0.90
INDEXS&T	0.23	0.44
INDEXT	0.47	0.58
INDEXN	0.86	0.03

[1]See table 2.

[2]See table 4.

(broadly defined). Competition seems to be channeled into price for these procedures.

Daily charges, however, encompass a multitude of afflictions, and consumers may benefit by staying in a hospital with a variety of capabilities. Hospital beds are more likely to be tied to other services offered, causing consumers to be more responsive to variation in hospital quality. Here, hospitals would be more likely to stress nonprice competition.

2. Consumer Information

Consumer information variables were very important in explaining lab charges, with the block proving significant at the 5 percent level in four out of the six cases. On the other hand, effects on daily room charges were minor, as the INF block was significant at only the 16 percent level (see Table 3).

Individually, the proportion of female headed households, FEMH, varied directly with prices while PHONE varied indirectly, both performing as expected. MOVED, however, varied indirectly with prices, a result opposite to that which was expected, and had a much more pronounced effect on lab charges. The cause of this may be selection. Moving is a costly investment in a better future, much like higher education. Thus, consumers who have recently moved may be more able than those who have not. The movers may also be more efficient in searching.

3. *Demand and demographic variables*

A higher value for INSUR, the proportion of medical expenses paid by third parties, including Medicare and Medicaid, unexpectedly led to lower prices. Possibly, because INSUR includes Medicare and Medicaid payments, it may pick up low income as well as third party reimbursement.

Probably more important is the difficulty in measuring insurance completeness. Not only is INSUR measured with error, but many determinants of INSUR, such as age, education and income, are measured well.

As one would expect, a high value for AGED, the proportion of the population over the age of 64, also led to higher prices.

4. *Other*

Length of stay proved to be important in determining average daily room charge, where a 1.3 day rise (one standard deviation) reduced average daily room charge by about $0.60, more than 1 percent.

Certificate of Need legislation had a strong positive affect on the lab charges. A three year increase in CON (about one standard deviation), raised lab charges an average of 5 percent, with the strongest effect being a 10 percent increase in upper gastrointestinal lab charges. This indicates that CON laws indeed reduce competition among hospitals, probably by restricting future entry.

B. *Nonprice competition*

Regression estimates for the models of nonprice competition are presented in Table 4.

1. *Average cost*

Concentration is negatively related to average cost and is significant at the 1 percent level. The estimated coefficient implies that the standard merger (Herfindahl index increase of 0.22) would decrease cost by roughly $2.17 per day or 3.1 percent. Consumer information played an insignificant role explaining variation in this measure of nonprice competition.

2. *Services index*

Hospitals, compete by offering increased services and technology as well as lower prices. While we have excellent data on 29 services offered, it is very awkward to deal with 29 variables when each of them plays the same role in the theoretical analysis. To summarize these variables, we created indexes, weighting each service by its respective coefficient in a daily room price equation. These indexes weight the services according to their relative importance in explaining price variation in a sort of hedonic price equation for hospital prices. Indexes were created for all services, INDEXS&T and for

Table 4. The effect of selected variables on hospital average costs and services and technology indexes

DEP VAR	AVGCOST	INDEXS&T	INDEXT	INDEXN
	Average Cost	Services & Technology	Technology	Nursing Personnel
HERF	-9.705 (3.469)	-2.405 (1.287)	-2.646 (0.974)	-2.227 (0.842)
FEMH	76.836 (63.540)	11.356 (23.571)	2.437 (17.836)	9.786 (15.419)
MOVED	23.440 (17.421)	10.300 (6.462)	6.583 (4.890)	1.387 (4.228)
PHONE	21.341 (20.460)	-2.251 (7.590)	-1.146 (5.744)	-0.104 (4.965)
GOVT	1.294 (2.902)	-0.641 (1.076)	-0.297 (0.815)	1.840 (0.704)
PROFIT	-1.175 (9.711)	4.144 (3.602)	2.708 (2.726)	-2.099 (2.356)
CON	0.151 (0.254)	0.052 (0.094)	0.030 (0.071)	0.073 (0.062)
GOVHEALTH	42.213 (28.231)	3.525 (10.472)	10.463 (7.925)	6.827 (6.851)
Equation				
R^2	0.693	0.288	0.342	0.388
Adj R^2	0.641	0.167	0.230	0.284
N	173	173	173	173

high technology services only, INDEXT. Similar indexes were created using the average cost equation and performed similarly.

Regression results indicate that hospitals in more concentrated markets offer fewer services and lower technology. Concentration is significant at the 10 percent level for the index of all services and at the 1 percent level for the index of technical services.

Quantitatively, the standard merger leads to a 0.53 decrease in the services index, INDEXS&T, which corresponds to a $0.53 decline in daily room charges or 17 percent of the standard deviation of INDEXS&T. Concentration has an even stronger affect on the technology index, INDEXT. The same merger would cause a decline in the technical services index of 0.58. which corresponds to a $0.58 decline in daily room charges or 26 percent of one standard deviation of INDEXT. Of course, total expenses would decline far more because the costly services, being less available, would be used less often.

3. *Nursing personnel*

Hospitals attract customers and physicians by improving nursing care. To (imperfectly) measure this, we created a value-weighted measure of nursing personnel per patient day, INDEXN, by weighting registered nursing time and licensed practical nurses per bed-day by their average salaries.

The resulting reduced-form equations performed as expected. Increased concentration significantly reduced nursing intensity, as the standard merger would lead to a 4.8 percent decline in this index.

Overall, the evidence is clear. Increased hospital concentration reduces nonprice competition among hospitals. As a result, hospital quality declines.

C. *Price-cost margins*

The above analysis provides insight into the price-cost margins for hospitals. It is clear that hospital costs fall as concentration increases, with the standard merger (Herfindahl index increase of 0.22) leading to a 3.1 percent decline in average cost (see Table 5). The effect on price is smaller. Average daily room charges are estimated to drop 1.8 percent, while all estimates for laboratory charges show prices increasing. Since hospital revenues are the sum of these and other charges, it is likely that overall prices rise, or at least fall more slowly than average cost. These results indicate that hospital price-cost margins rise in more concentrated markets, evidence consistent with the traditional antitrust theory (Noether [1988], Woolley [1989]) and in direct conflict with the increasing monopoly theory.

We investigated this further using accounting data to construct the Lerner Index. Theoretically, it is defined as price minus marginal cost, divided by price, giving a measure of the extent of monopoly pricing. The Lerner Index can also be thought of as a normalized measure of net margin or profit. For statistical purposes, we define the Index as hospital revenues minus costs, divided by revenues. Unfortunately, it is measured with considerable error.[19]

Higher concentration among hospitals appeared to increase profitability although the estimated effect is both imprecise and small. More interesting is the effect of consumer information on the Lerner Index. The INF block is significant at the 1 percent level and most of the coefficients have the expected signs. Apparently, consumer information plays a greater role than previously believed, even in 1970 when consumer coinsurance was low and active insurers were rare. Consumers were never as passive as the strong version of the redundant resources theory claims.

D. *Sensitivity testing*

A variety of modifications of the basic specification were estimates to be sure that our results were robust. In one test, the various blocks of explanatory variables were dropped, both singly and in combination. The basic findings

Table 5. The impact of a standard merger (0.22 increase in the Herfindahl index) on selected dependent variables

Dependent Variable	Percentage Change	Standardized Coefficient[1]
Daily Room Price		
CHGDR	-1.8	-10.4
Lab Prices		
CHGCXR	1.8	12.3
CHGCBC	0.7	5.5
CHGEC	2.5	16.1**
CHGPS	4.1	22.1***
CHGUGI	2.4	13.7*
CHGU	2.7	10.5
Nonprice Competition		
AVGCOST	-3.1	-18.5***
INDEXS&T[2]		-18.8*
INDEXT		-26.3***
INDEXN	-4.8	-24.7***

Note: *** indicates significant at the 1 percent level.
      ** indicates significant at the 5 percent level.
       * indicates significant at the 10 percent level.

---

[1]A standardized coefficient is defined as

$$\frac{\beta_x * s_x}{s_y}$$

Thus, it describes the influence of a one standard deviation increase in concentration on the dependent variable, normalized by the standard deviation of the dependent variable. For example, a one standard deviation increase in concentration (0.224), multiplied by the estimated coefficient on concentration found in the daily room charge regression (-3.283), implies a 10.4 percent of a standard deviation drop in CHGDR (which has a standard deviation of 6.898).

[2]There is no useful interpretation of the percentage change in the index of services offered, INDEXS&T and INDEXT.

were unchanged; more concentration always cut costs more than it cut prices. One result stood out. Concentration had a larger effect on both costs and prices as more standardizing variables were dropped. Other studies have found larger effects of concentration, because they included fewer standardizing variables.

Also we added variables of questionable exogenity. Again, the basic findings were robust. Some of the results are discussed below.

More beds per capita were found to decrease both costs and prices. Other studies have shown that more beds reduce physician fees.

We found weak (statistically significant at about the 25 percent level) evidence that more physicians raise costs and prices. Apparently, increased physician population does not reduce hospital competition as early writers supposed. Or perhaps the role of physicians as complements in demand to hospitals simply dominates.

VIII. SUMMARY AND CONCLUSIONS

The results of the empirical analysis in this paper indicate that broadly defined hospital quality declines in more concentrated markets. The direction of the effect of concentration on hospital charges is smaller and the direction is less clear. Prices are little, if any, lower in more concentrated markets. Hospital price-cost margins are higher in more concentrated markets. Higher concentration discourages price competition.

The data do not support the increasing monopoly theory. Further, since hospital price-cost margins do not appear to remain constant, we must reject the redundant resources theory as well, though its stress on nonprice competition rings true. The empirical results are consistent with the traditional antitrust theory.

In addition, consumer information plays a surprisingly important role. Consumer information is important in explaining hospital prices, and less important in hospital quality. Consumers are not passive; they do play a role in hospital choice.

It is likely that more recent innovations in health insurance will increase consumer awareness. With an increase in consumer copayments, and more active insurer contracting, it is likely that future hospital competition is more likely to stress price, and future antitrust activity could lead to price reductions in addition to declining hospital price-cost margins.

NOTES

1. Studies of actual medical shopping behavior support this view. Alan Booth and Nicholas Babchuk (1972, p. 94) found patients making a choice among hospitals or health service providers turning to friends and family for recommendations 73 percent of the time. Fredric Wolinsky and Steven Steiber (1982, p. 765) found social networks and the lay referrals to be important in the patient's search for physicians.
2. For our purposes, modelling hospitals as if they were all profit-seeking is a useful and appropriate simplification. Mark Pauly (1974, 1987) has shown that the hospitals' response to the external environment is similar whether they maximize profits or some other goal such as prestige or physicians' incomes.
3. With insurance that pays 100 percent of costs, consumers search only for higher quality, more pleasant amenities or more convenience. There is no price low enough to induce them to switch to another hospital, even if it were almost as favored, because they would keep none of the price savings themselves.
4. For more on the effect of insurance on competition *see* H. E. Frech (1984), Frech and Ginsburg (1978) and Joseph Newhouse (1981). For more on the impact of the growth of PPOs, HMOs and consumer copayment, *see* Frech (1988) and Frech and Ginsburg (1988).

5. A number of studies have stressed the importance of consumer information in health care markets including Booth and Babchuk (1972), Newhouse (1981), Pauly and Satterthwaite (1981), and Wolinsky and Steiber(1982).

6. For a survey of research on hospital competition, *see* Woolley and Frech (1989–90).

7. Individual physician level price elasticities of demand have been calculated in a similar way. The elasticities for physician services range from −1.75 to −5.20, slightly higher than those for hospital services (Frech 1984, fn. 12, p. 10).

8. These firm level demand estimates are far more elastic than those at the industry level. If there were no competition, the demand facing the individual hospital would reflect the lack of ability to attract customers from other hospitals by dropping price, thus the elasticity of demand would be identical to the elasticity of demand for hospital care in general, perhaps − 0.1 to −0.3.

9. Previous studies have not been able to directly examine prices, as this paper does. The closest other study is that of Noether (1987, 1988). Her dependent variable was the total gross charges per admission (price times quantity), standardized for diagnostic class. Her measure could not distinguish high pricing from high service intensity.

10. It is questionable whether all hospitals managed by a particular firm should be aggregated for analysis of competition. In many cases, the managing company cannot set pricing, quality or other policies.

11. Concentration is treated as exogenous with respect to cost and price. This is traditional (Noether [1987], Melnick and Zwanziger [1988], Zwanziger and Melnick [1988], Joskow [1982]). Also, it is difficult to imagine what additional data would be necessary to identify concentration as an endogenous variable. Further, the assumption is probably quite reasonable. Frech (1974) was able to explain very little of quantity supplied in cross section with the usual economic variables. He interprets that result as indicating that hospital supply is determined by variations in the strength of local hospital cartels. Shalit (1977) argues that local doctor-hospital cartels are important and would want to restrict hospital entry. He and others find empirically that where hospitals are more numerous, physician fees are lower.

12. Includes hospital amenities, range of services, convenience, *etc.*

13. The cost of living was generated by Glandon and Marder (1981) using econometric techniques and it is for 1978, the only year for which a full set is available. This cost of living index was adjusted so that the mean cost of living index value equals one. Thus, it corrects for cost of living variation across SMSAs, not over time.

14. While it has been often used, nursing intensity is ambiguous as a measure of quality or amenity. A hospital can have more nurses per bed-day either because it supplies high quality, responsive nursing services or because it is inefficient.

15. There are two sources of error in measuring INSUR. First, the HIAA data is estimated from partial information. Second, the process of assigning state data to SMSAs based on population is imperfect. Thus, INSUR is measured with error, while variables that are highly correlated with the true level of insurance coverage and are well measured are also included in the regressions.

16. There is some evidence that profit-seeking hospitals' costs are close to those of nonprofit ones. There is more evidence that profit-seeking hospitals' charges and margins exceed nonprofit firms' (Sloan, 1988). This implies a degree of unused monopoly power for the average nonprofit firm.

17. Analyses of patient origins for such cities show that a very high proportion of the residents receive their care within the SMSA, perhaps 75 to 90 percent, while very few of the patients in the SMSA's hospitals are from out-of-town. California Medicaid (MediCal) uses a 30–minute auto commute to define the maximum distance that they require their beneficiaries to travel to a lower-priced hospital. In small or medium SMSAs, this is usually long enough to drive from one end of the market to the other. There is some small patient flow from small cities to large ones. This has been interpreted as implying that the distant hospitals are in the same market (Morrisey, Sloan, and Valvona [1988]). We believe that most of

this flow is due to quality reputation, esoteric services, or personal connections, not competition within one market.

18. Complete regression results can be obtained from the authors.
19. There are three potential sources of error here. First, both revenues and costs include income and expenses related to other business interests. Second, as Fisher and McGowan (1983) have pointed out, there are grave logical problems in using accounting rates of return to proxy for monopoly rents. The Lerner index suffers some of the weaknesses of accounting rates of return, but since it relies more on operating costs, it is a better measure. Third, the assumed constancy of marginal costs is not correct, especially for the smaller hospitals.

REFERENCES

Booth, Alan and Nicholas Babchuk, "Seeking Health Care From New Resources," *Journal of Health and Social Behavior*, 13 (1), 90–99, March 1972.

Dranove, David, Mark Shanley, and Carol Simon, "Is Health Care Competition Wasteful? No!", unpublished paper, Graduate School of Business, University of Chicago, March 1, 1990.

Farley, Dean E., "Competition Among Hospitals: Market Structure and Its Relation to Utilization, Costs and Financial Position", Research Note 7, Hospital Studies Program, U.S. Department of Health and Human Services, National Center for Health Services Research and Health Care Technology Assessment, 1985.

Feldman, Roger and Bryan Dowd, "Is There a Competitive Market for Hospital Services?", *Journal of Health Economics*, 5 (3), 277–292, 1986.

Fisher, Franklin M., and John J. McGowan, "On the Misuse of Accounting Rates of Return to Infer Monopoly Profits", *American Economic Review*, 73 (1), 82–97, March 1983.

Frech, H. E., III, *The Regulation of Health Insurance*, Ph.D. dissertation, University of California, Los Angeles, 1974.

Frech, H. E., III, "Competition in Medical Care: Research and Policy", *Advances in Health Economics and Health Services Research*, 5, 1– 27, 1984.

Frech, H. E., III, "Preferred Provider Organizations and Health Care Competition", in: H. E. Frech, III, ed. *Health Care in America: The Political Economy of Health Care*, San Francisco: The Pacific Research Institute for Public Policy, 353–370, 1988.

Frech, H. E., III and Paul B. Ginsburg, "Competition Among Health Insurers", in: *Competition in the Health Care Sector: Past, Present and Future*, ed. by Warren Greenberg, Washington, D.C.: Federal Trade Commission, 210– 237, reprinted by Aspen System, Germantown, Maryland, 1978.

Frech, H. E., III and Paul B. Ginsburg, "Competition Among Health Insurers, Revisited," *Journal of Health, Politics, Policy and Law*, Special Issue on Competition in the Health Care Sector: Ten Years Later, ed. by Warren Greenberg, 13 (1), 279–291, Summer 1988; reprinted in: *Competition in the Health Care Sector: Ten Years Later*, ed. by Warren Greenberg, Durham, N.C.: Duke University Press, 57–70, 1988.

Glandon, Gerald D. and William D. Marder, "A Comprehensive Set of Cost of Living Estimates", unpublished paper, Center for Health Policy Research, American Medical Association, 1981.

Hersch, Phillip L., "Competition and the Performance of Hospital Markets", *Review of Industrial Organization*, 1 (4), 324–340, Winter 1984.

Joskow, Paul L., "The Effects of Competition and Regulation on Hospital Bed Supply and the Reservation Quality of the Hospital", *Bell Journal of Economics*, 11 (2), 421–447, Autumn 1980.

Lee, Robert H., and Donald M. Waldman, "The Diffusion of Innovations in Hospitals", *Journal of Health Economics*, 4, 373–380, 1985.

Lucas-Roberts, D., "Results of the 1986 Eugene Clinic Image Survey", memo to Dr. Craig, Dr. Hirons and D. Vanberg, 1986.

Luft, Harold S., Susan C. Maerki, James C. Robinson, Deborah W. Garnick, and Stephen J. McPhee, "The Role of Specialized Clinical Services in Competition Among Hospitals", *Inquiry*, 23 (1), 83–94, Spring 1986.

Melnick, Glenn A. and Jack Zwanziger, "Hospital Behavior Under Competition and Cost-Containment Policies", *Journal of the American Medical Association*, 260 (18), 2669–2675, November 11, 1988.

Morrisey, Michael A., Frank A. Sloan and Joseph Valvona, "Defining Geographic Markets for Health Care", *Law and Contemporary Problems*, 51 (2), 165–194, Spring 1988.

Mullner, Ross and Jack Hadley, "Interstate Variations in the Growth of Chain-Owned Proprietary Hospitals: 1973–1982." *Inquiry*, 21 (2), 144–151, Summer 1984.

Nelson, Phillip, "Information and Consumer Behavior", *Journal of Political Economy*, 78 (2), 311–329, March/April 1970.

Newhouse, Joseph P., "The Erosion of the Medical Marketplace." *Advances in Health Economics and Health Services Research*, 2, 1–34, 1981.

Noether, Monica *Competition Among Hospitals*, Staff Report of the Bureau of Economics, Federal Trade Commission, 1987.

Noether, Monica, "Competition Among Hospitals", *Journal of Health Economics*, 7 (3), 259–279, 1988.

Olson, Mancur, "Commentary: Organization and Financing of Medical Care," *Medical Care*, 23 (5), 432–437, May 1985.

Pauly, Mark V., "Behavior of Nonprofit Hospital Monopolies: Alternative Models of the Hospital", in: Clark C. Havighurst ed. *Regulating Health Facilities Construction*, Washington D. C.: American Enterprise Institute, 143–161, 1974.

Pauly, Mark V., "Nonprofit Firms in Medical Markets", *American Economic Review*, 77 (2), 257–262, May 1987.

Pauly, Mark V. and Mark A. Satterthwaite, "The Pricing of Primary Care Physicians' Services: A Test of the Role of Consumer Information", *Bell Journal of Economics*, 12 (2), 488–506, Autumn 1981.

Pyndyck, Robert S. and Daniel L. Rubinfeld *Econometric Models and Economic Forecasts*, New York: McGraw-Hill, 1976.

Rappaport, John, "Diffusion of Technological Innovation Among Non-Profit Firms: A Case Study of Radioisotopes in U.S. Hospitals", *Journal of Economics and Business*, 30 (2), 108–118, Winter 1978.

Robinson, James C., and Harold S. Luft, "The Impact of Hospital Market Structure on Patient Volume, Average Length of Stay, and the Cost of Care", *Journal of Health Economics*, 4 (4), 333–356, 1985.

Robinson, James C., and Harold S. Luft, "Competition, Regulation, and Hospital Costs, 1982–1986", *Journal of the American Medical Association*, 260 (18), 2676–2681, November 11, 1988.

Robinson, James C., Deborah W. Garnick, and Stephen J. McPhee, "Market and Regulatory Influences on the Availability of Coronary Angioplasty and Bypass Surgery in U.S. Hospitals", *The New England Journal of Medicine*, 317 (2), 85–90, July 9, 1987.

Romeo, Anthony A., Judith L. Wagner, and Robert H. Lee, "Prospective Reimbursement and the Diffusion of New Technologies in Hospitals", *Journal of Health Economics*, 3 (1), 1–24, April 1984.

Russell, Louise B. *Technology in Hospitals: Medical Advances and Their Diffusion*, Washington D.C.: The Brookings Institution, 1979.

Salkever, David D., "Competition Among Hospitals", in: Warren Greenberg, ed., *Competition in the Health Care Sector, Past, Present, and Future*, Germantown MD: Aspen Systems Corporation, 159–162, 1978.

Satterthwaite, Mark A., "Consumer Information, Equilibrium Industry Price, and the Number of Sellers", *Bell Journal of Economics*, 10 (2), 483–504, Autumn 1979.

Shalit, Sol., "A Doctor-Hospital Cartel Theory." *Journal of Business*, 50 (1), 1–20, January 1977.

Sloan, Frank A., Joseph Valvona, and James M. Perrin, "Diffusion of Surgical Technology", *Journal of Health Economics*, 5, 31–61, 1986.

Sloan, Frank A., "Property Rights in the Hospital Industry", in: H. E. Frech II ed. *Health Care in America: The Political Economy of Hospitals and Health Insurance*, San Francisco: The Pacific Research Institute for Public Policy, 103–141, 1988.

Stiglitz, Joseph E., "Competition and the Number of Firms in a Market: Are Duopolies More Competitive than Atomistic Markets?", *Journal of Political Economy*, 95 (5), 1041–1061, October 1987.

Wolinsky, Fredric D., and Steven R. Steiber, "Salient Issues in Choosing a New Doctor," *Social Science and Medicine*, 16 (7), 759–767, 1982.

Woolley, J. Michael, "The Competitive Effects of Horizontal Mergers in the Hospital Industry." *Journal of Health Economics*, 8 (3), 271–291, September 1989.

Woolley, J. Michael and H. E. Frech III, "How Hospitals Compete: A Review of the Literature", *Journal of Law and Public Policy*, 2 (1), 57–79, 1989.

Working For Patients, CM555, Department of Health, London: Her Majesties Stationary Office, 1989.

Zaretsky, Henry W., *Preliminary Results of Analysis of Modesto City Hospital and the Economic Impact of Its Acquisition*, Sacramento: Henry W. Zaretsky and Associates, 1984.

Zwanziger, Jack and Glenn A. Melnick, "The Effects of Hospital Competition and the Medicare PPS Program on Hospital Cost Behavior in California", *Journal of Health Economics*, 7 (4), 301–321, 1988.

APPENDIX

Data Definitions and Sources

Dependent Variable

Prices

CHGDR Average daily charge for an adult inpatient in a two-bed room (1970 American Hospital Association Survey of Hospital Charges, AHASHC). Dollar values here and throughout the data are adjusted by the cost of living within the SMSA. The index is from Glandon and Marder (1981).

CHGU Average charge for urinalysis, including professional fees (AHASHC).

CHGCBC As above for a complete blood count.

CHGEC As above for an electrocardiogram.

CHGCXR As above for a chest x-ray.

CHGPS As above for a pap smear.

CHUGI As above for an upper gastrointestinal series.

Nonprice Competition

AVGCOST Average hospital expense per adjusted patient day in 1970 (1970 American Hospital Association Survey of Hospitals, AHASH).

INDEXS&T Index of services, with weights taken from regression of full model, including services, on daily charges.

INDEXT Index of technical services (COBALT, EEG, ICU, INTCRD,

ORGNBK, RADISO, RADIUM, RENLIP, RENLOP), constructed as INDEXS&T, above.

INDEXN Index of nurses per adjusted bed-day, weights equal to average annual salaries of RNs ($6712) and LPNs ($4795) (1970 Bureau of the Census, BC and 1971 *Statistical Abstract*).

Independent Variables

Concentration

HERF Herfindahl index constructed with adjusted patient days (AHASH).

Information Block

FEMH Proportion of families with a female head (CCDB)
MOVED Proportion of housing units moved into between 1965 and 1970 (CCDB).
PHONE Proportion of households with telephone available (CCDB).

Demand Block

INCOME Mean income (BC).
INSUR Proportion of hospital costs paid by Blue Cross, Medicare, Medicaid, or private insurers, 1969 (Data set used in Russell (1979).
POP Population, 1970 (CCDB).
POPCHNG Proportion of 1970 to 1960 population (BC).
Property Rights Block

GOVT Proportion of adjusted patient days in a government controlled hospital (AHASH).
PROFIT Proportion of adjusted patient days in a profit seeking hospital (AHASH).

Input Prices Block

WNURSE Index of nurse wages. Calculated as a weighted average salary of registered nurses, licensed practical nurses, and aides and orderlies. The weights are 0.51, 0.16, and 0.32 respectively (BC, and *The* 1971 *Statistical Abstract*).
PHOUSE Median price of a home in 1970 (CCDB).

Demographic Block

AGED Proportion of population age 65 or over (BC).
KIDS Proportion of population age 14 and under (BC).

FEMALE Proportion of population that is female (BC).
WHITE Proportion of population that is white (BC).
COLLEGE Proportion of population with a college degree (BC).
PAFDC Proportion of population receiving aid to families with dependent children (CCDB).

Other Block

LOS Average length of stay (AHASH).
UNION Proportion of adjusted patient days in hospital with a collective bargaining agreement (AHASH).
CON Number of years that certificate of need legislation had been in place (LR).
BCSHARE Market share of Blue Cross in 1973 (The Blue Cross - Blue Shield Fact Book).
MEDSCH Proportion of adjusted patient days in hospital affiliated with a medical school (AHASH).
GOVHEALTH Local government health expenditure per capita (CCDB).
PROPDROP Proportion of statistical beds in hospitals which did not report either adjusted patient days, expenses, or revenues (AHASH).

Services Block

COBALT Proportion of adjusted patient days in hospitals with cobalt therapy (AHASH).
EEG As above for electro-encephalography units.
ICU As above for intensive care units
INTCRD As above for intensive cardiac care facilities.
OPENHT As above for open heart surgery facilities.
ORGNBK As above for an organ bank.
RADISO As above for radioisotope therapy facilities.
RADIUM As above for radium therapy facilities.
RENLIP As above for inpatient renal dialysis facilities.
RENLOP As above for outpatient renal dialysis facilities.
BLODBK As above for a blood bank.
ECU As above for extended care units.
HISTO As above for histopathology laboratories.
INHAL As above for inhalation therapy departments.
XRAY As above for x-ray therapy facilities.
EMBAS As above for a basic emergency department.
EMMAJ As above for a major emergency department.
EMPRV As above for a provisional emergency department.
PHYSTH As above for a physical therapy department.
PRENUR As above for premature baby care facilities.
PSYEM As above for emergency psychiatric facilities.

PSYOP As above for psychiatric outpatient units.
PSYPIP As above for psychiatric inpatient units.
REHBIP As above for inpatient rehabilitation facilities.
SELFCR As above for self-care facilities.

VARIABLE MEANS AND STANDARD DEVIATIONS

Block	Variable	Mean	Standard Deviation
DEPENDENT			
Daily Room Price			
	CHGDR	40.581	6.898
Lab Prices			
	CHGCXR	16.497	2.279
	CHGCBC	6.763	0.917
	CHGEC	15.861	2.457
	CHGPS	5.805	1.056
	CHGUGI	36.611	6.117
	CHGU	3.275	0.802
Nonprice Competition			
	AVGCOST	69.998	11.746
	INDEXS&T	1.131	2.876
	INDEXT	3.002	2.195
	INDEXN	10.163	1.935
INDEPENDENT			
Concentration			
	HERF	0.347	0.224
*Information*t			
	FEMH	0.106	0.020
	MOVED	0.514	0.077
	PHONE	0.889	0.050
Demand			
	INCOME	3031.471	318.811
	INSUR	0.802	0.136
	POP	661.798	1257.492
	POPCHNG	0.190	0.191
Property Rights			
	GOVT	0.141	0.212
	PROFIT	0.029	0.071
Input Prices			
	WNURSE	5.411	0.502

	PHOUSE	16.288	3.197

Demographic

	AGED	0.095	0.028
	KIDS	0.288	0.025
	FEMALE	0.513	0.012
	WHITE	0.901	0.086
	COLLEGE	0.057	0.019
	PAFDC	0.047	0.022

Other

	LOS	8.074	1.314
	UNION	0.859	0.253
	CON	2.665	2.773
	BCSHARE	34.992	14.931
	MEDSCH	0.209	0.291
	GOVHEALTH	0.235	0.042
	PROPDROP	0.163	0.155

Services

	COBALT	0.412	0.284
	EEG	0.756	0.279
	ICU	0.901	0.166
	INTCRD	0.760	0.255
	OPENHT	0.226	0.254
	ORGNBK	0.099	0.190
	RADISO	0.850	0.168
	RADIUM	0.714	0.255
	RENLIP	0.291	0.278
	RENLOP	0.191	0.215
	BLODBK	0.798	0.260
	ECU	0.135	0.229
	HISTO	0.910	0.127
	INHAL	0.917	0.153
	XRAY	0.730	0.256
	EMBAS	0.407	0.285
	EMMAJ	0.441	0.297
	EMPRV	0.133	0.245
	PHYSTH	0.931	0.144
	PRENUR	0.778	0.233
	PSYEM	0.373	0.297
	PSYOP	0.250	0.268
	PSYPIP	0.467	0.277
	REHBIP	0.215	0.238
	SELFCR	0.153	0.218

PART FOUR

Health care in the political arena

Cost containment in health care: Justification and consequences*

KLAUS-DIRK HENKE

FB Wirtschaftswissenschaften, Universität Hannover, Wunstorferstrasse 14, DW-3000 Hannover 91, Germany

I I I

I I 8

I. Cost containment as a principle of health care policy

1. The Issue

Cost Containment has been for more than a decade one of the major objectives of health care policy in almost all industrial nations. For many experts cost figures and their annual growth rates are the most important criterion to assess the health care sector. To politicians as well as to the public cost containment per se establishes a success of health care policy.

At the same time economists claim that cost containment itself is not an objective per se and not a sensible aim to pursue (Culyer 1989). A cost containment policy takes as its starting point a given cost figure. Yet as long as health care resources are not allocated on markets via the price mechanism it remains an open question whether this figure represents an appropriate and desired level of health care spending. Spending might in fact be too high but it might also be too low, so that cost containment is out of place. The appropriateness of a given sum of health care expenditures cannot be judged without reference to the benefit side, *i.e.* the outcome of health care expenditures.

However there are also economists who argue that even if expenditures and their outcome are considered simultaneously an optimal quota of health expenditures can only be derived from a perspective of welfare economics. In reality an optimal rate of health care expenditures or an optimal payroll tax rate cannot be determined (Sachverständigenrat für die Konzertierte Aktion im Gesundheitswesen, 1987). As the preferences are concealed, the economist can only ask for a system of health care that is both effective and

---

*I would like to thank Cornelia Behrens, Fredrich Breyer, and Peter Zweifel for valuable comments.

efficient. How much society is willing to spend for health care depends on
its willingness to pay in a given institutional arrangement (Gäfgen 1984).

2. Cost Concepts and Approaches to Cost Containment

In health care, different cost concepts and consequently different approaches
to cost containment do exist. It is a widespread practice to consider as
costs, health expenditures expressed as a percentage share of GDP. Cost
containment policy then focuses on this indicator whereas the necessity for
and the range of cost containment are established by comparing health
expenditure figures across different countries. Even if the several problems
connected to cross national comparisons of health expenditure ratios (*e.g.*
definition of health care sectors, price adjustments, inclusion or non-inclusion
of various transfer payments, tax expenditures) can be solved these input
oriented ratios are of limited importance. They only give some preliminary
information about the magnitudes of resources absorbed for health care. In
regard to questions of employment and growth, however, these figures reflect – if GDP is growth adjusted – some initial information on the opportunity costs of allocating these resources to the health care sector (Appendix
1, Figure 1).

Often the expenditures are reported as *per capita* figures to account for
different population sizes. Using this information Appendix 2 (Table 1)
shows the "success" of cost containment in different nations. As can be seen
from the data West Germany appears to be most successful in cost control,
a fact not easy to be explained as many influences (cost containment laws,
"concerted actions" to control expenditures, expenditures caps, prospective
budgets, co-payments) overlap.

Cost containment could also refer to the payment of production factors
like labor and capital. In this case of value added being the indicator, wages,
salaries, and profits of the participants in health care services must be kept
under control. In a market economy, however, this approach of cost containment would not have to be taken into account because factor pricing is left
to competition and market forces, expecting that they are leading under
certain conditions to cost efficient solutions. In reality, however, there are
labor markets with trade unions and employer associations defining the level
of wages. This is true for nurses and salaried doctors but not the case for
office-based physicians working under fee-for-service arrangements. Their
negotiations with the funds are determined to a large extent by the state of
the general economy and their bargaining power.

Thirdly cost containment can mean setting fixed premiums or as it is the
case in countries with Bismarck-type social security system stabilizing payroll
tax rates (Appendix 3, Figure 2). Revenue oriented expenditure policy is
e.g. the approach to stabilize health care costs in Germany. Instead of
controlling expenditures directly, Germany is trying to control them by freezing the payroll tax rate. Depending on the definition of the tax base, its upper

and lower limits and the size of the insured population, annual revenue, and annual expenditure will indeed fluctuate according to the level of business activity in the economy.

Finally cost containment could refer to the transaction costs for the patient, an almost neglected concept in health care. Transport, information cost, and waiting costs are concepts on which cost containment could focus, too (Adam 1983). This approach, however, is rarely included in the debate on cost containment. It is not even clear whether the transaction costs decline as one would assume with an increasing supply of doctors, beds *etc.*.

Up to this point cost concepts and approaches to cost containment basically refer to the health care sector as a whole. It is also possible and necessary to consider cost containment in selected areas of health care, *e.g.* dental care, ambulatory care, in-patient care, or pharmaceutical care. In case of budgets being allocated to different types of care, it is very likely that sub-budgets and quotas will be the consequence of cost containment; measurement problems change accordingly. In these cases cost containment refers to the relative expenditure shares in the total budget respectively sub-budgets.

Furthermore the disaggregation of cost containment may lead to a measurement that is related to population groups (*e.g.* by age), regions, health services, diseases, *etc.*. The need for disaggregation of the measurement of cost containment depends furthermore on the specific organization of the health care sector (*e.g.* England, Germany, United States) and the different strategies of cost containment.

3. *Containment of Direct or Indirect Costs?*

Cost containment policy is usually related to direct costs which represent the resources used in health care (Appendix 4, Table 2), not to indirect costs which represent the loss for resources due to premature death and avoidable morbidity (Appendix 4, Table 3). The indirect costs of illness are rarely mentioned in discussions of cost containment. Indirect costs of mortality and morbidity comprise the estimated cost or value to society of all deaths and the loss of output imposed upon society by illness and disability during a certain period of time. As the human capital approach to quantify the value of a human life in monetary terms is not unanimously accepted it should be mentioned that the indirect costs due to disability (morbidity) and premature death (mortality) could alternatively be measured in real terms by
– the number of deaths,
– total life years lost,
– total work-years lost in production due to short-term illness of the currently employed, due to disability, and due to premature mortality (Appendix 4, Table 4).
Total economic costs of diseases thus consist of direct and indirect costs. The shape of the respective cost curves is given in Figure 1.

Indirect Costs (C^{ind}) are inversely related to the health status of the

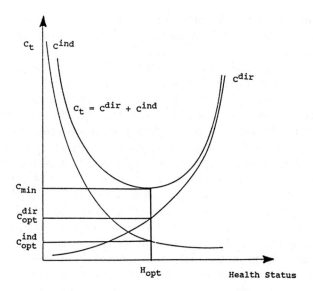

C^{dir}:	direct health care costs
C^{ind}:	indirect costs
C_t:	total health care costs
C_{min}:	minimum combination of direct costs and indirect costs
H_{opt}:	optimal health status
C^{dir}_{opt}:	Optimal direct cost of "health production"
C^{ind}_{opt}:	Optimal indirect cost of "health production"

Fig. 1. Direct and Indirect Costs in Health Care.

population. Direct costs (C^{dir}) on the other hand increase, because it is more and more costly to realize additional gains in the health status of the population. Total health care costs (C_t) are at a minimum where health status reaches its optimal level, thus giving the cost minimal budget H^{opt}. As the figures in Appendix 4, Table 2 and 3, are in relative terms they cannot be used to infer deviations from the optimum in Figure 1. In case of absolute figures a ratio of direct and indirect costs would represent an ex-post-relation for a disease-specific health status. To obtain the optimum in Figure 1, the shape of the curves must be known for each disease. Furthermore it has to be taken into account that the utility function is not fully specified.

As traditional cost containment policy is restricted to cutting back expenditures, risk prevention and the loss of value added by illness play only a minor role in health policy and in public opinion. Containing expenditures could mean that savings occur at the wrong end, in particular if a health policy is called for which places greater emphasis on prevention and health instead of traditional health care (Rice, *et al.* 1985; Henke, Behrens 1986; Hodgson 1989). Avoiding diseases and accidents, postponing illnesses, reducing the risk of morbidity, and achieving a higher life expectancy are objectives of prevention. Their realization may be important for the future development of expenditures as well. Thus cost containment may require a broader concept than just controlling direct costs (Appendix 5, Table 5).

On the other hand it can be argued that measuring indirect costs and taking them as an objective is nothing more than asking for an output-oriented perspective of health policy. Reducing avoidable morbidity and mortality is nothing else but pursuing the objectives of medicine and health policy. Avoiding a loss of resources due to premature death and avoidable morbidity is an objective of health policy. Thus a reduction of indirect costs ("cost containment") is the same as an increase in the population's level of health. The important question, however, refers to the influence of direct costs (expenditures) on the health status. Direct costs as represented in Figure 2 are only one factor influencing the health status of a population. Additional factors influencing the health status are listed in Figure 2 and should be included in a functional approach to avoid mortality and morbidity.

It is possible that further extensions in health care expenditures would not necessarily improve the health status any more and that we might have reached the limits of medicine and health care as a vehicle to improve the health status (*see* for an analytical framework according to this kind of approach Evans and Stoddart 1990).

II. THE JUSTIFICATION OF COST CONTAINMENT

1. *The Antagonism between Medicine and Economics as a Crucial Issue*

Different arguments are put forward to justify or reject cost containment in the sense of controlling health care expenditures. Perhaps the most important arguments have their roots in the antagonism between medicine and economics. This antagonism is best described by the fact that physicians regard cost containment as being inhuman because it seems to refuse medical services to potential patients. These arguments are used by medical associations to resist cost containment. Considering the broadly defined objectives of medicine
- postponing avoidable death,
- preventing, curing, relieving of disease, pain and indisposition,
- rehabilitation of physical and mental functions,
- safeguarding of the dignity and freedom of the individual even during illness and dying,
- physicians will basically always try to provide a maximum amount of services, *e.g.* all services with a positive marginal benefit to the health status of the population. The demand for resources as seen from the perspective of medical science is unlimited. Furthermore it also reflects income interests of the individual physician whereby the realization of

1. Demographic and socioeconomic determinants.

Age	Income
Sex	Occupation
Skin color	Education
Marital status	Place of residence
Family size	Position in working process

2. Individual determinants
Hereditary factors
Medical history
Family situation
Life style
Eating and drinking habits
Health awareness
Attention to symptoms

3. Structural determinants
Working conditions
Living conditions
Road safety
Insurance coverage
Sick pay
Health care expenditures (direct costs)

4. Medical determinants
Availability of medical services
Utilization of medical services
Level of medical knowledge
Development of medical technology

Concerning the importance of various determinants *see e.g.* Auster, *et al.* 1969 and Dever 1976.

Fig. 2. Main determinants of the population's level of mortality and morbidity.

demand and income interest also depend on the character of incentives of the financing systems and the overall organization of the health care sector.

In addition the individual patient expects maximum treatment. Besides, the individual is guided by the ideal of "healthy aging" which may be reached by successful prevention. The ambitious WHO definition of health as a state of unlimited physical, mental, and social well-being and not just as the absence of illness and handicaps can also be referred to in this context. This is of course an important aspect if illness in this very unspecified sense is covered by health insurance (Schwartz 1988).

Finally a potentially unlimited social need does exist deriving from the adjunction of insurance claims handled by a system of special courts, dealing with industrial relations and social security disputes (Sozialgerichte). These courts are generally inclined towards a generous interpretation of the claimer rights and play a major role in W.-Germany.

This argumentation leads to several conflicts and consequences as society is not likely and sometimes will resist to spend more than a certain share of

GDP for health. Health versus other objectives is the first level of the antagonism from an economic perspective. Besides the effectiveness of medical services has to be doubted and compared to other means. The fact that diagnostic and therapeutic services are often arbitrary, leads to the possibility of a supplier induced demand respectively supplier induced morbidity. Thus health care versus other means is the second level of the antagonism from an economic perspective.

If society is not able to make adequate public use of private interest (Schultze 1975), cost containment in the sense of expenditure and revenue control might be the only answer to the conflict between economics and the scarcity of resources on the one hand and the objectives and the unlimited demand of medicine, and the patients on the other. An adequately organized health care system, however, would install incentives to produce an efficient and effective provision of health care in a less arbitrary manner in contradiction to reality in most nations right now. Thus cost containment appears as a means of controlling the unlimited claim on resources by medicine.

To draw a conclusion the conflict between the objectives of medicine and the scarcity of resources could be used as an argument for, but at the same time as an argument against cost containment. Even in countries with already high expenditures there is still some scope for extending treatment which in fact yields additional benefits. From an economic perspective the necessity of rationing is indispensable giving the scarcity of resources. Only if the benefit-cost ratio is higher for additional treatment than anything else, the antagonism disappears.

In reality there is a dilemma that takes on different forms and calls for different solutions according to the perspectives taken of the health care sector. The rationing process with all its ethical consequences present in the individual relationship between doctors and patients differs from the rationing process reflected in the negotiations between doctors and funding bodies over contracts and remuneration. These levels are again different from the global perspective of a regional or federal authority matching needs with available resources (Henke 1986). On all these levels of the allocation process in health care the conflict between medicine and economics is existent, but rarely solved in a functional approach by referring to a production function of health (*see* pages 5–7).

2. *Arguments in Favor of Cost Containment*

Apart from the argument that cost containment in the form of given budgets or quotas may be considered as an answer to the "arbitrariness" of medicine there are other arguments to state the case for cost containment.

One argument accepts cost containment through a parliamentary process as a political decision about a desirable use of income. This is in particular true for tax funded national health services. Health care expenditures are treated like any other kind of public expenditures. In countries with a social security system this argument is also valid if the parliament controls expenditures either directly or indirectly by defining the total revenue available for health care, *e.g.* by payroll tax rate stability as part of the health insurance law as it is the case in Germany since 1977.

Fixed expenditures and sub-budgets, *i.e.* strict cost containment, may lead to more efficiency than a system with open-end financing in the sense that all participants may find this an incentive to use the resources more effectively and more efficiently. It leads to a tendency to reimburse only the most important services, seen from a medical point of view. This argument is especially important if signs of waste and inefficiency are evident in health care. Here savings are possible without reducing the quality of health care.

The political demand for payroll tax rate stability in statutory health insurance systems - as it is the case in Germany - is justified with different arguments. Lower contributions to the social security system will not only reduce labor costs but will also reduce the public share of the economy and thus stimulate market forces. Along these lines taxation in general and payroll taxes in particular should be reduced to promote growth, employment, and competition (Sachverständigenrat für die Konzertierte Aktion im Gesundheitswesen 1988). A high burden of social security taxes enforces the shadow economy leading to lower contributions into the social security system. This in turn raises the burden for the payroll tax payer to an inequitable level.

In addition the payroll tax burden and the distribution of income taxation are interrelated and should be coordinated within the overall tax policy of a country. For example a major income tax reform leading to a large tax reduction should not be undermined by increasing payroll tax rates. Cuts in income taxes are not a means to finance increasing payroll taxes for health care expenditures, although there might be a tendency to demand more health care with a higher net income. Thus there are some arguments in favor of cost containment which do not relate directly to the health care sector but to the economy as a whole.

3. *Arguments Against Cost Containment*

The first argument against cost containment derives from the discussion about the antagonism between medicine and economics. As long as medical services yield benefits to society cost containment is regarded as inhuman and unjustifiable. In particular if the population does want to spend more on health, organizational structures are needed to allow them to do so. In tax funded systems the population does not decide directly on the amount and structure of health care expenditures and in insurance based systems which rely on global budgets and extensive planning processes there is no adequate participation of the insured population either

This argument is further developed in Figure 3. For a situation in which

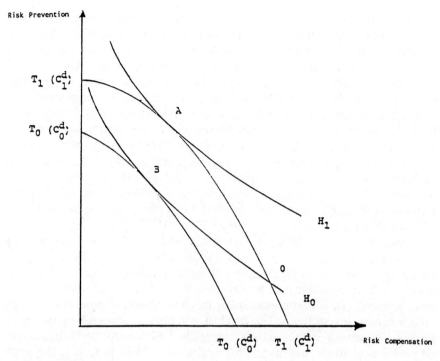

C = Direct Costs.
H = Health Status.
T = Production Possibility Curve.

Fig. 3. Higher Health Status with a given Budget (A) versus given Health Status with a lower Budget (B).

inefficiency in health care is prevailing it is shown that society has got two alternative strategies to choose from. In Figure 3 risk prevention and risk compensation are the two forms of risk provision. Risk prevention (RP) aims at reducing the incidence of losses whereas risk compensation (RC) of unavoidable losses increases the costs of treatment.

If the production of health (H_0, H_1) consists of these two goods, A and B represent two optimal solutions. Starting from the initial inefficient situation O of a country, society has to choose in which direction to go. The same amount of money T_1 (C_1^d) can buy more health at A, whereas alternatively the same health status could be realized with less money at B. A cost minimizing strategy will go for B and employs expenditure cuts to realize possible efficiency gains; maximizing the health status means to reach the highest health status possible with a given budget. In reality situations between A and B may occur and could be evaluated with the help of cost-effectiveness-studies (*see* in detail Henke 1991).

Apart from the argument according to Figure 3 that cost containment always involves opportunity costs (a) in terms of the health status in not reaching A on H_1, and (b) in regard to the reduction of the payment to the factors of production and of the purchase of commodities and services (buildings, equipment, beds per room, quality of infrastructure, *etc.*), in the case of B on H_0 there exist other arguments to reject cost containment.

Payroll taxes are not only a component of labor costs. Since these taxes are in turn spent, they also constitute demand for commodities and services. Health care is a growing industry; in Germany almost all of the newly created jobs during the last 15 years may be found in this sector. Thus cost containment could lead to less employment and growth. Yet resources not employed in health care would not be idle, but used for other areas of public or private economic activity (for a detailed discussion of this aspect *see* Evans 1990 and Zweifel 1985).

Another argument relates to payroll tax and – to a lesser extent – to tax financed systems. If revenue orientation is the basis for the growth of expenditures, this means that in times of increasing employment and growth more money is available for health care than in times of recession and unemployment. Thus cost containment through revenue oriented measures is not a convincing strategy. The level of revenues determined by the level of economic activity is then only accidentally sufficient to match the needs and preferences of the population for health care. Most probably, the level of business activity and the health status are positively correlated as it is known that unemployment deteriorates the health status. A revenue oriented system financed by an income related payroll tax, is insofar not an adequate basis to finance the system, as it links the health care budget to the business cycle and thus is pro cyclical.

A major argument against cost containment in the form of payroll tax rate stability refers to the danger of discouraging innovation. The status quo will be stabilized, if all participants claim additional income according to the development of wages and salaries, *i.e.* the current tax base of social insurance systems. If this is the case, all sectors in health care maintain their respective shares of the total budget, so that a necessary restructuring between sectors and subsectors will not take place. As long as this function is fulfilled neither by the market nor by parliaments economic and medical guidelines are needed to steer the health care sector. Thus cost containment requires macro and micro management in regard to the structure of the expenditures. Certain institutions (*e.g.* health care conferences, advisory bodies) are called for to equate marginal benefits of different categories of health care expenditures. This process is further complicated since it might involve a consideration of benefits of expenditures in other sectors than the health sector as well. These benefits may exceed or fall short of the benefits in health care. This illustrates again how arbitrary it is to start cost containment at a given level if an optimal health quota is and will be unknown.

Finally cost containment is a misleading principle. Against the background of the variety of expenditure carriers in health care, *e.g.* public households, statutory health-, statutory pension- and statutory accident insurance, private households, or public and private employers, containing costs in one or several sectors may in other sectors set off adjustment processes leading to increasing costs. Stable payroll tax rates alone are no proof or criterion of a successful cost containment policy.

4. Who is interested in achieving cost containment?

This question can be answered straightforwardly by identifying those participants in health care who support the various arguments for cost containment. In regard to the first two arguments in favor of cost containment those groups are favoring cost control who opt for public solutions and decisions in health care. In case of an inefficient and ineffective health care system only those participants who believe in more elaborate planning methods and more interventions are in favor of cost containment. In regard to the third line of reasoning according to which cost containment is justified by arguments that do not refer to the immediate benefits of health expenditures, those groups are interested in cost containment who profit from low labor costs. Here the demand of cost containment is voiced by private and public employers who pay part of the contribution rates to the social security system and who want to keep labor costs under control. The insured population gains from cost containment only if the same overall health status can be realized with lower expenditures and if there is no trade-off between health and other objectives. In case the status quo is already efficient in the health care sector, they only gain from the non-health benefits of cost containment. Finally those politicians are in favor of cost containment who believe that this strategy increases their power to intervene into and to manage the health care sector.

An alternative system steered by incentives and self-regulating mechanisms reduces the influence and power of politicians. This argument carries a different weight in the UK, Spain and the nordic countries on the one hand and continental middle and southern European nations on the other hand. National health systems being among the most important areas of public employment in the countries in question have a particular interest in cost control and planning processes. This is one of the explanations why management of health care plays such a dominant role in these countries. It is not by chance that the evaluation of health care, cost-effectiveness studies, league tables, *etc.* are so advanced in these countries compared to the other European countries. The latter, however, seem to go into the same direction if cost control is something that can be accomplished only through planning rather than by better incentives. For this reason the planning and management literature is more advanced in the UK and the nordic countries. In European countries with social insurance systems other issues are at the center of the debate. The role of incentives in the context of organizational reforms of health insurance, the principle of self employment of health care providers, especially office-based physicians, the future of self government in health care, the autonomy of the participants in health care or the relative importance of payroll tax funding are examples.

5. *Better Incentives as the Alternative to Cost Containment*

The discussion of the various arguments for and against cost containment indicates that a politically defined ratio is not necessarily matching the need respectively the preferences of the population. The opportunity costs of cost containment reveal the burden society may carry *e.g.* in terms of growth, employment and innovation. Modifications are necessary in regard to tax funded and payroll tax funded systems. In tax funded systems there automatically exists an overall budget, defined by parliament, whereas in social security systems the level of annual expenditures is not known *ex ante*. Furthermore there are important differences between the two systems as to how the supply side (hospitals, doctors, pharmaceutical care, *etc.*) is financed and regulated through contracts with federal, regional and/or local Governmental or self-governmental agencies.

Cost containment is not an objective *per se*. Even as a principle of health care policy it is merely an ultimate political answer to the future challenges of health care. From an economic and medical perspective better incentives are required for providing and financing health services in the different sectors and through the overall financing of the system. Before outlining a proposal to reduce the importance of cost containment and to increase the "self regulating power" of the system, however, some consequences of cost containment in health care will be discussed. They demonstrate the importance to substitute mere cost containment by better incentives.

III. ECONOMIC EVALUATION AND PRIORITY SETTING AS THE CONSEQUENCES
   OF COST CONTAINMENT

In almost all industrialized nations health care cost containment can be considered as the major concern of social and economic policy. Legislative measures of cost control were taken despite the opposition from professional and industrial interest groups. Instruments and incentives employed for controlling expenditures differ among nations. Countries with national health services and planned systems are relying more upon fixed budgets and politically defined rates of growth of health care expenditures. Countries relying on social security systems try to achieve cost containment by freezing the contribution rates, by negotiating expenditure caps for providers of health care and by moral suasion.

In West Germany *e.g.* a number of cost containment acts were passed in 1977, 1981, 1983, 1985 and again within the context of a more basic health care reform in 1988. Similar developments are typical of the health care systems of other European Countries; the number and intensity of cost control interventions, and other reforms are increasing. Budgeting and global macro economic management, quantity controls, a strengthening of the insurance principle and elements of an indemnity insurance are the strategies being applied at the same time. The consequences of these developments are obvious: economic evaluation, managed care, priority setting being the keywords to characterize the time to come. Without the introduction of better incentives, new insurance systems and structural adjustments, cost-effectiveness considerations and health care planning will be in the center of health policy issues. Against this background the two types of health care systems will converge.

In order to secure cost containment global and sectoral budgets are needed. As a consequence of sectoral budgets there is also a growing need for defining the structure of expenditures within the subbudgets. Thus allocating the resources means setting priorities by quotas for the different health care purposes. This development is a challenge for the management of health care. It will be expected that health care managers and planners in federal, regional and local agencies will try to monitor and promote the health of their population. They have to define the health needs and to find strategies to ensure that the health needs are met, *i.e.* that there are effective and efficient services for preventive and curative medicine, the control of diseases and the promotion of health. Economic appraisal in health care, developing economic and medical guidelines, the rational diffusion and use of health care technology and all methods of economic, medical and ethical evaluation will gain importance. "League tables" of costs and QALYs for selected health care interventions will be used in health promotion and disease prevention strategies (Appendix 5). This will be the environment for management and planning of health care in particular in tax funded systems with public provision of services but also in systems with social insurance and mixed provision of health care (Williams 1988). The "self regulating power" of the system will diminish and interventionism in health care will spread in the years to come.

IV. HOW TO REDUCE THE IMPORTANCE OF COST CONTAINMENT: A PROPOSAL FOR A GOVERNMENT MANDATED HEALTH INSURANCE

Arguing that this process of increasing interventionism is not desirable, and aiming at a more pluralistic and decentralized system a government mandated private health insurance is suggested through which, at the same time, the importance of cost containment will be reduced.

As shown above a health insurance system with the adequate incentives is needed in order to lead all participants *quasi* automatically to a cost efficient health care system providing the services on the basis of need rather than tradition and history or on the basis of an elaborate planning process.

The system likely to achieve includes mandatory insurance coverage for everybody, the volume and the structure of coverage being defined politically. Insurance then is provided by private insurance enterprises. This could be regarded as the pioneer system of health insurance for highly developed nations substituting in the decades to come the Bismarck type social security system (in case of less developed countries see Korea Development Institute, 1989). Its objective would be the introduction of incentives into health care so as to abolish permanent public interventions and parliamentary actions. It provides an effective as well as efficient health care whereas cost containment as an objective or principle of health policy loses a lot of importance (for a specific case *see* Frech, Ginsburg 1975).

What are the characteristics of this proposal which cannot be labelled as private or public, since it contains elements of both? The following elements characterize the proposal:

- total population is covered by obligatory insurance.
- types of services are defined politically as it is the case today. Indemnity tariffs should be used where possible (*e.g.* in dental care; Knappe, Leu, v. d. Schulenburg 1988).
- allocation and distribution elements are separated with the mandated insurance coverage being then restricted to the original *i.e.* the allocation function of health insurance,
- each individual pays a risk-oriented premium which substitutes compulsory income-related payroll taxes,
- obligatory insurance provides a variety of insurance plans offered by competing insurance companies,
- in cases of unemployment, rehabilitation, disability and low income the premiums are paid out of general revenues or for practical reasons by other branches of the social security system, if they exist,
- private insurances have to accept any individual for insurance (Kontrahierungszwang) and are not allowed to discriminate among different risks (Diskriminierungsverbot),
- financing and administrating of the suppliers is left to the health insurers and market forces again with federal control of minimum standards in regard to the provision of health services to all citizens.

This model would strengthen the self regulating capacity of the health care system and would thus reduce the number and intensity of discretionary (*ad hoc*) interventions. At the same time it is a socially balanced insurance system.

The new system could also respond better to future demographic challenges (Behrens 1991). Reserves are accumulated to compensate for high expenditures in old age. The funded system thus has advantages over the pay-as-you-go financing in the current statutory health insurance system. A related demographic problem, namely nursing home care for the elderly can be solved in the same way as some proposals for parliamentary action show in West Germany. Other challenges (medical technology, oversupply of doctors, beds, *etc.*) can be dealt with by competition among insurance firms. Innovations in providing health care are to be expected. The role of the private health insurers, however, would change. The administration of the system would gradually switch from the statutory system to a government controlled private system. Cream skimming has to be prevented to ensure solidarity and efficiency at the same time (Van de Ven, Van Vliet 1991). The question of cost containment in such a funded system refers only to the politically defined indemnity tariff. Economic evaluation and priority setting is no longer in the center of health policy. Its role is diminishing as an instrument of health care planning and growing as a means of informing the public. As the proposed insurance is provided by a variety of suppliers the process of competition will provide more effective and efficient solutions. As an optimal quota of health expenditures does not exist in reality, we do not know whether in such a system the quota would be higher or lower and how much will be spent in this sector. The insured population will have more freedom to choose. Their preferences play a larger role than in the existing system. Prevention will become more important as the incentives for a healthier life style will increase. The government mandated health insurance could be a model for the future organization of health care in industrialized countries. From this perspective the issue of cost containment loses its relative importance on the political agenda.

REFERENCES

Adam, H., "Ambulante ärztliche Leistungen und Ärztedichte. Zur These der anbieterinduzierten Nachfrage im Bereich der ambulanten ärztlichen Versorgung", *Beiträge zur angewandten Wirtschaftsforschung*, Berlin, 1983.
Auster, R. D., I. Leveson, D. Sarachek, "The Production of Health: An Exploratory Study", in: *Journal of Human Resources*, Vol. 4, pp. 411, 1969.
Behrens, C., "Intertemporale Verteilungswirkungen in der gesetzlichen Krankenversicherung der Bundesrepublik Deutschland", Frankfort/M u.a. 1991.
Bundesverband der Betriebskrankenkassen, (ed.), "Krankheitsarten und Arbeitsunfallstatistik 1987", Essen 1988.
Culyer, A.J., "Cost Containment in Europe", in: *Health Care Financing Review*, 1989 Annual Supplement, pp. 21–32, Baltimore M.D., 1989.
Dever, G.E.A., "An Epidemiological Model for Health Policy Analysis", in: *Social Indicators Research*, Vol. 2, pp. 461, 1976.
Evans, R.G., "Tension, Compression, and Shear: Directions, Stresses and Outcomes of Health Care Cost Control", in: *Journal of Health Politics Policy and Law*, Vol. 15, No. 1, pp. 101–128, Spring 1990.
Evans, R.G., G.L. Stoddart, "Producing Health, Consuming Health Care", Discussion Paper, The University of British Columbia, April 1990.
Frech III, H.E., P.B. Ginsburg, "Imposed Health Insurance in Monopolistic Markets. A Theoretical Analysis", in: *Economic Issues*, Vol. 13, pp. 55ff, 1975.
Gäfgen, G., "Die optimale Gesundheitsquote. Ein Problem der Verwendungsstruktur des Sozialprodukts", in: *Jahrbuch für Sozialwissenschaft (Zeitschrift für Wirtschaftswissenschaften)*, Vol. 35, 1984.
Henke, K.-D., "Alternativen zur Weiterentwicklung der Sicherung im Krankheitsfall", in: Hansmeyer, K.-H., (ed.), *Finanzierungsprobleme der sozialen Sicherung II*, Berlin, pp. 117–175, 1991.
Henke, K.-D., "A concerted approach to health care financing in the Federal Republic of Germany", in: *Health Policy*, Vol. 6, No. 6, pp. 341–351, 1986.
Henke, K.-D., C. Behrens, "The economic cost of illness in the Federal Republic of Germany in the Year 1980", in: *Health Policy*, Vol. 6, No. 2, pp. 119–143, 1986.

260   *Klaus-Dirk Henke*

Hodgson, T. A., "Cost of illness studies: no aid to decision making?", Comments on the 2. Opinion by Shiell *et al.*, in: *Health Policy*, Vol. 11, No. 1, pp. 57–60, 1989.

Killoran, A.J., "The Context of Health Promotion in the NHS", in: *Health Services Management*, pp. 36–40, February 1990.

Knappe, E., R.E. Leu, J.-M. v. d. Schulenburg *Der Indemnitätstarif, Wege zur Sozialverträglichkeit und Wirtschaftlichkeit beim Zahnersatz*, Berlin, 1988.

Korea Development Institute, "Policy Issues in Social Security", *Conference Series* 89–2, Seoul, 1989.

Organization for Economic Cooperation and Development (ed.), "Financing and Delivering Health Care", *Social Policy Studies*, No. 4, Paris, 1987.

Organization for Economic Cooperation and Development, Health Data File 1989.

Rice, D.P., T.A. Hodgson, A.N. Kopstein, "The economic costs of illness: A replication and update", in: *Health Care Financing Review*, Vol. 7, No. 1, pp. 61–80, 1985.

Sachverständigenrat für die Konzertierte Aktion im Gesundheitswesen, Jahresgutachten 1987 und 1988: "Medizinische und ökonomische Orientierung"; "Herausforderungen und Perspektiven der Gesundheitsversorgung"; Baden-Baden, 1990.

Schieber, G.J., J.P. Poullier, "Data Watch", in: *Health Affairs*, pp. 169–177, Fall 1989.

Schultze, Ch., *The public use of private interest*, Washington D.C., 1975.

Schwartz, F.W., "Chancen und Kostenfragen einer verstärkten Prävention in der Krankenversicherung", in: *Argument-Sonderband 178: Grenzen der Prävention*, pp. 31–49, Hamburg, 1988.

Van de Ven, P.M.M., R.C.J.A. van Vliet, "How can we prevent cream skimming in a competitive health insurance market?" Zweifel, P., H.E. Frech III, *Health Economics Worldwide*, Dordrecht, this volume.

Williams, A., "Priority setting in public and private health care, a guide through the ideology jungle", in: *Journal of Health Economics*, No. 7, pp. 173–183, 1988.

Zweifel, P., "Technology in Ambulatory Medical Care: Cost Increasing or Cost Saving?", in: *Social Science Medicine*, Vol. 21, No. 10, pp. 1139–1151, 1985

APPENDIX 1:

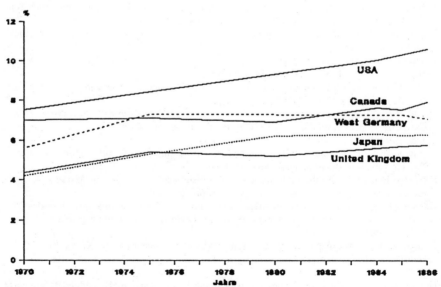

Fig. 1. Total Expenditures for Health Care in Percent of the GDP, Selected Countries 1970–1986.

Organization for Economic Cooperation and Development, Health Data File 1989.

APPENDIX 2:

Table 1. Growth in Actual per Capita Health Spending (Compound Annual Growth Rate)

	1960–87	1960–70	1970–80	1980–87
Canada	10.7	9.3	12.5	9.9
France	13.4	12.2	15.9	10.9
Germany	9.1	9.1	12.0	5.1
Italy	16.8	13.7	21.9	14.1
Japan	14.5	20.1	15.4	5.4
United Kingdom	12.4	12.6	19.0	9.3
Average	12.8	12.8	16.1	9.1
United States	10.2	8.1	11.5	9.4

Schieber, G.J., Poullier, J.P., Data Watch, in: Health Affairs, Fall 1989, p. 174.

APPENDIX 3:

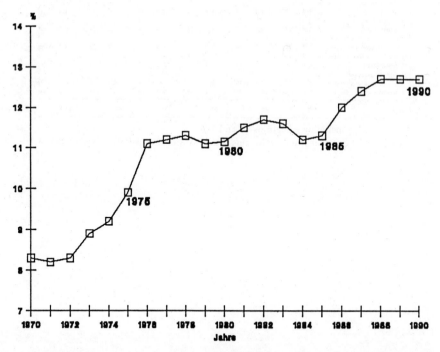

Fig. 2. Development of the Payroll Tax Rate in the German Statutory Health Insurance 1970–1990.

Sachverständigenrat für die Konzertierte Aktion im Gesundheitswesen, Jahresgutachten 1990, Herausforderungen und Perspektiven der Gesundheitsversorgung, Baden-Baden 1990, p. 228.

APPENDIX 4:

Table 2. Results of Cost of Illness Studies in 5 OECD Countries (D = Direct Costs in Percent, R = Rank)

	FRG (80)		Finland (2)		Sweden (75)		USA (80)		Japan			
	D	R	D	R	D	R	D	R	D(80)	R	D(83)	R
1 Diseases of the digestive system	28,6	1	5,3	7	13,7	2	14,7	2	13,1	2	13,0	2
2 Diseases of the circulatory system	15,0	2	17,1	2	13,7	2	15,4	1	21,2	1	22,8	1
3 Accidents, poisonings and violence	7,7	3	6,5	5	7,8	5	8,8	4	7,0	8	7,2	5
4 Diseases of the musculoskeletal system and connective tissue	7,6	4	4,8	9	5,3	6	6,2	7	7,1	6	7,2	5
5 Diseases of the respiratory system	5,6	5	5,3	7	5,1	8	7,9	6	10,6	3	8,9	3
6 Mental disorders	5,1	6	23,3	1	15,7	1	9,4	3	7,1	6	7,1	7
7 Diseases of the nervous system	4,8	7	4,1	10	4,4	9	8,1	5	5,5	9	5,8	9
8 Neoplasms	4,4	8	6,9	4	5,3	6	6,2	7	7,9	5	8,9	3
9 Diseases of the genito-urinary system	4,2	9	4,1	10	3,6	10	5,8	10	8,4	4	6,6	8
10 Endocrine and metabolic diseases	3,6	10	2,4	12	2,5	13	3,5	11	3,1	11	3,5	10
11 Complications of pregnancy and childbirth	3,3	11	5,9	6	2,6	12			1,2	13	1,2	13
12 Infective and parasitic diseases	3,0	12	7,6	3	1,5	14	2,0	13	3,5	10	3,2	11
13 Symptoms and ill-defined conditions	2,8	13	2,5	11	3,0	11	1,8*	14	0,6	15	0,8	15
14 Diseases of the skin and subcutaneous conditions	1,9	14	1,0	13	1,5	14	2,8	12	2,2	12	2,1	12
15 All others and unallocated	1,5	15	-	-	13,2	4	6,1	9	-	-	-	-
16 Congenital anomalies	0,3	16	1,0	13	0,4	16	0,6	15	0,5	16	0,4	16
17 Certain causes of perinatal morbidity and mortality	0,3	16	0,5	16	0,3	18	-	-	0,2	17	0,3	17
18 Diseases of the blood	0,2	18	0,7	15	0,4	16	0,5	16	0,7	14	0,9	14
Total (100%)	100		100		100		100		100		100	

() = year, * = including categories 11 and 17.
OECD (ed.) Financing and Delivering Health Care, Social Policy Studies No. 4, Paris 1987, p. 51.

Table 3. Results of Cost of Illness Studies in 4 OECD Countries (I = Indirect Costs in Percent, R = Rank)

	FRG (80)		Finland (72)		Sweden (75)		USA (80)	
	I	R	I	R	I	R	I	R
1 Accidents,poisonings and violence	20,7	1	14,2	4	12,7	4	26,4	1
2 Diseases of the circulatory system	15,4	2	25,0	1	16,0	2	21,5	2
3 Diseases of the musculoskeletal system and connective tissue	11,7	3	17,7	2	19,4	1	3,1	8
4 Diseases of the respiratory system	10,8	4	4,6	6	9,1	5	6,8	4
5 Neoplasms	10,1	5	5,1	5	8,3	6	15,4	3
6 Diseases of the digestive system	9,7	6	1,7	11	5,3	7	4,7	5
7 Mental disorders	3,7	7	17,1	3	14,2	3	4,5	6
8 Symptoms and ill defined conditions	3,6	8	0,3	16	1,8	12	2,8*	9
9 Diseases of the nervous system	3,5	9	4,2	7	4,0	8	2,4	10
10 Diseases of the genito-urinary system	2,4	10	0,8	13	1,9	11	1,3	14
11 Infective and parasitic diseases	2,4	10	2,4	8	2,2	9	2,4	10
12 Endocrine and metabolic diseases	1,4	12	1,6	12	2,1	10	2,3	12
13 Diseases of the skin and subcutaneous conditions	1,3	13	0,4	14	0,8	14	0,3	16
15 Certain causes of perinatal morbidity and mortality	1,0	14	2,0	10	0,5	15		
16 Complications of pregnancy and childbirth	0,8	16	0,2	17	0,4	16		
17 Diseases of the blood	0,4	17	0,1	18	0,3	17	0,4	15
18 All others and unallocated	0,1	18	0,4	14	-	-	3,8	7
	100		100		100		100	

() = year, * = including categories 15 and 16.
OECD (ed.) Financing and Delivering Health Care, Social Policy Studies No. 4, Paris 1987, p. 51.

Appendix 5:

Table 4. Case and Days of Illness Due to Inability to Work per 100 Compulsory Insured by Type of Illness, Federal Republic of Germany, 1987

Type of Illness	Inability to work		
	cases	days	days per case
1 Infective and parasitic Diseases	5,28	51,07	9,67
2 Neoplasms	1,20	54,59	45,33
3 Nutritional and metabolic diseases	1,04	24,35	23,32
4 Diseases of the blood	0,09	2,46	27,86
5 Mental disorders	2,42	78,37	32,33
6 Diseases of the nervous system and the sensory organs	4,05	60,58	14,97
7 Diseases of the circulatory system	7,77	213,31	27,44
8 Diseases of the respiratory system	40,75	413,83	10,15
9 Diseases of the digestive system	18,70	216,19	11,56
10 Diseases of the genito-urinary system	3,63	64,04	17,62
11 Complications of pregnancy	0,76	15,32	20,17
12 Diseases of the Skin and subcutaneous tissue	3,05	42,98	14,07
13 Diseases of the musculoskeletal system and connective tissue	32,46	710,22	21,88
14 Congenital anomalies	0,09	2,96	2,47
15 Perinatal morbidity and mortality	0,04	0,70	18,06
16 Symptoms and ill defined conditions	8,12	78,76	9,70
17 Injuries and poisonings[1]	19,38	346,16	17,86
Total	148,86	2 375,89	15,96

[1]Including accidents at work.
Bundesverband der Betriebskrankenkassen, ed., Krankheitsarten und Arbeitsunfallstatistik 1987, Essen 1988, p. 8.

Table 5. Burden of Avoidable Illness

Selected Diseases *ICD Code	Mortality (England & Wales 1988)		Costs to NHS		Estimates of Preventable Components
	Rate per 100,000 popultion	% Total deaths	Average No. of beds used daily	Est. Treatment costs (£)	% of deaths preventable through risk factor intervention/or early detection & treatment of disease
Coronary Heart Disease (410–414)	64	22	3283	500 m (3)	25% "of deaths under 70 years are probably preventable by the application of existing knowledge" (7)
Cerebrovascular disease (including Strokes) (430–438)	13	5	15809	550 m (4)	50%
All Cancers (140–205)	90	45	12776	290.2–497 m (5) (smoking related)	85% of all cancers (8)
Lung Cancer (162)	22	8	1713		90% attributed to smoking
Breast Cancer (174)	26	12	1385		30% over 50 years Preventable through screening programmes (9)
Cervical Cancer (179–182)	6	3	572		50% (10)
All Accidents (800–999) inc those caused by:	25	9	13643	326.4 m (6)	attributed to:
Fire					39% alcohol/smoking (11)
Drowning					15%
Homicide					50% alcohol
Suicide					30%
Road Traffic Accidents (E810–E819)	8	3		112.2 m (5) (Alcohol related)	35%
Alcohol Diseases (571)	3	1			100% alcohol
AIDS/HIV	2351 cases up to July 1989				

Killoran, A.J., The context of Health Promotion in the NHS, in: Health Services Management, February 1990, p. 37.

Political Economy of Hospital Financing

FRIEDRICH BREYER

Fakultät für Wirtschaftswissenschaften und Statistik, Universität Konstanz,
Postfach 5560, D-7750 Konstanz and FB Wirtschaftswissenschaft, FernUniversität
Hagen, Postfach 940, D-5800 Hagen

and

FRIEDRICH SCHNEIDER

Institut für Volkswirtschaftslehre und Politik, Johannes-Kepler-Universität Linz,
A-4040 Linz-Auhof

1. INTRODUCTION[1]

In health economics as in many other areas of economics there is a large gap between the policy recommendations often made quite unanimously by academic experts and the measures eventually taken by political decision-makers. Thus there is the persistent danger that academic health economists will get frustrated and withdraw from the unrewarding business of policy counseling. A better understanding of the laws of political decision-making would perhaps lower expectations and thus prevent illusions regarding the realization of policy proposals.

In this paper we concentrate on a specific branch of the health system, which has in recent years been the subject of important political decisions in Germany, namely the financing of hospital services. Using the recent changes in the financing law[2] as an illustrative example, we can examine both experts' proposals and the preferences of the interest groups concerned and thus gain insights into the structure of political decision-making in the health field.

The paper is organized in the following manner. In Section 2 we describe five basic types of hospital payment systems, which were available alternatives at the time when the decision on the reform of the hospital financing system was made in the early 1980s. We also identify the types of actors whose interests could have influenced the legislative process. Section 3 is devoted to a theoretical analysis of how these groups of actors might evaluate the respective payment systems. This is done on the basis of a very simple model of the provision and financing of hospital services. In Section 4 these theoretical hypotheses are empirically tested using the official statements made by the respective interest groups prior to the legislation in 1984/85. In Section 5 we confront the group interests with the actual result of the legislation in an attempt to explain the influences of the groups on the legislation within a public-choice model. And, finally, Section 6 contains some conclusions.

P. Zweifel and H. E. Frech III (eds.), Health Economics Worldwide. 267–285.

2. IDENTIFICATION OF THE ALTERNATIVES AND OF THE AGENTS

2.1. Basic Types of Hospital Payment and their Evaluation by Health Economists

It would go far beyond the scope of this paper to describe in detail either the hospital payment system in force in Germany until 1984 or the reform proposals put forward as alternatives, during this period. Instead, we omit the problem of the financing of hospital investment and confine our analysis to the payment for hospital services which is meant to be a counterpart of the operating expenses of the hospital. In the following we shall distinguish five ideal types of payment systems for hospital services:

A. the retrospective reimbursement of all costs incurred by the hospital (*cost reimbursement*),
B. the granting of a fixed *budget* for an entire accounting period,
C. the payment of a predetermined fee per admission (*per case payment*), normally differentiated according to patient type or diagnosis,
D. the payment of a predetermined fee per patient day (*per diem payment*), and
E. the application of a negotiated fee schedule on all services - medical and ancillary - provided by the hospital (*fee for service*).

Unlike system A which is clearly "retrospective", all other payment modes are called "prospective" (*e.g.* by Dowling 1974). This characterization refers to the price component of total hospital receipts, *i.e.* to the payment per unit of service provided by the hospital (where in the case of a fixed budget, B, the willingness to admit patients is considered as the relevant service of the hospital). Since system A, as formulated above, contains an invitation to incur costs, its application is usually restricted to the reimbursement of the costs "of an economically working hospital".[3] Such a legal qualification, however, normally entails the supervision of the efficient operation of hospitals by an authorized public agency.

Among academic health economists there is widespread agreement that a payment system should not only provide hospitals with the funds required to guarantee the provision of sufficient hospital services to the population, but should also be fair with respect to the performance of hospitals and contain incentives for an efficient production of services.

The latter aspect leads to the rejection of retrospective cost reimbursement. Furthermore, most economists prefer that payment be linked to "output-related" indicators of hospital activity (cases) rather than be distributed with no relation to activity (budget) or even be tied to indicators of "input" (patient days, medical and other services).[4] One of the motivations for this preference is the consideration that hospitals have little incentive to work efficiently if they have the power to extend the base of payment and thus their total revenue (as in systems D and E). Consequently one can safely conclude that the majority of academic health economists in the field (subscript H) would propose the rank order

$$C >_H B >_H D >_H E >_H A. \tag{2.1}$$

2.2. *The Interest Groups Concerned*

When analyzing the process of political decision-making we shall distinguish the following groups of actors with homogeneous interests within each group:
1. hospital physicians,
2. hospital owners or trustees,
3. hospital managers,
4. sickness funds and private health insurers, and
5. public supervisory agencies.

Each hospital will not be treated as an organism with a will of its own, but we shall take account of the differences of interest between doctors, managers and owners.[5] On the other hand, the above classification disregards (for the sake of transparency) possible further divisions, *e.g.*
- of hospital physicians into medical directors and others.
- of hospitals into public and private or commercial and non-profit-making institutions.

Furthermore the classification takes into account that statutory sickness funds are not necessarily perfect representatives of their insurers, but bureaucracies with their own targets. However, sickness fund members are not listed as a group because they have a very low degree of organization and thus were probably not able to articulate their interests in the legislative process.

Finally, the public bureaucracy is also affected by the hospital financing legislation because, as mentioned above, it can be entrusted with additional functions like the supervision of efficiency.

3. THE INTERESTS OF THE CONCERNED GROUPS: THEORY

In the following section we shall present an economic model of the hospital, which will enable us to infer the interests of some of the concerned groups from their basic preferences and the economic relations ruling in the hospital. The model is extremely simple in order to facilitate clear-cut answers to the questions related to our problem. Therefore, some aspects of the problem will necessitate further theoretical considerations not explicitly contained in the formal model.

3.1. *A Simple Economic Model of the Hospital*

We ignore the multi-product nature of hospitals and assume that there is only one type of patient (cases), the number of which per period, X, is exogenous to the hospital.[6] In contrast, the hospital itself chooses the quantity of medical and ancillary services Y delivered to the patients. (This includes the number of patient days.) Output quality Q is assumed to depend upon the number of services per patient:

$$Q = f(Y/X) \geq \underline{Q}, \tag{3.1}$$

where f is an increasing and strictly concave function and $\underline{Q}$ denotes the minimum level of quality which is just tolerated by the patients.

For the sake of simplicity we do not distinguish between different inputs (physician and non-physician labor, capital, medical supplies *etc.*) but assume that there is only one variable factor of production, the quantity of which is denoted by K and the purchasing price by w. The fixed factors K^f cause fixed costs of C^f, so that the cost equation for the hospital is given by

$$C = C^f + w \cdot K \tag{3.2}$$

In the production of services, the hospital does not necessarily combine the factors efficiently so that with given production function F:

$$Y = F(K + K^f) - s = : g(K,s), \quad g_K > 0, g_s < 0,[7] \tag{3.3}$$

where s ("slack") measures the difference between the maximum possible and the actual quantity of services with given inputs.

In the following we shall derive the set of feasible combinations of quality Q, slack s and profits π among which the hospital can choose. Solving (3.2) for K and inserting into (3.3) yields the relation between service quantity, total costs and "slack"

$$Y = g[(C - C^f)/w,s] = : g^*(C,s), \tag{3.4}$$

or, using (3.1):

$$Q = f[g^*(C,s)/X] = : h(C,s), \quad h_C > 0, h_s < 0 \tag{3.5}$$

when the number of patients X does not vary.

The following general equation for total revenue R includes all of the payment systems defined above as special cases:

$$R = B^f + p_X \cdot X + R^v \tag{3.6}$$

where

$$R^v = p_Y \cdot Y + \alpha \cdot C. \tag{3.7}$$

Here, B^f denotes a fixed budget, p_X a per-case payment, p_Y a fixed fee per unit of service[8], and α is a number between 0 and 1. R^v denotes the variable part of the revenue, *i.e.* the part which depends upon the behavior of the hospital. The "pure" systems A-E are therefore defined as follows (where the parameters B^f, p_X, p_Y and α are determined prospectively, *i.e.* before the beginning of the accounting period):

– retrospective cost reimbursement (A): $\alpha = 1$, $B^f = p_X = p_Y = 0$.

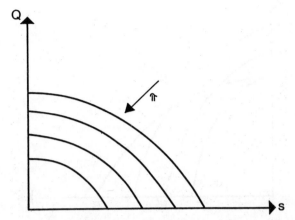

Figure 1. Iso-profit-curves when revenue is given.

- fixed budget (system B): $B^f > 0$, $p_X = p_Y = \alpha = 0$;
- per-case payment (C): $p_X > 0$, $B^f = p_Y = \alpha = 0$;
- per-diem rate (D) or fee-for-service (E): $p_Y > 0$, $B^f = p_X = \alpha = 0$;

If the definition of hospital profits, π,

$$\pi = R - C, \tag{3.8}$$

is inserted into (3.5),

$$Q = h(R - \pi, s) \tag{3.9}$$

one obtains an equation that specifies - with given revenue R - a relation between the quality of treatment Q, the degree of inefficiency s and the maximum possible profit π:

$$Q = h^*(\pi, s|R), \quad h^*_\pi < 0, h^*_s < 0. \tag{3.10}$$

Equation (3.10) can be represented graphically by iso-profit-curves in an (s,Q) diagram (*see* Figure 1). The slope of these curves is negative owing to $h^*_s < 0$, and from $h_{R-\pi} > 0$ we know that they are the further away from the origin the *smaller* π is. Furthermore, the strict concavity of f implies that the iso-profit curves are concave to the origin.

The assumption of a fixed revenue, however, applies only to the payment systems B and C (fixed budget and per-case payment). When payment is tied to services as in D and E, (3.9) becomes due to (3.1)

$$Q = h[p_Y \cdot Y - \pi, s] = h[p_Y \cdot f^{-1}(Q) - \pi, s] \tag{3.11}$$

or, after solving for Q,

$$Q = \varphi(\pi, s) \tag{3.12}$$

with[9]

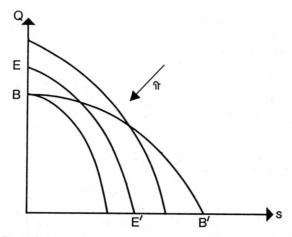

Figure 2. Iso-profit-curves for fixed revenue and fee-for-service.

$$\varphi_s(\pi, s) = \left.\frac{dQ}{ds}\right|_\pi = \frac{h_s}{1 - h_C \cdot p_Y/f'} < h_s = \left.\frac{dQ}{ds}\right|_{\pi,R} = h_s^*(\pi, s) \quad (3.13)$$

This inequality states that in each point (s,Q) the iso-profit-curve under fee-for-service (*e.g.* EE' in Figure 2) is steeper than the one corresponding to fixed revenue (*e.g.* BB').

The system of retrospective cost reimbursement represents a degenerate case, since due to R = C the profit π is always 0 and thus always identical. A restriction on feasible levels of Q and s exists only when the quantity of the variable factor, K, is bounded from above by K^{max}.[10]

3.2. *The Objectives of the Agents in the Hospital*

Having derived limitations on the feasible levels of the variables quality, slack and profit under alternative payment systems, it is necessary to specify plausible assumptions on the preferences of the various hospital agents, *i.e.* physicians, managers and owners (trustees), with respect to these variables.

The satisfaction of hospital physicians will be affected both by the medical quality of the treatment provided to their patients – the component of their objective system related to professional ethics –[11] and by the effective income obtained.[12] As the nominal income of an employed hospital physician in Germany is contractually fixed, effective income is the higher the lower the actual work load per physician is.[13] This in turn falls, at a given number of patients and services per patient, when the level of inputs is increased, and this applies both to physicians and – except in the extreme case of perfect complementarity – to non-physician inputs. Factor input at given output, however, can be inferred in this model – due to (3.3) – from the variable "slack". Therefore we propose the following utility function for physicians (superscript P):

$$U^P = U^P(Q,s), \qquad U^P_Q, U^P_s > 0 \qquad (3.14)$$

Among hospitals it is natural to distinguish between commercial and non-profit-making institutions (both public and voluntary) because of the differing attitudes between owners of the former and trustees of the latter type towards earning profits. However, as the first group is of little importance quantitatively,[14] the analysis can be limited to the second group, which is relatively homogeneous in their attitudes towards profits: positive profits are either unwelcome (as with public ownership) or legally prohibited (with voluntary tax-exempt institutions), while losses lead to conflicts with other objectives (like the financing of nursery schools, public swimming pools *etc.*) and are therefore not desirable either. On the dimension "profit", the objective function has therefore a maximum at the value zero.

Besides that, trustees are interested in the reputation of their hospital, which is positively related to quantity and quality of output, so that it can be measured by the variable Q, whereas slack, *i.e.* input without corresponding output, can not be as desirable for them as for the physicians. Thus the utility function of trustees (T) is:

$$U^T = U^T(Q,\pi), \qquad U^T_Q > 0, \pi \cdot U^T_\pi < 0 \qquad (3.15)$$

With respect to the objectives of hospital managers, the literature exhibits the greatest amount of disagreement. On one side it is argued that the performance of the manager of a non-profit-making firm is not measured by the profit, so that profit can not be an argument in his objective function (*see, e.g.* Newhouse 1970, S.65). In this vein, the manager's utility is identified with the status of the hospital and the latter is sometimes measured even by the level of inputs (Lee 1971), which justifies including "slack" in his utility function. On the other hand, the empirical observation (in particular in the U.S.) that non-profit hospitals persistently achieve considerable profits (*e.g.* Davis 1972, Sloan 1991), suggests that the crucial decision-makers – and according to our above considerations this can be neither physicians nor trustees – must have an interest in positive profits.

Bearing in mind that a hospital manager has normally been educated at a business school, it is quite likely that at least he himself measures his professional success by the level of profits achieved. Moreover, if the hospital has been permanently "in the red" and has to be put back on its feet again, his interest coincides with that of the owner, and the profit (or the reduction of losses) will have an impact on his income via premiums.

Besides this indicator of performance the manager will also be interested in his position in the power structure within the direction of the hospital. Obviously, this position is strengthened by the tightness of the external economic constraints which the hospital is subject to. Or, more pronounced: If the survival of the hospital is at stake, the manager as the economic expert becomes a dictator. If, on the contrary, any pressure to behave economically is absent (as with retrospective cost reimbursement), the physicians will degrade the manager to a chief purchaser. A good indicator for the strength (or, more precisely, the absence) of economic pressure from outside is R^v/R, the fraction of revenues which are variable, *i.e.* subject to choice by the hospital. We therefore postulate the following utility function for managers (M):

$$U^M = U^M(\pi, R^v/R), \qquad U^M_\pi > 0, U^M_{RV/R} < 0. \qquad (3.16)$$

3.3. *The Preferences of Hospital Agents for Payment Systems*

In Section 3.1 we outlined for each of the alternative payment systems the combinations of the variables Q (quality of treatment), s (slack) and π (profit) which are feasible for the individual hospital. The utility functions discussed in Section 3.2 serve to construct a set of indifference curves with respect to these variables for each group of agents. In order to draw conclusions as to which of the payment systems (A–E) each of the groups will prefer it is now necessary to know which of the feasible sets of parameter values will be actually *realized* in each of the five cases. To achieve this, the process of decision-making within the hospital – given the payment system – must be analyzed.

As a first step we shall make the following – necessarily somewhat arbitrary – assumptions on the ability of the respective groups to push through their claims:
1. The interests of the hospital trustees are respected insofar as realized profits will be zero in any case:

$$\pi^A = \pi^B = \pi^C = \pi^D = \pi^E = 0. \qquad (3.17)$$

   (A possible justification for this assumption is that the interests of the managers, who want to maximize profits, and those of the physicians, who are opposed to profits, block each other).
2. With respect to the other variables, the optimum for the physicians will be chosen. (Notice that managers are not interested in either quality or slack).

In comparing the respective utility maxima from the physicians' point of view, everything depends upon the location of the two zero-profit-curves (for fee-for-service, EE′, and for fixed revenue, BB′ in Figure 3) and of the curve which represents the resource constraint $K = K^{max}$ for the system of cost reimbursement (AA′). With respect to the two zero-profit-curves all three logically possible cases are a priori conceivable: EE′ can lie entirely above or entirely below BB′, or the two can intersect. Clearly, the location of a zero-profit curve depends not only on the basis of payment, but also on the generosity of the payment rates. As we are interested in a statement on the evaluation of payment *types* in most general circumstances, it is natural

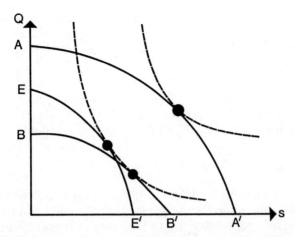

Figure 3. Optimum solutions with alternative payment systems.

to assume comparable generosity of rates, and so there should be some (intermediate) combination of quality and slack where the two curves intersect.

Furthermore, it depends upon the shape of the physicians' utility function whether

a) the optimum with payment for services (systems D and E) has higher quality $Q^E(= Q^D)$ and lower slack $s^E (= s^D)$ than the optimum with fixed revenue (systems B and C), or.

b) both values are higher (lower) in the payment-for-services optimum than otherwise.

Here it is somewhat more plausible (and with homothetic preferences it is certain) that the situation a) applies:

$$Q^E = Q^D > Q^B = Q^C; \qquad s^E = s^D < s^B = s^C \tag{3.18}$$

But even then it is not clear in which of the two optima hospital physicians reach the higher utility level (*see* Figure 3 which depicts the limiting case of indifference.).

Furthermore it will be supposed that the curve AA' is located entirely above the other two constraint curves and that the corresponding optimum for the physicians is characterized by higher values of both endogenous variables (*see* Figure 3):

$$Q^A > Q^E = Q^D > Q^B = Q^C; \qquad s^A > s^B = s^C > s^E = s^D. \tag{3.19}$$

Using these assumptions and their consequences we can now draw conclusions as regards the preferences of the concerned groups with respect to the payment systems A–E.

These are least straightforward for the *physicians*: It is certain only that they reach their highest utility under system A (retrospective cost reimbursement). On the other hand, it is not possible to rank their utility maxima under the systems B to E unambiguously. An additional consideration (not implied by the formal model) is that under pure fee-for-service (system E) revenues are based on their own activity so that this system will give them more power within the hospital than the other systems and is therefore a good candidate for second choice. Similarly, as they are the ones who decide on the length of stay of patients, the per-diem system (D) gives them at least some discretion to increase hospital revenue and so should be their third preference:

$$A >_P E >_P D >_P B,C \qquad (3.20)$$

For the *hospital trustees* it follows from (3.15) and (3.17) that their preference is uniquely determined by the levels of quality achieved in the respective optima. Therefore, according to (3.19), they too will favor cost reimbursement (system A) and will consider the payment-for-services systems, D and E, second-best:

$$A >_T D,E >_T B,C \qquad (3.21)$$

In stark contrast, *hospital managers* will consider a payment system less desirable – by (3.16) and (3.17) – according to the strength of the influence of the hospital itself on its revenues. So by this criterion system A is definitely worse than D and E (see the location of the budget curves in Figure 3). Better still are those systems in which the whole revenue is exogenously fixed (B and C). Which of these two systems a manager will prefer is not clear from the model, but an additional criterion could be the predictability of revenues, which facilitates the planning of factor inputs. Under this aspect the predetermined budget (B) is preferable to the per-case payment where the revenue level is revealed only in the course of the accounting period (according to the number and types of patients admitted). We thus get the rank order for managers:

$$B >_M C >_M D,E >_M A \qquad (3.22)$$

3.4. *The Evaluation of the Alternatives by the Other Groups*

From the point of view of *sickness funds*, a hospital payment system is the more attractive,
– the less it leads to expenditure increases which have to be passed on to their members via higher contributions, and
– the more precisely total expenditures can be predicted already at the beginning of an accounting period.
The second aspect makes the fixed budget (system B) appear ideal to them, while the first makes them reject both retrospective cost reimbursement (A) and the payment for activities chosen by the hospital itself (systems D and E). However, while there is a natural limit to the number of patient days a

hospital can generate, *viz.* the number of beds times 365, the number of services can be raised almost beyond limit, and this is even more true for costs, so that system D should appear more palatable than E or even A. So their preferences (with subscript I for insurers) are largely identical to those of the managers:

$$B >_I C >_I D >_I E >_I A \qquad (3.23)$$

The *public agencies*, finally, will favor a system which exerts a permanent pressure on the politicians to arrange for external supervision of the efficiency of hospitals since this provides them with functions of high priority and considerable power. Obviously, this requirement is ideally fulfilled by retrospective cost reimbursement (A), which fails to convey to the decision-makers in the hospitals any incentives for efficient behavior. Among the other alternatives, the supervisors might prefer fixed budgets insofar as they expect to act as mediators in the necessary negotiations between hospitals and sickness funds, whereas any self-regulating allocation process via prices must appear unattractive to them. So their preferences are

$$A >_S B >_S C,D,E \qquad (3.24)$$

4. THE INTERESTS OF THE CONCERNED GROUPS: EMPIRICAL EVIDENCE

4.1. *Preliminary Remarks*

In the following we shall confront the theory developed in Section 3 with the statements made by the respective interest groups in the course of the legislative process. In principle, we can distinguish two phases of this process:
- phase 1 (1983 and earlier): the period before the first draft of the hospital financing law (KHNG) was published by the Ministry of Labor and Social Affairs,
- phase 2 (January 1984 - August 1985): the period between the publication of the first draft of the KHNG and the final enactment of the decree on the reimbursement of hospital services (BPflV).

As a general problem, the statements made by the interest groups during the proper legislative process including the parliamentary hearings, *i.e.* in phase 2, are extremely numerous (because several drafts of the law were launched by the Ministry within a few months), but not very informative for our purposes. In the greatest part they refer, quite naturally, to individual paragraphs of the law rather than the basic principles of reimbursement. Moreover, they consist mainly of a critique of the Ministry's draft without presenting their own proposals in greater detail.

These, in contrast, were mainly offered during the first, the pre-legislative phase, and a very useful survey can be found in Chapter D. of the so-called "Wannagat-Report"[15]. Hence this is the main source of the following empirical examination of the theory developed in Section 3.

4.2. Official Statements made in the Pre-Legislative Phase

The statements of the several professional associations of *physicians* (general, hospital and leading hospital physicians) "officially" agree both in the rejection of the system of retrospective cost reimbursement existing until 1984 (system A) and in their support of the fee-for-service system E (BMA 1983, pp. 101–107). Some statements even suggest a separation of the payment for physicians' services from the payment for the remaining services (pp. 102, 104).

The association of hospital *managers* rejects the per-diem payment (system D) and demands an output-oriented system (*ibid.*, p. 92). In particular it proposes the introduction of a price schedule where each price refers to a specific bundle of services, *e.g.* appendectomy (p.93). Therefore, in terms of the classification used here, their proposal is equivalent to a differentiated case-based payment system (C).

Each type of non-profit-making hospital *trustees* (municipalities, churches and private charities) has its own association, but their proposals towards the reform of hospital reimbursement in the early 1980s exhibit a striking amount of agreement (*ibid.*, pp. 70–83). They all favor a modified version of the principle of cost reimbursement, in which payment is based – prospectively – upon the costs calculated in advance rather than – retrospectively – upon actual costs. Furthermore, they all propose to retain the use of the patient day as the basic unit of output measurement, whereas only "very expensive services" should be paid for on the basis of a fee schedule. Their proposal can, therefore, be considered as a combination of the systems A, D and E.

The association of statutory *sickness funds* rejects the system of cost reimbursement and proposes prospectively fixed per-diem rates (system D), whereas any empirical evidence on the interests of *public agencies* mandated with the supervision of hospitals is lacking because they were not explicitly admitted as concerned groups in the legislative process.

4.3. Is the Theory Consistent with the (Revealed) Evidence?

The examination of the empirical evidence in the last section shows a large amount of agreement but also some disagreement with the theoretical predictions put forward in Section 3. Table 1 shows both the theoretical and the actual (*i.e.*, revealed) preferences of the affected groups for the alternative payment systems. For each group we have two columns. The first column contains the rank order of payment systems derived from the theoretical model developed in Section 3, ranging from (1) for first preference to (5) for last preference. In the second column we summarize the statements made

Table 1. Theoretically predicted rank order and revealed preferences[1]

Payment System	Group										
	Physicians P th.pr.	r.p.	Managers M th.pr.	r.p.	Trustees T th.pr.	r.p.	Sickness funds I th.pr.	r.p.	Supervisors th.pr.	r.p.	Health Economists H
Cost reimbursement A	(1)	–	(5)	–	(1)	++	(5)	–	(1)	n.a.	(5)
Granted fixed budget B	(4)	0	(1)	0	(4)	0	(1)	0	(2)	n.a.	(2)
Per case payment C	(4)	0	(2)	++	(4)	0	(2)	0	(3)	n.a.	(1)
Per diem payment D	(3)	0	(3)	–	(2)	++	(3)	++	(3)	n.a.	(3)
Fee for service E	(2)	++	(3)	0	(2)	+	(4)	0	(3)	n.a.	(4)

[1]Explanations th.pr. = theoretically predicted rank order

r.p. = revealed preference

( ) = ranking, 1 = best, 5 = least preferred

++ = strongly supported

+ = supported

– = rejected

0 = not explicitly mentioned

n.a. = no statement available

by these groups in the pre-legislative process. As they typically did not make explicit statements on every single alternative, this "revealed preference" can not be expressed as a ranking but is represented by plus and minus signs for support and rejection.

Table 1 clearly shows that in several cases the revealed preference deviates from the theoretically most preferred solution. There are two possible explanations for this finding: First of all, the theoretical model analyzed in Section 3 of this paper may be too simple to capture the complicated relations among the hospital actors and their interests so that the empirical evidence would suggest rejecting the theory. Secondly, however, it is conceivable that the statements of some of the groups may not exactly express their "true" preferences. As this second view is certainly the more controversial, it is worth-while to expound it in greater detail.

According to this view, the legislative process itself was a highly interactive game so that official statements can already be regarded as the result of an intensive bargaining and logrolling process. Therefore, it will quite often be the case that an "official statement" is made strategically in order to reach a compromise which comes as close as possible to the most preferred solution. As we did not have an independent empirical source which would have told us the "true" preferred solutions, we always have to examine whether tactical or logrolling considerations may explain the discrepancy between the true preference (unknown to us) and the revealed preference expressed in the official statements of the group.

For example, physicians' incomes are a highly political (and also emotional) issue in Germany. Hence physicians will avoid as best they can to openly state their most preferred solution which will maximize their income. So for purely tactical reasons they will "officially" support a solution with which they can live quite well but this fact cannot be so easily detected by the public. In this particular case, the first part of our prediction made in (3.20) on the preferences of hospital physicians – that cost reimbursement should be favored – is rejected,[16,17] whereas the second part – that fee-for-service should be preferred to the three remaining systems – is confirmed.

Turning to hospital managers, it is again the second and not the first choice theoretically predicted in (3.22) that comes out first in revealed preference. This might quite well be a tactical statement in the process of logrolling, especially between hospital managers and physicians.

In contrast to these two groups, the hospital trustees, who in general have the strongest support from government (more than 50 per cent of all hospital beds are in public hospitals), may have much less incentive to engage in logrolling or to make tactical statements. Quite often they can be sent forward by the government as a pressure group which more or less covers the interests of the government, too. As they have a better knowledge of the positions of the other groups, they might be an ideal partner for the government to come out with a compromise with which all other groups can finally "live". Therefore it is not surprising that their proposal corresponds to a combination of the three best choices according to our theory (*see* (3.21)).

As to the sickness funds, their support for system D is, at least at first glance, an open contradiction to our theoretical considerations made in Section 3.4, which made fixed budgets (system B) appear more attractive to them. But on the other hand, the sickness funds know quite well that they would get no support for this position (except from the hospital managers), and as they most strongly desire a general change of the system, they are in a weak bargaining position so that they are inclined to offer what seems to be an acceptable compromise, *viz.* system D.

5. THE OUTCOME OF THE LEGISLATION

Using the Public Choice approach, the objectives of a selfish government with regard to this new legislation can be put forward in the following way.
(1) The government has to demonstrate to the voters that it undertakes concrete policy measures to fight the cost explosion in the health care system. Whether these are effective or not does not play a role, but the voters must be given the impression that the government cares about this important problem and is trying to find a solution, which at least can be regarded as a step towards fighting the cost explosion.
(2) On the other side, the government has no intention to provoke an open conflict with the interest groups because it relies upon these groups in several ways. Also if a conflict breaks out, it might be quite costly for the government because the interest groups are quite capable of destroying a possible compromise.
(3) Moreover, the governments want to keep the group of regulatory supervisors and other bureaucrats dealing with these matters busy. As this group may be the most important to the government, the latter has to find a compromise which will not offend them or infringe in their field of work.

In order to evaluate the outcome of the legislation, we shall first give a short description of the payment system enacted by the legislation before trying to explain why certain groups have received a result closer to their optimum than others.

The payment system enacted by the law of 1984 (KHNG) and the decree of 1985 (BPflV) is characterized by two main features:
a) a "flexible budget", *i.e.* total hospital revenue consists of a fixed part (75 percent on average) and a variable part which varies with the number of patient days;
b) the determination of the budget on the basis of the total costs estimated by the hospital management and subject to negotiations with the third-party payers.

Property a) means that the payment system represents a compromise between a fixed budget and a per-diem payment (systems B and D). Since actual costs in the preceding period will play a dominant role in estimating future costs, property b) adds a strong element of cost reimbursement, even if in the "prospective" version (a variant of system A).

Looking at Table 1, we can draw some preliminary conclusions, although it is difficult to say which of the groups have achieved their targets. Starting again with the physicians: they will be satisfied with the element of cost-reimbursement (system A) that is inherent in the determination of the budget on the basis of estimated total costs. Obviously the physicians achieved one of their main targets, although in a modified version. Looking at the group of managers, their most preferred solution B (and the less preferred one, D) have been realized, but they had to accept the compromise with elements of the system A, which they favor least. As to the hospital trustees, we see that they most prefer system A and then rank D and E in second place. Of these three systems, A and D have been at least partly realized. Finally, we find for the sickness funds that their theoretically most preferred solution B is partly implemented and also some parts of their "revealed" first preference, system D.

If we summarize our findings, again looking at Table 1, it is justifiable to claim that all groups have at least partly realized their targets. The fact that cost reimbursement has not been given up will please hospital trustees and public supervisors. However, while sickness funds and hospital managers are surely dissatisfied with cost reimbursement, they will be content with the "budget" element of the new legislation. The per-diem element, finally, is welcomed by the sickness funds, although theory says it should not be.

So, taken together we get the puzzling result that none of the concerned interest groups can be completely satisfied with the new hospital financing law in Germany. Quite to the contrary, it constitutes a compromise which seems to offer a little bit for everyone, but this may have been precisely the strategy of the government, which in any case wanted to avoid a deep conflict with one of the interest groups. Overall this law seems to be an extremely clever compromise between the conflicting interests of the different groups, and the government were quite successful in arranging for the different interest groups to play against each other so that finally such a compromise could be reached. Looking at the available evidence, one can conclude that the hospital payment legislation of the mid-1980s has achieved the three governmental targets mentioned above to an admirable extent.

6. SUMMARY AND PRELIMINARY CONCLUSIONS

In this paper we tried to explain the recent reform in the law of financing German hospitals. We first described five basic types of hospital payment systems which were available as alternatives to the decision on the reform in the early 1980s. In the next step we identified five concerned interest groups whose actions certainly had a great influence on the legislative process. We proposed a simple theoretical model to examine how these groups of actors evaluated the different payment systems.

After deriving a preference ranking for each actor, we confronted these rankings with the respective revealed preferences, which could be inferred from their official statements towards the reform. It could also be shown that quite often the actual statements deviated strongly from the theoretically expected preferences because all groups were engaged in a highly interactive lobbying game.

In the last step we compared these preferences to the actual outcome of the legislation and found that all groups have at least partly realized their targets. So in contrast to the typical results of interest group theory, the differences in bargaining power do not appear to have led to a solution which unambiguously benefits some groups of actors at the expense of others.

It has to be repeated that the empirical analysis was limited to statements from the interest groups in the *pre-legislative* stage of the whole process. From this point the most promising procedure would appear to be the step-by-step analysis of the statements of the groups during the legislative process as well. This would give the researcher a chance to evaluate whether or not the theoretical hypotheses can be confirmed, whether or not our simple theoretical model is an appropriate way to understand the behavior of the affected groups and what was finally responsible for the outcome of the legislation. Therefore this paper should be seen as a first attempt to apply the framework of public choice theory to the field of health care financing and to demonstrate that much more research is needed.

NOTES

1. Valuable comments by participants of the Second World Congress on Health Economics and by the editors of this volume are gratefully acknowledged.
2. "Gesetz zur Neuordnung der Krankenhausfinanzierung" (KHNG) of 20.12.1984 and "Verordnung zur Regelung der Krankenhauspflegesätze" (BPflV) of 21.8.1985.
3. *See* § 17 No. 1 of the German hospital financing law (KHG) of 1972.
4. *See, e.g.,* Cleverley (1979), Breyer (1985), Robert-Bosch-Stiftung (1987), Heess (1989), Neubauer (1991). Notice, however, that Newhouse (this volume) proposes mixtures of fixed and service-related reimbursement.
5. On this distinction, *see* Jacobs (1974).
6. In the German hospital sector, there is considerable excess capacity so that an individual hospital could in general not raise its number of admissions by cutting the length of stay. Furthermore, as few physicians practice both in the hospital and in ambulatory care, the typical hospital has no way of "inducing" admissions.
7. Here and henceforth we use the subscript K to indicate the partial derivative with respect to the variable K, *etc.*
8. As explained in Section 2.1, our model does not distinguish analytically between patient days and other measures of hospital services provided to a patient. So the variable p_L can mean either the application of a fee schedule or a fixed per-diem rate.
9. Totally differentiating (3.11) with respect to s yields

$$\frac{dQ}{ds} = \frac{\partial h}{\partial C} \cdot p_y \cdot \frac{1}{f'(L)} \cdot \frac{dQ}{ds} + \frac{\partial h}{\partial s} \; .$$

10. Such a limitation can be caused, *e.g.*, by imperfections in the factor markets, by limited area of hospital grounds and buildings or by external supervision of "efficiency".
11. The variable "quality" in the objective function of physicians and hospital owners/trustees is emphasized throughout the literature on the economics of the hospital. *See*, *e.g.*, Newhouse (1970), Jacobs (1974), Feldstein (1977). Due to equation (3.1), the variable "quantity of services" used by Sloan/Steinwald (1980, Chap.2) has analogous meaning. On the "quality preference" of non-profit-making firms in general *see* James/Rose-Ackerman (1986, Chap.4).
12. The income objective is emphasized, *e.g.*, by Pauly/Redisch (1973).
13. A low work-load can be used, at least by medical directors, for providing ambulatory treatment to privately insured patients and thereby for earning additional income.
14. In 1983 only 3.8 per cent of all acute-care hospital beds were in private hospitals (*see* Daten des Gesundheitswesens 1985, p. 250).
15. *See* Bundesminister für Arbeit und Sozialordnung (1983), henceforth quoted as BMA (1983).
16. This negative conclusion is qualified to some extent when the interests of non-physician hospital employees are included. The union ÖTV, in which nurses and other hospital workers are organized, explicitly supports the principle of cost reimbursement (*ibid.*, p. 101).
17. Mark Pauly suggested to us that cost reimbursement might not be all too attractive to physicians if they dislike the interference of public supervisors entailed in this system, as described above.

REFERENCES

Breyer, F., "Die Fallpauschale als Vergütung für Krankenhausleistungen - Idee, Formen und vermutete Auswirkungen" (Per-Case-Payment for Hospital Services - Idea, Types and Expected Consequences), *Zeitschrift für Wirtschafts- und Sozialwissenschaften*, 105: 743–767, 1985.
Bundesminister für Arbeit und Sozialordnung, "Gutachten zur Neuordnung der Krankenhausfinanzierung (Expertise on the Reform of Hospital Financing)", erstattet von der beim Bundesminister für Arbeit und Sozialordnung gebildeten Beratergruppe ("Wannagat-Report"), 1983.
Cleverley, W.O., "Evaluation of Alternative Payment Strategies for Hospitals: A Conceptual Approach", *Inquiry*, 16: 108–118, 1979.
"Daten des Gesundheitswesens 1985 (Health Sector Data)", Schriftenreihe des Bundesministers für Jugend, Familie und Gesundheit, Band 154, Stuttgart.
Davis, K., "Economic Theories of Behavior in Nonprofit Private Hospitals", *Economic and Business Bulletin*, 24: 1–13, 1972.
Dowling, W.L., "Prospective Reimbursement of Hospitals", *Inquiry*, 11: 163–80, 1974.
Feldstein, M.S., "Quality Change and the Demand for Hospital Care", *Econometrica*, 45: 1681–1702, 1977.
"Gesetz zur Neuordnung der Krankenhausfinanzierung - KHNG (Law on the Hospital Financing Reform)", *Bundesgesetzblatt*, Jg. 1984, Teil I: 1716–1722, 1984.
Heess, M., "Formen der Krankenhausvergütung. Eine mikroökonomische Analyse alternativer Systeme (Types of Hospital Reimbursement. A Microeconomic Analysis of Alternative Systems)". Bern, *et al.*, 1989.
Jacobs, P., "A Survey of Economic Models of Hospitals", *Inquiry*, 11: 83–97, 1974.

James, E., and S. Rose-Ackerman, "The Nonprofit Enterprise in Market Economics", *Fundamentals of Pure and Applied Economics*, Vol. 9. Chur *et al.*, 1986.

Lee, M.L., "A Conspicuous Production Theory of Hospital Behavior", *Southern Economic Journal*, 38: 48–58, 1971.

Neubauer, G., "Bausteine eines rationalen Krankenhaus-Vergütungssystems" (Building Blocks of a Rational System of Hospital Reimbursement), in: Neubauer G., and G. Sieben (eds.) *Alternative Entgeltverfahren in der Krankenhausversorgung* (*Alternative Payment Systems for Hospital Services*), Beiträge zur Gesundheitsökonomie der Robert Bosch Stiftung, Gerlingen, 1991.

Newhouse, J.P., "Toward a Theory of Nonprofit Institutions: An Economic Model of a Hospital", *American Economic Review*, 60: 64–74, 1970.

Pauly, M.V., and M. Redisch, "The Not-For-Profit Hospital as a Physicians' Cooperative", *American Economic Review*, 63: 87–99, 1973.

Robert-Bosch Stiftung, "Krankenhausfinanzierung in Selbstverwaltung (Hospital Financing and Self-Government)", Kommissionsbericht, Gerlingen, 1987.

Sloan, F.A., "The American Experience with Case-Based Payment for Hospital Care: The DRG Experiment", in: Neubauer G., and G. Sieben (eds.) *Alternative Entgeltverfahren in der Krankenhausversorgung*, Beiträge zur Gesundheitsökonomie der Robert Bosch Stiftung, Gerlingen, 1991.

Sloan, F.A., and B. Steinwald, "Insurance, Regulation, and Hospital Costs". Lexington/Mass., 1980.

"Verordnung zur Regelung der Krankenhauspflegesätze - BPflV (Decree on the Hospital Reimbursement Rates)", Bundesgesetzblatt, Jg. 1985, Teil I: 1666–1694, 1985.

A pooled cross-section analysis of the health care expenditures of the OECD countries*

ULF-G. GERDTHAM

Department of Economics, Stockholm School of Economics, Sweden.

JES SØGAARD

Department of Economics, Odense University, Denmark.

BENGT JÖNSSON

Department of Economics, Stockholm School of Economics, Sweden.

and

FREDRIK ANDERSSON

Battelle Medical Technology and Policy Centre, England.

ABSTRACT

This paper has two purposes. The first, empirical purpose is to estimate and evaluate the effects of aggregate income, institutional and socio-demographic factors on health care expenditures in the OECD countries. The second purpose is methodological, and comprises assessment of temporal instability, the choice of functional form, and misspecification of the estimated relationships. Data compiled over three years (1974, 1980 and 1987) from 19 OECD countries are used in a pooled cross-section regression analysis. Like previous studies, this one concludes that aggregate income measured by Gross Domestic Product per capita is the statistically most important factor in cross-national variation in health care expenditures, and that the aggregate income elasticity exceeds one. However, the data analyzed in this study also show some evidence that public financing of health care services is associated with lower expenditures per capita, and that countries with fee for service as the dominant form of remuneration have higher expenditures. The examined relationships appear to be temporally stable over the three years except for upward shifts, and there is no indication of statistical misspecification. This does not necessarily imply a correct specification, and we do note the presence of measurement errors in some of the variables. Moreover, the selected log-linear functional form appears to be non-optimal according to a likelihood criterion, and is rejected against a quadratic form. Based on

---

*We would like to thank the Editors, H.E. Frech III and Peter Zweifel for many helpful comments and encouragement. Constructive criticism from participants in the Second World Congress on Health Economics is also appreciated, in particular from Thomas Getzen, Robert Leu, Joseph Newhouse and Jean-Pierre Poullier.

P. Zweifel and H. E. Frech III (eds.), Health Economics Worldwide. 287–310.
© 1992 *Kluwer Academic Publishers. Printed in the Netherlands.*

the analyses from this study the results do not appear to be sensitive to use of the quadratic form specification.

1. INTRODUCTION

The substantial differences in health care expenditures across the Organization for Economic Cooperation and Development (OECD) countries have attracted much attention among health economists in recent years. Empirical analyses of these differences have usually been based on cross-sectional data, [Kleiman (1974), Newhouse (1977, 1987), Leu (1986), OECD (1977, 1987a), Parkin et al. (1987), Andersson and Gerdtham (1988), Gerdtham et al. (1988, 1991), Jönsson (1989), Culyer (1988, 1989); Parkin (1989)]. A major result of these studies concerns the importance of aggregate income per capita. Use of cross-national data offers an opportunity to investigate impacts of institutional factors of health care systems on health care expenditures, and Leu (1986) recently demonstrated that such factors also show measurable influence on health care expenditures.

The present paper continues this line of empirical research, and seeks in particular to shed light on some econometric aspects such as temporal stability of the estimated relationships and their functional form. Previous studies have paid little attention to these issues. The paper is organized as follows. An analytical framework is outlined in the next Section. The third Section concerns data and measurement, and an outline of the regression methods is presented in Section four. Results are reported in the fifth Section, and Section six summarizes the major findings of the analysis and its conclusions.

2. ANALYTICAL FRAMEWORK

Observed differences in health care expenditures in the OECD countries are the outcome of: 1) measurement errors, 2) random factors and 3) systematic factors. In this Section we discuss factors belonging to the latter group. Systematic differences in health care expenditures are the outcome of a composite of economic, demographic, social and political factors [Schieber and Poullier (1989)]. Any explanation that does not take all of these factors into account will necessarily be incomplete. The problem in practice is how to operationalize and hence assess the quantitative impact of those factors where conceptual and measurement difficulties abound. Differences in health care expenditures must ultimately reflect some combination of differences in demand/need for health care and the differences in costs of supply. But for these factors to be translated into differences in health care expenditure across countries, account should be taken of the historical, social and political context within which competing demands/needs and other pressures are determined. For the present study, attention focuses on factors that have featured most prominently in the literature. The factors are categorized in the following seven broadly defined groups: 1) aggregate income, 2) the relative price of health care, 3) demand/need for health care services, 4) substitution of formal for informal care, 5) supplier-induced demand, 6) delivery of health care, and 7) the financing of health care.

Aggregate income

Numerous studies at the micro level reveal a weak relationship between income and utilization [Andersen and Benham (1970), Grossman (1972), Newhouse and Phelps (1974), Muurinen (1982), Wagstaff (1986)]. This contrasts with evidence obtained from aggregate data. The individual consumer is not faced with the full resource cost of utilization due to subsidies, whereas the nation as a whole is. Culyer (1988) draws attention to the presence of non-price rationing such that health care is not consumed to the point of zero marginal value when the price is zero to the consumer. If such non-price-rationing is relaxed with increasing *aggregate* income, the income elasticity at the macro level is larger than the income elasticity at the individual level, and may exceed unity as in fact most empirical studies have reported.

Relative price

The demand for health care services is usually considered to be relatively inelastic with respect to the effective consumer price. The Health Insurance Experiment [Manning *et al.* (1987)] provided strong empirical support for this result. For similar reasons as above this result may not generalize to the macro level. Under fixed budget regimes the price elasticity is -1, and Gerdtham and Jönsson (1991) recently reported estimates of the aggregate price elasticity with respect to the quantity of health care as close to -1.

Demand/need for health care services

Two additional variables introduced in the model are age-distribution and urbanization. It is well known that the consumption of health care services is unevenly distributed over the life cycle. The hospitalization prevalence rate ratio of persons over 75 to persons about 50 years is 10 [Denton and Spencer (1975), Maxwell (1981)]. Therefore it is commonly agreed that changes in age-distribution affect the utilization of health care services. However, these utilization rates depend in turn on a variety of factors inherent in the health care system [Barer *et al.* (1987)], so the relationship between age distribution and demand for health care services is by no means certain. Actually, only one fifth of the growth of health care expenditures in Sweden between 1970 and 1985 is explained by changes in age distribution [Gerdtham (1990a,b), Gerdtham and Jönsson (1990)].

It has been argued that urbanization increases the demand for health care services. One argument refers to the spread of contagious diseases and industrial pollution in urban areas [Kleiman (1974)]. Secondly, the time and travel costs are lower in urban areas [Leu (1986)]. Thirdly, urbanization implies social change, as a result for instance, of the size and composition of households, which reduce the capacity of the households to take care of sick and debilitated persons [Pfaff and Nagel (1986)].

Substitution

A part of the observed increase in health care expenditures might be explained by the transition of health care from the family to institutions. Care of the elderly was previously the responsibility of the multi-generation family, while today it has been taken over by health care institutions [Fuchs (1972), Maxwell (1981), Ståhl (1986)]. We expect this substitution of formal for informal care to progress with increasing female labor supply and urbanization.

Supplier-induced demand

According to *the target income hypothesis*, physicians subject to fee for service remuneration adjust their workload in response to changes in the environment in order to maintain a target income [Evans (1974)]. When the stock of physicians increases and workload decreases, physicians may attempt to induce patients to use more services, *e.g.* by more contacts per medical service episode. The supplier-induced demand and target income hypotheses remain controversial, and they are difficult to assess empirically. Empirical relationships have been reported between the stock of physicians, the remuneration system and the number of surgical operations, and between the number of hospital beds, hospitalization rates and average length of stay in hospital, and between the physician stock and total out-patient expenditure, [Feldstein (1977), Reinhardt (1985)]. However, these findings are often not accepted as unambiguous evidence, at least not in favor of the target income hypothesis. The reported relationships between number of physicians and utilization may reflect true demand factors, for instance that more physicians increase the availability of health care, *i.e.* less distance to travel and less time to wait.

Delivery

The relative efficiency of public versus private (and non-profit versus for-profit) provision cannot be determined a priori, and empirical comparisons suffer from difficulties in standardizing for case mixes. From a public choice view, Leu (1986) argued that public provision increases health care expenditures through two different positive effects on the supply side: 1) the effect on the amount of health care services provided; and 2) the effect on unit costs at each level of activity. The former of these effects arises because bureaucrats in public or private non-profit institutions act like budget maximizers who are maximizing their own utility (status, better pay, promotion possibilities, reduced average work load, *etc.*) [Niskanen (1971)]. The effect on unit costs is expected to be positive owing to less intensive competition in the public sector, which in turn reduces incentives for cost minimization at each level of activity. These are Leu's propositions. His regression analysis of data for 19 OECD countries (1974) showed that an increase in the share of public and non-profit hospital beds by 10 percent was associated with a 8–9 percent increase in health care expenditures per capita. So Leu could present empirical evidence in favor of his propositions.

It has not been possible to test this result with later cross sections due to lack of data for shares of public and non-profit hospital beds [Gerdtham *et al.* (1988)]. Culyer (1989) questions Leu's arguments, and notes that private sector bureaucrats are not necessarily better controlled than their colleagues in the public sector; that costs in the private sector may be larger due to advertising and selling costs; and that market pressures may be less reliable than professional ethics and regulation (p 28). He also quotes the conclusion from a review of empirical comparisons [Stoddart and Labelle (1985)] that privately owned for-profit hospitals do not operate at lower production costs than do non-profit hospitals.

Financing

Leu (1986) also proposes that health care expenditures increase with the increasing share of public finance, - assuming implicitly that this share reduces the price to the consumer; and Culyer (1989) continues this line of reasoning. Both of Leu's hypotheses (public finance and public provision increase expenditure), states Culyer, depend on a passive response from the financing agent to adjust the supply of finance to the quantities and prices of health care services. Culyer suggests that the financing mechanism, in particular the degree of open-endedness of finance, is more relevant than the distribution per se of finance and provision on public and private institutions. Open-ended financing systems are characterized by multiple finance sources (insurance companies) and by fee for service remunerations. Conversely, closed systems are characterized by one or few finance agents, prospective payments such as capitation for outpatient services, and global budgets for hospitals. Open-ended systems provide little incentive for providers and little opportunity for financiers to contain expenditures; the converse is true for closed systems [Glaser (1987)]. The conclusion of all this appears to be that the impacts of share of public finance and/or provision on health care expenditures cannot be determined *a priori*. However, countries with more closed health care financing systems are anticipated to have lower expenditures.

The discussion above has served to identify potentially important factors to be included along with observable measures in the regression model for health care expenditures. They are summarized in the following 'theoretical model'

$$HE = f(Y,RP,AGE,URB,SUBST,SID,PP,PF,OPEN) \qquad (1)$$

where notation and anticipated signs of partial derivatives are

   HE = Health care expenditure per capita
    Y = Aggregate income per capita   +
    RP = Relative price of health care   +/0
   AGE = Age of population   +
   URB = Urbanization   +
  SUBST = Substitution of informal care   +
    SID = Supplier-induced demand   +
    PP = Public provision   ?
    PF = Public financing   ?
  OPEN = Open-endedness of financing   +

Having encircled a group of theoretical variables, the next step is measurement and data collection.

3. DATA AND MEASUREMENT ERRORS

Data for three years (1974, 1980 and 1987) have been compiled from either OECD or World Bank sources. Definitions and sources of the variables and proxy variables used in the empirical analysis are listed in Table 1. More detailed descriptions of the measurements are found in the data sources, and Poullier (1989) is of particular relevance. Note that the two monetary variables are both converted into US dollars by purchasing power parities (GDP-PPP) as calculated by the OECD [Ward (1985)].

Rigorous assessment of the quality (validity, reliability and precision) of such aggregate archival data is difficult. However, we would like to point out the following problems.

First; "Data are generally not comparable." [Schieber and Poullier (1989), p. 1]. Such a statement from researchers closely involved in compiling and processing data at the international level is of obvious concern to us. Poullier (1989) further describes the prevailing data compiling approach as: "An analyst attempts to 'massage' data from various countries, using as closely comparable units as can be obtained from the information readily accessible.", (p. 111). So there is ample scope for imperfect reliability with respect to cross section comparisons due to differential classifications, especially in the borderlands of health care services such as old age care. The differences, for instance, between Denmark and Sweden are well-known. Certainly, full homogeneity is not achieved by present approaches in international data compiling, although from the viewpoint of reproducibility of empirical analy-

Table 1. Definitions of variables in the empirical model for health care expenditure per capita

Theoretical variable	Measure/ proxy	Description and sources of data
HE	HEpc	Total expenditure for health care per capita converted by purchasing power parities for gross domestic product (GDP-PPP). Deflated by the GDP deflator, 1980 prices. (1974,1980,1987). Poullier(1989), Table 1. (Population data, same source, Table 61; GDP price index, same source, Table 64; purchasing power parities for GDP same source, Table 67)
Y	GDPpc	Gross domestic product at market prices per capita, converted by GDP-PPP, deflated by the GDP deflator, 1980 prices. (1974,1980,1987). Poullier(1989), Table 63.
RP	RPhc	Relative price index in 1985: Ratio of PPP for medical care to GDP-PPP's in 1985. (1985,1985,1985). (PPP for medical and health care in 1985, OECD(1987b)).
Age	AGE	Ratio of population 65 and over to population between 15 and 64 years. Multiplied by 100. (1974,1980,1986). OECD(1988).
URB	URB	Percentage of population living in cities with more that 500.000 inhabitants in 1980. (1980,1980,1980). World Bank(1989).
SUBST	FP	Female labor force participation: Percentage of female labor force to total number of females between 15 and 64. (1974,1980,1986). OECD(1988).
SID	DOCpc	Number of practicing, active physicians per 1000 inhabitants. (1974,1980,1987). (Number of physicians, Poullier (1989), Table 27).
PP	IP	Percentage of inpatient health care expenditures to total health care expenditures. (1974, 1980, 1987). (Total inpatient health care expenditures, Poullier (1989), Table 3).
PF	PF	Percentage of public health care expenditures to total health care expenditures. (1974,1980,1987). (Public health care expenditures, Poullier (1989), Table 2).
OPEN (1)	FEE	Dummy variable, one for countries with fee for service as the dominant means of remuneration, zero otherwise. (Identical for all years. The following countries have·been coded with one: Australia, Austria, Belgium, Canada, France, Germany, Greece, Ireland, Japan, Portugal, and the USA).
OPEN (2)	GLO BAL	Dummy variable, one for countries where global budgets dominate the financing of hospital services, zero otherwise. (Identical for all years. The following countries have been coded with one: Australia, Canada, Denmark, France, Greece, Ireland, Italy, Netherlands, New Zealand, Norway, Portugal, Spain, Sweden, and the UK).
	D80	Time dummy variable, 1 for 1980, zero otherwise.
	D87	Time dummy variable, 1 for 1987, zero otherwise.

ses we prefer the present situation to earlier practices where individual investigators performed their own 'massage' of the data.

Secondly, the measure of relative prices of health care services is based upon OECD's PPP's for health care, which is usually considered to be much less reliable than their GDP-PPP's. As we have not wanted to use the very unreliable health care PPP's for 1980, we only have a measure for the price variable for one year (1985).

Thirdly, only crude proxies are available for some of the theoretical variables, and their face validity is questionable. No exact measurement is available for shares of public (or of non-profit) provision of total health care. Leu (1986) used the shares of public and non-profit hospital beds in his analysis of 1974 cross section data. Unfortunately, our efforts to reproduce these data for 1974 or any other year were in vain. As an admittedly poorer proxy variable for share of public provision, we have used the percentage of inpatient care expenditures to total expenditures (IP). We motivate this choice of proxy measurement by a belief that more inpatient services than outpatient services are provided by public or non-profit institutions. As a proxy for substitution of formal for informal care, we use female labor force participation rates (FP). The number of physicians per capita is used as a proxy for the degree of supplier induced demand, and the other unobservable variable, degree of open-endedness in the financing of health care expenditures, is measured by two dummy variables, FEE and GLOBAL. The face validity of these two dummy variables is hardly low, but the underlying theoretical construct is of course not discrete, let alone dichotomous.

The relevant trade-off here is whether to omit variables for which only crude proxies are available or to include them with even poor proxies, and in the statistical analysis this is equivalent to a trade-off between a bias due to measurement errors and an omitted variable bias. With respect to the coefficients to regressor variables without measurement errors, the bias induced by measurement errors in proxy regressors is under fairly general assumptions smaller than the bias induced by omitting the proxy regressor [McCallum (1972), Kinal and Lahiri (1983)].

Data were missing for one or more variables for five countries (Finland, Iceland, Luxembourg, Switzerland and Turkey), and we decided to exclude these countries from the entire analysis. This leaves 19 countries, and a total sample size of 57.

4. STRATEGY OF REGRESSION ANALYSIS

Previous cross section regression analyses of health care expenditures pay much more attention to matters of theory than to econometric considerations such as the various restrictions more or less implicitly imposed on their data by choice of functional form and regressor variables, the question of temporal stability, and whether the statistical assumptions are satisfied or not (*i.e.* misspecification assessment). Our aim here is also to pay some attention to these econometric questions, and our reference is the emergent tradition in applied time-series econometrics [Hendry and Richard (1982,1983), Gilbert (1986)]. Before the results are presented the steps in the analysis are summarized.

General model and simplification searches

The two key concepts are simplification (or reduction) and misspecification analysis (or model evaluation). A general model is formulated to constitute a statistical framework for tests of theoretically or otherwise interesting hypotheses which can be expressed as (linear) restrictions on the general model. At each stage of reduction the restricted model is tested for emergent misspecification, and the acceptance of a set of restrictions depends both on the outcome of the hypothesis test of H_o: $R\beta = r$, and on the outcome of misspecification tests in $y = X\beta + u$ subject to $R\beta = r$. Both the general model and the sequence of reductions are designed to serve some particular purpose(s). If the purpose is to compare some previously published rival models for y, the general model is designed so as to provide a common distributional framework for a series of encompassing tests of the rival models [Mizon (1984)], - *see* Gerdtham *et al.* (1988, 1991) for applications in this field.

In this study one purpose is to assess the temporal stability of health care expenditure equations (slopes and variance), and the general model therefore allows all coefficients and the regression variances to vary over the three cross-section years, *i.e.*

$$\ln HC_{it} = \beta_0 + \partial_{01}D80_{it} + \partial_{02}D87_{it} + (\beta_1 + \partial_{11}D80_{it} + \partial_{12}D87_{it})FEE_{it}$$

$$+ (\beta_2 + \partial_{21}D80_{it} + \partial_{22}D87_{it})GLOBAL_{it} + (\beta_3 + \partial_{31}D80_{it}$$

$$+ \partial_{32}D87_{it})\ln GDPpc$$

$$+ (\beta_4 + \partial_{41}D80_{it} + \partial_{42}D87_{it})\ln PF_{it} + (\beta_5 + \partial_{51}D80_{it} + \partial_{52}D87_{it})\ln IP_{it}$$

$$+ (\beta_6 + \partial_{61}D80_{it} + \partial_{62}D87_{it})\ln DOCpc_{it} + (\beta_7 + \partial_{71}D80_{it}$$

$$+ \partial_{72}D87_{it})\ln RPhc_{it} \qquad (2)$$

$$+ (\beta_8 + \partial_{81}D80_{it} + \partial_{82}D87_{it})\ln FP_{it} + (\beta_9 + \partial_{91}D80_{it}$$

$$+ \partial_{92}D87_{it})\ln URB_{it}$$

$$+ (\beta_{10} + \partial_{101}D80_{it} + \partial_{102}D87_{it})\ln AGE_{it} + \epsilon_{it}$$

$$\epsilon_{it} \sim N(0,\sigma_t^2)$$

$$i = 1, 2, \ldots, 19, \quad t = 1974, 1980, 1987. \quad N = 19 * 3$$

The β_j parameters refer to the 1974–cross section, and the ∂_{ji} parameters are slope change coefficients, *i.e.* they measure *deviations* in corresponding coefficients in the 1980 and 1987 cross sections relative to the 1974 base coefficient. For example, the income elasticity in 1987 is measured by $\beta_3 + \partial_{32}$. Note also that the regression variances are allowed to vary over the three cross section years.

Stability tests as a simplification search

The stability hypothesis amounts to an equality restriction on the regression variances and on all triples of coefficients to the same regressor variables. First, the equal variance hypothesis is tested, and then the equal slope vector hypothesis. The model is parameterized so that the coefficient stability tests can be carried out as a joint significance test on the ∂ parameters. The actual tests are carried out in a sequence starting with the 18 ∂ coefficients associated with the regressor variables minus GDPpc and the constant; then the two slope change coefficients for the GDPpc variable, and finally for the constant.

Further simplification

It turns out that we cannot reject the stability hypothesis except for upward proportional shifts in the equation, and the next task is to reduce a model with 10 regressor variables and two time dummy variables for 1980 and 1987. Except for the most restrictive model with only the two time dummies and income per capita, the reduction sequence is not organized according to any particular theoretical considerations. Insignificant variables have been excluded. We are aware that this is not an ideal approach, and that alternative approaches are possible which pay more consideration to theory or policy relevance. The reason for using individual insignificance as an exclusion criterion is to assess a) whether a set of individually insignificant coefficients is also jointly insignificant, b) whether their exclusion induces misspecification, and c) whether the other parameter estimates are sensitive to zero restrictions on the insignificant ones.

The restrictions discussed so far involve regression parameters. It is also relevant to consider more systematically the functional form of the health care expenditure equations. Previous equations in the literature have assumed either linear or log-linear form (double-log), and this whole issue has not been explored much except for Parkin *et al.* (1987). They report R^2s for 4 different functional forms, and discuss the matter in relation to the estimation of income elasticities in aggregate health care expenditures. They claim theoretical justification for the linear functional form, in which case we may have a clash between such justification and data admissibility, because a linear functional form model does not ex ante estimation exclude negative health care expenditures in the outcome space. For the present analysis we assume a logarithmic functional form, but after the tests of temporal stability this assumption is carefully investigated within the framework of Box-Cox transformation analysis [Box and Cox (1964), Zarembka (1974), Spitzer (1982)]. The idea in the extended Box-Cox analysis is to parameterize functional form by two transformation parameters, one for the dependent variable and one for a relevant subset of the regression variables. Given estimates of the transformation parameters, hypotheses about particular values of these (and hence functional form) can be tested.

The extended Box-Cox model for health care expenditures is expressed

$$HC_{it}(\lambda_y) = X_{it}'\beta_1 + (Z_{it}(\lambda_z))'\beta_2 + \epsilon_{it} \tag{3}$$

$$\epsilon_{it} \sim N(0,\sigma^2)$$

where the X_{it} vector contains values for the constant and the four dummy variables (D80, D87, FEE and GLOBAL) which are not subject to transformation; Z_{it} contains values for all the other regressor variables, which are all positive and subject to Box-Cox power transformation; β_1 and β_2 are the associated 4*1 and 8*1 parameter vectors. The two lambda parameters (λ_z is **not** a vector but a scalar) represent the Box-Cox power transformation parameters, defined by the operations

$$Y_i(\lambda) = \begin{matrix} (Y_i^\lambda - 1)/\lambda \text{ for } \lambda \neq 0 \\ \ln Y_i \text{ for } \lambda = 0 \end{matrix} \tag{4}$$

The extended Box-Cox regression model in (3) encompasses a wide range of functional forms, including the four considered in Parkin *et al.* (1987): linear $(\lambda_y;\lambda_z) = (1;1)$; semi-log $(1;0)$; exponential $(0;1)$ and the double-log $(0;0)$. Unfortunately the model is non-linear in the lambda parameters, and they must be estimated either by iterated ordinary least squares or by a gradient optimization technique. Our primary concern here is to obtain ML point estimates of the lambda parameters for the purpose of likelihood ratio tests of null hypotheses about the transformation parameters, and a correct estimate of the asymptotic variance-covariance matrix of the parameter estimates (slope and transformation parameters) is not important to us. Therefore maximum likelihood estimates of the two lambda parameters have been computed by iterated ordinary least squares in successively narrower two dimensional grids using the following concentrated log likelihood function as the maximization criterion

$$L_c(\lambda_y,\lambda_z,\beta_1,\beta_2; HC, Z, X) = -\frac{N}{2}(\ln(2\pi) + 1) - \frac{N}{2}\ln\hat{\sigma}^2 \tag{5}$$

$$+ (\lambda_5 - 1)\sum_{j=1}^{N}\ln HC_j$$

where $\hat{\sigma}^2 = \Sigma\hat{e}_j^2/N$ and the last term $(\lambda_y-1)\Sigma\ln HC_j$ is the Jacobian of the Box-Cox transformation of the dependent data

When the ML estimates of λ_y and of λ_z have been determined, null hypotheses about certain values, say $(0;0)$, can be tested by a conventional likelihood ratio test computed as twice the difference between the log likelihood with unrestricted lambda parameters (ML estimates) and the log likelihood with the lambda values under the null hypothesis, *i.e.*

$$2(L(\hat{\lambda}_y,\hat{\lambda}_z - L(\lambda_{y0},\lambda_{z0})) \sim \chi^2(2) \tag{6}$$

This procedure is carried out for each model considered after temporal stability has been assessed. Ideally the general model should also have been subject to Box-Cox transformation analysis, but this was impractical for a model with 33 parameters and 57 observations.

Misspecification analysis as model evaluation

Misspecification analysis involves a checking of the assumptions laid down for consistent estimation and inference. Here it is obvious that particular attention should be paid to heteroskedasticity, but statistics are also reported which should have power against non-normality, against functional form, and Ramsey's RESET test is also reported. See Table 2 for a summary description.

The heteroskedasticity and non-normality tests refer to the regression *residuals*, and may upon significant outcome indicate either heteroskedastic or non-normal regression *errors*, or - just like the RESET and Box-Cox tests - some misspecification in the systematic part of the regression equation. However, if the residuals from a restricted equation show heteroskedastic residual behavior while the less restricted equation did not, it is likely that the particular (mis)behavior was induced by the restrictions, and the resulting model should therefore either be rejected or interpretations and inferences from it be flagged with warnings. Non-significant misspecification statistics may simply reflect low power, and are therefore no guarantee for a correctly specified model. Yet we do consider misspecification statistics as an important part of the information reported from regression exercises, and hopefully our knowledge about power in relatively small sample sizes such as we have here will improve with practice.

5. RESULTS OF REGRESSION ANALYSIS

The empirical results are based on observations for 19 OECD countries for three years, 1974, 1980 and 1987. Ten regressor variables are included, *see* Table 1 for a description.

We start by estimating eq. (2) above for the purpose of testing temporal stability in the slope coefficients and the regression variances, *see* Table 3. Please note that acronyms used in equation (2) above and (7) below are avoided in the tables. 'Fem.lab.part' is awful, but bears closer resemblance to 'Female labor force participation rate' than does 'FP'. Coefficients in * D80 rows are slope change coefficients for 1980, *i.e.* ∂_{j1} parameters, and similarly for *D87 rows. The equations are estimated in double-log form, so the coefficients can be interpreted directly as elasticities (subject to a constant elasticity restriction). The first column reports the coefficient estimates for the general model. The coefficient 1.12 to the GDPpc variable is the 1974 cross section estimate of the income elasticity. This had not changed in the 1980 cross section, but had increased by 0.34 in the 1987 cross section to

Table 2. Overview of statistics used in misspecification analysis in regression equations based on data for 19 cross section observations for three years. $n = 19$; $T = 3$; $N = 57$. Fitted regression; $Y_{it} = X'_{it}b + e_{it}$. k = number of regression coefficients. Y and X represent possibly transformed data. Below $s^2 = \Sigma^N e^2_{it}/N$, (ML estimate of the regression variance).

Test against	Type[1] and distr.	Description and textbook references
Heteroskedasticity groupwise	LR $X^2(2)$	Test for equal regression variances in the T cross section years; $X^2(2) = N\{\ln(s^2) - \Sigma^T \ln(s^2_t)\}/\text{adj}$ s^2 = variance under homoskedasticity assumption for all N observations. s^2_t = variance for the t'th cross section under heteroskedasticity assumption. [Johnston (1984) pp. 298–9, Greene (1990), pp. 422–3.]
B–P: 80–87	LM $X^2(2)$	Breusch–Pagan test against heteroskedastic residuals due to groupwise variance differences. $g_{it} = e^2_{it}/s^2$. B-P auxiliary regression
B–P: GDPpc	LM $X^2(2)$	Breusch–Pagan test against heteroskedastic residuals as a fucntion of aggregate income per capita. $g_{it} = e^2_{it}/s^2$. B–P auxiliary regression $g_{it} = \alpha_1 + \alpha^*_2\{GDPpc(\lambda_z)\}_{it} + \alpha^*_3\{GDPpc(\lambda_z)\}^2_{it} + v_{it}$. $X^2(2) = 0.5*ESS$.
B–P: X	LM $X^2(k - 1)$	Breusch–Pagan test against heteroskedastic residuals as a linear function of all X-variables. $g_{it} = e^2_{it}/x^2$. B-P auxiliary regression $g_{it} = X'_{it}\alpha + v_{it}$; $\quad X^2(k - 1) = 0.5*ESS$. [Johnston (1984), p. 300, Greene (1990), pp. 421–2]
Non-normality	W $X^2(2)$	Browman–Shelton test of the joint hypothesis that residual skewness is 0 and kurtosis in 3 (mesokurtic). $BS = N\{Skewness^2/6 - ((Kurtosis - 3)^2)/24\} - X^2(2)$ [Greene (1990), pp. 328–30]. The approximation is poor even for medium samples, and more precise critical values have been numerically determined [Bera and Jarque (1981)]. For $N = 57$ the 10% and 5% critical values are 2.95 and 4.26, respectively.
Specification	LR $F_{3;N-k-3}$	Ramsey's RESET test against omitted variables and functional form error, joint significance test of a_1, a_2 and a_3 in the auxiliary regression: $Y_{it} = X'_{it}c + a_1(X'_{it}b)^2 + a_2(X'_{it}b)^3 + a_3(X'_{it}b)^4 + v_{it}$. [Kmenta (1986), p. 452].
Functional form	LR $X^2(2)$	Hypothesis test of Box–Cox transformation parameters, see the text for further details, equation (6).

[1] LM denotes Lagrange multiplier test, LR likelihood ratio test, and W a Wald test.

Table 3. Temporal stability in pooled regressions of health care expenditures per capita: 19 OECD countries", 1974, 1980 and 1987. N = 57. Log-linear functional form (double-log)

Equations Regressor variable	Unrestricted H_g WLS[w] coef	t	restricted H_{01} OLS coef	t	H_{02} OLS coef	t	H_{03} OLS coef	t
Constant	-4.75	-1.75	-4.55	-3.28[a]	-4.24	-3.78[a]	-5.68	-4.88[a]
*D80	2.17	0.56	0.97	0.63	0.15	3.00[a]	-	-
*D87	0.85	0.26	0.56	0.38	0.21	3.39[a]	-	-
Fee/service	0.04	0.33	0.12	1.97[c]	0.11	1.99[c]	0.11	1.70[c]
*D80	0.09	0.50	0		0		0	
*D87	0.15	0.89	0		0		0	
Global budget	-0.10	-0.60	-0.03	-0.42	-0.04	-0.47	-0.01	-0.13
*D80	0.03	0.12	0		0		0	
*D87	0.19	0.92	0		0		0	
GDPpc	1.12	4.29[a]	1.30	9.03[a]	1.26	12.00[a]	1.35	12.04[a]
*D80	0.00	0.00	-0.09	-0.53	0		0	
*D87	0.34	1.08	-0.04	-0.25	0		0	
Public finance	-0.08	-0.20	-0.36	-1.93[c]	-0.34	-1.90[c]	-0.20	-1.00
D80	-0.35	-0.57						
*D87	-0.63	-1.25						
Inpatient/total	0.40	1.50	0.29	2.51[b]	0.28	2.54[b]	0.22	1.78[c]
*D80	-0.06	-0.17						
*D87	-0.19	-0.59						
Physicians/pop	-0.16	-0.62	-0.17	-1.96[c]	-0.17	-1.96[c]	-0.00	-0.11
*D80	-0.11	-0.34						
*D87	0.00	0.03						
Rel. price HC	0.50	1.33	0.22	1.31	0.23	1.39	0.23	1.27
*D80	-0.25	-0.47						
*D87	-0.52	-1.14						
Fem. lab. part	0.14	0.57	-0.01	-0.10	-0.01	-0.13	0.00	0.00
*D80	-0.06	-0.20						
*D87	-0.37	-1.19						
Urbanization	-0.26	-1.27	-0.26	-3.06[a]	-0.26	-3.09[a]	-0.19	-2.15[b]
*D80	-0.10	-0.36						
*D87	0.03	0.10						
Age: 64+/15-64	0.15	0.23	1.70[c]	0*.22	1.68[c]	0.20	1.42	
*D80	0.07	0.18						
*D87	0.25	0.64						

Statistics[$] (k)	H_G (33)	H_{01} (15)	H_{02} (13)	H_{03} (11)
Standard error of regression (SSE/(N − k))	0.165	0.143	0.141	0.156
R^2	0.946	0.925	0.928	0.908

Heteroskedasticity

Groupwise LE-X^2 (2)	2.16			
B-P::80,87 LM-X^2 (2)	1.90	1.14	1.05	0.60
B-P:GDPpc LM-X^2 (2)	1.58	0.45	1.20	2.68
B-P:all X LM-X^2 (k − 1)	29.9	17.4	15.9	11.8

Slope restrictions

H_{0j} against H_G		$F_{18;24} = 0.43$	$F_{20;24} = 0.40$	$F_{22;24} = 0.78$
H_{0j} against H_{0j-1}			$F_{2;42} = 0.14$	$F_{2;44} = 6.41^a$

\# Excluded countries are Finland, Iceland, Luxembourg, Switzerland and Turkey.
[a,b,c] Significance at 1%, 5% and 10% levels.
[w] Weights are 1 (1976), 0.999 (1980) and 0.717.
[$] See Table 2.

1.46. However, the estimate of ∂_{32} of 0.34 is statistically insignificant as judged by the t-ratio value of 1.08. Actually, most coefficients appear to be statistically insignificant, which is to be expected in a model with 33 parameters estimated with 57 data points.

Temporal stability

The interesting information is in the lower part of Table 3 (the statistics section). The groupwise heteroskedasticity LR-test, see top of Table 2, is the statistic most frequently used for assessment of equal regression variances over several groups, and it is clearly insignificant (less than half the critical 10% value), so we infer equal variance over the three cross sections. The model is then re-estimated with OLS, and the other test statistics are based on the OLS residuals. Of course the parameter (point)estimates do not change, and since the t-ratios only changed slightly they are not reported. The Breusch-Pagan LM test of temporal shifts in the regression variance (B-P:80,87) is asymptotically equivalent to the LR-test just mentioned, and, as expected, is also insignificant. The other two heteroskedasticity tests are also insignificant. Slope stability over time will now be examined.

In the first step the joint significance of 2*9 ∂_{ij} parameters is tested (H_{o1}), *i.e.* all slope change coefficients except for function shifts and changes in the income elasticities. This null hypothesis cannot be rejected; the F-test statistic (second row from bottom of Table 3) is only 0.43, and the 18 zero restrictions do not induce heteroskedasticity in the residuals. This step may have been too large, that is we may not have done justice to some change parameters. On the other hand, if we begin a search for change parameters, we are sure to find some, but without much knowledge of the type I error. We did make an exception with the income elasticity parameter, because the GDPpc variable has been very important in these health care expenditure equations. However, neither 1) the estimated sizes and their individual t-ratios for the two income elasticity change coefficients, 2) the joint significance test against the entire H_G model (0.40) and against the H_{o1} model (incremental test) (0.14), nor 3) the heteroskedasticity tests provide any empirical justification for such changes in the income elasticity from 1974 to 1980 or 1987. So H_{o2} is also accepted. Finally also the two function shift parameters are set to zero under the third and most restrictive model with respect to temporal stability, H_{o3}. The joint F-tests are actually redundant because the two individual t-ratios are both high, and therefore the joint hypothesis test of H_{o3} against the H_{o2} model also becomes highly significant, (6.41 with 2 degrees of freedom in the numerator and 44 in the denominator). The joint test statistic for all 22 zero restrictions against the general model H_G is only 0.78 and statistically insignificant, and reflects but deflated power in large joint tests - in our opinion. Note also that there is no indication in the residuals estimated under H_{o3} where no parameter is allowed to vary over time.

The temporal stability part of the analysis concludes with a rejection of H_{o3} and an acceptance of H_{o2}. Consequently, all slope coefficients are inferred to be stable over the three time points, but it appears that the health care expenditure function has shifted upwards. The two shift parameters amount to an average autonomous increase of 2.5% annually from 1974 to 1980, and 0.8% annually after 1980. The statistical significance of the autonomous increase after 1980 has not been tested.

Analysis of a health care expenditure equation with constant slope parameters

The analysis now proceeds with H_{o2} from above as the maintained model (H_M) for further simplification, *see* Table 4. Note that the coefficients and heteroskedasticity statistics under H_M in Table 4 are identical to those under H_{o2} in Table 3. The estimated coefficients are hardly promising for further analysis; three coefficients (to the Global budget dummy variable, physicians per capita and urbanization) have 'wrong' signs, two of them 'significantly wrong'! Although the test statistics against residual heteroskedasticity and non-normality (skewness and non-mesokurtosis), and the RESET specification error statistic are insignificant, there is indication that the double-log form is non-optimal. The pair of maximum likelihood estimates for λ_y and λ_z are (0.44;1.525), and the Box-Cox likelihood ratio test for the functional form null hypothesis

$$H_o: (\lambda_{oy};\lambda_{oz}) = (0;0)$$

yields a $X^2(2)$ value of 10.7, $p < 0.01$.

The simplification search continues, and β_2 (Global budget dummy variable) and β_8 (female labor force participation rate) are set to zero in the first step (H_{o1}) because their estimates are very insignificant sizewise and statistically. This reduction does not induce any indication of misspecification, and the remaining coefficients hardly change at all, while their t-ratios increase. The hypothesis test of the double-log functional form is still significant but the X^2-statistic is much lower. Under H_{o2} β_7 (relative price of health care services) is also set to zero, and except for the public finance share coefficient the remaining coefficients change little bit as a result of this exclusion. Again there is no indication of misspecification and the double-log form hypothesis is accepted at the 10% level but not at the 5% level.

Further simplification appears unwarranted. Under H_{o3}, β_6 (physicians per capita) and β_{10} (age) are also set to zero, but these additional restrictions are rejected against H_{o2} at the 10% level, and the Breusch-Pagan X^2 statistic for heteroskedasticity as a function of all included regressor variables is significant at the 5% level. Finally, the simplest model including only the temporal shift dummy variables and Gross Domestic Product per capita, is also rejected, both against the previous model and against H_M.

The simplification search suggests the equation under H_{o2} according to which three regressor variables, the dummy variable for Global budgets,

Table 4. Pooled regresions of health care expenditures per capita. Tests of slope restrictions. 19 OECD countries[#], 1974, 1980 and 1987. N = 57. Log-linear functional form (double-log). Ordinary least squares

Equations Regressor variable	Unrestricted H_M coef	t	restricted equations H_{01} coef	t	H_{02} coef	t	H_{03} coef	t	H_{04} coef	t
Constant	-4.24	-3.78[a]	-4.33	-4.07[a]	-4.17	-3.89[a]	-4.35	-4.09[a]	-6.19	-9.75[a]
Shift 1980	0.15	3.00[a]	0.15	3.05[a]	0.15	3.04[a]	0.12	2.56[b]	0.12	2.33[b]
Shift 1987	0.21	3.39[a]	0.20	3.41[a]	0.20	3.37[a]	0.15	2.94[a]	0.13	2.46[b]
Fee/service	0.11	1.99[c]	0.13	2.50[b]	0.12	2.32[b]	0.09	1.75[c]	0	
Global budget	-0.04	-0.47	0		0		0		0	
GDPpc	1.26	12.00[a]	1.28	17.80[a]	1.27	17.54[a]	1.29	17.24[a]	1.38	19.25[a]
Public finance	-0.34	-0.90[c]	-0.36	-2.08[b]	-0.48	-3.10[a]	-0.33	-2.26[b]	0	
Inpatient/total	0.28	2.54[b]	0.26	2.66[b]	0.31	3.46[a]	0.27	2.95[a]	0	
Physicians/pop	-0.17	-1.96[c]	-0.17	-2.07[b]	-0.17	-1.97[c]	0		0	
Rel. price HC	0.23	1.39	0.22	1.46	0		0		0	
Fem. lab. part	-0.01	-0.13	0		0		0		0	
Urbanization	-0.26	-3.09[a]	-0.26	-3.31[a]	-0.23	-2.96[a]	-0.19	-2.51[b]	0	
Age:65+/15-64	0.22	1.68[c]	0.23	2.00[c]	0.22	1.88[c]	0		0	

Statistics[$] (k)	H_M (13)	H_{01} (11)	H_{02} (10)	H_{03} (8)	H_{04} (4)
Standard error (SSE/(N − k))	0.141	0.137	0.140	0.144	0.154
R^2	0.928	0.928	0.925	0.916	0.896
Heteroskedasticity					
B-P:80,87 LM-X^2 (2)	1.05	1.13	1.79	1.39	0.57
B-P:GDPpc LM-X^2 (2)	1.20	0.42	2.12	4.00	3.96
B-P:all X LM-X^2 (k − 1)	15.9	13.5	13.9	14.5[b]	3.19
Non-normality, SK = 0, KS = 3 W-X^2 (2)	1.46	1.53	0.82	0.30	0.87
Specification error Ramsey's RESET $F_{3:(N-k-3)}$	0.89	1.11	0.88	0.76	
Functional form Box-Cox, Ly = Lz = 0 LR-X^2 (2)	10.7[a]	5.62[b]	5.27[c]	6.34[b]	5.37[c]
Slope restrictions					
H_{0j} againat H_M		$F_{2:44} = 1.43$	$F_{3:44} = 0.77$	$F_{5:44} = 1.55$	$F_{9:44} = 2.22$[b]
H_{0j} against H_{0j-1}			$F_{1:46} = 2.13$	$F_{2:47} = 2.72$[c]	$F_{4:49} = 2.92$[b]

Excluded countries are Finland, Luxenbourg, Switzerland and Turkey.
[a,b,c] Significance at 1%, 5% and 10% levels.
[$] See Table 2.

relative price of health care services, and the female labor force participation rate can be excluded as insignificant in the regression equation for health care expenditures. The insignificance of the relative price variable implies acceptance of the fixed budget hypothesis, *i.e.* a price elasticity of -1. The resulting model is

$$\ln HC_{it} = -4.17 + 0.15*D80_{it} + 0.20*D87_{it} + 0.12*FEE_{it}$$

$$+ 1.27*\ln GDPpc_{it} - 0.48*\ln PF_{it} + 0.31*\ln IP_{it}$$

$$- 0.17*\ln DOCpc_{it} - 0.23*\ln URB_{it} + 0.22*\ln AGE_{it}$$

$$+ e_{it}. \tag{7}$$

$$s_e = 0.14; \ R^2 = 0.925; \ i:19 \text{ OECD countries;}$$

$$t:1974,1980,1987;$$

(see table 1 for guidance to acronyms).

The two shift parameter estimates have not changed, and require no further comments. The *fee for service dummy variable* has a positive coefficient according to which health care expenditures are about 13% larger in countries with fee for service as the dominant remuneration. This result is fairly insensitive to exclusion of insignificant regressor variables. The estimated *income elasticity* is 1.27, which is significantly larger than unity (t-ratio for H_o: $\beta_3 = 1.0$ is 3.73), and both the size of the estimate and the rejection of a unit elasticity hypothesis are insensitive to exclusion of the other variables, although the elasticity estimate increases somewhat when *all* other regressor variables are excluded. The *public finance share* has a coefficient of -0.48, so that health care expenditures are predicted to fall by about 5% when the share of public health care expenditures to total expenditures increases by 10%. The sign is as expected, although the magnitude is unexpectedly large, and appears to be sensitive to exclusion of the relative price variable but not to exclusion of the dummy variable for Global budgets. Neither sign nor significance of this coefficient is affected by exclusion of the United Kingdom or of New Zealand. A shift in the *age distribution* in the population towards more elderly people is predicted to increase health care expenditure, and the estimated coefficient is rather insensitive to exclusion of other regressor variables. These were the relatively nonproblematic results. However, the remaining three coefficients are problematic either because of ambiguous measurement or an anomalous prediction or both.

The coefficient to the *share of inpatient care expenditures of total expenditures* is positive, but whether the elasticity coefficient of 0.31 really reflects a positive impact of share of public provision on health care expenditures is questionable. Also the number of *physicians per capita* is a proxy measure, and whether or not it is a satisfactory proxy measure for degree of supplier induced demand, the prediction that health care expenditures decrease by 1.7% when the number of physicians per capita increases by 10% is simply

Table 5. Assessment of multicollinearity by the internal coefficients of determination and the correlation matrix of estimated coefficients in model H_{02}

Internal coefficient of determination		\- Correlations between coefficients: $\mathrm{cor}(b_i b_j)$ \- regressor variable								
j'th regressor	$R^2_{j,x}/i$	1	2	3	4	5	6	7	8	9
1 Constant		1.0								
2 Shift-80		0.27	1.0							
3 Shift-87		0.36	0.62	1.0						
4 Fee/service	0.45	−0.12	0.01	0.10	1.0					
5 GDPpc	0.29	−0.74	−0.20	−0.02		1.0				
6 Public finance	0.58	−0.72	−0.23	−0.27	0.02	0.34	1.0			
7 Inpatient/total	0.49	0.27	0.06	0.18	0.45	−0.38	−0.46	1.0		
8 Physicians/pop	0.50	−0.20	−0.37	−0.56	−0.26	0.10	0.36	−0.23	1.0	
9 Urbanization	0.47	−0.59	−0.18	−0.26	−0.36	0.25	0.52	−0.44	0.33	1.0
10 Age 65+/15−64	0.31	−0.10	0.03	0.05	0.15	−0.04	−0.33	0.11	−0.37	−0.03

$R^2_{j,x}$ is the R^2 of the regression of the j'th regressor variable on the other regressor variables.

hard to explain. The case is similar with respect to the prediction that health care expenditures decrease by 2.3% when urbanization (the share of population living in very large cities) increases by 10%. We observe that the latter two coefficients with 'wrong' signs are as robust to exclusion of other regressor variables as are those with 'correct' signs.

Rather than embark on some speculations about theoretical explanations for the latter two coefficient estimates we shall discuss possible methodological explanations. First, the interpretation above focused on partial effects, and the validity of such interpretation depends on the degree of collinearity in the regressor data matrix. Secondly, we shall look more closely at the functional form issue to see whether the results may be sensitive to the choice of a double-log specification.

Multicollinearity

Multicollinearity is usually not comprised by misspecification analysis because it reflects a real life phenomenon, and except for perfect multicollinearity it is not included among the estimation assumptions. However, high but less than perfect multicollinearity 1) confounds the measurement of separate effects of individual regressor variables on health care expenditures per capita, 2) it may deflate the t-ratios, and 3) it may render the parameter estimates highly sensitive to addition or deletion of other regressor variables. The latter two consequences have been taken into account in the regression analysis above, but the first-mentioned has not. Some information about multicollinearity is presented in table 5.

The first column of Table 5 reports the internal coefficients of determination for the regressor variables, except for the two shift dummy variables. The remaining columns contain coefficients of correlation between the 10 regression coefficients in the regression equation under H_{o2}. Except for

Table 6. Functional form analysis of health care expenditure equations

			Double log		Linear $(\lambda_{yo}, \lambda_{xo})$		Exponential		Semilog		Square root linear	
	ML estimates											
Models	λ_y	λ_x	(0;0)		(1;1)		(0;1)		(1;0)		(0.5;1)	
			$x^2(2)$	p%	$x^2(2)$	p%	$x^2(2)$	p%	$x^2(2)$	p%	$x^2(x)$	p%
H_M	0.44	1.53	10.7	0.48	30.5	0	7.6	2.24	49.21	0	4.55	10.3
H_{01}	0.31	1.02	5.62	6.0	26.2	0	7.03	3.0	43.9	0	1.99	37,0
H_{02}	0.38	0.98	5.27	7.2	23.5	0	9.48	0.9	41.1	0	1.08	58.3
H_{03}	0.41	1.13	6.34	4.2	24.4	0	8.7	1.3	41.2	0	1.47	47.9
H_{04}	0.36	1.04	5.37	6.8	26.3	0	10.1	0.66	52.6	0	1.13	51.3

GDPpc and the AGE ratio variable, the internal determination coefficients are relatively high, about 0.50. On the other hand 0.5 is much lower than the R^2 for the health care expenditure data reported in Table 4, so the individual t-ratios should not be affected much by multicollinearity. How high these measures of collinearity can be before partial effect interpretation is severely hampered is yet to be determined, but we caution against too firm a partial effect interpretation for the 5 regressor variables with high internal R^2. The correlations between the regression coefficients also prompt moderate concern, and we reiterate the mild warning above. The coefficients to physicians per capita and to urbanization are highly correlated with several of the other coefficients, but hardly enough to explain their unexpected signs.

Functional form

A closer inspection of the functional form issue is justified because the chosen double-log form appeared to be non-optimal by a likelihood criterion. From a purely statistical view a regression of the square roots of health care expenditures on regressor data (linear) seems to be superior to any of the functional forms conventionally used in empirical analyses, see Table 6. The linear and the semi-log forms are conclusively rejected, while the exponential form yields significance test statistics a bit larger than those for the double-log form assumed above.

It appears that the functional form of these health care expenditure equations may be much more complicated than previously assumed and the estimates in Table 6 point at a quadratic form rather than linear or log-linear forms. A more detailed analysis of the issue is beyond the scope of this article. However, the entire regression analysis was replicated, with square roots of the health care expenditures and the regressor variables included linearly to examine sensitivity in the results to the choice of functional form. The alternative functional form did not alter the general results reported above. The signs of the coefficients are unchanged, and the outcomes of the model tests and misspecification analysis are similar to those in Tables 3 and 4. The major differences are some heteroskedasticity in the H_M and H_{o1} models but not in the others, and non-significance of the physician per capita variable in all the models, *e.g.* the t-ratio under H_{o2} is -1.45 compared to -1.97 under the double-log assumption. Due to this the joint F statistic of H_{o3} against H_{o2} is 2.41 compared to 2.72 in table 4, and is hence just insignificant at the 10% level (but the estimated p is 0.101 !).

6. CONCLUSIONS

International comparisons can be used to enlarge our understanding of the overall determinants of health care expenditure, and regression analyses of health care expenditures in the OECD countries on various socio-demographic and institutional factors have been published in the past with this purpose in mind. Yet another regression analysis has been presented here, and one aim has been to investigate some econometric issues which have not previously been considered systematically. These econometric issues comprise temporal stability of the estimated equations, previously estimated with pure cross section data and the important issue of functional form. Futhermore we have argued for more emphasis on misspecification testing and more explicitness about the process by which a model is obtained and evaluated. Production of plausible coefficients and canvassing conventional wisdom concerning empirical regularities are not the only legitimate purposes of empirical analysis. An important purpose of the work presented above has been to point out problems and issues to be followed up in future work by ourselves and others.

We began by outlining seven categories of potential determinants of systematic differences between health care expenditures, (aggregate income, the relative price of health care, demand/need for health care services, substitution of formal care for informal care, supplier-induced demand, delivery of health care and financing of health care services). Theorizing about aggregates is, however, sadly backward. Moreover, several of the factors believed to determine health care expenditures at the national level are difficult to measure due to lack of data or because they are inherently latent variables, and the potentially low validity of the proxy variables is an issue of concern for these and previously published empirical results.

Among the multitude of estimates and test statistics reported in the previous section, we want to emphasize only a few here. As far as can be judged from three years, 1974, 1980, and 1987, the specified health care expenditure equation is surprisingly stable over time, both in slopes and in variance. As in previous research, Gross Domestic Product per capita, with a coefficient of elasticity significantly larger than one, appears to be the most important statistical factor in cross-national health care expenditure variations. However, it is equally clear that aggregate income, and whatever it reflects, is not the only factor. Both institutional and socio-demographic factors do show measurable effects on health care expenditures. Unfortunately, measurement errors, multicollinearity and imperfect comprehension from our side make it difficult to disentangle the various effects from one another. Finally, it must be concluded that evidence for the conventional assumption of a double-log functional form for these OECD health care expenditure equations is weak. The evidence is very strong against the linear form which also is frequently applied in empirical analysis.

Originally, an impetus for this work was to investigate the important issue of public finance and provision in health care. For the latter we lack good data. For the former we have found some evidence in favor of lower expenditures the higher the public share of finance. Considering the measurement problems, and presence of an unexplained negative coefficient to the number of physicians per capita, the reported coefficients must be cautiously interpreted. Consequently, we do not wish to spell out any firm empirical conclusions with respect to the effects of open-endedness and of public share in finance and provision on health care expenditures in the OECD countries.

REFERENCES

Andersen, R., and L. Benham, "Factors affecting the relationship between family income and medical care consumption". In: Empirical Studies in Health Economics: Proceedings of the Second Conference on the Economics of Health. Ed. H. Klarman. The John Hopkins Press. Baltimore and London, 1970.

Andersson, F., and U-G. Gerdtham, "En studie av sjukvårdsutgifternas bestämmningsfaktorer - internationellt och nationellt perspektiv (A study of the determinants of health care expenditures in a national and international perspective)". CMT Report 1988:6, Center for Medical Technology Assessment, University of Linköping, 1988.

Barer, M.L., R.G. Evans, C. Hertzman, and J. Lomas, "Aging and Health Care Utilization: New Evidence on Old Fallacies", Social Science and Medicine, 24, 851–862, 1987.

Bera, A.K., and C.M. Jarque, "An Efficient Large-sample Test for Normality of Observations and Regression Residuals". Working Papers in Economics and Econometrics, No 049, Australian National University, 1981.

Box, G.E.P., and D.R. Cox, "An Analysis of Transformations". Journal of the Royal Statistical Society. Ser B, 211–243, 1964.

Culyer, A., "Health Expenditures in Canada: Myth and Reality; Past and Future". Canadian Tax Paper No. 82. Canadian Tax Foundation, Toronto, 1988.

Culyer, A., "Cost Containment in Europe". Health Care Financing Review. Annual Supplement, 21–32, 1989.

Denton, F.T., and B.G. Spencer, "Health Care Costs when the population changes". Canadian Journal of Economics, 8, 130–135, 1975.

Evans, R.G., "Supplier-induced demand: Some empirical evidence and implications". In: The Economics of Health and Medical Care. Ed. Perlman, M., Macmillan, London; John Wiley, New York, 1974.

Feldstein, M., "The high cost of hospitals - and what to do about it". Public interest, 48, 40, 1977.

Fuchs, V., "The basic forces influencing costs of medical care". In: *Essays in the economics of health and medical care*. Eds. V. Fuchs. Columbia University Press. New York and London, 1972.

Gerdtham, U-G., F. Andersson, J. Søgaard, and B. Jönsson, "Econometric analysis of health care expenditures - a cross-section study of the OECD countries". Paper presented at the 9th Nordic Meeting of the Health Economists' Study Group in Oslo 2–3 Sep. 1988. CMT report 1988:9. Center for Medical Technology Assessment. University of Linköping.

Gerdtham, U-G. "Den förändrade åldersstrukturens effekt på sjukvårdskostnaderna (The effect of the changing age-structure on health care expenditures)". CMT Rapport 1990:3. Center for Medical Technology Assessment. University of Linköping, 1990a.

Gerdtham, U-G., "The Problem of Analyzing Health Care Costs for Different Age Groups without the Requisite Data". Mimeo. University of Linköping, 1990b.

Gerdtham, U-G., and B. Jönsson, "Price and quantity in international comparisons of health care expenditures". *Applied Economics*, 23, 1519–1528, 1991.

Gerdtham, U-G., and B. Jönsson, "Sjukvårdskostnader i framtiden - Vad betyder åldersfaktorn? (Health care expenditures in the future - of what significance is the age-factor?)". Rapport till ESO Expertgruppen för studier i offentlig ekonomi, Finansdepartementet, Ds 1990:39, 1990.

Gerdtham, U-G., J. Søgaard, F. Andersson, and B. Jönsson, "Econometric Analysis of Health Expenditures - A Cross Section study of the OECD countries, forthcoming in *Journal of Health Economics*, 1991.

Gilbert, C.L., "Practitioners' corner - Professor Hendry's Econometric Methodology". *Oxford Bulletin of Economics and Statistics*, 48, 283–307, 1986.

Glaser, W.A. *Paying the hospital*, Jossey-Bass Inc., Publishers, California, 1987.

Greene, W.H. *Econometric Analysis*. MacMillan Publishing Company, New York, 1990.

Grossman M. *The Demand for Health: A theoretical and empirical investigation*. Columbia University Press, New York, 1972.

Hendry, D.F., and J.-F. Richard, "On the Formulation of Empirical Models in Dynamic Econometrics". *Journal of Econometrics*, 20, 3–33, 1982.

Hendry, D.F., and J.-F. Richard, "The Econometric Analysis of Economic Time Series". *International Statistical Review*, 51, 111–163, 1983.

Johnston, J. *Econometric Methods*. Third ed. McGraw-Hill. Auckland, 1984.

Jönsson, B., "What can Americans learn from Europeans?" *Health Care Financing Review*, Annual Supplement, 79–93, 1989.

Kinal, T., and K. Lahiri, "Specification Error Analysis with Stochastic Regressors". *Econometrica*, 51, 1209–1219, 1983.

Kleiman, E., "The Determinants of National Outlay on Health". In: *The Economics of Health and Medical Care*. Eds. Perlman, M., John Wiley and Sons, New York, 1974.

Kmenta, J. *Elements of Econometrics*. Second ed. Macmillan Publishing Company, New York, 1986.

Leu, R.E., "The public-private mix and international health care costs". In: *Public and private health services: Complementarities and Conflicts*. Eds. Culyer A.J. and B. Jönsson. Basil Blackwell, Oxford, 1986.

Manning, W.G., J.P. Newhouse, N. Duan, E.B. Keeler, A. Leibowitz, and M.S. Marquis, "Health insurance and the demand for medical care: Evidence from a randomized experiment". *American Economic Review*, 77, 251–277, 1987.

Maxwell, R.J. *Health and Wealth*. Lexington books, Lexington, Mass., 1981.

McCallum, B.T., "Relative Asymptotic Bias from Errors of Omission and Measurement". *Econometrica*, 757–758, 1972.

Mizon, G.E., "The Encompassing Approach in Econometrics". In: *Econometrics and Quantitative Economics*. Eds. Hendry, D.F., and K.F. Wallis, Basil Blackwell, Oxford, 1984.

Muurinen, J.M., "Demand for Health. A Generalised Grossman Model". *Journal of Health Economics*, 1, 5–28, 1982.

Newhouse, J.P., "Medical-care expenditure: A cross-national survey". *The Journal of Human Resources*, 12, 115–125, 1977.

Newhouse, J.P., "Cross National Differences in Health Spending - What Do They Mean?" *Journal of Health Economics*, 6, 159–162, 1987.

Newhouse, J.P., and C.E. Phelps, "Price and Income Elasticities for Medical Care Services". In: *The Economics of Medical Care*. Eds. Perlman, M. The Macmillan Press Ltd., London and Basingstoke, 1974.

Niskanen, W.A. *Bureaucracy and Representative Government*. Aldine-Atherton. Chicago, 1971.

OECD "Public Expenditure on Health". *OECD Studies in Resource Allocation*. No. 4. OECD. Paris, 1977.

OECD "Financing and delivering health care - A Comparative Analysis of OECD Countries". *OECD Social Policy Studies*. No 4. OECD. Paris, 1987a.

OECD "Purchasing power parities and real expenditures". OECD. Paris, 1987b.

OECD "Labor force statistics 1966–1986". OECD. Paris, 1988.

Parkin, D., "Comparing Health Service Efficiency Across Countries". *Oxford Review of Economic Policy*, 5, 75–88, 1989.

Parkin, D., A. McGuire, and B. Yule, "Aggregate health expenditures and national income - Is Health Care a Luxury Good?" *Journal of Health Economics*, 6, 109–127, 1987.

Pfaff, M., and F. Nagel, "Consequences for hospitals resulting from demographic, social and morbidity changes: A European perspective". *International Journal of Health Planning and Management*, 2, 311–333, 1986.

Poullier, J.-P., "Health Data File: Overview and methodology". *Health Care Financing Review/Annual Supplement* 1989, pp. 111–194, 1989.

Reinhardt, U.E., "The theory of physician-induced demand: reflections after a decade". *Journal of Health Economics*, 4, 187, 1985.

Schieber, G.J., and J.-P. Poullier, "Overview of international comparisons of health care expenditures". *Health Care Financing Review*, Annual supplement, 1–7, 1989.

Spitzer, J.J., "A Primer on Box-Cox Estimation". *Review of Economics and Statistics*, 64, 307–313, 1982.

Stoddart, G.L., and R.J. Labelle, "Privatisation in the Canadian Health Care System". Ottawa, Canada. Ministry of Supply and Services, 1985.

Ståhl, I. "Can Health Care Costs be Controlled?" Lund University, 1986.

Søgaard, J., "ETSRA: Computer programs for time-series and simple pooled cross section analysis". Odense University, Odense, 1990.

Wagstaff A., "The Demand for Health. Some New Empirical Evidence". *Journal of Health Economics*, 5, 195–233, 1986.

Ward, M., "Purchasing power parities and real expenditures in the OECD". OECD. Paris, 1985.

World Bank, "World Development Report". Oxford University Press. Washington D.C., 1989.

Zarembka, P., "Transformation of variables in Econometrics". In: *Frontiers in Econometrics*. Eds. Zarembka, P., Academic Press, New York, 1974.

Is there a Sisyphus Syndrome in Health Care?

PETER ZWEIFEL and MATTEO FERRARI

IEW Universität Zürich, Kleinstrasse 15, CH-8008 Zürich, Switzerland.

I 11 I 18

O E C D

1. INTRODUCTION

When discussing the causes of ever-rising costs of health care, policy makers sooner or later point to the failure of modern medicine. If modern medicine is so effective in increasing chances of survival, devoting additional resources to the health care sector must result in increased longevity. In turn, the increased number of aging survivors will exert an increased demand for medical services. Thus, modern medicine would result in a Sisyphus syndrome, reminiscent of the unfortunate Greek hero who never succeeded in pushing a rock to the top of the hill because it kept slipping off at the last moment. The more resources allocated to health, the greater the success of medicine in terms of longevity; the longer the lifespan, however, the higher the outlay on medical services. These two simultaneous relationships will be called the Sisyphus syndrome in health care henceforth.

Interestingly enough, this simple idea, sounded by Gruenberg in 1977, never seems to have been subjected to an empirical test. This is the more unfortunate as the policy implications of a Sisyphus syndrome in health care would be quite far-reaching. This paper is an attempt at such a test at the aggregate level of industrial countries. It consists of three parts. First, the relationship between the level of development of the health care system and life expectancy, particularly of middle and advanced age, will be examined. The second part will in turn be devoted to an analysis of the feedback relationship, running from the life expectancy of a population to outlays on health care. In the final part, a discussion and conclusion will be provided.

2. THE IMPACT OF HEALTH CARE ON LONGEVITY

The factors influencing mortality and longevity of a population are the theme of the "production of health" literature, to be reviewed below. In a certain

P. Zweifel and H. E. Frech III (eds.), Health Economics Worldwide. 311–330.
© 1992 *Kluwer Academic Publishers. Printed in the Netherlands.*

sense, this literature marks a return to the classical economics after a few decades of domination by the "medical model" with its emphasis on health care services as a determinant of health. For the classical writers and Malthus (1830) in particular, it was evident that the state of the economy determined to a great extent the health and survival of a population. Indeed, there is a fair amount of evidence suggesting that decreases in food supply, by undermining the resistance against communicable diseases, caused mortality rates to rise in the 19th century (Schofield, 1984). This knowledge was lost in the wake of the discovery of anti-infective drugs in the 1930's. The most influential criticism of the medical model came from McKeown (1976) who showed that most of the mortality decline in England and Wales preceded the development of effective forms of medical treatment; for a thorough update of this type of evidence, see McKinlay et al. (1989). This finding raises the more general question regarding the factors influencing the health status of a population, which is the topic of the following subsection.

2.1. Short literature review

From an economic point of view, health, although not tradable, is a good that can be produced using several inputs. The specific concept of a production function apparently was first introduced by Auster et al. (1969), who found standardized mortality rates of U.S. states to be unrelated to key medical inputs (such as physician density, capital endowment of hospitals, drug use per capita). In turn, below average mortality rates could be traced to additional years of schooling and low (rather than high) per capita income. The lacking effectiveness of medical inputs was again found in an exploratory study covering most OECD countries (Cochrane et al., 1978), whereas higher income turned out to have a lowering effect on mortality independently of variables relating to nutrition and alcohol and tobacco consumption. A study defining health, medical care, and nonmedical inputs as latent quantities reflected by multiple fallible indicators also pointed to a dominant (positive) influence of income in the case of Switzerland (Zweifel (1978)).

A more recent contribution by Peltzman (1987), based on data from industrial as well as developing countries, concludes that average income, along with a more equal income distribution (indicated by a ratio of median income/average income of households not very different from 1) contributes to a reduction of mortality. On the other hand, neither public spending on health nor regulation such as mandated prescription for dangerous drugs contributed to a reduction of mortality due to infection and poisoning. On the basis of OECD data again, Leu (1986) also produced evidence suggesting that income (along with education and the share of public finance in health care expenditure (HCE)) contributes to a lowering of mortality rates.

The role of publicly financed programs may be rather important in view of Hadley's (1988) finding that high U.S. Medicare expenditures go along with reduced regional mortality rates among beneficiaries, with differences in population and area characteristics controlled for.

Recently, Fries (1980) borrowed arguments from biology to advance the hypothesis that man is subject to a biologically determined maximum life span. Given such a maximum, there would have to be an ultimate limit to the contribution of medical care to life expectancy, suggesting decreasing marginal returns in the production of health. However, that ultimate limit will only be reached when the survival curve of a cohort runs fully rectangular, implying that no deaths occur prior to biologically determined maximum age.

Whether this limit really exists is a matter of some dispute. In particular, Schneider and Brody (1983) as well as Myers and Manton (1984) found that maximum age at death has still been on the increase in the U.S. during the last two decades. Moreover, they show that beyond the age of sixty, the variance of age at death has not been decreasing, which is at odds with the rectangularization hypothesis advanced by Fries. More specifically, Wolfe (1986) found changes of life expectancy at birth in 7 OECD countries to be related to changes in life style and HCE, a result that was replicated by Wolfe and Gabay (1987) for 22 industrial countries. However, none of the estimated coefficients reached conventional levels of significance.

At the microeconomic level, there is also some limited evidence that medical intervention does not have too much of an impact on health. Thus, Newhouse and Friedlander (1980) related physiological indicators such as blood pressure, cholesterol content and ECG score to utilization of medical care services, income, and education. These data originated from a health examination survey in the U.S. The indicators of physiological health did not seem to be influenced by medical inputs, whereas additional schooling at least appeared to contribute to a reduction of blood pressure and improved dental health.

In all, this evidence suggests that additional medical care does not contribute much to survival in general anymore. However, this does not preclude that certain subpopulations still may profit from more medical care services. Judging from the work by Hadley (1988), Schneider and Brody (1983), and Myers and Manton (1984), this could well be groups of rather high age.

This conjecture has implications in at least two respects. At the statistical level, the variable of interest should become mortality rates of higher age groups or remaining life expectancy at higher age rather than over-all mortality or life expectancy at birth. Accordingly, life expectancies at age 40 and 65 respectively will constitute the jointly dependent variables in the first part of this paper. At the policy level, the rationale of providing medical care at public expense is undercut if medical care were to contribute mainly to the longevity of those who have already enjoyed a long life. A key argument in favor of subsidizing medical care has always been the investment logic: To the extent that medical care enables a worker to get back on his job or a housewife to perform her duties in the household, it generates an external benefit that may merit subsidization or even free provision. However, if medical care should affect above all the health of people beyond retirement age, this motivation would be undermined. Therefore, the first link of the alleged Sisyphus syndrome, running from health care to remaining life expectancy at advanced age, is of considerable relevance for social policy.

2.2. *Empirical analysis using OECD data*

2.2.1. *Definition of the dependent variable*
The analysis of life expectancy poses two particular problems. First, there is the problem of cohort definition. Strictly speaking, life expectancy cannot be determined for those presently alive but only of the cohort born in 1890 or even earlier. The survival curve of that cohort would have to be related to the impacts of two World Wars, the introduction of anti-infective drugs as well as the improvement of living conditions due to economic growth. However, this type of analysis requires long time series not available in most OECD countries. As a substitute, survival curves are calculated that would result if a cohort born in the year in question were to pass through one age class after another while being subject to current age specific mortality rates (United Nations International Conference on Population, 1984). It should be noted that current age specific mortality rates continue to depend on influences of a distant past.

A second issue has to do with the question of whose life expectancy should be measured, touched upon in the literature review. As argued there, life expectancy at birth may not be the quantity of principal interest but rather remaining life expectancy at an advanced age. This calls for a definition of advanced age that will also be appropriate for analyzing the feedback relationship between age and HCE, to be undertaken in the third section of this paper.

From the point of view of a political decision maker, the planning horizon of his constituency is the decisive variable. When voters come to expect to live longer, their behavior at the polls may adjust at a rather young age. Voters at the age of forty, say, may well be aware of the fact that they will have much occasion to use medical care during a prolonged retirement phase, leading them to prefer public spending on health over competing uses. Among other things, the individual's rate of time preference enters this evaluation, a parameter about which little is known. The remaining life expectancies at ages 40 and 65, compiled by the OECD, may therefore be as appropriate a choice as any other.

2.2.2. *Results of econometric analysis*
The dependent variables to be analyzed are sex specific life expectancies at the ages of 40 and 65, (L40M, L40F; L65M, L65F). Due to lacking data, Luxembourg, New Zealand, Portugal and Switzerland had to be excluded

Table 1. Description of variables

Symbol	Definition	Mean	Min.	Max.
GDP70	Gross domestic product per capita, 1970, current prices, PPP converted, in 1,000 US $	3.512	1.756 (GR)	4.976 (S)
GDP84	as above, but 1984	12.133	6.300 (GR)	15.434 (S)
HCE70	Health care expenditure per capita, 1970, current prices, PPP converted, in 1,000 US $	0.208	0.070 (GR)	0.366 (US)
HCE84	as above, but 1984	0.917	0.287 (GR)	1.637 (US)
HCEG	Public HCE (=HCE · SH.PUBL), 1984, in 1,000 US $	0.705	0.228 (GR)	1.321 (S)
HCEP	private HCE, (=HCE · [1 – SH.PUBL]), 1984, in 1,000 US $	0.212	0.059 (GR)	0.959 (US)
L40F	Life expectancy of 40 year old women, in 1980	39.5	36.2 (IRL)	41.6 (ISL)
L40M	Life expectancy of 40 year old men, in 1980	33.9	31.8 (SF)	36.5 (ISL)
L65F	Life expectancy of 65 year old women, in 1980	18.0	15.8 (IRL)	19.4 (ISL)
L65M	Life expectancy of 65 year old men, in 1980	14.1	12.5 (IRL)	15.7 (JAP)
SH.PUBL	Share of publicly financed HCE, in 1984	0.784	0.414 (US)	0.916 (B)

Source:
OECD (1987), Financing and Delivering Health Care, Tables 10, 11, 18, 20.
The sample used here comprises Australia, Austria, Belgium, Canada, Denmark, Finland, France, Germany, Greece, Iceland, Ireland, Italy, Japan, Netherlands, Norway, Spain, Sweden, United Kingdom, United States.
Codes:
B = Belgium, GR = Greece, IRL = Ireland, ISL = Iceland, JAP = Japan, N = Norway, S = Sweden, SF = Finland, US = USA.

from the file. Among the 19 OECD countries retained, there are important differences in life expectancy as of 1980, with *e.g.* men of age 40 in Finland featuring the lowest value in the sample, a mere 32 years (L40M in Table 1). In Iceland, on the other hand, men of that age can look forward to another 37 years of life.

In a first attempt (not documented here), life expectancy at ages 40 and 65 was analyzed separately for either sex. In the four regression equations, comparable coefficients with regard to per capita gross domestic product (GDP) as well as health expenditure per capita (HCE) were obtained, with HCE remaining insignificant, however. This similarity suggested a merging of observations and using dummy variables for representing the differences between the sexes and ages 40 and 65, respectively. Equation (1) gives the results of this merged regression. It should be noted that the dependent variables refer to the year 1980, whereas GDP and HCE are for 1984.

$$
\begin{bmatrix} L40F \\ L65F \\ L40M \\ L65M \end{bmatrix}_{1980}
\begin{aligned}
= \quad & 33.0^{***} \\
& - 20.7^{***} \cdot (\text{AGE65}, = 1 \text{ if life expectancy at 65}) \\
& + 4.8^{***} \cdot (\text{SEXF}, = 1 \text{ if life expectancy of females}) \\
& + 0.078 \cdot (\text{GDP84, per capita GDP, 1984}) \\
& + 3.9 \cdot (\text{HCE84, per capita HCE, 1984})
\end{aligned}
\tag{1}
$$

$\bar{R}^2 = 0.99$; COND = 24.5; ***: significance level 0.001; OLS. (COND is an indicator of multicollinearity. Heuristically, values above 50 are considered critical. See *Judge et al.* (1985, p. 902) for details).

According to this estimate, the remaining life expectancy of a 65 year old person is 20.7 years less on average than that of a 40 year old. Since perfect rectangularization of the survival curve would call for a difference of 25 years, this result points to a considerable degree of rectangularization. Also, the remaining life expectancy of a female person appears to exceed that of a male by 4.8 years. Both of these differences are highly significant, while the coefficients of GDP and HCE cannot be distinguished from zero with sufficient certainty. The fact that roughly contemporaneous HCE do not leave a recognizable trace in life expectancy is evidence against an extreme variant of the "medical model" emphasizing the contribution of latest medical innovations to chances of survival.

In a more general model, standards of living and possibly medical care extend their influence over an entire life cycle. A full test of this more general model would require several orders of lags for GDP and HCE, which are not available on a PPP conversion basis. The one year for which the OECD (1987) prepared PPP conversions is 1970, an acceptable choice in terms of its business cycle characteristics. Reestimating equation (1) with such a lag of a decade's length, one obtains.

$$
\begin{bmatrix} L40F \\ L65F \\ L40M \\ L65M \end{bmatrix}_{1980}
\begin{aligned}
= \quad & 34.8^{***} \\
& - 20.7^{***} \cdot (\text{AGE65}, = 1 \text{ if life expectancy at 65}) \\
& + 4.8^{***} \cdot (\text{SEXF}, = 1 \text{ if life expectancy of females}) \\
& - 0.88^{*} \cdot (\text{GDP70, per capita GDP, 1970; e} = -0.12) \\
& + 12.4^{**} \cdot (\text{HCE70, per capita HCE, 1980; e} = 0.095)
\end{aligned}
\tag{2}
$$

$\bar{R}^2 = 0.99$; COND = 24.6; *(**): significance level 0.05 (0.01); OLS. e = Elasticity, calculated at arithmetic means.

This second estimate fully confirms the effects of age and sex noted in the context of equation (1). However, a higher GDP now appears to reduce rather than increase remaining life expectancy, a result that harks back to

Auster *et al.* (1969) for the U.S. The surprising result is that HCE of 1970 seems to have a positive effect on life expectancy in 1980, with an elasticity of about 0.1 that comes close in absolute value to the one of GDP.

Therefore, HCE might indeed benefit the upper age classes of the population of industrial countries, an effect that was not noticed in previous studies. One reason for this may have been their emphasis on standardized mortality rates covering the entire population. Another reason may have been their exclusive use of contemporaneous relationships whereas a crude attempt was made here to allow for influences extending over an entire life cycle.

Since the income data of the year 1970 may still have contained a sizable transitory component, more permanent values were formed using data from 1969 to 1971 (real, but not PPP converted). An average was calculated, which served as a correction factor for the PPP converted data as of 1970. This procedure required exclusion of Iceland and Spain from the data set due to unavailability of data. While the overall goodness of fit remained about the same, GDP lost significance entirely, HCE appreciably. Moreover, the same changes occurred when Iceland and Spain were eliminated from the original data set, which does not contain a permanent income variable. This finding suggests that the exclusion of countries from the data set might be far more crucial than differentiating *e.g.* between measured and permanent income.

As a first step towards more systematic testing of the robustness of estimates against sample variations, each of the 19 OECD countries of the sample was excluded while retaining the original specification of equation (2). The coefficient of GDP was found to vary (in absolute value) between 0.47 and 1.54, with values between 0.8 and 1.0 obtained in 14 out of 19 cases. Significance at the 5 percent level or better resulted in 16 of these 19 experiments. In a similar way, the coefficient estimates of HCE were bunched between 11 and 13, with three outlayers extending the range to 8 and 16. Statistical significance was retained in all but one experiment. Averages of coefficients and t-ratios based on these 19 experiments proved to just about coincide with the coefficients shown in equation (2).

As a second step, a bootstrapping exercise was performed, based on 100 and 500 iterations, respectively (Freedman and Peters, 1984; Efron, 1979). Bootstrapping consists in using calculated values of the endogenous variable and adding sample values of regression residuals as though the distribution of residuals were identical with the distribution of true error. In these experiments, the average of bootstrap estimated coefficients coincided with the initial OLS estimate shown in equation (2). More importantly, estimated standard errors of bootstrap coefficients did not exceed the estimated standard errors shown in equation (2).

In all, these results seem to indicate that equation (2) is unlikely to exhibit the instabilities found by Gerdtham *et al.* (1988) in their analysis of the Leu model. They also cast doubt on the hypothesis put forward by more medically oriented researchers such as Cochrane *et al.* (1978) who argued that clinically measured risk factors contribute more to the explanation of mortality rates than do indicators of economic well-being such as GDP.

3. AGING OF THE POPULATION AND THE HEALTH CARE SYSTEM

This section is devoted to the possible feedback link running from an increased life expectancy to health care expenditures (HCE) at the aggregate level. It is this second relationship that may lock a policy maker into an ever-growing health bill because part of the increased aggregate HCE will in all likelihood fall on the public purse. For this reason, the factors determining national outlay, and among them the aging of the population, are of considerable interest from a policy perspective.

3.1. Short literature review

The influence of age of a population on the health care system of a country has traditionally been analyzed at the aggregate level. Interestingly enough, the expected positive relationship between the population share of the aged and HCE most often failed to materialize. As will be shown in the second subsection, it also fails to materialize quite frequently at the microeconomic level.

3.1.1. Age and income as determinants of HCE at the aggregate level
In his early study of the determinants of national health outlays, Kleiman (1974) first identified income per capita (GDP) as the main explanatory variable, a result that will be replicated by all subsequent investigations. Originally, he had also introduced the percentages of the population less than 15 and more than 60 years old as explanatory variables. However, the partial estimated effect of the population share of the young on HCE turned out to be negative rather than positive, an unexpected result which seems to have led Kleiman to remain silent on the results concerning the population share of the elderly. Focusing on changes in life expectancies in OECD countries between 1960 and 1980 as independent variables, Wolfe and Gabay (1987) found positive (but insignificant) impacts on changes in HCE.

Age effects are also notably absent from the well-known study by Newhouse (1977), which however focused on the question of whether health care is a luxury good. There are indeed signs of an income elasticity of HCE above unity, which constitutes somewhat of a puzzle because at the microeconomic level, income and the consumption of medical care do not seem to be strongly related (Newhouse and Phelps, 1976 for the U.S.; Leu and Doppmann, 1986 and Zweifel, 1986 for Switzerland; van Doorslaer, 1987 for the Netherlands). This puzzle can be solved by noting that the great majority in all OECD countries is covered by some kind of health insurance, granting access to medical care regardless of income. At the aggregate level, however, high incomes translate into a high willingness to pay in the guise of contributions to social security or taxes when it comes to public provision of medical services.

This line of reasoning calls attention to the role of institutional factors permitting voters to influence public spending on health rather than other publicly provided goods, an issue taken up by Leu (1986). From such a public choice point of view, the population share of the elderly should be an important predictor of aggregate HCE because of their influence as a voting bloc. However, it was the share of the population below age 15 that turned out statistically significant in Leu's work. With more than 96 percent of the variance of HCE explained, there does not seem to be much room for an additional age variable.

While all the studies mentioned so far had used HCE and GDP data converted at exchange rates, Parkin *et al.* (1987) introduced purchasing power parity (PPP) converted figures prepared by the OECD (1985). This change was associated with a marked drop in coefficients of determination, opening up again the possibility, to be pursued below, that additional (among them age-related) explanatory variables could make a difference.

However, the link between aging and aggregate HCE cannot be viewed as a simple demand function in an ultimate sense. After all, the quantity of medical care that can be financed by (social) health insurance depends on the prices that have to be paid for the services performed. These prices mirror (although with a great amount of time lag in many OECD countries) scarcities on the market for health workers. The supply of such workers in turn depends on the age structure of the population as well as the wage rate. Thus, aging affects not only the demand but also the supply of medical care, suggesting the use of an interdependent macroeconomic model for simulation.

Such an interdependent model was developed by Denton *et al.* (1988) for Canada. In that model, the long-run effects of a reduction of the fertility rate from 3.5 to 2.1 children per woman are simulated. The concomitant aging of the population does not seem to increase the share of HCE in GDP in a noticeable way. Indeed, the share would even remain stable if the market for medical care services were competitive. If however physicians succeeded to keep their incomes relative to the average of the active population, then the simulation results in a 1 percentage point increase of HCE's share in GDP. In the very long run, *i.e.* after fifty years, this increase may come to 3 percentage points. In all, the evidence suggesting a positive relationship between HCE and mean age is surprisingly scarce at the macro level.

3.1.2. *Age and individual HCE*
As early as 1977, there was a great deal of international·data from health insurance sources compiled by the OECD (1977), showing that persons above

age 65 consumed a disproportionate share of health care services of all types, ranging from drugs to hospital days. Such tabulations fail to hold income and health status constant, however. Indeed, in their analysis of a rather comprehensive micro data set including income and self-assessed health status, Newhouse and Phelps (1976) found that age was negatively related to the probability of initiating a medical care episode. Neither does age play a significant role in their equations explaining the number of ambulatory care visits given initiation and the likelihood of a hospital admission. An age gradient becomes only evident in their equation for hospital days given admission. In an attempt at taking into account possible non-linearity in the gradient, Leu and Doppmann (1986) also entered the square of age in their analysis of a Swiss micro data set. However, the total age effect on the number of physician visits and hospital days (given health status) remains negative in the admissible domain.

In their interim report on the Health Insurance Study, Newhouse *et al.* (1982, Appendix) report 21 equations referring to the probability of initiating a medical episode and use given initiation, relating to different experimental sites. Distinguishing between age effects for males and females, they find positive age coefficients for both sexes in only four of these 21 cases. In two cases, they were both negative (although non-significant). Therefore, health status rather than age per se appears to be the crucial variable, a conclusion suggested also by a recent study by Wedig (1988); *see* also the estimates in van Doorslaer (1987, p. 76).

In all, the micro evidence regarding a pure age effect on utilization of health care services is less than overwhelming. To the extent that income increases and health deteriorates with age, however, one would still have expected a positive relationship between age and HCE at the aggregate level.

An interesting explanation of the failure of age effects on HCE to materialize is that calendar age may not be the appropriate variable to measure (Fuchs, 1984). If health care is regarded as improving the ratio of useful time to total time lived, the demand for it should be positively related to remaining life expectancy. For example, if an individual were to count on living only for a few months at any rate, the benefit from health care in terms of useful time would be too small to make major outlays on health care worthwhile. Conversely, health care will promise a sufficient payoff if the individual expects to live on for another few years.

The emphasis on remaining life expectancy rather than calendar age appears even more justified when one takes into account that much of health care is publicly financed. Espousing the public choice view advanced by Leu (1986), voting in favor of and paying taxes for facilities such as medical schools and hospitals amounts to an investment in public health. Given sufficiently long life expectancy, a 40 year old individual *e.g.* may well decide to vote in favor of such facilities in the hope of reaping the benefits during the remainder of his life. Failure of age-related variables to contribute to the explanation of aggregate HCE might thus be due to the choice of a variable that does not sufficiently reflect the decision making situation with regard to health care both in the private and public domain.

3.2. *Empirical analysis using OECD data*

3.2.1. *Analysis of total aggregate health expenditure*
The objective of this second empirical investigation is to find out whether there is evidence in favor of the hypothesis that high remaining life expectancy of a population results in increased HCE. Such a feedback from age to HCE would constitute the lock-in effect of the suspected Sisyphus syndrome in health care. Besides life expectancy (again conditional on having attained ages 40 and 65), there are two additional regressors appearing in equation (3) below. The first, per capita income (GDP), does not need justification in view of all the previous work reviewed in the previous section. The second, the share of public in total HCE was introduced by Leu (1986) on the grounds that public finance increases demand for and hence expenditures on health care by reducing its user price to the consumer. As reported by Culyer (1989), this variable also survived later scrutiny by Gerdtham *et al.* (1988), contrary to other variables used by Leu (1986) for characterizing institutional differences between OECD countries with regard to health.

Since equation (3) contains the two endogenous variables L65F and L65M, parameter estimates are biased and inconsistent. Two-stage estimation would in principle remedy inconsistency, but on the basis of 19 observations, this asymptotic property does not appear too relevant. Moreover, truly predetermined variables that could serve as instruments are difficult to come by. An attempt was made using GDP in the year 1970 and the ratio of retirement benefits to GDP as of 1980 as instruments. However, the statistical fit of the first stage was not good enough for allowing residuals to be interpreted as pure reflections of endogeneity. Therefore, there seemed to be the real risk of contaminating with error rather than purging from error. For these reasons, OLS estimates are presented here, with the simultaneity issue deferred to the last part of this section. The equation reads

$$
\begin{aligned}
\text{HCE}_{1984} = \quad & 0.052 \\
& + 0.099^{***} \cdot (\text{GDP84, per capita GDP, 1984; e} = 1.26) \\
& + 0.028 \cdot (\text{L65F, life expectancy of 65 year old women}) \\
& - 0.020 \cdot (\text{L65M, life expectancy of 65 year old men}) \\
& - 0.701^{*} \cdot (\text{SH.PUBL, public share in HCE; e} = -0.60)
\end{aligned}
$$
(3)

$\bar{R}^2 = 0.81$; COND $= 126.1$; OLS.

The coefficient of the income variable (0.099) corresponds quite closely to the one found by Parkin *et al.* (1987) who, using PPP converted GDP and HCE data as well, arrived at 0.092. Evaluated at the means, the income elasticity of HCE amounts to 1.26, which would make health care a "luxury good". In contrast to Leu (1986), a higher share of public finance in HCE appears to be associated with lower rather than higher outlays on health.

In this context, however, the two life expectancy variables are of primary interest. Neither of them contributes to the explanation of HCE to a statistically significant degree. Moreover, while L65F suggests a positive partial influence on HCE, its male counterpart L65M seems to have a negative one.

3.2.2. *Analysis of public and private health expenditure*

The high value of the condition number (COND) of equation (3) indicates a substantial amount of multicollinearity among explanatory variables, making precise estimates of regression coefficients impossible. An increase in sample size could again be effected by splitting total HCE in its public (HCEG) and private (HCEP) components and exploiting similarities between the two regressions.

Separately estimated regressions for HCEG and HCEP yielded comparable estimates of the coefficients pertaining to life expectancy variables. Indeed, HCEP was only weakly and insignificantly related to GDP, while HCEG showed a strong and highly significant relationship. This finding contrasts clearly with those of Kleiman (1974), whose sample also included eight developing countries, however (out of a total of 16). In seven of these eight countries, health care expenditures were mainly private at the time. Thus, differences in HCEP in Kleiman's sample were apt to be rather strongly correlated with income.

In order to allow for a differential impact of GDP on the two jointly dependent variables, GDP is multiplied by a dummy variable that takes on the value of 1 if the data refer to HCEG. Using HCEP and HCEG as jointly dependent variables resulted in the following regression,

$$
\begin{bmatrix} HCEG \\ HCEP \end{bmatrix}_{1984} = \begin{aligned} &-0.45 \\ &+ 0.027^{+} \cdot (\text{GDP84, per capita GDP, 1984; e} = 0.72) \\ &+ 0.040^{***} \cdot (\text{GDP84} \cdot \text{PUBL, PUBL} = 1 \text{ if public} \\ &\qquad \text{HCE; e} = 1.17) \\ &+ 0.029 \cdot (\text{L65F, life expectancy of 65 year old} \\ &\qquad \text{women}) \\ &- 0.013 \cdot (\text{L65M, life expectancy of 65 year old} \\ &\qquad \text{men}) \qquad\qquad\qquad\qquad\qquad\qquad (4) \end{aligned}
$$

$\bar{R}^2 = 0.76$; COND = 119; $^{+}$: significance level better than 0.10; OLS.

Equation (4) confirms the suspicion that the income elasticity of aggregate HCE as usually estimated may be an average of two rather different elasticities: One, lying clearly below 1, relates to private HCE, the other, lying somewhat above 1, to public HCE. Therefore, it may be the redistribution inherent in public HCE rather than health care as such that is a luxury good. Another, less far-reaching interpretation is that government in OECD countries has grown in general, a fact that is also reflected in growth of public HCE.

The main issue continues to be the possible feedback from remaining life expectancy to HCE, however. Both life expectancy variables fail to contribute significantly to the explanation of HCE, public or private. Before concluding that aging does not leave its trace in aggregate HCE, it must be admitted that there are pitfalls that may have prevented the expected feedback relationship to materialize.

A first issue concerns the splitting of HCE in its private and public components. For example, the share of public in total HCE in Australia jumped from 62.5 to 84.5 percent between 1980 and 1984, reflecting important changes in governmental policy (OECD, 1987, p. 55; Duckett, 1984). As in the context of equation (2), an attempt was made to obtain more permanent values for HCEP and HCEG. Average shares of public HCE were calculated based on the observations of 1980, 1982, and 1984 as well as 1975, 1980, and 1984 for deriving permanent values for HCEP and HCEG. In view of the high degree of multicollinearity noted below equation (3), these reestimations also provided a first test of coefficient stability. However, neither of the two modifications changed regression coefficients or t-ratios in an appreciable way.

Still with an eye on multicollinearity, one of the two life expectancy variables was deleted from the list of regressors. Deleting L65F *e.g.*, while halving the condition number and changing the coefficient of L65M from -12.7 to (a still insignificant) 9.93, did not affect overall goodness of fit. Only the two coefficients related to GDP became more strongly significant, with their values unchanged. Excluding L65M instead produced comparable results.

Bootstrapping experiments again served to complete the picture regarding robustness. First, these experiments were made on the separate equations for HCEP and HCEG. In neither equation was there any indication that the coefficients obtained from the original OLS regression were outliers. Therefore, pooling the equations was judged admissible once more. Finally, 1,000 replications of equation (4) were run, resulting in distributions of coefficient estimates whose means just about coincided with those shown in equation (4). Also, standard errors obtained in this way did not exceed those of equation (4), lending a measure of credibility to the significance tests applied to the coefficients.

A limited amount of specification search was also performed. First, newborns cause a substantial amount of HCE while OECD countries differ greatly in terms of birth rates (live births per 1,000 population), *cf.* United Nations (1987, p. 290–296). Thus, the aggregate health burden of aged countries may be considerably relieved by a low birth rate. This addition did not produce any changes in the remaining coefficients, and although the coefficient of the birth rate turned out positive, it failed to attain even a 10 percent significance level.

The second modification refers to the influence of the aged population in the political process. Whereas life expectancy at an advanced age certainly reflects the intensity of interest in public provision of health care, it fails to directly gauge the weight of the voting group thus affected. In an ultimate sense, a voting group is strong if it consists of a sufficiently large number of voters who are at the same time motivated to take part in elections and referenda. This argument calls for an interaction between remaining life expectancy (motivation) and the population share of those aged 65 and beyond (weight of numbers) (OECD, 1987, p. 16). However, interaction variables of the type (L65M*AGE65) did not change the main result flowing from equation (4), *viz.* that the aged population subgroup does not seem to exert a statistically recognizable influence on HCE.

4. ESTIMATING THE SISYPHUS SYNDROME AS A SYSTEM

The two relationships that jointly might constitute a Sisyphus syndrome in health care are conditioned by a host of factors that could not be taken into due account. Since health and health care services are non-tradeables, the production of health is likely to differ greatly among OECD countries. For example, the Scandinavian countries (with the exception of Finland) appear to use hospital services much more than other OECD countries (OECD, 1987, Table 24). This fact may simultaneously affect longevity and HCE in the countries concerned.

Due to the small number of observations, this and other factors linking the two equations to the rest of the system had to be relegated to the error terms, resulting in a likely correlation between them. One way to check whether these linkages are important enough to affect the estimates obtained is to run a seemingly unrelated regression (SURE, Zellner, 1962). The SURE procedure is usually employed in the hope of deriving more efficient estimates. In this context, however, it may serve to uncover the dependence of the two estimated equations upon a non-specified environment.

Simultaneous estimation of equations (2) and (4) poses a particular problem for estimating the covariance between the residual vectors because the first dependent variable has 76 ($=4 \times 19$) observations whereas the second has 38 observations. Following the recommendation by Judge *et al.* (1985, p. 480–483), the estimate proposed and tested (using Monte Carlo methods) by Schmidt (1977) is employed in the following. The estimated covariance matrix reads

$$\hat{\Sigma} = \begin{bmatrix} 0.024 & -0.013 \\ -0.013 & 1.27 \end{bmatrix}$$

The SURE regression on the basis of this covariance matrix is

$$
\begin{bmatrix} L40F \\ L65F \\ L40M \\ L65M \end{bmatrix}_{1980}
\begin{aligned}
= \quad & 34.9^{***} \\
& - 20.7^{***} \cdot (AGE65, = 1 \text{ if life expectancy at } 65) \\
& + 5.0^{***} \cdot (SEXF, = 1 \text{ if life expectancy of females}) \\
& - 0.97^{*} \cdot (GDP70, \text{ per capita GDP, } 1970; \text{ e} = -0.13) \\
& + 13.2^{**} \cdot (HCE70, \text{ per capita HCE, } 1970; \text{ e} = 0.105)
\end{aligned}
$$

$$(5)$$

$$
\begin{bmatrix} HCEG \\ HCEP \end{bmatrix}_{1984}
\begin{aligned}
= \quad & 8.80 \\
& + 0.078 \cdot (GDP84, \text{ per capita GDP, } 1984; \text{ e} = 2.08) \\
& + 0.073 \cdot (GDP84 \cdot PUBL, PUBL = 1 \text{ if public HCE;} \\
& \qquad \text{e} = 2.14) \\
& - 0.19 \cdot (L65F, \text{ life expectancy of } 65 \text{ year old women}) \\
& - 0.45 \cdot (L65M, \text{ life expectancy of } 65 \text{ year old men})
\end{aligned}
$$

$$(6)$$

SURE estimation.

The residuals generated by equations (5) and (6) can in turn be used to derive an unconstrained estimate of the residual covariance matrix. This matrix reads

$$
\hat{\Sigma} = \begin{bmatrix} 0.296 & 0.418 \\ 0.418 & 1.28 \end{bmatrix}
$$

It is now possible to find out whether the assumption of spherical errors implicit in previous OLS estimation was justified. Employing the Lagrange multiplier test given in Breusch and Pagan (1980) alternatively on the basis of 38 and 76 observations for checking the diagonality of the covariance matrix of SURE residuals, the chi-square values amount to 17.5 and 35, respectively, with a critical value of 6.6 (at the .01 significance level, with 1 d.f.). A general likelihood ratio test also indicates that the null hypothesis of sphericalness must be rejected. There, the two chi-square values are 73 and 146, respectively, to be again compared to a critical value of 6.6.

Despite the apparent importance of error covariance, equation (5), explaining remaining life expectancies, contains coefficients almost identical with equation (2); *see* also Table 2. Equation (6), explaining HCE, looks rather different when estimated as part of a system, however. Both GDP variables lose their significance, which is surprising in view of so many OLS-based inferences [among which also equation (4) above] pointing to GDP as the main determinant of HCE. Finally, while the coefficients of L65F and L65M do not diverge as much anymore, both clearly remain statistically insignificant. In all, it looks as though the relationship between HCE and its economic determinants is strongly embedded in a non-specified surrounding

326

P. Zweifel and M. Ferrari

Table 2. Overview of estimation results

	OLS4065	SUR4065	OLS40	SUR40	OLS65	SUR65
L. Equation No.	(2)	(5)	col. 3	col. 4	col. 5	col. 6
CONST	34.8*** (47.5)	34.9*** (56.5)	35.1*** (31.4)	35.1*** (254.0)	13.9*** (18.5)	13.9*** (101.0)
AGE65	-20.7*** (77.2)	-20.7*** (88.7)	-	-	-	-
SEXF	4.8*** (17.9)	5.0*** (22.0)	5.7*** (13.7)	5.7*** (110.0)	3.9*** (14.0)	3.9*** (76.2)
GDP70	-0.88* (-2.4)	-0.97** (-3.1)	-1.27* (-2.2)	-1.27*** (-18.0)	-0.49 (-1.3)	-0.48*** (-6.8)
HCE70	12.4** (3.4)	13.2*** (4.2)	15.8** (2.8)	15.7*** (22.2)	9.07* (2.3)	9.00*** (12.7)
H. Equation No.	(4)	(6)	col. 3	col. 4	col. 5	col. 6
CONST	-0.45 (-0.86)	8.80 (0.42)	-	-13.4** (-3.4)	-	-8.15** (-3.1)
GDP84	0.027 + (1.95)	0.078 (1.25)	-	-0.053 (-0.45)	-	-0.024 (-0.30)
GDP84·PUBL	0.040*** (9.81)	0.073 (0.43)	-	0.034 (1.08)	-	0.037 (1.72)
L65F	0.029 (0.46)	-0.19 (-0.07)	-	0.35 (0.73)	-	0.30 (0.93)
L65M	-0.013 (-0.22)	-0.45 (-0.19)	-	0.57 (1.28)	-	0.23 (0.77)
(CO)VARIANCE OF RESIDUALS	0.024 -0.013 -0.013 1.270	0.296 0.418 0.418 1.280	1.454 -0.019 -0.019 0.025	0.554 -0.729 -0.729 0.727	0.664 -0.015 -0.015 0.025	0.193 -0.299 -0.299 0.332

Notes:

L: Longevity equations, at ages 40 and 65.

H: Health care expenditure equation.

+, *, **. ***: Levels of significance (0.1, 0.05, 0.01, 0.001) or better.

OLS4065: Equation for **L** based on pooled longevity data at ages 40 and 65. Residuals vectors of length 76 (**L**) and 38 (**H**), respectively; see section 4 of text.

SUR4065: Joint estimation of equation for **L** and **H**.

OLS40: Equation for **L** based on longevity at age 40 only. Residuals vector of length 38.

SUR65: Joint estimation of equations for **L** (longevity at age 65 only) and **H**. Residuals vectors of length 38.

system whereas the first relationship, between life expectancy and its economic determinants, is more autonomous.

It must be admitted, however, that the above SURE estimation rests on a decision for dealing with residual vectors of unequal length that cannot be justified on theoretical grounds. Therefore, only remaining life expectancies at ages 40 and age 65 were retained as dependent variables in equation (5), resulting in vectors of equal length of 38 observations - both in equations (5) and (6). SURE reestimation produced coefficients reasonably close to either equation (5) or equation (2) for the first relationship; see cols. 3 to 6 of Table 2. In particular, HCE of 1970 continues to be a significant predictor (partially even at the 0.001 level of significance or better) of remaining life expectancies at ages 40 and 65. With regard to the feedback relationship, both GDP and life expectancies at age 65 continue to lack statistical significance. After all these refinements, it seems safe to conclude that the feedback from longevity to HCE cannot have been of overriding importance in OECD countries, at least in the recent past.

5. DISCUSSION AND CONCLUSIONS

The financiers of public health care are afraid of the successes of modern medicine that prolong life, threatening to increase the future cost of health care. Spelled out in detail, this fear rests on two hypothesized relationships.
1. The higher health care expenditures per capita (HCE), the longer remaining life expectancy, especially at an advanced age;
2. The higher life expectancy at an advanced age, the stronger the demand for private and especially public health care services, and the higher HCE.

Jointly, the two relationships make up what can be called the Sisyphus syndrome in health care. On the presumption that this syndrome is of sufficient force and general validity, it was attempted to find its traces in aggregate data from OECD countries. The statistical analysis produced two rather surprising results.

In contradistinction to earlier work focusing on mortality rates, there is some evidence suggesting that increased HCE does contribute to increased life expectancy beyond age 40, although with a sizable lag. Due to data limitations, this lag had to be fixed at ten years; in the future, it will have to be determined more precisely to see whether it is medical care received over the life cycle rather than the most recent (and hence modern) care that has an effect on longevity at the margin.

The feedback relationship, running from longevity to HCE, commands a great deal of *a priori* credibility. It is common experience that aged persons are strong users of medical care. At the same time, they form a sufficiently important voting bloc for pushing through demands for public provision or financing of health care services in today's Western democracies (Bös and von Weizsäcker, 1989). While several previous studies had been unable to unearth a relationship between the population share aged 65 and more and HCE, they could be criticized for using an inappropriate explanatory variable. Counting the numbers of the aged fails to take into account a much younger voter's motivation to opt for public HCE, deriving from an expectation to live on for quite a few years during which medical care might make a difference. Accordingly, remaining life expectancies (at the ages of 40 and 65, say) rather than pensioners' population share would constitute the appropriate explanatory variable. However, remaining life expectancies were not found to significantly contribute to the explanation of HCE either, regardless of a number of variations in terms of specification and estimation methods. Thus, the feedback link from age to HCE fails to materialize, at least for the time being.

There are at least two explanations for this failure. The first starts from the observation that the fertility decrease in OECD countries serves to reduce HCE on newborns and infants. This reduction might neutralize the increase of HCE on the elderly, thus masking the feedback link running from longevity to HCE. However, neither earlier work by Leu (1986) nor this investigation produced confirming evidence for this hypothesis.

The second explanation is based on the fact that a major share of medical care expenditure is concentrated in the last twelve months of the human life (Lubitz and Prihoda, 1984, but *see* also Scitovsky, 1988). If this statement should be true independent of age at death, it is the process of dying rather than aging that is costly. Accordingly, increasing (remaining) life expectancy would not have a great influence on lifetime HCE.

However, this explanation is not fully satisfactory either because at least for three OECD countries, there is evidence that at present HCE begin to rise at an earlier age than a decade or so ago; for Canada, *see* Barer *et al.* (1987); for Germany, *see* Sachverständigenrat (1987, p. 231–276); for Switzerland, *see* Zweifel (1989). This does not square well with the notion of the costly final year of life being deferred to higher and higher calendar age.

In conclusion, the Sisyphus syndrome in health care does not appear to exert enough force on today's developed economies as to leave its traces in their aggregate data. While it may in fact be operative, other influences such as increasing incomes seem to still have superseded the demands of the aged for more HCE both public and private. For the time being, the Sisyphus syndrome in health care can hardly be invoked for explaining the growth of health care expenditures.

REFERENCES

Auster, R., I. Leveson, and D. Sarachek, "The Production of Health, an Exploratory Study", in: *The Journal of Human Resources*, 4(4), 411–436, 1969.
Barer, M.L., *et al.*, "Aging and Health Care Utilization: New Evidence and Old Fallacies", in: *Social Science and Medicine*, 24(10), 551–862, 1987.
Bös, D., and R.K. von Weizsäcker, "Economic Consequences of an Aging Population", in: *European Economic Review*, 33, 345–354, 1989.
Breusch, T.S., and A.R. Pagan, "The Lagrange Multiplier Test and Its Applications to Model Specification in Econometrics", in: *Review of Economic Studies*, 47, 239–253, 1980.
Cochrane, A.L., A.S. St. Leger, and F. Moore, "Health Service Input and Mortality Output in Developed Countries", in: *Journal of Epidemiology and Community Health*, 32, 200–205, 1978.
Culyer, A.J., "Cost Containment in Europe", in: *Health Care Financing Review*, 1989 Annual Supplement, 21–32, 1989.
Denton, F.T., S. Neno Li, B.G. Spencer, "Health Care in the Economic-demographic System: Macro-effects of Market Control, Government Intervention, and Population Change", in: *Southern Economic Journal*, 55(1), 37–56, 1988.
Duckett, S.J., "Structural Interests and Australian Health Policy", in: *Social Science and Medicine*, 18(11), 959–966, 1984.
Efron, B., "Bootstrap Methods: Another Look at the Jackknife", in: *Annals of Statistics*, 7, 1–26, 1979.
Freedman, D.A., and S.C. Peters, "Bootstrapping a Regression Equation: Some Empirical Results", in: *Journal of the American Statistical Association*, 79 (385), 97–106, 1984.

Fries, J.F., "Aging, Natural Death, and the Compression of Morbidity", in: *New England Journal of Medicine*, 303(3), 130–135, 1980.

Fuchs, V.R., "Though Much is Taken. Reflections on Aging, Health, and Medical Care", *NBER Working Paper No.* 1269, Cambridge, MA: National Bureau of Economic Research, 1984.

Gerdtham, U.-G., F. Andersson, J. Sogaard, and B. Jönsson, "Economic Analysis of Health Care Expenditures: A Cross-sectional Study of the OECD Countries", *CMT Report No.* 1988-9, Linköping, Sweden, 1988.

Gruenberg, E.M., "The Failures of Success", in: *Health and Society*, 55(1), 3–24, 1977.

Hadley, J., "Medicare Spending and Mortality Rates of the Elderly", in: *Inquiry*, 25(4), 485–493, 1988.

Judge, G.G., W.E. Griffiths, R. Carter Hill, T.-C. Lee, and H. Lütkepohl, *The Theory and Practice of Econometrics*, 2nd ed., New York: John Wiley and Sons, 1985.

Kleiman, E., "The Determinants of National Outlay on Health", in: Perlman, M. (ed.), *The Economics of Health and Medical Care*, London: Macmillan, 66–81, 1974.

Leu, R.E., "The Public-private Mix and International Health Care Costs", in: Culyer, A.J. and B. Jönsson, (eds.), *Public and Private Health Services*, Oxford: Basil Blackwell, 41–63, 1986.

Leu, R.E., and R.J. Doppmann, "Gesundheitszustand und Nachfrage nach Gesundheitsleistungen (Health Status and Demand for Health Care Services)", in: Wille, E. (ed.), *Informations- und Planungsprobleme in öffentlichen Aufgabenbereichen*, Bern: P. Lang, 1–90, 1986.

Lubitz, J., and R. Prihoda, "Use and Costs of Medicare Services in the Last Years of Life", in: *Health Care Financing Review*, 6 (1), Spring 1984.

Malthus, T.R., *Essay on Population*, 1803. New York: Random House, 1960.

McKeown, T. *The Modern Rise of Population*, London: Edward Arnold, 1976.

McKinlay, J.B., S.M. Mc Kinlay, and R. Beaglehole, "A Review of the Evidence Concerning the Impact of Medical Measures on Recent Mortality and Morbidity in the United States", in: *International Journal of Health Services*, 19(2), 181–208, 1989.

Myers, G.C., and K.G. Manton, "Compression of Mortality: Myth or Reality?", in: *The Gerontologist*, 24(4), 346–353, 1984.

Newhouse, J.P., "Medical-care Expenditure: A Crossnational Survey", in: *Journal of Human Resources*, 12(1), 115–125, 1977.

Newhouse, J.P., *et al.*, "Some Interim Results from a Controlled Trial of Cost Sharing in Health Insurance", *Report No. R-2847–HHS*, Santa Monica: Rand Corporation, 1982.

Newhouse, J.P., and L.J. Friedlander, "The Relationship Between Medical Resources and Health: Some Additional Evidence", in: *Journal of Human Resources*, XV(2), 200–218, 1980.

Newhouse, J.P., and Ch.E. Phelps, "New Estimates of Price and Income Elasticities of Medical Care Services", in: Rosett, R.N. (ed.), *The Role of Health Insurance in the Health Services Sector*, New York: National Bureau of Economic Research, 261–312, 1976.

OECD, *Public Expenditure on Health*, Paris, 1977.

OECD, *Measuring Health Care. 1960–1983. Expenditure, Cost, and Performance*, Paris, 1985.

OECD, *Financing and Delivering Health Care. A Comparative Analysis of OECD Countries*, Paris, 1987.

Parkin, D., A. McGuire, and B. Yule, "Aggregate Health Care Expenditures and National Income: Is Health Care a Luxury Good?", in: *Journal of Health Economics*, 6, 109–127, 1987.

Peltzman, S., "Regulation and Health: The Case of Mandatory Prescriptions and an Extension", in: *Managerial and Decision Economics*, 8, 41–46, 1987.

Sachverständigenrat für die Konzertierte Aktion im Gesundheitswesen, *Medizinische und ökonomische Orientierung. (Medical and Economic Guideposts)*, Baden-Baden: Nomos, 1987.

Schmidt, P., "Estimation of Seemingly Unrelated Regressions with Unequal Numbers of Observations", in: *Journal of Econometrics*, 5, 365–377, 1977.

Schneider, E.L., and J.A. Brody, "Aging, Natural Death, and the Compression of Morbidity: Another View", in: *New England Journal of Medicine*, 309(14), 854–856, 1983.

Schofield, R., "Population Growth in the Century After 1750: The Role of Mortality Decline", in: Bengtsson, T., G. Fridlizius, and R. Ohlsson, (eds.) *Pre-industrial Population Change*, Stockholm: Almquist and Wiksell, 17–40, 1981.

Scitovsky, A.A., "Medical Care in the Last Twelve Months of Life: The Relation Between Age, Functional Status, and Medical Care Expenditures", in: *Milbank Memorial Fund Quarterly*, 66(4), 640–660, 1988.

United Nations *Demographic Yearbook* 1985, New York, 1987.

United Nations International Conference on Population *Mortality and Health Policy*, New York: UN, ST/ESA/SER.A/91, 1984.

Van Doorslaer, E.K.A. *Health, Knowledge, and the Demand for Medical Care. An Econometric Analysis*, Assum/Maastricht: Van Gorcum, 1987.

Wedig, G.J., "Health Status and the Demand for Health: Results on Price Elasticities", in: *Journal of Health Economics*, 7(2), 151–164, 1988.

Wolfe, B.L., "Health Status and Medical Expenditures: Is There a Link?", in: *Social Science and Medicine*, 22(10), 993–999, 1986.

Wolfe, B., and M. Gabay, "Health Status and Medical Expenditures: More Evidence of a Link", in: *Social Science and Medicine*, 25(8), 883–888, 1987.

Zellner, A., "An Efficient Method of Estimating Seemingly Unrelated Regressions and Tests of Aggregation Bias", in: *Journal of the American Statistical Association*, 57, 348–368, 1962.

Zweifel, P., "Zu den Folgen des Geburtenrückgangs für das Gesundheitswesen (Consequences of the Fertility Decline for the Health Care Sector)", in: Recktenwald, H.C. (ed.), *Der Rückgang der Geburten - Folgen auf längere Sicht*, Düsseldorf: Verlag Wirtschaft und Finanzen, 298–304, 1989.

Zweifel, P., "Die Kosten-Versicherungs-Spirale im schweizerischen Gesundheitswesen (The Cost-Insurance Spiral in the Swiss Health Care Sector)", in: *Schweiz. Zeitschrift für Volkswirtschaft und Statistik*, 3 (122), 555–583, 1986.

Zweifel, P., "Was ist eine zusätzliche Million für das Gesundheitswesen wert? (Another Million for Swiss Health Care: What Would it be Worth?)", in: *Schweiz. Zeitschrift für Volkswirtschaft und Statistik*, 114, 449–474, 1978.

Deaths from gastro-intestinal cancer in Mexico: probable cause for water sampling*

I 12 Q 15

Mexico

EDGAR LOPEZ

Centro de Investigaciones Economicas, Universidad Autonoma de Nuevo León

LLAD PHILLIPS

Department of Economics, University of California, Santa Barbara, CA 93106, U.S.A.

MANUEL SILOS

Facultad de Economia, Universidad Autonoma de Nuevo León

I. INTRODUCTION

The evidence from epidemiological studies of an ecological nature indicate that the incidence of cancer of the gastro-intestinal tract can be affected by the chemical pollution of water.[1] Frequently, of the carcinogenic organic chemicals that can be detected in water, the most dangerous is chloroform because of its relative high concentration. This is ironic, since the source is often chlorine, used to control bacteria in water and to prevent disease. However, if natural and/or synthetic organic chemicals are polluting the water, they evidently contribute to a chemical reaction involving chlorine to produce chloroform.

Specially conducted surveys in the United States of America show that the average concentration of chloroform in untreated water (no chlorine) is 1 microgram per liter. The average concentration of chloroform in treated water is 45 micrograms per liter. However, in city water supplies heavily contaminated with organic chemicals, the concentration of chloroform can exceed 300 micrograms per liter.[2]

Chloroform is not the only dangerous organic chemical contaminating water supplies. Insecticides and other chemicals may also be present. Potentially, pollution from synthetic compounds may originate from industrial use of chemicals that are improperly disposed of, agricultural use of insecticides

*We would like to thank Licencia Alejandra Vela for providing data on the deaths of each individual in the State of Nuevo León for 1980–1984. We are also indebted to Mario Leal, Centro de Investigaciones Economicas, for his able assistance in processing the data.

Llad Phillips would like to express his gratitude for support from the Universidad Autonoma de Nuevo León and from the Community Organization Research Institute, University of California, Santa Barbara, Harold L. Votey, Jr., Director.

P. Zweifel and H. E. Frech III (eds.), Health Economics Worldwide. 331–347.

and other organic compounds that find their way into the water supply, and household use of chemicals. Similarly, the contamination of water supplies from natural organic compounds can originate with the improper disposal of refuse, garbage, and sewage.

The detection of trace amounts of volatile organic compounds in water utilizes the technique of gas chromatography, applied to this purpose within the last fifteen years. The volatile fraction of organic chemicals in water is estimated to be on the order of 10%. Little is known of the other 90% containing heavier organic compounds.[3] They are difficult to detect and only a small fraction have been identified. Hence their potential contribution to carcinogenic contamination is unknown.

A serious difficulty in detecting contamination is that it may be geographically localized in "hot spots". The source may have been a disposal site or dump for chemicals, possibly used and abandoned decades ago, before it was realized how dangerous the chemicals were. The location may even have been forgotten. Another possibility is a particular industry which may be disposing dangerous chemical wastes. Once again, the disposal may have occurred in the past, but the contamination from these chemicals could be continuing in the present and into the future.

A feasible detection procedure, of course, is to sample drinking water at various locations, and conduct assays for trace amounts of volatile organic compounds and other contaminants. However, the water may not be contaminated at the source, or at plants where it is processed and treated. The contamination could occur in the distribution system before it is used. To detect the possibility of contamination at locations in the distribution system may require wide-spread sampling in numerous communities.

A potential aid to detecting possible chemical contamination of water is the use of vital statistics. Deaths from malignant tumors of the gastro-intestinal system, excluding the lips, mouth and pharynx (which are available as a separate category), are available by municipio in the state of Nuevo León for the years 1980–83.[4] The total number of deaths from this cause in the state of Nuevo León for the years 1980, 1981, 1982, and 1983 were 327, 318, 316 and 330 respectively. Using the total population of 2,513,044 for the state of Nuevo León in 1980, this amounts to an annual average death rate of 128 per million. This rate can be used to calculate the expected number of deaths from this cause during these four years for each municipio to search for those municipios with exceptionally high (or low) death rates.

Two precautions must be taken. First of all, approximately 93% of deaths from gastro-intestinal cancer afflict people aged 45 or more and the percentage of the population in this age bracket varies dramatically by municipio from, for example, a low of 9.6% for General Escobedo to a high of 30.0% for Paras, compared to 13.7% for Nuevo-León as a whole.[5] Consequently, age specific death rates for the population 45 and older are used. Deaths from gastro-intestinal cancer are available by age and the population for this age group from the 1980 Census was used for each municipio.[6]

Secondly, the sample of municipios is very heterogeneous, varying by income, the fraction of the economically active population engaged in agriculture and/or industry, and the percentage of the population possessing running water and sewage drainage, to mention just a few of many factors. Consequently, significant deviations in the number of deaths for a municipio from those expected, as based on the rate for the state as a whole, might be due to social, economic, and environmental conditions. As a consequence, average death rates are examined for more homogeneous groupings of municipios to search out possible "hot spots". Of course, one can never be sure that one has isolated, or controlled for, the true cause of higher death rates in a municipio. Our goal is to muster sufficient evidence that some municipios are exceptional, as an argument for further investigation and action, including water sampling and assay.

II. DEATHS FROM GASTRO-INTESTINAL CANCER BY MUNICIPIO IN NUEVO LEÓN

The number of deaths from gastro-intestinal cancer at ages 45 and above in the state of Nuevo León in the years 1980–1983 were 300, 296, 295, and 310 respectively. This is equivalent to an average annual death rate from this cause of 875 per million for the age group 45 and older using the 1980 population as a base.

This rate, p, was used to calculate the expected number of deaths, d, for each municipio,

$$d = n\,p\,t$$

where t is the number of years, 4, and n is the population (1980) age 45 or more of the municipio and the rate p is

$$P = \frac{D}{tN}$$

where D are the deaths, 1201, in Nuevo León and N is the population (1980) age 45 or more for the state. Hence the expected number of deaths in each municipio, is proportional to the fraction of the total population aged 45 or more, for that municipio

$$d = \frac{n}{N}D$$

The data for population age 45 and older, observed deaths for the period 1980–83, g, and expected deaths are listed in Table 1. The municipios for which observed deaths differ from expected deaths by more than 2 times the square root of expected deaths are also indicated in Table 1. This criterion was based on the binomial distribution where, as discussed above, expected deaths, d, equal npt, and the variance in deaths equals $np(1-p)t$, observing

Table 1.

Municipio	Population 45 & older (1980)	Observed deaths, g, from gastro-intestinal cancer 1980–1983	Expected deaths, d	$\frac{|g - d|}{\sqrt{d}} > 2^*$	Average annual death rate per 10,000 gastro-intestinal cancer
Abasolo	105	1	0.4		23.8
Agualegas	1,164	6	4.1		12.0
Los Aldamas	833	6	2.9		18.0
Allende	3,253	19	11.4	2.2	14.6
Anáhuac	2,781	20	9.7	3.3	18.0
Apodaca	3,932	23	13.8	2.5	14.6
Aramberri	2,604	5	9.1		4.8
Bustamonte	742	2	2.6		6.7
Cadereyta Jiménez	6,846	21	24.0		7.7
Carmen	538	2	1.9		9.3
Cerralvo	1,497	8	5.2		13.4
Ciénaga de Flores	679	4	2.4		14.7
China	2,161	5	7.6		5.8
Dr. Arroyo	6,153	8	21.5	−2.9	3.3
Dr. Coss	852	2	3.0		5.9
Dr. González	539	4	1.9		18.6
Galeana	6,181	6	21.6	−3.4	2.4
Garcia	1,440	4	5.0		6.9
Garza Garcia	11,112	24	38.9	−2.4	5.4
Gral. Bravo	1,252	2	4.4		4.0
Gral. Escobedo	3,614	11	12.6		7.6
Gral. Teran	3,458	16	12.1		11.6
Gral. Treviño	483	1	1.7		5.2
Gral. Zaragoza	919	2	3.2		5.4
Gral. Zuazua	614	6	2.1	2.7	24.4
Guadalupe	40,908	108	143.2	−2.9	6.6
Las Herreras	943	10	3.3	3.5	26.5

Municipality	Population	Observed deaths	Expected deaths	Difference	Std. dev.
Hildalgo, San Nicolas	1,448	3	5.1		5.2
Higueras	223	1	0.8		11.2
Hualahuises	1,203	3	4.2		6.2
Iturbide	547	4	1.9		18.3
Juárez	1,728	10	6.0		14.5
Lampazos de Naranjo	1,052	6	3.7		14.3
Linares	8,692	38	30.4		10.9
Marin	390	2	1.4		12.8
Melchor Ocampo	224	4	0.8	3.6	44.6
Mier y Noriega	1,112	0	3.9		0.0
Mina	645	5	2.3		19.4
Montemorelos	7,359	26	25.8		8.8
Monterrey	157,172	536	550.0		8.5
Parás	361	3	1.3		20.8
Pesqueria	1,190	5	4.2		10.5
Los Ramones	1,655	6	5.8		9.1
Rayones	681	4	2.4		14.7
Sabinas Hildalgo	4,323	17	15.1		9.8
Salinas Victoria	1,411	6	4.9		10.6
San Nicolas de los Garza	30,393	112	106.4		9.2
Santa Catarina	8,772	44	30.7	2.4	12.5
Santiago	5,373	25	18.8		11.6
Vallecillo	575	3	2.0		13.1
Villaldama	1,037	7	3.6		16.9
Not Specified		5			
Neuvo León	343,171	1,201			8.73

*Difference between observed and expected deaths greater than two times the standard deviation in deaths.

that 1−p is approximately one. With this criterion, for an observed number of deaths of zero to be significantly below the expected number of deaths, the latter must be at least 4, implying a population size of 1,143 for the municipio. Of the 51 municipios, 22 are smaller than this.

The probability of observing a given number of deaths, k, can be calculated using the Poisson distribution for the smaller municipios

$$P(k) = \frac{d^k e^{-d}}{k!}$$

where d is the number of expected deaths. For example, for a population of size 1,143 the expected number of deaths, d, is 4 and the probability of observing k = 0 deaths is .02, the probability of observing k = 1 death is .07, the probability of observing k = 2 deaths is .15, the probability of observing 3 deaths is 0.20, *etc.*, of course provided the death rate for the state of Nuevo León is apropos for this population.

The analysis represented in Table 1 suggests that seven municipios have significantly higher gastro-intestinal cancer rates than Nuevo León as a whole. However, the nature of these municipios ranges from metropolitan, such as Apodoca and Santa Catarina to rural, such as Anahuac and Las Herreras. Similarly the four municipios with cancer rates significantly below Nuevo León include metropolitan areas such as Garza Garcia and Guadalupe and rural areas such as Dr. Arroyo and Galeana. Are there other factors which can explain these strange comparisons and contrasts?

III. CONCEPTUAL FRAMEWORK

A number of factors could contribute to chemical pollution and its impact on cancer deaths. In addition to the use and disposal of chemicals by agriculture, industry and households, population density may be an important factor. A given amount of pollution may be more dangerous, and is certainly likely to affect more people, the higher the population density.

The same factors that may generate pollution, such as agricultural and industrial activity, also generate income, and people with a higher income will demand more of all goods, including a clean environment. Hence there will be a balance between the activities generating pollution and the activities abating pollution. This is illustrated in Figure 1. Very poor communities will not have the resources to reduce pollution but may not have the activities generating it as well. Wealthy communities will have the resources to combat pollution, and can afford running water in the house, sewage drainage, and a better location for better housing.

Bruce Forster developed an optimal control model of pollution and consumption tradeoffs.[7] A static version of this model is that a community maximizes utility, which depends on a good, consumption, and a bad, pol-

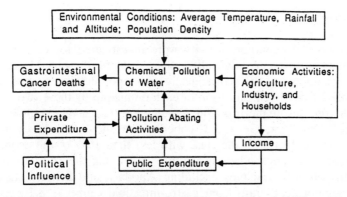

Figure 1. Causal and Remedial Factors Affecting Gastrointestinal Cancer Deaths.

lution, subject to pollution generation net of abatement activities, which depends on consumption. The community is presumed to have a fixed income, so that what is consumed is not available for expenditure on pollution abatement. This model is illustrated in Fig. 2. Thus, in this conceptual model there are two endogenous variables, consumption and pollution.

To implement this conceptual model, pollution, as indicated by cancer deaths, is presumed to vary with agriculture and industrial activity, which are taken to be exogenous. It also varies with pollution abatement activities, such as running water and sewage drainage, which are endogenous. Engel curves are specified for the latter. These relationships are examined, first descriptively, and then estimated statistically.

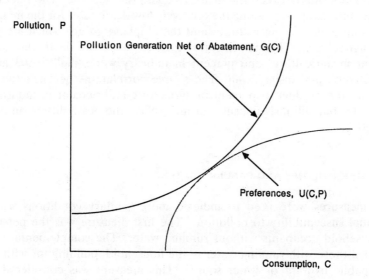

Figure 2. Tradeoffs Between Consumption and Pollution.

IV. ECONOMIC ACTIVITY AND CANCER DEATHS

Two measures of economic activity were investigated for each municipio, the percentage of the economically active population engaged in agriculture and the percentage of the economically active population engaged in industry.[8] Table 2 lists the classification of each municipio by these two measures. Note that the seven metropolitan municipios (Garza Garcia, Guadalupe, Monterrey, Apodaca, General Escobedo, San Nicolas de Los Garza, and Santa Catarina) all fall in the class with less than 10% of the economically active population engaged in agriculture. Grouping the population for the five metropolitan municipios excluding Apodaca and Santa Catarina, the average annual death rate from gastro-intestinal cancer is 8.1 per 10,000. The death rate for Santa Catarina is over 50% higher and the death rate for Apodaca is over 80% higher.

The other feature worth noting from this table is the grouping of municipios Aramberri, Dr. Arroyo, Galeana, Mier y Noriega, and General Zarogosa. All have less than 10% of the economically active population in industry and over 50% of the economically active population in agriculture. They are all located in the southern part of the state of Nuevo León on the higher altiplano or in the Sierra Madre Oriental mountains. As a group they have an average annual death rate from gastro-intestinal cancer of 3.1 per 10,000 and in contrast to the metropolitan area, are among the poorest municipios in Nuevo León.

Using the classification scheme in Table 2, one-way analysis of variance was conducted between the death rate and the percent of the economically active population in agriculture. There was a weak, but statistically insignificant relationship between the death rate and this variable. The relationship was not monotonic, reflecting the relatively low death rates for the metropolitan group with little agriculture, and the altiplano group, which are principally agricultural. The simple correlations between the death rate and the percent in agriculture, and percent in industry were small, $-.03$ and $.03$ respectively, and insignificant. The simple correlations between the death rate and the product of percent in agriculture and percent in industry was large, $.15$, but still insignificant, but may reflect the possibility of an interaction effect.

V. WATER UTILITIES AND CANCER DEATHS

Two measures were used to indicate more sanitary conditions with less potential susceptibility to pollution.[9] The first measure was the percentage of household occupants without running water. The complementary group included those with running water in the household, building, or with access to a public hydrant or water source. This measure was considered to be largely a privately provided good with the exception of those dependent on

Table 2. Average annual death rates from gastro-intestinal cancer, 1980–83, by municipio and economic activity

% of econ. active in agriculture	% of economically active in industry 0–9.99	10–19.99	20–29.99	30–39.99	40–49.99
0–9.99		Garza Garcia 5.4	Guadalupe 6.6 Monterrey 8.5	Apodaca 14.6* Gral. Escobedo 7.6 San Nicolas de los Garza 9.2 Santa Catarina 12.5*	Hildalgo, S.N. 5.2 Abasolo 23.8
10–19.88		Sabinas Hildalgo 9.8 Santiago 11.6	Garcia 6.9 Juarez 14.5	Carmen 9.3 Cienega De Flores 14.7 Salinas Victoria 10.6	
20–29.99	Montemorelos 8.8	Allende 14.6* Bustamonte 6.7 Cerralvo 13.4 Villaldalma 16.9	Cadereyta Jimenez 7.7 Marin 12.8		
30–39.99	Los Aldamas 18.0 China 5.8 Hualahuises 6.2 Lampazos 14.3 Linares 10.9 Melchor Ocampo 44.6*		Dr. Gonzalez 18.6 Gral. Zuazua 24.4* Higueras 11.2 Mina 19.4 Pesqueria 10.5		
40–49.99	Agualegas 12.9 Anahuac 18.0* Dr. Coss 5.9 Gral. Bravo 4.0 Gral. Teran 11.6 Gral. Treviño 5.2 Los Herreras 26.5* Iturbide 18.3 Paras 20.8 Los Ramones 9.1				
50–59.99	Aramberri 4.8 Dr. Arroyo 3.3 Galeana 2.4 Vallecillo 13.1				
60–69.99	Mier y Noiega 0 Rayones 14.7				
70–79.99	Gral. Zaragosa 5.4				

*Significantly higher than expected in Table 1.

a public hydrant or source. The second measure was the percentage of household occupants without sewage drainage of any type, sewer, septic tank, or drainage pipe to the soil. This measure was considered to be a mixture of a publicly provided good (because of the importance of sewers) and a privately provided good.

Table 3 depicts the classification of each municipio by these two measures. Note that the seven metropolitan municipios are in the top left of the table with a high percentage of the households having running water and sewage drainage. For six out of seven of the metropolitan municipios, more than 90% of the household occupants have running water. For the exception, Apodoca, more than 80% of the household occupants have running water. This reflects the relative affluence of the population in the metropolitan municipios and the amenities of an urban lifestyle.

There is more variation among the metropolitan municipios in the percentage of household occupants who have sewage drainage. Three municipios, Garza Garcia, Monterrey and San Nicholas de Los Garza are in the class where 80 to 90% of the occupants have sewage drainage while General Escobedo and Apodoca are in the class where only 50 to 60% of the occupants have sewage drainage.

Once again, Santa Catarina and Apodoca stand out among the metropolitan municipios as having a much higher death rate for gastro-intestinal cancer, while the other five metropolitan municipios tend to have more moderate death rates in the range 5.4–9.2 per 10,000 people.

In contrast to the metropolitan area, the municipios of the altiplano and the Sierra Madre have little in the way of amenities but they nonetheless have low gastro-intestinal cancer death rates. Galeana, Aramberri, Dr. Arroyo, General Zaragoza, and Mier y Noriega all fall in the class where only 10 to 20% of household occupants have sewage drainage. For this group of municipios, there is more variation in the percentage of occupants with running water, which ranges from 10 to 20% for Mier y Noriega to 50–60% for Galeana.

The simple correlation between the death rate and the percentage of household occupants without running water was -0.30, reflecting more the situation of the altiplano municipios than the sanitary advantages of running water in a polluted environment. The simple correlation between the death rate and the percentage of households without sewage drainage was −.06.

VI. ENGEL CURVES FOR RUNNING WATER AND SEWAGE DRAINAGE

The statistical estimation of the economic model depicted in Fig. 2 involves two aspects, the demand for abatement activities and pollution generation net of abatement. The demand for abatement activities is derived from the tangency condition depicted in Fig. 2 and is modeled in this section in terms of separate Engel curves for running water and sewage drainage. The

Table 3. Average annual death rates from gastro-intestinal cancer, 1980–83, by municipio, and occupants without running water and sewage drainage

% Without Running Water — Running Water	% Without Sewage Drainage								
	0–9.99	10–19.99	20–29.99	30–39.99	40–49.99	50–59.99	60–69.99	70–79.99	80–89.99
0–9.99	Garza Garcia 5.4 Monterrey 8.5 San Nicolas D.L.G. 9.2	Guadalupe 6.6		Santa Catarina 12.5	Gral. Escobedo 7.6	Bustamonte 6.7 Hidalgo, SN 5.2 Marin 12.8	Abasolo 23.8 Gral. Zuazua 24.4		
10–19.99					Apodaca 14.6 Sabinas Hildago 9.8	Santiago 11.6	Carmen 9.3 Gral. Trevino 5.2 Melchor Ocampo 44.6	Cienega D.F. 14.7 Higueras 11.2	Garcia 6.9
20–29.99						Allende 14.6	Agualegas 12.9 Los Aldamas 18.0 Cerralvo 13.4 Salinas Victoria 10.6	Los Herreras 26.5 Juarez 14.5 Villaldama 16.9	Pesqueria 10.5
30–39.99						Linares 10.9	Anahuac 18.0 Dr. Gonzalez 18.6 Montemorelos 8.8 Paras 20.8	Lampazos D.H. 14.3 Los Ramones 9.1	Mina 19.4
40–49.99						Cadereyta, J. 7.7	Gral. Bravo 4.0	China 5.8	
50–59.99								Hualahuises 6.2	Galeana 2.4 Iturbide 18.3 Vallecillo 13.1
60–69.99						Gral. Teran 11.6			Dr. Coss 5.9
70–79.99									Aramberri 4.8 Dr. Arroyo 3.3 Gral. Zaragosa 5.4 Rayones 14.7
80–89.99									Mier y Noriega 0

constraint depicted in Fig. 2 as pollution generation net of abatement is modeled in the following section. The cancer death rate is used as a proxy for pollution. Since the demands for running water and sewage drainage are endogenously determined along with the level of pollution (cancer deaths), these structural equations are estimated using instrumental variables (denoted with the variable underlined) for the endogenous variables. The variables mean income, industrial and agricultural activity, population density, illiteracy, the municipio's population as a portion of the state population, and the ratio of males to females were presumed to be exogenous.

Running water, for the most part, and sewage drainage, to some extent, are provided by private resources and demand for these goods will vary with income. The form of the Engel curve chosen for estimation was the natural logarithm, ln, of the odds of having the particular amenity in a municipio. For example, the proportion of households with running water, P_w, was divided by the proportion without, $1 - P_w$, and the logarithm of this ratio was regressed against mean income, y:

$$\ln(P_W/1 - P_W) = \beta_1 + \beta_2 y$$

Transforming the proportion to the logarithm of the odds increases the range of the dependent variable from zero to one to plus infinity to minus infinity. A similar formulation of the Engel curve was used for sewage drainage.

The potential health hazard from pollution, as well as income, should influence demand for running water and sewage drainage. A good proxy or measure for pollution was not available and hence the logarithm of the death rate from gastro-intestinal cancer, ln DRGIC, was used. Since this variable is postulated, in turn, to be affected by running water and sewage drainage, an instrumental variable or two stage least squares technique was utilized. Because the health hazards from pollution are exacerbated by population density, the logarithm of this variable, ln DEN was added to the regression.[10]

Since sewage drainage is to a considerable extent a publicly provided good, a measure of political influence or importance was added to the Engel curve for this good. The logarithm of the population of the municipio as a percentage of the population for the state was used for this variable, ln POP%. To compare and contrast results, this variable was also added to the Engel curve for running water.

Lastly, it was hypothesized that the public authorities tended to provide sewage drainage to those communities where a large proportion of the household occupants had running water. Hence an instrument for $\ln(P_w/1 - P_w)$ was added to the Engel curve for sewage drainage.

The Engle curves, estimated from data for 50 municipios using two stage least squares, are reported in Table 4. The sign and magnitude of the coefficients are comparable to those estimated using ordinary least squares. For the latter, the R^2 for the Engel curve for running water was .69 and the corresponding statistic for sewage drainage was 0.86.

The coefficient for income is positive and significant in both Engel curves

Table 4.

1. ENGEL CURVE FOR RUNNING WATER: TWO STAGE LEAST SQUARES

$$\ln(P_w/1-P_w) = -3.31 + 0004y + .476 \ln \underline{DRGIC} + .384 \ln DEN$$
$$(-5.4) \quad (3.5) \quad (1.7) \quad\quad\quad (3.9)$$

$$- .296 \ln POP\%$$
$$(-2.5)$$

t-distribution
statistics in parentheses

2. ENGEL CURVE FOR SEWAGE DRAINAGE: TWO STAGE LEAST SQUARES

$$\ln(P_D/1-P_D) = -2.18 + .00019y + .162 \ln \underline{DRGIC} -.02 \ln DEN$$
$$(-5.1) \quad (2.9) \quad\quad (1.2) \quad\quad\quad (-.3)$$

$$+ .20 \ln POP\% + .37 \ln \underline{(P_w/1-P_w)}$$
$$(3.2) \quad\quad\quad (4.0)$$

t-distribution
statistics in parentheses

and the death rate from gastro-intestinal cancer is positive and adds to the explained variance for both Engel curves.

The coefficient for population density is positive and significant in the regression for running water but is not significantly different from zero in the regression for sewage drainage.

As hypothesized, the relative size of a municipio in terms of population and the percentage of household occupants with running water both have a positive and significant influence on sewage drainage consistent with the notion that these factors influence the public authorities. The population of a municipio as a percent of the state has a negative and significant effect on the demand for running water, a result not anticipated. This variable could be a proxy for a significant omitted variable. For example, the price of running water may vary with the relative size of the municipio.

In sum, the results for the estimated Engel curves for running water and sewage drainage are satisfactory and largely as anticipated.

VII. A MULTI-FACTOR ANALYSIS OF GASTRO-INTESTINAL CANCER DEATH RATES BY MUNICIPIO

The cancer death rate is modelled as a balance of forces, economic activity being a potential source and running water and sewage drainage aiding abatement. The specification is in terms of the logarithms of the variables with the explanatory variables being represented with linear and second order terms and interaction effects. For example, the logarithm of the cancer

Table 5. Gastro-intestinal cancer death rate: Instrumental variables, dependent variable; ln DRGIC

Explanatory Variable		Coefficient	T-Statistic
Constant	C	−15.3	−1.8
Agricultural Activity	ln Ag	−14.9	−2.3
	$(\ln AG)^2$	−5.7	−2.2
Industrial Activity	ln IN	6.8	3.0
	$(\ln IN)^2$	0.63	3.3
	ln AG · ln IN	−1.5	−1.9
Population Density	ln DEN	−5.8	−2.4
	$(\ln DEN)^2$	−1.2	−2.1
	ln DEN · ln AG	−5.1	−2.2
	ln DEN · ln IN	−2.4	−2.4
Sex Ratio	ln M/F	10.2	3.3
Illiterate	ln ILL	−11.5	−2.5
Running Water	$\ln (P_W/1 - P_W)$	−3.2	−1.7
	$[\ln(\overline{P_W/1 - P_W})]^2$	−0.29	−1.3
Sewage Drainage	$\ln (\overline{P_D/1 - P_D})$	−6.1	−1.9
	$[\ln(\overline{P_D/1 - P_D})]^2$	0.58	0.4
	$[\ln(\overline{P_W/1 - P_W})]$ $[\ln(\overline{P_D/1 - P_D})]$	0.65	0.3

death rate, ln DRGIC, varies with the logarithm of the percentage of the active population in industry, ln IN, and their higher order terms:

$$\ln DRGIC = \beta_1 + \beta_2 \ln AG + \beta_3(\ln AG)^2 + \beta_4(\ln IN)$$
$$+ \beta_5(\ln IN)^2 + \beta_6 \ln AG \cdot \ln IN.$$

The pollution abatement variables are added in their log-odds specification, as in the Engel curves discussed above, $\ln(P_w/1-P_w)$ and $\ln(P_D/1-P_D)$ along with their second order and interaction terms. The complete specification of the variables is detailed in Table 5.

The logarithm of population density, along with its square and interaction terms with the agriculture and industry variables is introduced to capture the potentially greater danger of pollution in highly populated areas.

Lastly, the logarithm of the ratio of males to females, ln M/F, was added to standardize for demographic differences between municipios and the logarithm of the fraction of the population age 45 or older who are illiterate, ln ILL, was introduced to determine the long run effect of a lack of education.[11]

Since the Engel curves depend on the death rate and the death rate in turn is affected by pollution abatement through running water and sewage drainage, instrumental variables were used for the latter two variables.

In general, the results were quite significant. The cancer death rate is higher in municipios with a higher fraction of the active population in industry and lower in municipios with a higher fraction of the population in agriculture. Municipios where a higher proportion of household occupants have running water and sewage drainage have a lower cancer death rate, other things equal. Municipios with a higher ratio of males to females have a higher death rate.

There are some results which are unexpected. The higher the population density, the lower the cancer death rate. This could be because of the accessibility of goods such as bottled water, at a lower cost in terms of time spent for shopping, in more densely settled municipios.[12] Municipios with a higher proportion of population age 45 or older who are illiterate have a lower cancer death rate. This last variable may be proxy for the municipios of the altiplano and the Sierra Madre who have high illiteracy rates and low cancer death rates. However, the variable, average number of days per week that household occupants eat meat, was added to the analysis (the reduced form equation for the cancer death rate) and was insignificant and did not affect the sign, magnitude, or significance of the other exogenous variables, including the illiteracy rate which was highly significant.[13]

The estimated death rate from the equation reported in Table 5 is compared to the actual death rate from gastro-intestinal cancer for each municipio in Table 6. The standard error of estimate for the regression was 0.408 and those municipios whose actual death rates exceeded the estimated death rate by more than this amount are indicated by an asterisk. This is equivalent to having an actual death rate 50% higher than the estimated death rate. Although one cannot be certain, the excess may be due to exceptional chemical pollution or other unknown or unmeasured factors not included in the regression analysis.

Of the seven municipios identified in Table 1 as having gastro-intestinal cancer deaths more than two standard deviations above the expected number based on the population of the municipio relative to the state of Nuevo León, four remain in the group with exceptionally high rates in Table 6 (with asterisks) even after accounting for industrial activity, water, sewage and other factors.

VIII. CONCLUSIONS

A model has been constructed which explains the death rate from gastro-intestinal cancer in the municipios of Nuevo León. The conceptual basis of the model is a balance of forces, such as economic activity in manufacturing industry, which generates pollution, and investment in amenities such as running water and sewage drainage, which reduces the risks from pollution.

The model is helpful in explaining the variation in the gastro-intestinal cancer death rate among municipios. Nonetheless, there are municipios which have observed rates 50 percent higher than the estimates of the model. Of these, four have cancer deaths statistically significantly higher than one would expect based on their population and the gastro-intestinal cancer death rate for the state as a whole. Among these four is Apodaca, a metropolitan municipio with many people.

Table 6. Actual and estimated Gastro-intestinal cancer death rates per 10,000.

AVERAGE ANNUAL DEATH RATE
PER 10,000:

MUNICIPIO	Actual	Estimated	Ratio of Actual to Predicted
Abasolo	23.8	23.9	0.99
Agualegas	12.9	18.8	0.69
Los Aldamas	18.0	16.0	1.13
Allende	14.6	13.2	1.10
Anáhuac	18.0	11.1	1.62*#
Apodaca	14.6	8.7	1.67*#
Aramberri	4.8	5.5	0.87
Bustamonte	6.7	8.5	0.79
Cadereyta Jiménez	7.7	10.3	0.75
Carmen	9.3	10.8	0.86
Cerralvo	13.4	8.2	1.63*
Ciénaga de Flores	14.7	15.2	0.97
China	5.8	6.9	0.84
Dr. Arroyo	3.3	3.2	1.03
Dr. Coss	5.9	7.8	0.76
Dr. González	18.6	14.7	1.26
Galeana	2.4	3.1	0.78
Garcia	6.9	10.0	0.69
Garza Garcia	5.4	4.7	1.15
Gral. Bravo	4.0	7.1	0.57
Gral. Escobedo	7.6	7.9	0.96
Gral. Teran	11.6	6.5	1.77*
Gral. Treviño	5.2	9.8	0.53
Gral. Zaragoza	5.4	7.6	0.71
Gral. Zuazua	24.4	18.0	1.35
Guadalupe	6.6	7.3	0.91
Las Herreras	26.5	15.8	1.68*#
Higueras	11.2	12.2	0.92
Hildalgo, San Nicolas	5.2	6.9	0.76
Hualahuises	6.2	10.0	0.62
Iturbide	18.3	21.9	0.83
Juárez	14.5	8.2	1.76*
Lampazos de Naranjo	14.3	16.4	.87
Linares	10.9	10.6	1.03
Marin	12.8	15.9	0.81
Melchor Ocampo	44.6	21.9	2.04*#
Mina	19.4	12.7	1.53*
Montemorelos	8.8	6.8	1.29
Monterrey	8.5	9.5	0.89
Parás	20.8	25.9	0.80
Pesqueria	10.5	9.3	1.13
Los Ramones	9.1	9.2	0.98
Rayones	14.7	9.3	1.58*
Sabinas Hildalgo	9.8	15.0	0.65
Salinas Victoria	10.6	19.4	0.55
San Nicolas de los Garza	9.2	9.6	0.96
Santa Catarina	12.5	9.1	1.37
Santiago	11.6	12.7	0.91
Vallecillo	13.1	9.8	1.34
Villadama	16.9	16.0	1.06

*   More than one standard error of the regression estimate above the
        actual death rate.

More than two standard deviations above expected deaths in Table
        1.

The evidence presented here, although only indicative, suggests an effort should be undertaken to initiate water sampling for organic chemical pollution beginning with the large metropolitan municipios and extending to those that appear to have an unusually high number of deaths.

The gestation period for cancer is on the order of twenty years. Anti-pollution efforts begun now will be important in the future. As Mexico's population increases in average age, deaths from cancer will become even more significant. Investment in a pollution detection effort today will improve the welfare and health of future generations of Nuevo León's older citizens.

NOTES

1. *See* Hoel and Crump (1981), pp. 183–191 (including Table 4) and Page et al. (1981) p. 204.
2. *See* Hoel and Crump (1981) pp. 176 and 177.
3. *See* Hoel and Crump (1981), pp. 175 and 183.
4. *See* Secretaria (1983) for the data for 1981. Data for 1980, 1982, and 1983 were obtained from Licencia Alejandra Vela.
5. Death rates from gastro-intestinal cancer increase exponentially with age. *See* Phillips (unpublished manuscript).
6. *See* Secretaria (1986).
7. *See* Forster (1977).
8. These data were taken from the 1980 Census, Secretaria (1986).
9. These data were taken from the 1980 Census, Secretaria (1986).
10. The population density was calculated from the area in square kilometers of each municipio taken from Instituto Nacional de Estadistica Geografia e informatica.
11. These data were taken from the 1980 Census, Secretaria (1986).
12. I am indebted to a referee for this suggestion.
13. The data for the consumption of meat was not available by municipio for the 1980 Census and was taken from the 1970 Census, Secretaria (1970). The under-consumption of meat was shown to have a simple correlation of 0.43 with general mortality at the municipal level in Mexico in 1970, see Presidencia de La Republica (1983). The simple correlation between illiteracy (analfabetismo) and general mortality was 0.68.

REFERENCES

Hoel, David G., and Kenny S. Crump, "Waterborne Carcinogens: A Scientist's View", in *The Scientific Basis of Health and Safety Regulation*, edited by Robert Crandall and Lester Lave. The Brookings Institution, Washington, D.C. 1981.
Instituto Nacional de Estadistica Geografia e Informatica, *Carta Estatal En Relieve, Estado de Nuevo León*.
Forster, Bruce A., "On a One State Variable Optimal Control Problem – Consumption-Pollution Tradeoffs", in: John Pitchford and Stephen Turnovsky (eds.), *Applications of Control Theory to Economic Analysis*, Amsterdam, North-Holland, 1977.
Page, Talbot, Robert Harris, and Judith Bruser, "Waterborne Carcinogens: An Economist's View", in: *The Scientific Basis of Health and Safety Regulation*, edited by Robert Crandall and Lester Lave, The Brookings Institution, Washington, D.C., 1981.
Phillips, Llad, "The Use of Vita Statistics as Potential Social Indicators of Chemical Pollution of Water", in Nuevo León (unpublished manuscript).
Presidencia de La Republica *Necesidades Esenciales en Mexico: Salud*, Segunda Edicion, 1983.
Secretaria de Industria y Comercio, *IX Censo General de Poblacion* 1970, Estados Unidos de Mexico, Estado de Nuevo León.
Secretaria de Programación y Presupuesto, *Defunciones* 1981, Volume I, Numéro 1, Nuevo León, 1983.
Secretaria de Programación y Presupuesto, *X Censo General de Poblacion y Vivienda*, 1980, Estado de Nuevo León, Volumen I, Tomo 19. México, 1986.

Name Index

Subject Index